Environmental Criminology and
Crime Analysis

Crime Science Series

Series editor: Gloria Laycock

Published titles:

Superhighway Robbery: Preventing e-commerce crime, by Graeme R. Newman
and Ronald V. Clarke
Crime Reduction and Problem-oriented Policing, by Karen Bullock and Nick Tilley
Crime Science: New approaches to preventing and detecting crime, edited by
Melissa J. Smith and Nick Tilley
*Problem-oriented Policing and Partnerships: Implementing an evidence-based
approach to crime reduction*, by Karen Bullock, Rosie Erol and Nick Tilley
Preventing Child Sexual Abuse: Evidence, policy and practice, by Stephen Smallbone,
William L. Marshall and Richard Wortley
Raising the Bar: Preventing aggression in and around bars, pubs and clubs, by
Kathryn Graham and Ross Homel
Environmental Criminology and Crime Analysis, edited by Richard Wortley and
Lorraine Mazerolle

Environmental Criminology and Crime Analysis

Edited by Richard Wortley and Lorraine Mazerolle

Routledge
Taylor & Francis Group

LONDON AND NEW YORK

First published by Willan Publishing 2008
This edition published by Routledge 2011
2 Park Square, Milton Park, Abingdon, Oxon OX14 4RN
711 Third Avenue, New York, NY 10017

Routledge is an imprint of the Taylor & Francis Group

ISBN 978-1-84392-280-3 paperback
     978-1-84392-281-0 hardback

British Library Cataloguing-in-Publication Data

A catalogue record for this book is available from the British Library

Project managed by Deer Park Productions, Tavistock, Devon
Typeset by GCS, Leighton Buzzard, Bedfordshire

Contents

Figures and tables

Tables

Notes on contributors

Luc Anselin is Foundation Professor of Geographical Sciences, Director of the School of Geographical Sciences, and Director of the GeoDa Center for Geospatial Analysis and Computation at the Arizona State University in Tempe, Arizona. He holds a PhD in regional science from Cornell University. His research deals with various aspects of spatial data analysis and geographic information science, ranging from exploratory spatial data analysis to geocomputation, spatial statistics and spatial econometrics. He has published widely on these topics and is the developer of the SpaceStat and GeoDa software packages.

Patricia Brantingham, AB, MA, MS, PhD, a mathematician and urban planner by training, is RCMP University Professor of Computational Criminology and Director of the Institute for Canadian Urban Research Studies at Simon Fraser University. She served as Director of Programme Evaluation at the Department of Justice Canada in the mid-1980s. Dr Brantingham is the author or editor of two dozen books and scientific monographs and more than 100 articles and scientific papers. She is one of the founders of environmental criminology and is currently the leader of an international collaboration in computational criminology linking university research laboratories around the world.

Paul Brantingham, BA, JD, Dip. Crim., a lawyer and criminologist by training, is RCMP University Professor of Crime at Simon Fraser University. He taught at Florida State University prior to joining the School of Criminology at Simon Fraser University. Professor Brantingham was Director of Special Reviews at the Public Service Commission of Canada in the mid-1980s and has been a member of the California Bar since 1969. Professor Brantingham's best known books include *Juvenile Justice Philosophy* (West Pub. Co. 1974; second edition 1978), and *Environmental Criminology* (Waveland Press 1981; second edition 1991) and *Patterns in Crime* (Collier Macmillan 1984) both co-authored with Patricia Brantingham.

Ronald V. Clarke is a professor at Rutgers University and Visiting Professor at the Jill Dando Institute, University College, London. He worked for fifteen years in the Home Office and was head of the Research and Planning Unit from 1982–84. While at the Home Office he helped to develop situational crime prevention and to launch the British Crime Survey. He is author or joint author of more than 200 publications including *Designing out Crime* (HMSO 1980), *The Reasoning Criminal* (Springer-Verlag 1986), *Superhighway Robbery: Preventing e-commerce crime* (Willan Publishing 2003), *Become a Problem Solving Crime Analyst* (US Department of Justice 2005) and *Outsmarting the Terrorists* (Praeger 2006).

Derek B. Cornish joined the Department of Social Science and Administration at the London School of Economics in 1978 to teach psychology, criminology and research methods. While there he pursued an interest in rational choice approaches to criminal decision-making (cf. *The Reasoning Criminal*, Springer-Verlag 1986, with R.V. Clarke), and in 'crime scripts'. He took early retirement in 2002 and now lives in the United States. Dr Martha Smith and he recently edited *Theory for Practice in Situational Crime Prevention* (Criminal Justice Press 2003) and *Safe and Tranquil Travel: Preventing crime and disorder on public transport* (Willan Publishing 2006).

Paul Cozens has extensive research, policy and practical experience in crime prevention through environmental design (CPTED). He is currently a research fellow at Curtin University of Technology in Perth, Western Australia (WA) and is an internationally accredited Advanced CPTED Practitioner. He obtained his PhD in Crime and Design in 2000 and subsequently held a four year research fellowship analysing CPTED and peoples' perceptions of crime associated with UK railway stations. In March 2004 Paul migrated to Perth, WA. From 2004–06 he held the post of principal policy officer at the Department of Premier and Cabinet to develop the state's Designing Out Crime Strategy, published in 2000.

John Eck is a professor in the Division of Criminal Justice at the University of Cincinnati. His primary areas of interest are crime prevention, problem-oriented policing and police effectiveness. In the late 1980s he led the first study of the full scale implementation of problem-oriented policing. He has been instrumental in the development of many of the commonly used tools of problem-oriented policing, including the SARA process and the problem triangle. With Ronald V. Clarke, he co-authored *Crime Analysis for Problem Solvers in 60 Small Steps*. Eck is the author of many other articles, chapters, and books on policing, crime, and prevention.

Paul Ekblom read psychology and gained his PhD at University College, London. As a Home Office researcher, Paul worked on many crime prevention projects; also horizon-scanning, Design against Crime and developing the professional discipline of crime prevention. Paul has worked with the EU Crime Prevention Network, Europol, the UN and Council of Europe. He is currently Professor and Co-director of the University of the Arts, London, Research Centre on Design Against Crime. Here, he works on design and evaluation of products, places and communications whilst continuing to develop practical conceptual frameworks for general crime prevention. Both fields are covered on www.designagainstcrime. com. Email: p.ekblom@csm.arts.ac.uk.

Graham Farrell, PhD, is Professor of Criminology at the Midlands Centre for Criminology and Criminal Justice at Loughborough University in the UK. He previously worked at the University of Cincinnati, the Police Foundation (Washington, DC), Rutgers University, the United Nations International Drug Control Programme (Vienna), the University of Oxford, and the Home Office. His research includes repeat victimisation, crime prevention and international drug policy.

Marcus Felson is Professor of Criminal Justice at Rutgers University. He is author of *Crime and Nature, Crime and Everyday Life,* and co-author (with Ronald V. Clarke) of *Opportunity Makes the Thief.* He has authored 'A Theory of Co-Offending' (2003) in J. Knutsson (ed.), *Problem-Oriented Policing,* Crime Prevention Studies Vol. 15 (Criminal Justice Press) and 'Redesigning Hell: Preventing Crime and Disorder at the Port Authority Bus Terminal' (1997) in R.V. Clarke (ed.), *Preventing Mass Transit Crime,* Crime Prevention Studies Vol. 6 (Criminal Justice Press). Professor Felson is the originator of the routine-activity approach to crime rate analysis, and has lectured in over twenty different nations.

Herman Goldstein is Professor Emeritus at the University of Wisconsin Law School and the original architect of the problem-oriented approach to policing. He was a researcher with the American Bar Foundation's landmark Survey of the Administration of Criminal Justice. From 1960–64, he was executive assistant to Superintendent O.W. Wilson of the Chicago Police Department, the architect of the professional model of policing. Goldstein has published widely on problem-oriented policing, the police function, police discretion, political accountability of the police, and control of police misconduct. He was co-author of the American Bar Association *Standards Relating to the Urban Police Function* and author of *Policing a Free Society* (1977) and *Problem-Oriented Policing* (1990).

Elizabeth Griffiths is an assistant professor in the Department of Sociology at Emory University, Atlanta. Her research focuses on explaining spatial and temporal trends in homicide across urban areas, including Buffalo, NY, Chicago, Los Angeles, and Pittsburgh, PA. Dr Griffiths' work largely explores patterns in the diffusion of homicide across cities, examining how and why some neighbourhoods experience a vulnerability to violence from surrounding communities while others are better able to effectively buffer violence. She is also presently a co-investigator on a multi-year evaluation of a HOPE VI public housing redevelopment project in Atlanta.

George Kelling is a senior fellow at the Manhattan Institute, a professor in the School of Criminal Justice at Rutgers University, and a fellow in the Kennedy School of Government at Harvard University. In the 1970s he conducted several large-scale experiments in policing, most notably the *Kansas City Preventive Patrol*

Experiment and the *Newark Foot Patrol Experiment*. The latter was the source of his contribution to his most familiar publication, 'Broken Windows', with James Q. Wilson. His most recent major publication is *Fixing Broken Windows: Restoring order and reducing crime in our communities*, which he has published with his wife, Catherine M. Coles (Free Press 1998).

Johannes Knutsson received his PhD in Criminology at Stockholm University. Presently he is Professor in Police Research at the Norwegian Police University College in Oslo and at the Swedish National Police Academy, where he has a part-time position. He is also a visiting professor of the Jill Dando Institute of Crime Science, University College, London and TRANSCRIME (Joint Research Centre on Transnational Crime) Università di Trento-Università Cattolica di Milano, Italy. Knutsson has published several evaluation studies of crime preventive measures as well as studies on different aspects of policing – uniformed patrol, crime investigations and police use of firearms.

Lorraine Mazerolle is the Director of the Australian Research Council (ARC) Centre of Excellence in Policing and Security (CEPS) and a Professor in the School of Criminology and Criminal Justice at Griffith University, Brisbane. She is the recipient of numerous US and Australian national competitive research grants on topics such as problem-oriented policing, police technologies (e.g. crime mapping, gunshot detection systems, 3-1-1 call systems), community crime control and street-level drug enforcement. Professor Mazerolle is a Fellow of the Academy of Experimental Criminologists and the author of three books and many scholarly articles on policing, drug law enforcement, displacement of crime, and crime prevention.

Ken Pease is a Chartered Forensic Psychologist and was Professor of Criminology at Manchester University. After retirement he has held visiting professorships at Loughborough University, University College, London and Chester University. He also sits on the Home Secretary's Design and Technology Alliance against Crime. The bulk of his published work has been on crime reduction. A volume in his honour was recently published under the title *Imagination for Crime Prevention* (Criminal Justice Press 2007).

Jerry H. Ratcliffe is a professor in the Department of Criminal Justice, Temple University, Philadelphia. He was a police officer with the Metropolitan Police in London for eleven years until a winter mountaineering accident prompted a move to academia. He has a PhD from the University of Nottingham that focused on spatial and temporal crime analysis techniques, and is a Fellow of the Royal Geographical Society. He has published over 50 research works including four books, the most recent of which is *Intelligence-Led Policing* (Willan Publishing 2008). He publishes and lectures on environmental criminology, intelligence-led policing and crime reduction.

Sacha Rombouts is a forensic psychologist and an associate of the Australian Research Council (ARC) Centre of Excellence in Policing and Security (CEPS) at

Griffith University, Brisbane. His research interests focus on recidivism among juvenile sexual offenders, terrorism, profiling and the development of risk assessment instruments. He is an expert in a number of sophisticated statistical techniques including time series, meta-analysis, and multi-level modeling. Dr Rombouts is trained in crime scene reconstruction and behavioural evidence analysis of unsolved crimes and in GIS software.

D. Kim Rossmo is the Roy F. and Joan Cole Mitte Endowed Chair in Criminology and the Director of the Center for Geospatial Intelligence and Investigation in the Department of Criminal Justice at Texas State University. He has researched and published in the areas of environmental criminology, policing and offender profiling. Dr Rossmo was formerly the Director of Research for the Police Foundation and the Detective Inspector in charge of the Vancouver Police Department's Geographic Profiling Section. He is a member of the IACP Advisory Committee for Police Investigative Operations and is currently writing a book on criminal investigative failures.

Michael Scott is the director of the Center for Problem-Oriented Policing and clinical associate professor at the University of Wisconsin Law School, specializing in research and teaching in policing. Scott was formerly a police chief in Lauderhill, FL, and served in various civilian police administrative positions in St. Louis, MO; Ft. Pierce, FL, and New York City; and was a police officer in Madison, WI. He was a Senior Researcher at the Police Executive Research Forum (PERF) in Washington, DC. Scott holds a JD from Harvard Law School and a BA in Behavioural Science and Law from the University of Wisconsin.

William Sousa is an assistant professor in the Department of Criminal Justice at the University of Nevada, Las Vegas. He received his PhD from Rutgers University, Newark, his MS in Criminal Justice from Northeastern University, Boston, and his BA in Criminal Justice from Stonehill College, Easton, MA. His current research projects involve police order-maintenance practices, police management, and community crime prevention.

George Tita is an associate professor in the Department of Criminology, Law and Society at the University of California, Irvine. His research is anchored in the community and crime literature with a special focus on the causes and correlates of interpersonal violence. In addition to exploring how youth gangs impact spatial dimensions of crime, he is also interested in examining how racial and ethnic change at the neighbourhood level impact levels and patterns of crime. In addition to spatial analysis, Dr Tita has employed diverse set of methodologies in his research including quasi-experimental methods (propensity score matching), hedonic models, agent-based models, and social network analysis.

Michael Wagers is an assistant professor in the Department of Political Science and Criminal Justice at The Citadel, the Military College of South Carolina. He received his BS and MS in Criminal Justice from the University of North Carolina at Charlotte and his PhD from the Rutgers School of Criminal Justice, Newark. He consults with police across the United States, including most recently departments in Los Angeles, Denver, Milwaukee and Allentown, PA.

Richard Wortley is a professor in the School of Criminology and Criminal Justice at Griffith University, Brisbane. He was a prison psychologist for ten years before moving to academia. It was observing the reactions of prisoners to the prison environment that initiated his interest in situational approaches to explaining and preventing crime. Recent books include *Situational Prison Control: Crime prevention in correctional institutions* (Cambridge University Press 2002) and *Preventing Child Sexual Abuse* (co-authored with S. Smallbone and W. Marshal, Willan Publishing 2008). He is a past national chair of the Australian Psychological Society's College of Forensic Psychologists.

Foreword

by Gloria Laycock

This book offers both a retrospective and a prospective contribution to the control of crime. Retrospective in that it looks back over the development of some of the key theories and ideas in use today, and brings them up to date. Prospective in that it offers an exciting promise of the potential for bringing crime under some sort of control without the excessive use of imprisonment or of oppressive security. Its underlying assumption is that, like all scientists, we need to understand the problems we are trying to solve, measure them, articulate them, reduce them to the lowest common denominator and then respond to them. In doing this, again like all scientists, we use theories, models and concepts that help us to refine the problem and point to the potential solution. And like all scientists we want to know whether that solution was correct – did it work? This entire approach is grounded in scientific method. That is why this book is a wholly appropriate addition to the Crime Science Series.

Crime science is a new approach to crime reduction, drawing on science in many forms: its methods – testing hypotheses, drawing on and building theories but also questioning and rebuilding them – its rigour, its many challenges and its excitement. Increasingly government officials, policy-makers and advisers, as well as law enforcement staff and security practitioners, are realising that there are real gains to be made if we can better understand the drivers of crime and disorder – and one of these is opportunity. Crime opportunities are everywhere if you are looking for them, as many of the more prolific offenders are, but they are also there to fall into, as young people can readily testify. We need to ensure that in our societies such opportunities are brought under some sort of control; that we do not create crime waves by mistake. The contributors to this book will provide the tools – both conceptual and practical – to do just that.

Gloria Laycock
Series Editor
Jill Dando Institute of Crime Science, UCL
London 2008

Preface

The nature of crime is changing. Emerging transnational terrorist threats and crimes such as sex-worker trafficking, identity theft, and illicit goods smuggling have joined an array of already established state-centric crime and disorder problems, challenging police and security agencies to forge closer partnerships, better coordinate their interventions, and develop innovative responses in the interests of national security. Federal and state governments throughout the world spend billions of dollars to control and prevent terrorism and associated criminality. Many new domestic laws and programs have been implemented and dozens of offshore and global initiatives are under way to create greater global security.

Environmental Criminology and Crime Analysis offers an exciting and fresh approach to the understanding of and response to contemporary crime problems. It has much to offer those engaged in the task of investigating, controlling and preventing crime and our book is an important resource for practitioners, students, researchers and others in the field. For the first time, the foundational theories, concepts and techniques that comprise the environmental perspective in criminology – presented in chapters written by the leading researchers in the field – have been brought together into one volume.

As we detail in this book, the great appeal of the environmental perspective is its applied focus and the engagement by researchers with criminal justice agencies and crime prevention practitioners. Adherents make no bones about their desire to reduce crime and are prepared to get their hands dirty in the process. And there is clear evidence that the environmental perspective is gaining increasing traction among end-users in criminal justice agencies. For example, a dedicated website (www.popcenter.org) that posts evidence-based guides for tackling crime problems experiences some two million hits, and 60,000 downloads of its pdf files, per month.

The worldwide popularity of the environmental perspective is growing among academics and researchers. In North America, the School of Criminal Justice at Rutgers University, with Ron Clarke and Marcus Felson, and Simon

Fraser's School of Criminology, with Pat and Paul Brantingham, remain intellectual centres for the environmental perspective. In order to provide a forum to exchange research and ideas, and to encourage new researchers in the field, these researchers founded an annual symposium in Environmental Criminology and Crime Analysis (ECCA) that draws members from around the world.

Prominent ECCA researchers from the US include Gisela Bichler (California State University San Bernardino), Rachel Boba (Florida Atlantic University), Sharon Chamard (University of Alaska), Derek Cornish (Jill Dando Institute of Crime Science), Marti Smith (Wichita State University), John Eck (University of Cincinnati), Rob Guerette (Florida International University), Keith Harries (University of Maryland Baltimore County), Jim LeBeau (Southern Illinois University), Steve Lab (Bowling Green State University), Mangai Natarajan (John Jay College of Criminal Justice), Graeme Newman (SUNY Albany), Jerry Ratcliffe and George Rengert (Temple University), Jennifer Robinson (Northeastern University), Kim Rossmo (Texas State University) and Jacqueline Schneider (University of South Florida).

In the UK, the Jill Dando Institute of Crime Science at University College London is home to leading figures in the field such as Gloria Laycock, Nick Tilley, Ken Pease, Kate Bowers, Shane Johnson and Spencer Chainey. JDI was founded by broadcaster Nick Ross (co-presenter with Jill Dando of the BBC *Crimewatch* programme) in 2001 with the explicit aim of bringing the scientific method to bear on the problem of crime reduction. Other notable British contributions to the environmental perspective have been made by Alex Hirschfield and Andrew Newton (University of Huddersfield), Paul Ekblom (University of the Arts London), Graham Farrell (Loughborough University) and Barry Webb (British Home Office).

In Australia at Griffith University, the editors of this volume (Lorraine Mazerolle and Richard Wortley), along with colleagues including Mike Townsley and Ross Homel, belong to a new Australian Research Council-funded Centre of Excellence in Policing and Security (CEPS) devoted to furthering the cause of evidence-based crime prevention. On the other side of the country, Frank Morgan heads an active research team at the University of Western Australia's Crime Research Centre.

Johannes Knutsson (National Police Academy, Norway), Tadashi Moriyama (Takushoku University, Japan), Tinus Kruger (Council for Scientific and Industrial Research, South Africa) and Henk Elffers (Netherlands Institute for the Study of Crime and Law Enforcement) lead the advance of the environmental perspective in other parts of the world and have been active ECCA participants for many years.

Each year the ECCA symposium is held in a new location, and in recent years there have been particular efforts to take the symposium to countries showing an emerging interest in the environmental perspective. Past locations have included Japan, Norway, Spain, South Africa, Chile and Turkey, with future meetings planned for Brazil and India. The participation of local academics and criminal justice practitioners is actively encouraged. The challenge taken up by ECCA is to shake free of the North American- and Euro-centric bias of traditional criminology and raise the profile of crime prevention on the international policy reform agenda. Our hope is that this book can contribute in some small way to this aim.

Richard Wortley and Lorraine Mazerolle

Brisbane, 2008

1. Environmental criminology and crime analysis: situating the theory, analytic approach and application

Richard Wortley and Lorraine Mazerolle

Introduction

Environmental criminology is a family of theories that share a common interest in criminal events and the immediate circumstances in which they occur. According to Brantingham and Brantingham (1991a: 2), 'environmental criminology argues that criminal events must be understood as confluences of offenders, victims or criminal targets, and laws in specific settings at particular times and places'. Environmental criminologists look for crime patterns and seek to explain them in terms of environmental influences. From these explanations they derive rules that enable predictions to be made about emerging crime problems, and that ultimately inform the development of strategies that might be employed to prevent crime.

Crime analysis is an investigative tool, defined as 'the set of systematic, analytical processes that provide timely, pertinent information about crime patterns and crime-trend correlations' (Emig *et al.* 1980). It uses crime data and police reports to study crime problems, including the characteristics of crime scenes, offenders and victims. Crime patterns are analysed in terms of their socio-demographic, temporal and spatial qualities, and may be represented visually using graphs, tables and maps. Using these findings, crime analysts provide tactical advice to police on criminal investigations, deployment of resources, planning, evaluation and crime prevention.

Where the job of the crime analyst is to describe crime patterns, the job of the environmental criminologist is to understand them. These two tasks are highly interdependent and each informs the other. On the one hand, crime analysts provide the facts that are the focus of environmental criminology and which are needed by environmental criminologists to develop and test their theories. On the other hand, environmental criminology is increasingly used by crime analysts to guide them in the questions they ask of crime data and in the interpretations that they place on their findings. Together, the tasks of describing and understanding crime patterns comprise the environmental perspective on crime.

1

The concerns of the environmental perspective contrast sharply with those of most other criminological approaches. Traditional criminological theories are concerned with *criminality*. They seek to explain how biological factors, developmental experiences and/or social forces create the criminal offender. In this, they take a historical perspective, focusing on the distant causes of crime. The occurrence of crime is understood largely as an expression of the offender's acquired deviance, which may be a function of events that occurred many years beforehand. Once the criminal has been created, crime is seen as more or less inevitable: the exact location and timing of the criminal act is of little interest. The prevention of crime is viewed in terms of changing offenders' fundamental criminality through enriching their childhoods, removing social disadvantage, and – once they have offended – providing them with rehabilitation programmes.

The environmental perspective takes a very different view. Here *crime* is the object of interest. The offender is just one element of a criminal event, and how offenders come to be the way they are is of little immediate relevance. Instead, the focus is on the current dynamics of crime – where did it happen, when did it happen, who was involved, what did they do, why did they do it, and how did they go about it? The aim of the environmental perspective is to prevent crime, not to cure offenders.

The environmental perspective is based on three premises.

1 Criminal behaviour is significantly influenced by the nature of the immediate environment in which it occurs. The environmental perspective depends upon the principle that all behaviour results from a person–situation interaction. The environment is not just a passive backdrop for criminal behaviour; rather, it plays a fundamental role in initiating the crime and shaping its course. Thus, crime events result not only from criminogenic individuals; they are equally caused by criminogenic elements of the crime scene. Environmental criminology explains how immediate environments affect behaviour and why some environments are criminogenic.

2 The distribution of crime in time and space is non-random. Because criminal behaviour is dependent upon situational factors, crime is patterned according to the location of criminogenic environments. Crime will be concentrated around crime opportunities and other environmental features that facilitate criminal activity. Crime rates vary from suburb to suburb and from street to street, and may peak at different times of the day, different days of the week, and different weeks of the year. The purpose of crime analysis is to identify and describe these crime patterns.

3 Understanding the role of criminogenic environments and being aware of the way that crime is patterned are powerful weapons in the investigation, control and prevention of crime. This knowledge allows police, crime prevention practitioners and other interested groups to concentrate resources on particular crime problems in particular locations. Changing the criminogenic aspects of the targeted environment can reduce the incidence

of crime in that location. Environmental criminology and crime analysis combine to provide practical solutions to crime problems.

Across these three domains of theory, analysis and practice, the environmental perspective is multi-disciplinary in its foundations, empirical in its methods and utilitarian in its mission. The environmental perspective draws on the ideas and expertise of sociologists, psychologists, geographers, architects, town planners, industrial designers, computer scientists, demographers, political scientists and economists. It embraces measurement and the scientific method, and it is committed to building theories and providing advice based on rigorous analysis of the available data. Finally, environmental criminologists and crime analysts actively engage with law enforcement personnel and crime prevention practitioners to help reduce crime.

The purpose of this volume is to bring together the key components of environmental criminology and crime analysis and, in doing so, comprehensively map the field. Despite the apparently unifying definitions and attributes outlined above, the environmental perspective encompasses a varied collection of approaches. Beneath a shared concern with crime patterns and the environment are differing levels of analyses, methods of enquiry and explanatory models. In this chapter we unpack the historical roots of the environmental perspective on crime and outline the key concepts that have emerged within the field. In the process, we demonstrate our logic for showcasing the work of leading theorists and researchers in environmental criminology and crime analysis. We begin with an analysis of the early influences on the environmental perspective on crime. We then describe the chronology of work that has shaped our contemporary understanding of environmental criminology and crime analysis. We conclude with a synopsis of the sections and chapters of this edited volume that are structured and guided by the three basic premises of the environmental perspective.

Historical roots of the environmental perspective

The contemporary array of approaches in environmental criminology and crime analysis reflects the diverse roots from which the perspective has sprung. The influences have come down through different disciplines that in turn have viewed the relationship between crime and the environment through an analytic lens set at different levels of magnification. Brantingham and Brantingham (1991b) identified three levels of analysis in the environmental perspective – macro, meso and micro – and it is useful to trace the foundations of the field in terms of these categories.

Macro-analytic roots

Macro analysis 'involves studies of distribution of crime between countries, between states or provinces or cities within a particular country, or between the counties or cities within a state' (Brantingham and Brantingham 1991b: 21). Analysis at this highly aggregated level constituted the earliest way of conceptualising environmental influences on crime, and indeed, studies of this sort represented some of the first 'scientific' criminological research.

Pioneering this line of research in the late 1820s, André-Michel Guerry and Adolphe Quetelet independently conducted detailed analyses of French crime statistics (see Beirne 1993). From this research came the first recognisable examples of crime maps, depicting crime rates for the provinces of France. The maps were shaded to reflect various socio-demographic features such as poverty and education levels. Guerry and Quetelet both found that crime was not evenly distributed across the country, and further that the distribution varied according to the crime in question. Contrary to expectations, violent crime was highest in poorer rural areas while property crime was highest in wealthy, industrialised areas. From this they reasoned that poverty did not cause property crime, but rather opportunity did. Wealthy provinces had more to steal. Their observation about the role of opportunity has remained a central principle of environmental criminology through to the modern era. Likewise, the use of maps to represent crime trends has become the standard technique of crime analysis.

Similar studies in other countries soon followed, as did comparisons between countries (see Brantingham and Brantingham 1991b). For example, research in England in the late nineteenth century found wide differences in crime rates across counties, again with higher rates reported for urban and industrialised areas than for rural areas. Macro-level analysis of crime trends continued into the twentieth century. In the US, significant and stable differences in crime rates and patterns were found among cities and states. However, there are limits to what such aggregated data can show. Inevitably, as we will see in the following sections, there was a trend towards analysis at higher levels of resolution.

Meso-analytic roots

Meso analysis 'involves the study of crime within the subareas of a city or metropolis' (Brantingham and Brantingham 1991b: 21). These areas represent intermediate levels of spatial aggregation, and may range from suburbs and police districts down to individual streets and addresses. We present two seminal contributions to the meso-level analysis of crime and the environment, the first from sociology and the second from architecture.

The sociological roots of the environmental perspective can be traced to the human ecology movement, known as the Chicago School, in the early part of the twentieth century. Ecology is a branch of biology that examines the intricate balance achieved by plant and animal life within their natural habitat. The basic premise of ecology – that individual organisms must be studied as part of a complicated whole – was adopted by a group of sociologists at Chicago University and applied to the study of human behaviour. Members of this group included Robert Park, Ernest Burgess, Clifford Shaw and Henry McKay. In particular, this group is noted for its research on migration trends within urban communities and the effects on criminal activity and other forms of social disorder. In this research, the city was conceptualised as a super-organism comprising a collection of sub-communities based around ethnic background, socio-economic class, occupation, and so on. Members within these sub-communities were bound together by symbiotic relationships, and the sub-communities in turn were in symbiotic relation with one another (Park 1952). However, ecological equilibrium is subject to change. In the natural world, a new plant may invade and dominate an area until it becomes the successor species. A similar pattern occurs in cities. Burgess (1928) proposed that the city could be divided into five concentric rings or zones. At the centre, Zone I, was the business district; around this was Zone II, where the poorest citizens lived in old, run-down houses; then came Zone III, where workers lived in modest houses; there was another step up the social ladder in Zone IV; and finally, Zone V comprised satellite suburbs from where relatively affluent commuters travelled. With population growth, there is a natural process of invasion, domination and succession as citizens migrate from inner to outer zones.

During the 1930s Shaw and McKay built on these observations to investigate the relationship between neighbourhoods and delinquency (see Shaw and McKay 1969). They found that delinquency was greatest in Zone II. The neighbourhoods in Zone II contain the poorest citizens, have the least effective social and economic support systems, and offer the most criminal opportunities. In addition, these neighbourhoods are subject to two kinds of invasion. First, because they are adjacent to the industrial and commercial centre they are put under pressure as the central area expands and fewer buildings are available to live in. Second, because Zone II has the cheapest housing new immigrants are drawn to it. The influx of immigrants, many with adjustment problems associated with their immigrant status, increases the social disorganisation of the neighbourhood through cultural transmission. However, as residents of Zone II make their gradual journey to outer zones, they do not take their delinquency with them. That is, the lesson for the environmental perspective is that the social problems exhibited in Zone II are features of the neighbourhood conditions rather than inherent features of the individuals who reside there.

The second significant influence on the environmental perspective at the meso level was the work of Jane Jacobs. Like members of the Chicago School, she was interested in cityscapes and the built environment, but at a more local, street level. Moreover, her work contained clear prescriptions for reducing crime. In 1961 she published *The Death and Life of Great American Cities* in which she argued that many of the orthodox indices of poor city planning – the intermingling of industrial, commercial and residential areas; the division of neighbourhoods into small city blocks divided by a criss-cross of streets; the presence of ageing buildings; and the reliance on high-density living with the corresponding absence of open, green spaces – did not actually predict social disorganisation. Using the North End district of Boston as an example, she demonstrated that an area regarded by many as a slum could in fact be well maintained, vibrant and relatively crime-free. Despite breaking the accepted rules of good urban design – or more accurately, because these rules were broken – the environment of North End created opportunities for residents to interact and to develop mutual support systems. Based on these observations, Jacobs proposed a radical rethink of urban design principles.

Crime occurs, Jacobs argued, when residents feel isolated and anonymous, and believe that they have no stake in their neighbourhood. What mattered, therefore, were planning policies that helped bring people together and to foster a sense of community. Jacobs set out four conditions of urban design to put these principles into practice. First, the district should cater to a multitude of purposes. The inclusion of commercial, industrial and recreational activities in residential areas means that streets and parks are in constant use and residents can interact with each other at all times of the day. Second, districts should be divided into small blocks with frequent corners and interconnecting streets that permit residents to readily access all areas. Such a configuration unifies the district and ensures that there are no deserted backstreets and other dead zones. Third, there should be a mixture of new and older buildings to ensure a diversity of enterprises that the district can support. While banks, chain stores and the like can afford the infrastructure costs of new buildings, restaurants, bookstores, antique shops and other establishments that are essential to the cultural life of the district are typically found in older buildings. Finally, population density needed to be sufficiently concentrated to support diversity and to facilitate the interaction among residents. The problems often associated with high-density living, she argued, have often more to do with the nature of the featureless tower blocks that residents are forced to inhabit rather than population density *per se*. Together, these planning principles were designed to get people on to the streets. This not only helped build social networks for their own sake, it also encouraged residents to notice outsiders and to provide informal surveillance of the neighbourhood. This she referred to as having 'eyes on the street'. An important consequence, therefore, was increased community safety. In advancing these proposals, Jacobs foreshadowed the explicit crime prevention mission of the environmental perspective.

Micro-analytic roots

Micro analysis examines specific crime sites, focusing on 'building type and its placement, landscaping and lighting, interior form, and security hardware' (Brantingham and Brantingham 1991b: 21–2). In comparison to ecological approaches, micro-level analysis reflects an increasingly reductionist philosophy where the whole is broken down into its smaller constituent parts. At this level, the focus is on the effects that specific elements of the immediate environment have on specific decisions and behaviours of individuals. Crucial in the development of this line of analysis are the debates in psychology about the locus of the causes of behaviour.

Psychology as a discipline has been traditionally concerned with the investigation of individual differences. A great deal of psychological theory and research is devoted to the study of internal constructs, or traits – personality, attitudes, beliefs and so on – that are assumed to drive behaviour and to differentiate one person from the next. In classic trait theory, the psychological make-up of each individual is seen to comprise various dimensions, and on each dimension an individual can be located somewhere along a continuum. For example, everybody is presumed to fall somewhere along an extroversion/ introversion dimension. Once acquired, a person's psychological attributes are viewed as being more or less fixed. Everybody can be described in terms of their characteristic personality profile and on this basis their behaviour in new situations can be reliably predicted. Someone described as extroverted will behave in an extroverted fashion in most circumstances, and can be readily distinguished from a person who is described as introverted. It is the person's psychological make-up that determines how they behave.

This theoretical focus on dispositions parallels the way human beings intuitively account for events. In our everyday experience, we have a natural tendency to see individuals as being fully in charge of their actions. This is particularly so where the outcomes are negative. Psychologists call this cognitive bias fundamental attributional error (Jones 1979; Ross 1977). We typically overestimate the role of other people's personal characteristics when assessing their responsibility for undesirable behaviour, while at the same time we discount the role of immediate environmental factors. Interestingly, this does not apply when we assess our own bad behaviour – we are only too happy to cite the role of extenuating environmental circumstances in our own case. This ingrained faith that behaviour is caused largely by an individual's psychological disposition can make it difficult to sell the environmental perspective on crime.

However, though dominant, the dispositional model has never been universal in psychology, and there is simultaneously a long history of theory and research that has been interested in the way that behaviour is influenced by the immediate environment. This alternative tradition was cogently articulated by Walter Mischel in 1968. Mischel brought to prominence the so-called cross-situational consistency debate, which revolves around the extent to which people possess underlying traits that remain stable from one situation to the next. Drawing particularly on the conditioning models in learning theory, Mischel advocated a position of behavioural specificity. According to Mischel, the way an individual behaves can vary dramatically from one situation to the next, depending upon the nature of the immediate environmental influences. For example, Michael Jackson can be extroverted on stage but painfully introverted when being interviewed. If we think for a moment about our own behaviour we similarly recognise that we behave differently in different contexts – for example, we may act one way with our colleagues and another with our family.

Applied to criminal behaviour, the principle of behavioural specificity has important implications. In the first place, it suggests that the performance of criminal behaviour is not restricted to a small, definable group of offenders with criminal dispositions – given the right circumstances, most people are capable of illegal conduct. Rape, for example, is a frequent occurrence in war zones and is often carried out by soldiers who in other circumstances would never have contemplated such behaviour. But furthermore, even chronic,

7

predatory offenders do not commit crime all of the time nor indiscriminately – in fact they offend relatively infrequently and only under certain favourable conditions. Knowledge of the precise circumstances in which crime occurs is crucial for a complete understanding of criminal conduct and traditional theories of criminology that are devoted to explaining the development of criminality as a fixed attribute are missing a key ingredient. Micro-level analysis has become particularly influential in the development of crime prevention strategies within the environmental perspective.

Contemporary environmental approaches

The aim of this section is to examine the contemporary development of the environmental perspective and show how various contributions intersect. This is not a straightforward task. The history of the environmental perspective is by no means an orderly or linear progression of ideas, and a strict chronology of contributions would be of little value. Instead, we trace developments that have taken place, more or less in tandem, within a number of different approaches. Four basic ways of conceptualising the crime–environment interaction were identified in the previous section and each of these has generated a research tradition in the contemporary environmental perspective. Building on the architectural insights of Jacobs and others, some researchers have focused on the design of the built environment. Based on the principle of behavioural specificity, other researchers have examined specific offences in specific locations. Others, following the socio-demographic research of Guerry and Quetelet, have focused on the impact of broad social forces on crime trends. And, in the tradition of the Chicago School, still other researchers have investigated urban crime patterns. To these four approaches one more has emerged, and that is a focus on the delivery of environmental strategies through enhancements to policing practice. We examine each of these five approaches in turn. We do not discuss each contribution in detail: that is the task of the chapters in our book. Rather, our aim is to highlight the chronology of intellectual thought within each approach, and to indicate the key areas and time periods of overlapping development among the approaches.

Designing the built environment

By general agreement, the birth of the modern environmental perspective in criminology can be dated quite precisely to 1971/72. In the space of a year two books appeared, written independently of one another by authors working at the same university, that systematically set out frameworks for reducing crime by modifying immediate environments. Even their titles bore striking similarity. The first book, *Crime Prevention Through Environmental Design* was written by criminologist C. Ray Jeffery (1971); the second, *Defensible Space: Crime Prevention Through Urban Design*, was written by architect Oscar Newman (1972).

Both authors, but Newman in particular, presented meso- to micro-level architectural solutions to crime. Newman's concept of defensible space extends Jacob's ideas about the need for residents to take responsibility for crime in their immediate neighbourhoods. Defensible space can be created in a number of ways. First, Newman proposed strategies for increasing in residents their sense of ownership over private and semi-public space by more clearly defining territorial boundaries. This might be achieved through the erection of real and symbolic markers such as fences and gates, or through displaying conspicuous signs that an area is occupied and cared for. Second, he suggested ways of increasing opportunities for natural surveillance so that criminal activity might be better observed. This might be achieved through the placement of windows, the routing of pedestrian traffic, the elimination of blind-spots and so forth. In Newman's model of defensible space, the built environment affects the behaviour of offenders indirectly. Environmental design primarily aims to change the behaviour of residents, who then, through their increased vigilance, deter potential offenders.

Of the two authors, Jeffery presented a wider vision. In addition to architectural and urban planning solutions to crime, he suggested strategies ranging from broad social policies at one extreme to micro-level psychological interventions at the other. He was particularly influenced by the operant conditioning models of Skinner (1953), which had provided much of the theoretical and empirical support for the situational side of the cross-situational consistency debate. Skinner argued that behaviour was controlled by its consequences, and Jeffery thought the key to crime control was through the design of environments and the implementation of social policies that systematically decreased the rewards for criminal behaviour and increased the risks. He also recognised that criminal behaviour cannot occur without opportunity, which he saw as a necessary but not sufficient condition for crime. Jeffery's position was perhaps the most radical in the environmental perspective, amounting to situational determinism. 'There are no criminals,' he declared, 'only environmental circumstances that result in criminal behaviour. Given the proper environmental structure, anyone will be a criminal or a non-criminal' (Jeffery 1977: 177).

Although Jeffery's term Crime Prevention Through Environmental Design (CPTED) has stuck, it has been Newman's narrower architectural approach that has proved the more popular and enduring. CPTED has gone through some modifications and remains widely used today, especially among architects and urban planners (see Cozens, Chapter 9, this volume). Moreover, CPTED was a catalyst for a flurry of activity in the environmental criminology field, and core ideas within the model were widely adopted by subsequent theorists. Within a decade of the publication of Jeffery's and Newman's books, most of the foundational approaches of the environmental perspective had appeared.

Focusing on specific offences and settings

The next major contribution to the environmental perspective came in the mid 1970s with Ron Clarke's development of situational crime prevention.

Situational crime prevention represents the micro-level extreme of the environmental perspective. Clarke argued that the key to crime prevention was to focus on very specific categories of crime, and to understand their precise situational dynamics. His approach incorporated aspects of Newman's defensible space, but philosophically it owes a greater debt to the psychological theories examined by Jeffery. Like Jeffery, Clarke saw reduction of opportunity and the manipulation of the costs and benefits of crime as the bases for prevention. However, Clarke offered what Jeffery did not, and that was a comprehensive set of concrete strategies for operationalising his crime prevention principles.

The impetus for Clarke was his research on absconding from residential training schools for delinquents (Clarke and Martin 1975). Unable to find consistent personal variables that predicted absconding, he found instead that absconding rates varied according to a number of institutional factors. The best way to prevent absconding was not to identify potential absconders but rather to change the way that institutions were built and run. While head of the British Home Office Research Unit during the 1970s, Clarke developed this idea into a comprehensive model of situational crime prevention and set about putting the prevention principles into practice (Clarke 1980).

The psychological basis of situational prevention was made more explicit with the development of the rational choice perspective (Cornish and Clarke 1986, and Chapter 2, this volume), which was formulated retrospectively to underpin the model. In rational choice perspective, offenders are portrayed as active decision-makers who use environmental data to make purposive decisions about engaging in crime. These decisions can be considered rational inasmuch as the offender seeks to benefit in some way from the contemplated behaviour. Crime will occur when the perceived benefits outweigh the perceived costs. The practical implication of rational choice perspective, delivered through situational crime prevention, is that crime can be reduced by reducing criminal opportunities by designing environments that make crime an unattractive option from the perspective of the decision-maker.

Over the years, Clarke's original crime prevention model has evolved and expanded to account for additional theoretical insights on offender decision-making. His original taxonomy of prevention strategies – involving the three dimensions of reducing of rewards, increasing risks and increasing effort – appeared in 1992, (Clarke 1992). In 1997, in collaboration with Ross Homel, he added a fourth column that examined techniques for removing excuses for crime (Clarke and Homel 1997). The basis for this strategy was the observation that, aided by environmental conditions, offenders may seek to reduce personal inhibitions by minimising the perceived criminality of their behaviour. An additional column, reducing provocations, was added in 2003, (Cornish and Clarke 2003). This was in response to Richard Wortley, who argued that situations can actively precipitate criminal behaviour (Wortley 2001, 2002). Wortley drew on a range of psychological theories that supported the principle of behavioural specificity. According to his argument, offenders do not necessarily enter the crime scene motivated to exploit criminal opportunities. Situational factors, such as peer pressure and environmental stress, can induce individuals to commit crimes they might not have otherwise considered (see Wortley, Chapter 3, this volume). The most recent situational crime prevention model involves a five-column matrix of 25 techniques (Cornish and Clarke 2003; Clarke, Chapter 10, this volume).

The situational crime prevention model has been applied to a wide variety of crimes and situations (see Clarke 1992, 1997 for collections of case studies). One particular spin-off has been in the area of product design. An early insight of Clarke's was that some products were inherently criminogenic because they were attractive and easy to steal. Based on this observation, Paul Ekblom (then part of Clarke's research team at the Home Office) wrote an article speculating on the design of the crime-free car, and this was the forerunner for an active research programme in designing products against crime (Ekblom 1979; Chapter 11, this volume).

Examining wider social trends

While Clarke was taking the environmental perspective to more fine-grained levels, Cohen and Felson (1979) were examining crime patterns and trends in terms of broad social forces. Cohen and Felson set out to explain the apparent paradox that crime rates after World War Two rose substantially at the same time that economic conditions improved. According to traditional criminological theories that associated crime with poverty, crime rates might have been expected to fall during this period. Paying explicit homage to the demographic research of Guerry and Quetelet, and to the ecological theories of the Chicago School, they argued that higher crime rates could be explained by the changes in the routine activities of everyday life that accompanied economic prosperity. Crime was caused, they said, by 'the convergence in space and time of the three minimal elements of direct-contact predatory violations: (1) motivated offenders, (2) suitable targets, and (3) the absence of capable guardians against a violation' (1979: 589). Improved economic conditions often had the incidental effect of bringing these three elements into alignment. For example, with the increased participation of women in the workforce, there was an accompanying increase in the number of houses left unattended during the day. At the same time, growing affluence and technological advances meant that there were more valuable personal possessions available to steal. These factors helped explain why rates of daytime residential burglaries doubled between 1960 and 1975, while the rates for commercial burglaries almost halved.

While the routine activities approach was pitched largely at the macro-analytic level, it has been very influential in the environmental perspective generally. Subsequent refinements by Felson (1994, 1998, and Chapter 4, this volume) explored the micro-level implications of the approach, and the compatibility of routine activities with rational choice and situational crime prevention (Clarke and Felson 1993). It was realised that the three necessary elements for crime – an offender, a target and an absent guardian – provided a framework for analysing the dynamics of individual crime events and for determining points of intervention for crime prevention. For example, some crimes occur because of the easy accessibility of vulnerable targets and so intervention requires target-hardening strategies; other crimes are the result of poor management of facilities and so require interventions that strengthen guardianship. The familiar crime triangle ('hot' offenders, 'hot' locations, 'hot' targets) used in operational policing is based on the routine activities approach (Clarke and Eck 2003).

Exploring crime patterns

As we have learned, some of the earliest research on crime–environment relationships involved examination of the geographic distribution of crime. Since the pioneering work of Guerry and Quetelet, there has been a continuous line of research that has focused on mapping crime patterns. The idea of mapping the spatial distribution of crime was picked up by the Chicago School, whose focus on intra-city crime patterns reflected a trend away from macro- to meso-level analysis. For the most part, though, this research remained largely peripheral to mainstream criminology. However, since the 1980s there has been a resurgence of interest in understanding and analysing the geo-spatial dimension of crime. This renewed activity is related to two main factors – the development of new theories of crime patterns, and the advent of powerful geographic software.

From the early 1980s, Patricia and Paul Brantingham began developing their ideas on the movement of offenders in time and space that would eventually become crime pattern theory (Brantingham and Brantingham 1984, 1993, and see also Chapter 5, this volume). Showing the influence of the routine activities approach in particular, but focusing on the meso level, crime pattern theory attempts to account for the non-uniformity and non-randomness that characterises the criminal event. According to Brantingham and Brantingham, crime is associated with the distribution of key activities in a community (e.g. work and recreation) and an offender's familiarity with the urban environment. Crime is argued to occur in predictable locations defined by the intersection of crime opportunities and an offender's awareness space. The work of the Brantinghams and others has provided much of the theoretical bases for crime analysis.

Advances in crime analysis were further aided by the widespread availability by the 1990s of geographic information system (GIS) software for personal computers. Mapping technology allowed the spatial and temporal distribution of crime to be readily modelled, and in particular, for crime concentrations, or hot spots, to be identified. The publication by Sherman, Gartin and Bueger (1989) of an analysis of hot spots for predatory crime heralded a new era of applied mapping research. Hot spots became the obvious priority for policing resources and crime prevention efforts (see Anselin, Griffiths and Tita, Chapter 6, this volume).

One phenomenon that emerged from hot spot analysis was repeat victimisation. It was observed that some places or people had particular vulnerabilities and were victimised on multiple occasions (Farrell and Pease 1993). For example, a burgled house may be soon re-burgled. Similarly, many victims of assault have experienced prior episodes of victimisation. These people or locations are sometimes call 'hot dots' (Pease and Laycock 1996). Policing repeat victims is an especially efficient way of allocating resources to crime prevention (see Farrell and Pease, Chapter 7, this volume).

Another variation of hot spot analysis is geographic profiling. Building on the general crime pattern theories of Brantingham and Brantingham, geographic profiling maps the behaviour of an individual serial offender. By examining the geographic distribution of offences, estimations can be made of the likely area where the offender resides, or other places (e.g. work location) that serve as an anchor point or base of operations. Based on the distributions of their crimes, the analyst derives clues about where the offender is likely to live, work and move (see Rossmo and Rombouts, Chapter 8, this volume).

Working through the police

Some contributions to the environmental perspective were less concerned with the mechanics of the person–situation interaction or descriptions of crime patterns than with the methods of delivery of crime prevention strategies. They focused on equipping police with the necessary methods and tools to implement environmental interventions. The seminal model in this regard is Herman Goldstein's (1979) problem-oriented policing (POP). POP provides a problem-solving framework for police to intervene to prevent crime problems within their jurisdiction before those problems develop or get out of control. But, insisted Goldstein (1990), it is also more than this: 'In its broadest context, it is a whole new way of thinking about policing that has implications for every aspect of police organization, its personnel, and its operations' (1990: 3). POP seeks to transform fundamentally the way that policing is conceptualised.

Goldstein's colleagues John Eck and Bill Spelman operationalised the problem-oriented policing approach by setting out an action model for tackling crime problems. They summarised the steps in this model using the acronym SARA, standing for scanning, analysis, response and assessment (Scott, Eck, Knutsson and Goldstein, Chapter 12, this volume). The first step is to scan for recurring crime problems, grouping similar incidents into clusters. Information about the crime problem must then be collected and analysed, and the underlying causes identified. Based on this intelligence, a tailor-made response is formulated. Finally, the effectiveness of the response is assessed, and if necessary (i.e. the response is ineffective), the process starts again. Within this framework, the actual strategies available to police are not prescribed. Rather, the officer is encouraged to search for new and exciting alternatives to traditional policing responses. After careful analysis of the problem, the responses are only limited by the officer's enthusiasm and creativity.

Shortly after Goldstein's original paper appeared, James Q. Wilson and George Kelling (1982) published the article *Broken Windows: The Police and Neighborhood Safety*, which stemmed from the research of Kelling and his colleagues on the Fear Reduction Experiments in Newark and Houston, funded by the National Institute of Justice in the US Department of Justice.

The foot patrol experiment in Newark was particularly influential in creating the foundations of the 'broken windows' metaphor. With echoes of Jacobs and Newman, Wilson and Kelling addressed the role of neighbourhood decay in crime and the implications for policing. They argued that lack of attention to small signs of neglect and petty crime can lead to more serious crime problems. Fixing broken windows is a metaphor for addressing these criminogenic incivilities. In contrast to POP, the broken windows approach is built on a central idea about crime causation and also contains explicit crime prevention instructions. The approach was famously institutionalised as an operational police tactic when it was espoused as the justification for the policing strategies employed by police chiefs such as William Bratton and Howard Safir under the mayorship of Rudolph Giuliani in New York City during the 1990s (see Wagers, Sousa and Kelling, Chapter 13, this volume). Most controversially, the broken windows approach was operationalised as the vigorous enforcement of laws against disorderly behaviour and other minor offences. Some commentators credit the broken windows approach as being instrumental in contributing to New York City's significant drop in crime rate.

The most recent contribution to the policing and environmental criminology field is the intelligence-led policing model (see Ratcliffe, Chapter 14, this volume). It is difficult to pinpoint the precise introduction of this approach, but the term began being used in the policing literature during the 1990s (e.g. Smith 1994). Its implementation coincided with, and was to a considerable extent dependent upon, the development of the crime analysis techniques described in the previous section. Intelligence-led policing is a model of police management and law enforcement that makes strategic use of crime data and criminal intelligence. Like POP, then, intelligence-led policing presents a style of police practice, rather than a model of crime events.

Conclusion

From these disparate beginnings, the environmental perspective has emerged to become arguably the fastest growing approach in criminology and criminal justice. Once regarded by many criminologists as esoteric and largely peripheral to the main game, the approach has increasing acceptance and influence. The relatively small and scattered group of original researchers in the field has been joined by a new wave of academics and practitioners from around the world, making the approach truly international. The perspective itself continues to evolve and expand, with new research and ideas published almost daily. Technology is changing the face of crime and the environmental perspective is well placed to respond to the new challenges that this poses (see Clarke 2004). The crimes of the twenty-first century are increasingly organised in nature and global in scope. Terrorism (Clarke and Newman 2006), internet fraud (Newman and Clarke 2003), internet child pornography (Wortley and Smallbone 2006), organised crime (van de Bunt and van der Schoot 2003), and smuggling of immigrants (Guerette and Clarke 2005) are just some of the problems to which environmental criminology and crime analysis have been applied in recent years.

The organisation of this book

There is to date no book that collects the seminal contributions to the environmental perspective into a single volume. With this volume we fill this gap. In addition to this introductory chapter, we present thirteen original chapters by leading theorists and practitioners in the field, most of whom are identified with developing the original concept which they present.

The order in which the contributions are arranged can play an important role in helping to bring coherence to the field. In the introduction to this chapter, we outlined three premises on which the environmental perspective is founded: that crime is best understood in terms of an interaction between the offender and the immediate environment; that crime is therefore patterned according to the criminogenic nature of the environment; and that knowledge of crime patterns is useful in the prevention and control of crime. Working sequentially through these three domains of theory, analysis and practice seems to us to be a logical way of unfolding the environmental perspective story.

The first section we have labelled 'Understanding the Crime Event'. Four ways of conceptualising the contribution of immediate environments to crime are presented in this section. Chapters 2 and 3 examine the psychology of the individual offender. We have previously argued that environmental criminology is concerned with crime, not criminality. While this true, the perspective only makes sense if one begins with a model of human action that explains how offenders might moderate their behaviour according to the demands of moment. In Chapter 2 Derek Cornish and Ron Clarke present 'Rational Choice Perspective', examining the decision-making processes of offenders as they contemplate criminal involvement. In Chapter 3, Richard Wortley argues that 'Situational Precipitators of Crime' augment rational choice by readying the individual to offend. Two chapters then examine crime patterns at the macro and meso levels. In Chapter 4, Marcus Felson outlines 'Routine Activity Approach', examining variations in crime rates in terms of broad social trends. Chapter 5 presents 'Crime Pattern Theory' by Paul and Patricia Brantingham. This chapter drills down to explain crime patterns at the neighbourhood and street level. Rather than presenting contradictory views on the crime–environment nexus, these four models present explanations at different levels of analysis. Together they provide the theoretical bases for the environmental perspective that underpin the practices of crime analysis and crime prevention.

The second section, 'Analysing Crime Patterns', covers approaches that focus on the geo-spatial distribution of crime and the selection of specific crime targets by offenders. The section begins with an overview by Luc Anselin, Elizabeth Griffiths and George Tita, in Chapter 6, of 'Crime Mapping and Hot Spot Analysis'. Graham Farrell and Ken Pease, in Chapter 7, then examine the phenomenon of 'Repeat Victimisation' and its implications for crime prevention. Finally, in Chapter 8, Kim Rossmo and Sacha Rombouts set out the principles and techniques of 'Geographic Profiling'. These chapters present the key analytical techniques of environmental criminology and crime analysis.

In the third and final section, 'Preventing and Controlling Crime', we examine the end-use application of environmental criminology and crime analysis. Understanding and analysing crime patterns can tell us where and when crime is likely to occur, but this understanding on its own is not necessarily sufficient to suggest effective intervention strategies. The perspectives covered in this section are concerned with what we actually do to address crime problems in those locations that are identified as criminogenic. The first three chapters examine methods of crime prevention. Chapter 9, by Paul Cozens, covers the architectural approach embodied in 'Crime Prevention Through Environmental Design'. Chapter 10, by Ron Clarke, is on 'Situational Crime Prevention', taking an offence-specific approach to prevention. Chapter 11 by Paul Ekblom, looks at a sub-category of situational prevention in the form of 'Designing Products Against Crime'. The final three chapters then examine the delivery of crime prevention and control strategies from within a policing context. Chapter 12 by Michael Scott, John Eck, Johannes Knutsson and Herman Goldstein, is on 'Problem-oriented Policing'. In Chapter 13, 'Broken Windows', Michael Wagers, William Sousa and George Kelling make the case that attending to minor disorder prevents the development of major crime problems. Finally, in Chapter 14, Jerry Ratcliffe examines the utilisation of the results of crime analysis via 'Intelligence-led Policing'.

References

Beirne, P. (1993) *Inventing Criminology*. Albany, NY: SUNY Press.

Brantingham, P.J. and Brantingham, P.L. (1984) *Patterns in Crime*. New York: Macmillan.

Brantingham, P.J. and Brantingham, P.L. (1991a) 'Introduction to the 1991 Reissue: Notes on Environmental Criminology', in P. Brantingham and P. Brantingham (eds) *Environmental Criminology*, 2nd edn. Prospect Heights, IL: Waveland Press, pp. 1–6.

Brantingham, P.J. and Brantingham, P.L. (1991b) 'Introduction: The Dimensions of Crime', in P. Brantingham and P. Brantingham (eds) *Environmental Criminology*, 2nd edn. Prospect Heights, IL: Waveland Press, pp. 7–26.

Brantingham, P.L. and Brantingham, P.J. (1993) 'Environment, Routine and Situation: Towards a Patterns Theory of Crime', in R.V. Clarke and M. Felson (eds) *Routine Activity and Rational Choice. Advances in Criminological Theory, Vol. 5*. New Brunswick, NJ: Transaction Publishers.

Burgess, E.W. (1928) 'The Growth of the City', in R.E. Park, E.W. Burgess and R.D. McKenzie (eds) *The City*. Chicago, IL: University of Chicago Press.

Clarke, R.V. (1980) 'Situational Crime Prevention: Theory and Practice', *British Journal of Criminology*, 20: 136–47.

Clarke, R.V. (ed.) (1992) *Situational Crime Prevention: Successful Case Studies*. Albany, NY: Harrow and Heston.

Clarke, R.V. (ed.) (1997) *Situational Crime Prevention: Successful Case Studies*, 2nd edn. Albany, NY: Harrow and Heston.

Clarke, R.V. (2004). 'Technology, Criminology and Crime Science', *European Journal on Criminal Policy and Research*, 10: 55–63.

Clarke, R.V. and Eck, J. (2003). *Become a Problem-solving Crime Analyst*. London: Jill Dando Institute of Crime Science.

Clarke, R.V., and Felson, M. (eds) (1993) *Routine Activity and Rational Choice. Advances in Criminological Theory, Vol. 5*. New Brunswick, NJ: Transaction Publishers.

Clarke, R.V. and Homel, R. (1997) 'A Revised Classification of Situational Crime Prevention Techniques', in S.P. Lab (ed.) *Crime Prevention at the Crossroads*. Cincinnati, OH: Anderson, pp. 17–27.

Clarke, R.V. and Martin, D.N. (1975) 'A Study of Absconding and its Implications for the Residential Treatment of Delinquents', in J. Tizard, I.A. Sinclair, and R.V. Clarke (eds) *Varieties of Residential Experience*. London: Routledge and Kegan Paul, pp. 249–74.

Clarke, R.V. and Newman, G.R. (2006) *Outsmarting the Terrorists*. Westport, CT: Praeger Security International.

Cohen, L.E. and Felson, M. (1979) 'Social Change and Crime Rate Trends: A Routine Activity Approach', *American Sociological Review*, 44: 588–608.

Cornish, D.B. and Clarke, R.V. (1986) *The Reasoning Criminal: Rational Choice Perspectives on Offending*. New York, NY: Springer-Verlag.

Cornish, D.B., and Clarke, R.V. (2003) 'Opportunities, Precipitators and Criminal Dispositions: A Reply to Wortley's Critique of Situational Crime Prevention', in M.J. Smith and D.B. Cornish (eds), *Theory for Practice in Situational Crime Prevention. Crime Prevention Studies, Vol. 16*. Monsey, NY: Criminal Justice Press.

Ekblom, P. (1979) *A Crime Free Car?* Home Office Research Bulletin 7. London: Home Office.

Emig, M., Heck, R. and Kravitz, M. (1980) *Crime Analysis: A Selected Bibliography*. Washington, DC: US National Criminal Justice Reference Service.

Farrell, G. and Pease, K. (1993) *Once Bitten, Twice Bitten. Repeat Victimisation and its Implications for Crime Prevention*, Crime Prevention Unit Paper 46. London: Home Office.

Felson, M. (1994) *Crime and Everyday Life: Insights and Implications for Society*. Thousand Oaks, CA: Pine Forge.

Felson, M. (1998) *Crime and Everyday Life*, 2nd edn. Thousand Oaks, CA: Pine Forge.

Goldstein, H. (1979) 'Improving Policing: A Problem-oriented Approach', *Crime and Delinquency*, 25: 236–58.

Goldstein, H. (1990) *Problem-oriented Policing*. New York: McGraw Hill.

Guerette, R. and Clarke, R.V. (2005) 'Border Enforcement, Organized Crime, and Deaths of Smuggled Migrants on the United States–Mexico Border', *European Journal on Criminal Policy and Research*, 11: 159–74.

Jacobs, J. (1961) *The Death and Life of Great American Cities*. New York: Random House.

Jeffery, C.R. (1971) *Crime Prevention Through Environmental Design*. Beverly Hills, CA: Sage.

Jeffery, C.R. (1977) *Crime Prevention Through Environmental Design*, 2nd edn. Beverly Hills, CA: Sage.

Jones, E.E. (1979) 'The Rocky Road from Acts to Dispositions', *American Psychologist*, 34: 107–17.

Mischel, W. (1968) *Personality and Assessment*. New York, NY: Wiley.

Newman, G.R. and Clarke, R.V. (2003) Superhighway Robbery: Preventing E-commerce Crime. Cullompton, UK: Willan Publishing.

Newman, O. (1972) *Defensible Space: Crime Prevention Through Urban Design*. New York: Macmillan.

Park, R.E. (1952) *Human Communities*, Glencoe, IL: The Free Press.

Pease, K. and Laycock, G. (1996) *Revictimization: Reducing the Heat on Hot Victims*. Washington, DC: National Institute of Justice.

Ross, L. (1977) 'The Intuitive Psychologist and his Shortcomings: Distortions in the Attribution Process', in L. Berkowitz (ed.) *Advances in Experimental Psychology, Vol. 10.* New York, Academic Press.

Shaw, C.R. and McKay, H.D. (1969) *Juvenile Delinquency and Urban Areas.* Chicago, IL: University of Chicago Press.

Sherman, L., Gartin, P. and Bueger, M. (1989) 'Hot Spots of Predatory Crime: Routine Activities and the Criminology of Place', *Criminology,* 27: 27–55.

Skinner, B.F. (1953) *Science and Human Behavior.* New York: Macmillan.

Smith, A. (ed.) (1994) *Intelligence-led Policing: International Perspectives on Policing in the 21st Century.* Lawrenceville, NJ: International Association of Law Enforcement Intelligence Analysts.

van de Bunt, H. and van der Schoot, C. (2003) *Prevention of Organised Crime: A Situational Approach,* WODC Report 215. Netherlands: Ministry of Justice.

Wilson, J.Q. and Kelling, G.L. (1982). 'Broken Windows: The Police and Neighborhood Safety', *The Atlantic Monthly,* March: 29–38.

Wortley, R. (2001) 'A Classification of Techniques for Controlling Situational Precipitators of Crime, *Security Journal,* 14(4): 63–82.

Wortley, R. (2002) *Situational Prison Control: Crime Prevention in Correctional Institutions.* Cambridge: Cambridge University Press.

Wortley, R. and Smallbone, S. (2006) *Child Pornography on the Internet,* Problem-oriented Guides for Police Series. Washington, DC: US Department of Justice.

Part One

Understanding the Crime Event

2. The rational choice perspective

Derek B. Cornish and Ronald V. Clarke

Introduction

Asked why he robbed banks, Willie Sutton is said to have replied, 'Because that's where the money is' (Cocheo 1997). His wisecrack was later elevated into a rule-of-thumb – Sutton's Law – to guide physicians when making diagnoses: 'Go first for the most likely explanation.' Curiously there seems to be no equivalent Sutton's Law in criminology, where one might most expect to find one.

Maybe, though, by responding to a question about motivation with an answer about target selection, Willie Sutton has a message for the discipline. By turning a question about motivation into an answer about criminal decision-making, the wisecrack pinpoints the disconnect between traditional criminological theory – preoccupied with the development of criminality and the supposed roots of crime – and a newer crime science, more concerned with the practical business of understanding how to prevent crime here and now. If there were to be a Sutton's Law for crime science, it might run along the following lines: 'If you want to develop practical ways of preventing criminal activity, go for the obvious: pay less attention to theorising about criminal motivation, and more attention to finding out about how crimes happen.'

The rational choice perspective provides just one such theory for practice. Instead of viewing criminal behaviour as the outcome of stable criminal motivations, it views the desires, preferences and motives of offenders and potential offenders as similar to those of the rest of us, and as in continual interaction with contemporary opportunities and constraints to produce, reinforce and sometimes reduce criminal behaviours. At its core are the concepts of choice and decision-making, present-centredness, and the centrality of the crime event to continued criminal activity – success in offending driving the development of criminal lifestyles, and failure leading to reduction and change in criminal activity, or to desistance.

Background and history

The rational choice perspective was one outcome of a general shift of focus in British criminology that took place during the 1970s (Clarke and Cornish 1983). In the 1960s criminal behaviour was believed to be primarily the result of long-standing criminal predispositions and psychopathologies that caused individuals to offend. Research efforts were therefore heavily invested in programmes to prevent the development of criminality, viewed as a complex of attitudes, personality traits, and dispositions to offend. Criminality, it was thought, could be changed through appropriate treatments, and these changes once made would then persist.

When evaluations of existing programmes failed to find convincing evidence of their effectiveness, it called into question this prevailing medico-psychological model of the causation of offending. Many of these programmes, including the ones we studied (Cornish and Clarke 1975), often removed offenders from their natural environments, treated them in residential institutions, and reinserted them with varying degrees of support into their post-treatment environments. Once released, relapse was commonplace, but one of the puzzling features of the failure of rehabilitation to bring about lasting change was the fact that offenders were clearly affected by their treatment environments during their stay. Whether because of the rewards and punishments handed out by staff or as a result of other features of the treatment environment, such as the opportunities it offered to misbehave, institutional regimes varied in the effects they had on the behaviour of their inmates during treatment.

One positive by-product of the failure of the rehabilitative ideal, then, was the realisation that even if the effects of treatment were not permanent – that is, not generally maintained in the post-treatment environment – the treatment environments themselves seemed to have an influence on behaviour while the offender was exposed to them. Sinclair's (1971) study of probation hostels, for example, indicated that hostels varied in their failure rates – that is, proportions of boys leaving prematurely as the result of absconding or other misbehaviour – while Clarke and Martin's (1975) study of absconding from residential schools for delinquent children showed widely differing rates. Taken together these studies provided striking evidence of the effects of the immediate environment on inmates' behaviour.

Although offering little support to medico-psychological models of rehabilitation, such findings pointed to the influence of the current environment on behaviour. The resulting 'environmental/learning theory' explanation that was developed (Clarke and Martin 1975; Cornish and Clarke 1975) had four main elements (Clarke and Cornish 1983: 37):

1 While an individual's emotional inheritance and upbringing play some part in delinquency, the major determinants are those provided by the current environment.

2 The current environment provides the cues and stimuli for delinquency, as well as the reinforcements. Thus, a temporary mood of unhappiness,

anxiety or euphoria, resulting from recent crises or events, may place someone in a state of emotional readiness to commit an initial delinquent act. Whether in fact he or she does so will depend to a large extent on opportunity and the example of others. Once committed, a delinquent act, like any other behaviour, will become part of the individual's behavioural repertoire. Thereafter, reinforcement as well as opportunity becomes salient to its maintenance.

3 Since delinquent acts are learned in particular environments, they will only be repeated under closely similar conditions. Consistencies in behaviour over time are therefore dependent on consistencies in environments.

4 Delinquent acts of different kinds do not serve equivalent functions for the actor; each is acquired and maintained by situational variables specific to it, and it alone. This is not to deny, however, that some individuals, by virtue of their particular circumstances, may learn a range of delinquent behaviours.

The environmental/learning theory was specifically designed to explain the shortcomings of the medico-psychological model and redirect future efforts. Though rudimentary, the theory seemed to point to important influences on criminal behaviour that had been neglected, revealing it as being much more malleable, and dependent on environmental contingencies than had previously been supposed. As such, the theory provided an initial way of thinking about how the immediate environment influenced the likelihood of offending, and how it might be manipulated in order to prevent or reduce crime (see Clarke, Chapter 10, this volume).

Even so, the theory suffered from its use of concepts drawn from radical behaviourism, a theoretical orientation which was rapidly losing traction within psychology because of its reluctance to investigate cognitive aspects of behaviour. The rapid growth of situational crime prevention practice demanded a revised explanatory framework within which both developments in situational crime prevention and the criticisms which it was already attracting could be properly examined. Situational crime prevention was already beginning to use the language of choice and decision-making, and a simple choice model had been developed (Clarke 1980) as an opening move to counter the common criticism that situational measures would merely – and inevitably – lead to displacement. This was the notion that, stopped from committing a particular offence, the offender would simply displace the offending by choosing another time or place, a different target, a different modus operandi, or a different form of crime (Reppetto 1974). The adoption of the language of choice and decision-making allowed a more nuanced discussion of the circumstances under which displacement might or might not be expected to occur.

The transition from a radical behaviourist to a rational choice perspective was also mandated by practical considerations. The language of intentionality and choice is the discourse of the criminal justice system and of everyday life. Getting inside the offender's head to look at his or her decision-making was a far cry from the black box approach adopted by radical behaviourism. But the move to a new conceptual framework was needed to handle the burgeoning research on offenders' perceptions and decision-making that was taking place in the early 1980s (Bennett and Wright 1984; Maguire and Bennett 1982; Walsh 1980), especially given its relevance to situational crime prevention.

By this time the choice model was on its way to becoming a rational choice one (Clarke and Cornish 1983: 50). A study of gambling provided support for this development. Traditionally, psychiatrists had depicted much gambling as pathologically motivated, while economists and decision theorists had often found gamblers' choices to be apparently irrational in financial terms when measured against outcomes. Viewed in the light of gamblers' real-life motives, needs and options, however, gambling emerged as both more complex and more rational than suspected, especially given the circumstances under which gambling took place and given the difficulty of making decisions under conditions of uncertainty, using partial and sometimes deliberately misleading information (Cornish 1978).

A survey of the criminological literature of the time (Clarke and Cornish 1985: 149) described 'the convergence of interest among a variety of academic disciplines – the sociology of deviance, criminology, economics, and cognitive psychology – upon a conception of crime as the outcome of rational choices' on the part of offenders. This view was further developed in a volume that assembled original papers from researchers working, broadly speaking, within a rational choice perspective (Cornish and Clarke 1986). The picture that emerged was one of offenders as reasoning criminals, using cues present in potential crime settings to guide their decisions about whether (or not) to commit particular crimes and, if so, how to commit them.

Core concepts of the rational choice perspective

The rational choice perspective is a heuristic device or conceptual tool rather than a conventional criminological theory. (We will return to this important point later.) Its purpose has always been to offer a way of looking at offending that is both present-centred and recognises the influence of the environment on behaviour. This environment is both the environment of everyday life – lifestyle and its motives, needs and inducements – and the more particular environment of instrumental action to achieve particular goals. As currently conceptualised the rational choice perspective consists of six core concepts and four decision-making models embodying them.

- Criminal behaviour is purposive.
- Criminal behaviour is rational.
- Criminal decision-making is crime-specific.
- Criminal choices fall into two broad groups: 'involvement' and 'event' decisions.
- There are separate stages of involvement.
- Criminal events unfold in a sequence of stages and decisions.

Criminal behaviour is purposive

When trying to make sense of human behaviour, we seem to make use a rather simple theory of action. People have needs and desires, and beliefs about how these can be fulfilled. Guided by these beliefs, they take actions to achieve their particular goals. This relationship between desires, beliefs and actions gives behaviour its purposive character, and we go about making behaviour intelligible to ourselves by trying to establish the purposes of actions and by identifying the nature of desires and beliefs that fuel and guide them.

When it comes to crime, however, we often lose sight of the instrumental nature of much action. Media reports of crime – particularly of violent crimes against persons, animals, and property – are replete with descriptions of offending as senseless, incomprehensible, irrational or thuggish when applied to offences as diverse as joyriding, domestic violence, assault, rape, football hooliganism and vandalism. While these may rightly reflect our horror and outrage, the emotions they arouse do little to help us understand and prevent criminal behaviour. The rational choice perspective takes the view that crimes are purposive and deliberate acts, committed with the intention of benefiting the offender. The benefits of offending include satisfying the usual human motives, such as desires for sexual gratification, excitement, autonomy, admiration, revenge, control, reduction of tension, material goods and so on. Money, of course, can buy many of these satisfactions – sex, drugs, freedom from control by others – so it becomes a convenient and important goal of offending in its own right.

Criminal behaviour is rational

In daily life we assume most of the time that people's actions are not only purposive and intelligible, but also rational: that, given their motives and goals, individuals will try to select the best available means to achieve them. This presumption of rationality underpins explanations of human action. As Herrnstein (1990: 356) has commented, it 'comes close to serving as the fundamental principle of the behavioral sciences. No other well articulated theory of behavior commands so large a following in so wide a range of disciplines.' Karl Popper also emphasised the advantages of using the presumption of rationality as an essential methodological principle (Knepper 2007).

Presuming rationality is not, however, the same as presuming perfect rationality. It is here that the rational choice perspective departs from the normative models of rational choice found in modern economics and decision theory. Instead, the perspective offers a more nuanced view of rationality in practice, borrowing from Herbert Simon (1990) the notion of a more limited or bounded rationality. This recognises that in the real world action often has to be taken on the basis of decisions made under less than perfect circumstances. Offending is inherently a risky business, and the possible costs and benefits are difficult to estimate in advance. To these uncertainties are added time pressures, and differences in skill and experience on the part of individual offenders in interpreting what information there is. Under these conditions,

25

which are far from perfect, and despite offenders' best efforts, decisions are likely to produce 'satisficing' – that is, satisfactory and sufficient – outcomes rather than optimal ones most of the time.

The presumptions of purposiveness and (bounded) rationality put criminal behaviour on the same footing as any other human activity. Of course, offenders vary in their skills, experience and intelligence, sometimes make mistakes, act rashly, fail to consider all sides of a problem, ignore or downplay risks, or act while under the influence of drugs and alcohol. But these departures from rationality hardly make offenders more fallible than anyone else. And criminal decision-making is by its very nature likely to be prone to error because of the constraints under which it often has to operate.

Criminal decision-making is crime-specific

Crime is often treated as though it were one unitary phenomenon, rather than a set of rather diverse behaviours. There is a place for generalising about crime – aggregate crime rates, for example, can be used as indicators of societal malaise – and all crime by definition involves law-breaking. But treating crime as a unitary phenomenon often leads to the development of simple theories to explain crime and simple policies to combat it. Practical crime-control efforts are forced to be less ambitious and better focused. When called upon to do something about crime, distinctions start to be made in terms of type, degree and consequences within the general category of crime. What people want is to be protected from particular types of crime events. At the local level, getting tough on crime is shorthand for dealing with a shopping list of specific criminal activities that people want stopped.

In fact, offenders don't commit crime, but carry out specific crimes, each of which has its own particular motives, purposes and benefits. Rape may gratify sexual need and desires for dominance, control and humiliation; burglary may satisfy a need for cash or goods, but also a desire for 'sneaky thrills' (Katz 1988). In other words, specific offences bring particular benefits to offenders and are committed with specific motives in mind. Because crimes differ from one another, the factors weighed by offenders, and the variables influencing their decision-making, will also differ greatly with the nature of the offence. This is especially noticeable when considering the choices and decisions made when committing the crime itself. The circumstances surrounding the passing of a dud cheque – the nature of the risks, efforts and rewards, the activities undertaken and the locations within which they take place – are very different from those surrounding the planning and committing of a terrorist event.

This means that even the ostensibly finer distinctions among crimes, made by lawyers and statisticians – such as violent crime, computer fraud or sex offending – may be too broad to use as a basis for understanding criminal decision-making. This is because they may still include many differently motivated offences, committed by a wide range of offenders, using a variety of methods with varying degrees of skill. Even offences that seem to cluster into natural groupings – car thefts, for example – will be found to differ in important ways according to the purposes for which they are committed and the ways they are carried out. Therefore, it is always important to distinguish the choices and decisions made in relation to joyriding from those related to vehicle theft for temporary transport, for parts, or for selling on to various markets. How crime-specific one needs to become will ultimately be a pragmatic decision, based upon the purpose at hand. While it may be important for theory to draw finer distinctions, for practical crime prevention purposes the stop-rule might well be the extent to which this would improve the prospects for designing more successful interventions.

The need to be crime-specific does not ignore the fact that many offenders are generalists, in the sense that they may commit a wide range of crimes over the course of their careers. Indeed, in order to support a criminal lifestyle an experienced offender may be engaging in many different crimes over the same period – from illegal parking and receiving stolen property to burglary, social security fraud, mugging drunks and aggravated assault – all to support and facilitate the different aspects of his or her life. But each of these crimes has its own purposes and its own methods of crime-commission at which the offender can hope to become more proficient over time, and out of which certain ones may become preferred solutions to particular needs.

Distinguishing criminal involvement from crime event decisions

The decisions that offenders and potential offenders make can be divided into two broad categories: involvement decisions and event decisions. Event decisions are crime-centred and concentrate upon crime-commission; as mentioned previously, they are crime-specific, and concern choices and decisions made when preparing for, carrying out and concluding the commission of a particular type of crime. Although the timescales of these decisions may differ for various types of crime, they are only as long as is necessary to complete these activities. The factors considered by offenders are also limited, being concerned primarily with the immediate tasks at hand, such as selecting a potential robbery victim, or choosing a safe location for a rape. Involvement decisions, on the other hand, concern the offender's criminal career, and include decisions about initial involvement (initiation), continued involvement (habituation) and desistance. Because of this they extend over longer timescales and, while they incorporate decisions about, and reactions to, offending, they are also concerned with a wider range of variables.

Involvement decisions, like event ones, are crime-specific, and must be studied separately for different crimes. Contemplating whether or not to get involved in a terrorist attack on a subway train is clearly very different from thinking about whether or not to fiddle one's tax returns, in terms of the relative complexities of the undertakings, the risks involved, the skills required, the alternatives to the crime in question, the moral considerations involved, and the costs of discovery. Similar considerations apply to decisions about continuation and desistance from particular crimes. One form of crime (a parking violation, for example) may play a relatively marginal role in sustaining a life of crime, while another (such as drug-dealing) may be economically vital. And the centrality of a crime, such as paedophilia, to other aspects of a person's life is likely to give decisions about continuation and desistance a special significance.

Distinguishing the separate stages of criminal involvement

Separating an offender's involvement in a particular form of crime into the three broad stages of initiation, habituation and desistance serves to emphasise the fact that at each stage different sets of variables influence the offender's decisions. For example, decisions about getting involved for the first time in that form of crime might be influenced by prior experience of having committed other kinds of crime, and by a range of background factors, such as personality and upbringing, and current circumstances, such as the individual's lifestyle and the needs and motives it generates, together with the opportunities and inducements available to the potential offender.

On the other hand, decisions to continue offending or to desist will be most powerfully affected by the criminal's success or failure in continuing to carry out the chosen crime, and by their impact on his or her lifestyle. Nor in real life are the transitions from initiation to desistance likely to be inevitable, smooth or sequential, since changes of pace and lulls in offending may also be affected by extraneous factors, such as ill health, marriage, divorce, death of a family member and other life events and crises.

In practice, too, an offender may be involved to varying degrees in a number of different forms of crime. In such cases, he or she will be making many different choices and decisions simultaneously, and existing experience at committing one form of crime may influence decisions about committing others. Decisions about desistance provide good examples of these issues. Lack of success at committing a particular type of crime – say, auto theft – may lead to a reduction in its frequency or even to desistance. But, if the offender is experienced and skilled at that form of offending, it may also lead to displacement. Thus, an offender may be able to continue committing the same type of offence, albeit at different times of day, at different locations, or towards different targets. Alternatively, especially if the offender has a wide repertoire of offending skills, he or she may turn to other methods – as from simple car theft to key theft (Copes and Cherbonneau 2006) or car-jacking – some of which may involve innovation. Finally, some offenders may turn to totally different forms of crime, especially where these share some of the important characteristics of previously preferred ones.

Multi-stage decision-making during the crime event

Identifying the *modus operandi* used by an offender in furtherance of a particular crime has long been recognised as an important aspect of both crime detection and crime prevention, but attention has often been confined to decision-making in relation to the central stages of a crime event, without equivalent attention to its opening and closing stages. But even beginning-middle-and-end conceptualisations of the process are too simple to capture the dynamic unfolding of criminal events, and the detailed requirements of the crime in terms of the resources and actions needed during each of its stages.

Empirical research during the 1980s and 1990s began to provide some of the necessary detail. Walsh's (1980) study of residential burglary, for example, drew attention to how offenders made use of local criminal knowledge networks when looking around for opportunities to burgle; and Rossmo's (2000) studies of serial murder have indicated just how complex are the demands of successful offending in terms of choice of locations for different stages of the crime event.

The decision-making models

We developed a set of simple flow diagrams to illustrate the decision processes for the three stages of criminal involvement, and for the criminal event. In the choice of crime to be modelled in the diagrams, we were guided by both theoretical and practical considerations: we wanted to be as crime-specific as existing knowledge allowed, but also to select an offence that was sufficiently common and serious to justify special preventive efforts. For these reasons we chose burglary as a volume crime over which there was considerable concern, and in relation to which considerable empirical research had been generated. In terms of crime-specificity, we chose suburban burglary, rather than residential burglary or simply burglary because we believed that burglaries committed in suburbs were quite different from those committed in the city centre. This belief was subsequently confirmed by Poyner and Webb (1991) who found that inner-city burglaries tended to be committed by offenders on foot who were looking for cash and jewellery, whereas those in the suburbs were committed by offenders who used cars and targeted electronic goods. Differences in the methods used to gain access were also found. Because there is restricted access to the side and rear of older town houses in England, entry was often gained through the front door or a front window. In the suburbs, however, burglars were as likely to enter from the back or side of the house as the front.

Initiation

Figure 2.1 illustrates the factors influencing the initial decision to become involved in suburban burglary. Box 1 lists various psychological and sociological background factors traditionally thought to influence the values, attitudes and personality traits that dispose people to commit crime. In terms of the rational choice perspective these factors are viewed as having more of an orienting function. On the one hand, they contribute to ongoing processes of learning and experience (Box 2) that influence the individual's perceptions and judgements about the attractiveness and viability of criminal activity. On the other hand the background factors also influence the individual's material conditions and the particular problems and opportunities to which they will be exposed. Thus, Box 3 deals with the offender's current life circumstances, such as his or her friends, employment, housing, marital status, aspects of lifestyle, and so on. These help to shape an individual's current needs and motives (Box 4), as well as current opportunities for meeting these needs, and the inducements that may trigger or increase them (Box 5). The other boxes

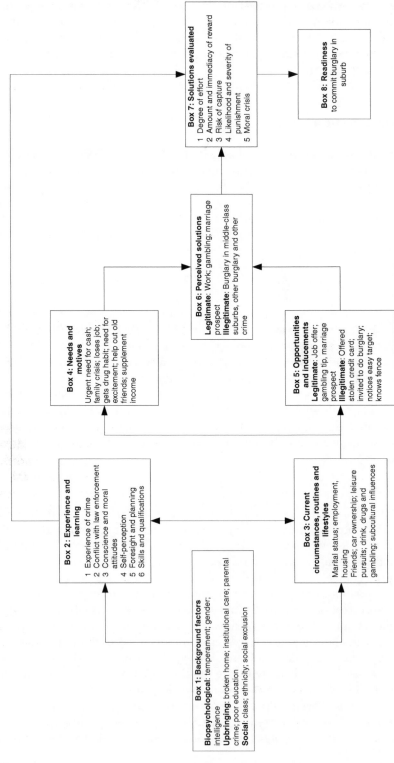

Figure 2.1 Initiation model (example: suburban burglary)
(*Source*: adapted from Clarke and Cornish 1985)

indicate how these needs are translated by the offender, based on his or her accumulated experience and learning, through a process of identifying and evaluating alternative courses of action (Boxes 6 and 7) into a readiness to become involved in this form of crime (Box 8). During this stage, background factors have their greatest influence, since they shape both the nature of the individual's accumulated learning and experience, and his or her current life circumstances.

Habituation

During habituation (Figure 2.2), background factors play less of a part in decisions. Instead, the dominant roles are exercised by contemporary ones: by the rewards of crime and by consequent changes in the offender's circumstances, such the acquisition of new friends, increased professionalism, and changes in lifestyle and associated values.

Desistance

At the stage of desistance (Figure 2.3), background factors have ceased to play any significant part in decision-making. Rather, it is lack of success in bringing crimes to satisfactory completion (including brushes with the law) and increasing reluctance to take risks, together with further changes in current life circumstances (such as marriage and increasing family responsibilities) that play the important roles in decisions to desist.

The crime event

For an experienced offender, decision-making in relation to the crime event (Figure 2.4) will tend to concentrate solely on those situational factors that hinder or advance instrumental action in fulfilment of the criminal goal. Since questions of needs and motives, moral scruples and readiness have already been addressed, they are unlikely to intrude into the decision-making process at this point unless the offender is inexperienced, or the action has been disrupted in some way – perhaps by unanticipated opposition or additional criminal opportunities that require a change of plan. But although the source of the variables considered during crime-commission may narrow, the decision-making process is not a simple one.

Crime scripts

In Figure 2.4, attention is focused on just two of the steps involved – the selection of area and target house – but as mentioned earlier offenders are presented with a much more complex sequence of decisions. To assist analysis of this process, Cornish (1994) subsequently proposed the concept of crime scripts, which are step-by-step accounts of the procedures used by offenders to commit particular crimes. Crime scripts are designed to help identify every stage of the crime-commission process, the decisions and actions that must be taken at each stage, and the resources – such as criminal cast, props and suitable locations – required for effective action at each step. By providing a

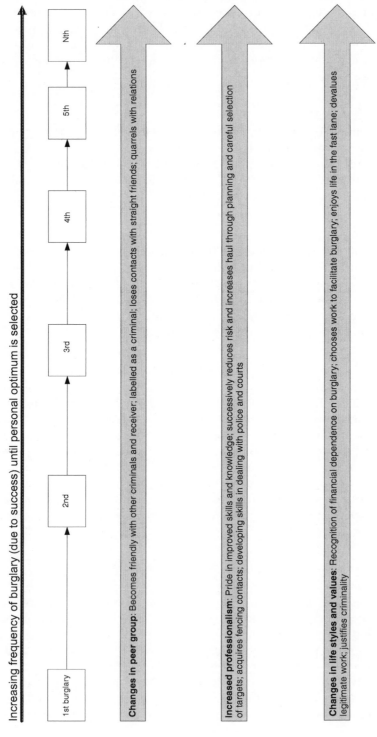

Increasing frequency of burglary (due to success) until personal optimum is selected

| 1st burglary | 2nd | 3rd | 4th | 5th | Nth |

Changes in peer group: Becomes friendly with other criminals and receiver; labelled as a criminal; loses contacts with straight friends; quarrels with relations

Increased professionalism: Pride in improved skills and knowledge; successively reduces risk and increases haul through planning and careful selection of targets; acquires fencing contacts; developing skills in dealing with police and courts

Changes in life styles and values: Recognition of financial dependence on burglary; chooses work to facilitate burglary; enjoys life in the fast lane; devalues legitimate work; justifies criminality

Figure 2.2 Habituation model (example: suburban burglary)
(*Source*: adapted from Clarke and Cornish 1985)

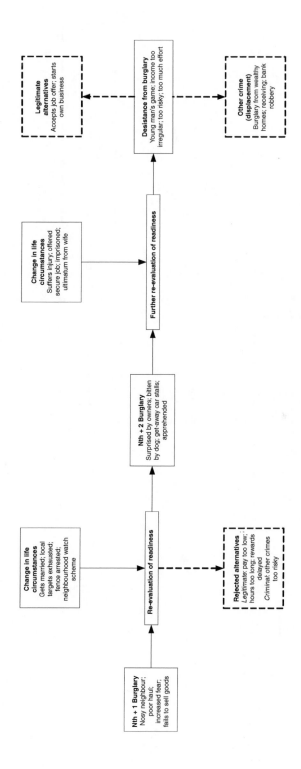

Figure 2.3 Desistance model (example: suburban burglary)
(*Source*: adapted from Clarke and Cornish 1985)

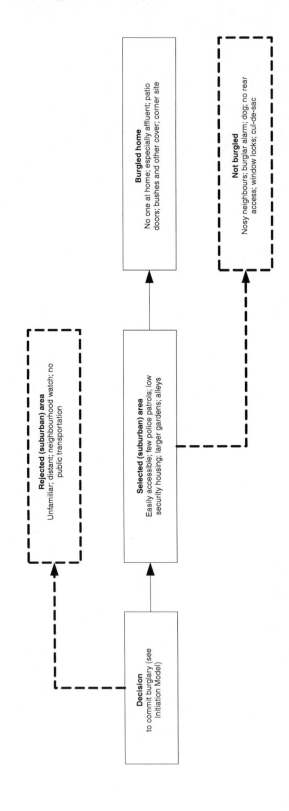

Figure 2.4   Event model (example: suburban burglary)
(*Source*: adapted from Clarke and Cornish 1985)

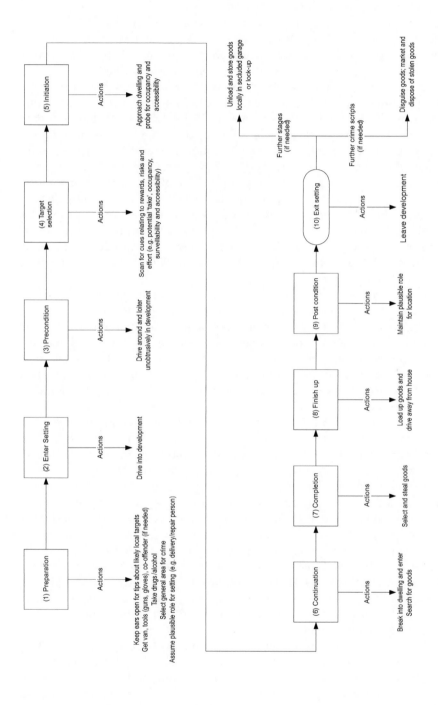

Figure 2.5 A simple crime script (example: suburban burglary)
(*Source*: adapted from Cornish and Clarke 2006)

template that outlines the necessary steps involved in any kind of successful offending, crime scripts can reveal the rationality in even ostensibly 'senseless' crimes, and the complexities of even simple ones.

One such possible sequence is briefly sketched out in Figure 2.5's crime script for suburban burglary. Notice that the stages of the crime script are relatively uniform across crimes, while their contents – the cast, props, locations and actions – are specific to the crime being described.

A need for cash, a chance meeting between burglars, or a hot tip about a suitable target may start the crime event. Preparations may include assembling tools for a break-in, and the theft of a vehicle for the trip to the suburban development. The next steps involve entering the neighbourhood, adopting a plausible reason for being there, and selecting a house to enter – ideally, one for which the promise of reward is high, and the effort and risks of breaking in are low. Getting into the house, systematically searching for, and rapidly choosing the goods to steal follow this stage. The goods must then be carried out to the van or car without being seen by neighbours or passers-by. Afterwards, they may have to be stored in some safe location while buyers are found. Finally, they must be delivered to the buyers in exchange for cash. Where they occur, the 'further stages' referred to in Figure 2.5 often constitute crime scripts of their own.

Such crime scripts range from comparatively simple sequences to more complex ones where many participants, locations and actions may be involved, and within which a number of crime scripts may be merged – as where vehicles and guns are stolen for a robbery, witnesses injured or killed, and the spoils are afterwards marketed (see, for example, the script for professional auto theft, or 'ringing': Cornish and Clarke 2002). The crime scripts themselves are subject to further development as new empirical data come to light. For example, Nee and Meenaghan (2006) have recently provided new data on methods of search used by burglars within targeted houses; and, in the context of auto theft, Cherbonneau and Copes (2006) have described in detail some of the strategies used by offenders to avoid detection ('hiding in the open') while driving a stolen vehicle. As well as making important contributions to our understanding of specific crime scripts involving auto theft, such research also suggests the need to pay more attention to analogous strategies used by offenders to establish and maintain plausible roles before, during and after the commission of other types of crime.

The concept of crime scripts has helped to provide further evidence of the importance of offender decision-making, its pervasive presence in criminal activity and its rational, purposeful nature. It also provides a detailed understanding of the crime-commission process – from the analysis of body switching, which involves the switching of vehicle identity numbers from crashed but legitimate vehicles to the bodies of stolen ones (Tremblay *et al.* 2001), to the hunting process of serial sex offenders (Beauregard *et al.* 2007), or the *modus operandi* of adolescent sex offenders (Leclerc and Tremblay 2007). The use of script analysis can be particularly illuminating when used in relation to complex crimes, such as terrorism (see, for example, the elaborate script developed by Clarke and Newman (2006) for suicide bombing).

Distinguishing characteristics of the perspective

In this section we describe some of the characteristics that distinguish the rational choice perspective from traditional criminological theories. It shares many of these distinguishing characteristics with routine activity theory (Felson, Chapter 4, this volume) and crime pattern theory (Brantingham and Brantingham, Chapter 5, this volume).

A theory for practice

The failure of rehabilitation programmes in the 1960s and 1970s was as much a failure of theory as of practice, and the need to find new means of reducing crime involved a search for new ways of thinking about the problem. The rational choice perspective that eventually emerged was intended to provide the conceptual framework for a new form of crime prevention practice – situational crime prevention (see Clarke, Chapter 10, this volume) – that was already being developed. Four contributions in particular to situational prevention should be mentioned:

1 It is the source of the injunction, when thinking about prevention, to examine crime from the offender's perspective as a series of decision points that can be influenced by changes in the immediate settings for crime. Ekblom's (1995) term, 'think thief', helps make this process more tangible.

2 It has provided the rationale for the classification of 25 situational interventions that fall under the five main headings of increasing the effort needed for crime, increasing the risks, reducing the rewards, removing excuses and reducing provocations and temptations.

3 It has helped to deal with the displacement criticism so frequently levelled at situational prevention. To the extent that this criticism relies on simplistic assumptions about the nature of criminal motivation, it can be countered by more realistic ones relying on criminal decision-making. The concept of choice-structuring properties for different crimes also helps to determine the likely boundaries for displacement in any particular case. These theoretical contributions have been backed up by studies of the empirical evidence for displacement (Hesseling 1994), and research suggesting that offenders are often be reluctant to shift between crimes (Tunnell 1992) or even to change where they offend (Weisburd et al. 2007b).

4 It has helped to alert situational prevention researchers to two other quite commonly observed consequences of situational interventions: diffusion of benefits, which refers to the spread of the beneficial results of interventions beyond the focus of the interventions themselves (Clarke and Weisburd 1994), and anticipatory benefits, which refers to the fact that crime often declines in anticipation of a situational intervention (Smith et al. 2002). In both cases the explanations for these phenomena derive from the rational choice perspective. Diffusion of benefits results from offenders being uncertain about the precise scope or reach of the situational intervention

and anticipatory benefits from offenders being unsure when anticipated measures are to be introduced.

A good-enough theory

Rather than setting out to provide a complete explanation of criminal behaviour, the rational choice perspective has been more concerned with how to prevent or disrupt it. Just as situational strategies have evolved pragmatically, so too has the underlying theory developed in a pragmatic and piecemeal way. We have termed this style of approach 'good-enough theorising' to emphasise its orientation towards policy-relevant theory and practice. We have chosen clarity and parsimony over comprehensiveness, tending to prefer simple assumptions to complex ones, making distinctions only where they seem necessary. We have also elaborated new concepts only when required. For example, the notion of choice-structuring properties was introduced in order to explain the likely limits to crime displacement (Cornish and Clarke 1987). The term refers to the ways in which different crimes vary in terms of a whole range of features and requirements. For the potential offender, these may include availability and accessibility of targets, knowledge necessary to carry out the crime, skills required, moral evaluation, resources needed, and so on. An understanding of the choice-structuring properties of different crimes helps explain what makes these crimes differentially available and attractive to certain individuals at certain times and why it is not a simple matter for offenders to switch to (i.e. displace to) another type of crime when newly introduced situational measures make it hard for them to continue committing a particular form of crime.

An emphasis on the person–situation interaction

Traditional theories of criminal behaviour tend to view it as driven by long-standing and stable criminal dispositions. In this view, current lifestyles, needs and motives are merely long-term manifestations of these influences, and current opportunities and inducements simply act as triggers that call out long-standing criminal motivation. As a result the primary ways of dealing with criminal behaviour involve attempts to prevent the development of such criminal dispositions, re-engineer the individual or incapacitate him or her. In contrast, the rational choice perspective is concerned to understand, prevent and disrupt criminal actions. Since actions are a function of opportunity as well as motivation, the rational choice perspective focuses upon those points where the individual has to interact with the current environment in order to achieve his or her goals by getting things done. Hence its appreciation of the role of opportunity in offending, its detailed analysis of the role of situational factors throughout the crime-commission process, and its use of the concepts of choices, decisions and actions highlight the ways in which offenders interact with situational factors.

A present-centred focus

The decision-making models are notable for their concentration on the immediate precursors of criminal activity. In the event model and in crime scripts the timescale is short and the action immediate; in habituation, certain aspects of the offender's current lifestyle are developed and maintained by continued success at committing a particular type of crime. Desistance depicts an unravelling of this steady state as criminal activity falters and, together with a variety of other pressures, renders the criminal lifestyle less easy to sustain and leads ultimately to a re-evaluation of readiness to continue committing this particular type of crime.

Even in the initiation model it is the offender's current lifestyle and current environment that play the most important role in generating the needs and motives, inducements and opportunities that take the potential offender to the 'invitational edge' (Matza 1964) – the state of readiness that precedes the first tentative forays into a particular criminal activity. We have also chosen to emphasise the role of the current environment because this draws attention to those variables which we regard as the immediate and most accessible causes of criminal actions and crime events. As Laub and Sampson (2003: 34–5) have suggested, compared to traditional developmental models of criminal behaviour, the present-centred focus of the rational choice approach makes it more compatible with their life-course perspective. With its emphasis on turning points and on the unpredictability and social malleability of human lives, their approach invites a similar comparison to the role of criminal decision-making in the involvement models.

This is not to say that earlier influences do not continue to play some role in the likelihood of becoming involved in a particular crime. But these influences are transmitted via their effects on the individual's experience and learning, and on the quality of his or her subsequent material circumstances and associated options. The role of personality traits or stable dispositions, on the other hand, is less certain, and we view them more as convenient but misleading summary descriptions of behaviour than as explanations for it.

The nature of the offender

The rational choice perspective has had rather little to say about the nature of the offender. In accordance with good-enough theorising the original depiction of the offender was of an individual bereft of moral scruples – and without any defects such as lack of self-control that might get in the way of rational action. He (or she) was assumed to arrive at the crime setting already motivated and somewhat experienced in committing the crime in question, and to evaluate criminal opportunities on the basis of the likely rewards they offered, the effort they required, and the risks they were likely to involve. Although this picture has been modified over the years (Cornish and Clarke 2003) the offender as anti-social predator has remained the perspective's default view. There is a practical reason for this reluctance to qualify this bleak picture. In many cases situational crime prevention knows little or nothing about the offenders whose activities it is trying to stop, reduce or disrupt. Under these circumstances the most effective measures may be those that credit the as yet unidentified offender with few qualities other than rationality.

Misperceptions and criticisms

Partly because of its perceived association with economics, and partly because it does not fit in with conventional views about what constitutes a criminological theory, the rational choice perspective has faced a range of misunderstandings, misperceptions and criticisms. Many arise from misunderstandings about, or objections to, its metatheoretical assumptions and practical goals. Psychologists often criticise it for not paying sufficient attention to the development and importance of criminal motivation, and to the merits of early prevention. Sociologists tend to criticise it for failing to contextualise offending and its meaning(s) within the rich tapestry of offenders' lives and lifestyles, and for being too policy-oriented – that is, too concerned with preventing crime. These differences in preoccupations, theoretical goals and orientations towards practice exist and have to be recognised. Some of the most common ones are briefly noted here.

Offenders act rationally less often than is claimed

As was noted earlier, because of the conditions under which they make them, the decisions made by offenders tend to evidence limited rather than perfect rationality. Since they may very well be doing the best they can in the circumstances, however, it is generally conceded that this is enough to qualify their behaviour as rational. A review of research on property offenders, such as auto thieves, burglars and robbers, for example, concluded that there was considerable support for this conclusion (Gibbons 1994). Many times, however, offenders are reported as acting without much forethought – failing to do much planning, acting impulsively, ignoring consequences and making mistakes. They are also reported as offending under the influence of drugs or drink, or as having been spurred on to act recklessly by their peers (see, for example Wright *et al.* 2006).

It is often difficult to determine how widespread or significant are these alleged departures from the norm of bounded rationality, and the extent to which they should be allowed to qualify the general picture. Since abandoning the view that offenders act rationally can lead to a subtle re-pathologisation – or, just as dangerous, a romanticisation – of their behaviour and a reopening of the debate over the extent to which delinquents and criminals are different from the rest of us, this is a serious step for social scientists to take. Before doing so, it might be wise to ask the following questions:

- Are the respondents a representative sample of those committing the offence in question, or are they those who have been particularly unsuccessful at offending?

- Do they have reasons for concealing evidence of prudential behaviour? Are they, for example, trying to assert spontaneity, daring and carelessness of consequences as a way of impressing their peers or questioners?

- Is evidence of deliberate heedlessness of consequences necessarily evidence of irrationality?

- Is lack of evidence of planning, evidence of lack of planning? Could the lack of evidence be explained by a failure on the part of the researcher to seek it in the details of how such crimes are carried out?

- Is an apparent lack of overt planning on the part of experienced offenders evidence of irrationality? Or does it denote routinisation of much of the crime script in question?

- Is evidence of thrill or pleasure seeking in offending, or offending to support a partying lifestyle, evidence of irrationality?

Issues such as these are difficult to resolve since they turn not only on the quality of the empirical data but also on questions of the definition of rationality, the correct identification of motives and purposes, the truthfulness of respondents, the knowledge and expertise of researchers in relation to what is going on, and the extent to which they buy into the presumption of rationality as a necessary discipline when theorising in the social sciences.

Ironically, since so much effort has been expended over it, the whole debate is only of tangential importance to the rational choice perspective itself. This is because its interest is not so much in the extent to which offenders are, in fact, rational actors as in the more relevant question for situational crime prevention of whether reliable information about how particular crimes are successfully committed can be gleaned and reconstructed from offenders' accounts of their criminal activities. If this can be done, then there is a good chance that situational measures can be designed on the basis of this information – and, indeed, from information relating to failures and attempts – to successfully prevent or disrupt the crime events in question. It scarcely needs adding that measures designed to prevent or disrupt purposeful, rational action will be even more likely to prevent or disrupt purposeful action that falls short of this degree of rationality. Indeed, actions that do not conform to the logic of the situation will tend to fail of their own accord.

Some crimes are not rational

Predatory property crimes, organised crime and white-collar crimes are generally perceived as rational, instrumental activities with commonplace, easily understood motives and clear material objectives. Crimes involving sex and violence, on the other hand, raise issues in all these areas. Consistent with the desire to distance ourselves from these offenders, there is often a reluctance to explore the motives in question, or to view any means associated with their fulfilment as rational and instrumental. This is particularly the case in relation to violent offending where, despite (or perhaps because of) most people's experiences in schoolyard and workplace, the notion that violence could be an attractive instrumental option for achieving valued goals is an uncomfortable one.

This reluctance appears to stem from three sources. The first is the belief that only economically motivated crimes should be considered rational. This view is patently absurd since it rules out from consideration a whole swathe of criminal activity fuelled by common human desires and motives (Clarke and Cornish 2001: 33, Table 1) – for example, to assert dominance or control, to avenge an insult, to hurt or frighten someone, to prove toughness and bravery, to have fun, to gain status and admiration and so on. The second source of reluctance arises when the process of correctly identifying a motive is replaced by one of labelling it – for example, as senseless, inconceivable, inhuman and so on. Since the motive cannot be contemplated, the observer is absolved from the business of judging whether either the motive is intelligible or the means taken to secure its fulfilment are rational. The third reason for reluctance is similar, and arises from the failure to make distinctions between means, ends and motives. In the case of serial sexual murder, for example, if certain elements of the crime seem pathological – e.g. the motive itself and the use of disproportionate or even frenzied violence to complete the crime – then the whole crime-commission process may be dismissed as irrational, even when there is considerable evidence of planning, target selection, disposal of evidence and other attempts to avoid discovery.

Judging the rationality of a particular criminal action can only be done after the motive has been properly identified: a 'senseless' mugging may become viewed as intelligible or even rational once its motive has been correctly determined. This having been done, the rationality of the methods used can then in turn be assessed. To take another example, the issue of lack of overt planning is still cited by many researchers as evidence of irrational decision-making, despite the well-attested fact that, especially during habituation – the stage of involvement during which crime scripts are likely to be most well developed – experienced offenders may routinise many aspects of their decision-making. These useful rules of thumb might include adopting standing decisions to offend, going equipped with weapons as a routine self-protective precaution by those living a criminal lifestyle, as well as a routine preparation for offending if the circumstances arise, and using pattern planning. As Sommers and Baskin put it:

> As the circumstances of the women's lives changed, it became less and less likely that they actively considered alternatives to committing crimes. Decisions concerning the execution of violent crimes became routine or 'patterned,' relying largely on their ability to recognize and seize situational opportunities. (Sommers and Baskin 1993: 157)

Lack of attention to the details of crime-commission and to the multi-tasking nature of offenders' lifestyles may often be responsible for researchers' failures to see rational decision-making where it is present. Nevertheless, given that, to our mind, the best and most persuasive evidence for the rationality of offending comes from the many ethnographic studies of particular crimes, how is it that their authors regularly come to conclusions about the rationality of offenders' decision-making that are so much at variance with our own, especially when their data would appear to conform so closely to all the assumptions of the rational choice perspective? The issues discussed above go some way to explaining this, but ultimately they may well reflect the mutual tensions inevitable in a field of interdisciplinary studies such as that of criminology, where conceptual frameworks collide and disciplinary preoccupations and missions vary. Radically divergent views on the relative importance of explaining as opposed to controlling crime, on criminal justice policy matters, and on the status and value of policy-oriented theory and practice may all reduce mutual respect and the inclination to cooperate (see Clarke 2004). Some of these issues are explored briefly below.

The rational choice perspective is pallid and boring, listless and inert

This comment featured recently as an aside in a manifesto to launch 'a criminology of energy and tension' (John Jay College 2007), and is the subtext of many long-standing sociological critiques of the rational choice perspective and, more generally, of policy-oriented research. It highlights a series of interlocking differences of emphasis as between what could be termed an 'appreciative' stance towards crime and criminality as opposed to a criminal justice and crime science one. Set against the vivid depictions of criminal lifestyles given by Wright and his colleagues (2006), the preoccupations of the rational choice perspective with crime prevention and the reduction of harm to victims, together with its somewhat dry focus on means and ends, inevitably pale in comparison. But there are good reasons for these differences, as the brief points below explain.

In fact, much crime is rather mundane, both in terms of its motives and its commission. The early decision by the rational choice perspective to focus attention on volume crimes such as burglary and vandalism rather than on those with more human interest (rape, murder, child sexual abuse, terrorism) was a pragmatic one, but may have fostered the view that it was not interested or could not deal with the full range of criminal activity – a notion that still lingers even after its expansion into these areas has proved otherwise. Another source of criticism has been its handling of the question of offender motivation. First, it is true that, for the purposes of studying the crime event, the rational choice perspective is more interested in correctly identifying offenders' motives and preferences than explaining them. When it comes to tracing their origins, it leaves this task to sociological and psychological theorists. And while its initiation model locates offenders' motives within the context of their current lifestyles (Clarke and Cornish 2001), it once more leaves the task of describing these lifestyles to others.

As for being listless and inert, terms such as governmentality, managerialism and administrative criminology, all of which convey the impression of a system of bureaucratic control that is concerned solely with restricting and disciplining rather than enriching and liberating human lives have also been applied to the rational choice perspective. Yet the offender's benefits are always taken at the victim's costs, and an essential part of the process of maintaining a civil society lies in the regulation of social interaction in the interests of protecting its citizens from harm. In its emphasis upon the need to regulate interactions among people and between people and their environments, the rational choice approach also has much in common with social control theory, and its roots in radical behaviourism and its affinities with the assumptions and mode of explanation in evolutionary psychology make it clear where its preoccupations lie.

Lastly, what could be more redolent of listlessness and inertia than to extol the merits of piecemeal tinkering over the attractions of sweeping radical solutions to the crime problem? Why is it that the procedure of making incremental advances popular in other sciences is so despised in some areas of criminology? Perhaps it is because the idealogues of right and left are so set on imposing their utopian visions on the pragmatic middle. To the rational choice perspective, other approaches often seem dangerously disregarding of the unintended consequences of blanket solutions. Virtuous motives are, after all, no guarantee of beneficial results. While analyses of societal structures are necessary and illuminating, how to change these is less well understood. The rational choice perspective takes a cautious view of many issues – free will vs determinism; the nature of human nature; nature vs nurture. All these uncertainties favour a policy of cautious tinkering and one that manipulates the environment – where the rewards and punishments lie – rather than a potential and unidentified offender.

Conclusion

The core concepts of the rational choice perspective outlined above are a set of working assumptions, and the perspective itself is more a set of sensitising concepts than a conventional criminological theory. Its main purpose is to provide a heuristic device for analysing the conditions leading to the occurrence of crime events: fruitfulness rather than empirical truth is therefore its primary objective. Treating offending 'as if' it is rational involves viewing offenders as reasoning criminals. This in turn suggests the utility of a decision-making approach, and of the development of decision-making models which explore further the implications of the rationality presumption in the context of criminal involvement and crime-commission. Such models provide a framework within which to synthesise the results of ethnographic research on offending, and a perspective by means of which new research directions can be identified. In particular, by providing a way of identifying some of the conditions under which crimes occur, novel ways of preventing or disrupting criminal activity can be developed.

As we have made clear, the rational choice perspective was conceived primarily to assist the development of situational prevention, but it has also made some other, specific contributions to criminology. Thus, it has been able to provide plausible explanations, backed by empirical data, for phenomena such as repeat victimisation (Farrell *et al.* 1995), the preferences of thieves for particular types of products (Clarke 1999), and the dramatic fall in the suicide rate following the substitution of natural gas for coal gas in the UK (Clarke and Mayhew 1988).

More generally, the rational choice perspective itself and allied approaches such as crime pattern analysis have gradually extended their analyses of criminal behaviour from property crimes such as burglary and auto theft into the area of so-called expressive offending, such as opioid addiction (Bennett 1986), serial murder (Rossmo 2000) and child sexual abuse (Wortley and Smallbone 2006) – all crimes often cited as being inaccessible to a rational choice analysis because of their allegedly irrational, impulsive or pathologically motivated aspects.

The rational choice perspective is still very much a work in progress – a theory that is good enough for the present rather than simply 'good enough'. As a theory for practice it has always tended, once its initial assumptions were in place, to be reactive rather than proactive, growing alongside the development of situational crime prevention and developing as the result of the need to better understand criminological phenomena: the role of displacement, the details of the crime-commission process and the different aspects of criminal decision-making. Growth and change is also occurring in response to critiques of its minimalist view of the offender (Wortley 2001; Cornish and Clarke 2003; Ekblom 2007). The recognition that crime prevention practice has implicitly assumed the existence not only of the sociopathic predator, but also of offenders with less determination and moral scruples, has led to progressively greater recognition of the roles of excuses, and situational pressures and provocations in decisions to offend. We hope that this openness to new ideas and concepts will be maintained in the future.

References

Beauregard, E., Proulx, J., Rossmo, K., Leclerc, B. and Allaire, J.-F. (2007) 'Script Analysis of the Hunting Process of Serial Sex Offenders', *Criminal Justice and Behavior*, 34: 1069–84.

Bennett, T. (1986) 'A Decision-making Approach to Opioid Addiction', in D.B. Cornish and R.V. Clarke (eds) *The Reasoning Criminal: Rational Choice Perspectives on Offending*. New York: Springer-Verlag.

Bennett, T. and Wright, R. (1984) *Burglars on Burglary: Prevention and the Offender*. Aldershot, UK: Gower.

Cherbonneau, M. and Copes, H. (2006) ' "Drive it Like You Stole it": Auto Theft and the Illusion of Normalcy', *British Journal of Criminology*, 46: 193–211.

Clarke, R.V. (1980) ' "Situational" Crime Prevention: Theory and Practice', *British Journal of Criminology* 20: 136–47.

Clarke, R.V. (1999) *Hot Products: Understanding, Anticipating and Reducing Demand for Stolen Goods*, Police Research Series, Paper 112. London: Home Office.

Clarke, R.V. (2004) 'Technology, Criminology and Crime Science', *European Journal on Criminal Policy and Research*, 10: 55–63.

Clarke, R.V. and Cornish, D.B. (1983) 'Editorial Introduction', in R.V. Clarke and D.B. Cornish (eds) *Crime Control in Britain*. Albany, NY: State University of New York Press.

Clarke, R.V. and Cornish, D.B. (1985) 'Modeling Offenders' Decisions: A Framework for Research and Policy', in M. Tonry and N. Morris (eds) *Crime and Justice: An Annual Review of Research, Vol. 6*. Chicago, IL: University of Chicago Press.

Clarke, R.V. and Cornish, D.B. (2001) 'Rational Choice', in R. Paternoster and R. Bachman (eds) *Explaining Criminals and Crime: Essays in Contemporary Criminological Theory.* Los Angeles, CA: Roxbury.

Clarke, R.V. and Martin, D.N. (1975) 'A Study of Absconding and its Implications for the Residential Treatment of Delinquents' in J. Tizard, I.A. Sinclair and R.V. Clarke (eds) *Varieties of Residential Experience.* London: Routledge and Kegan Paul.

Clarke, R.V. and Mayhew, P. (1988) 'The British Gas Suicide Story and its Criminological Implications', in M. Tonry and N. Morris (eds) *Crime and Justice: An Annual Review of Research, Vol. 10.* Chicago, IL: University of Chicago Press.

Clarke, R.V. and Newman, G.R. (2006) *Outsmarting the Terrorists.* Westport, CT: Praeger Security International.

Clarke, R.V. and Weisburd, D. (1994) 'Diffusion of Crime Control Benefits: Observations on the Reverse of Displacement', in R.V. Clarke (ed.) *Crime Prevention Studies, Vol. 2.* Monsey, NY: Criminal Justice Press.

Cocheo, S. (1997) 'The Bank Robber, the Quote and the Final Irony', *ABA Banking Journal,* Vol. 89, March (www.banking.com/aba/profile_0397.htm).

Copes, H. and Cherbonneau, M. (2006) 'The Key to Auto Theft: Emerging Methods of Auto Theft from the Offenders' Perspective', *British Journal of Criminology,* 46: 917–34.

Cornish, D.B. (1978) *Gambling: A Review of the Literature and Its Implications for Policy and Research,* Home Office Research Studies 42. London: HMSO.

Cornish, D.B. (1994) 'The Procedural Analysis of Offending, and its Relevance for Situational Prevention', in R.V. Clarke (ed.) *Crime Prevention Studies,* Volume 3. Monsey, NY: Criminal Justice Press.

Cornish, D.B. and Clarke, R.V. (1975) *Residential Treatment and its Effects on Delinquency,* Home Office Research Studies 32. London: HMSO.

Cornish, D.B. and Clarke, R.V. (eds) (1986) *The Reasoning Criminal: Rational Choice Perspectives on Offending.* New York, NY: Springer-Verlag.

Cornish, D.B. and Clarke, R.V. (1987) 'Understanding Crime Displacement: An Application of Rational Choice Theory', *Criminology* 25(4): 933–47.

Cornish, D.B. and Clarke, R.V. (2002) 'Analyzing Organized Crimes', in A.R. Piquero and S.G. Tibbetts (eds) *Rational Choice and Criminal Behavior: Recent Research and Future Challenges.* New York: Routledge.

Cornish, D.B. and Clarke, R.V. Clarke (2003) 'Opportunities, Precipitators and Criminal Decisions: A Reply to Wortley's Critique of Situational Crime Prevention', in M.J. Smith and D.B. Cornish (eds) *Theory for Practice in Situational Crime Prevention. Crime Prevention Studies, Vol. 16.* Monsey, NY: Criminal Justice Press.

Cornish, D.B. and Clarke, R.V. (2006) 'The Rational Choice Perspective', in S. Henry and M.M. Lanier (eds) *The Essential Criminology Reader.* Boulder, CO: Westview Press.

Ekblom, P. (1995) 'Less Crime, by Design', *Annals of the American Academy of Political and Social Science,* 539: 114–29.

Ekblom, P. (2007) 'Making Offenders Richer', in G. Farrell, K. Bowers, S. Johnson and M. Townsley (eds) *Imagination for Crime Prevention: Essays in Honour of Ken Pease. Crime Prevention Studies, Vol. 21.* Monsey, NY: Criminal Justice Press.

Farrell, G., Phillips, C. and Pease, K. (1995) 'Like Taking Candy. Why Does Repeat Victimization Occur?', *British Journal of Criminology,* 35: 384–99.

Gibbons, D. (1994) *Talking About Crime and Criminals: Problems and Issues in Theory Development in Criminology.* Englewood Cliffs, NJ: Prentice-Hall.

Herrnstein, R.J. (1990) 'Rational Choice Theory: Necessary but not Sufficient', *American Psychologist,* 45(3): 356–67.

Hesseling, R.B.P. (1994) 'Displacement: A Review of the Empirical Literature', in R.V. Clarke (ed.) *Crime Prevention Studies, Volume 3*. Monsey, NY: Criminal Justice Press.

John Jay College (2007) 'On the Edge: Transgression and the Dangerous Other. A Celebratory Exploration of Intellectual and Artistic Transgression'. Conference, 9–10 August, New York City. (www.jjay.cuny.edu/ontheedge/OnTheEdgeConferenceProgram.pdf).

Katz, J. (1988) *Seductions of Crime*. New York: Basic Books.

Knepper, P. (2007) 'Situational Logic in Social Science Inquiry: From Economics to Criminology', *Review of Austrian Economics* 20(1): 25–41 (www.springerlink.com/content/a761072678017n83/fulltext.pdf).

Laub, J.H. and Sampson, R.J. (2003) *Shared Beginnings, Divergent Lives: Delinquent Boys to Age 70*. Cambridge, MA: Harvard University Press.

Leclerc, B. and Tremblay, P. (2007) 'Strategic Behavior in Adolescent Sexual Offenses Against Children: Linking Modus Operandi to Sexual Behaviors', *Sexual Abuse: A Journal of Research and Treatment*, 19: 23–41.

Maguire, M. and Bennett, T. (1982) *Burglary in a Dwelling*. London: Heinemann.

Matza, D. (1964) *Delinquency and Drift*. New York: Wiley.

Nee, C. and Meenaghan, A. (2006) 'Expert Decision Making in Burglars', *British Journal of Criminology*, 46: 935–49.

Poyner, B. and Webb, B. (1991) *Crime Free Housing*. Oxford: Butterworth Architecture.

Reppetto, T.A. (1974) *Residential Crime*. Cambridge, MA: Ballinger.

Rossmo, D.K. (2000) *Geographic Profiling*. Boca Raton, FL: CRC Press.

Simon, H.A. (1990) 'Invariants of Human Behavior', *Annual Review of Psychology*, 41: 1–19.

Sinclair, I.A.C. (1971) *Hostels for Probationers*. Home Office Research Studies No. 6. London: HMSO.

Smith, M.J., Clarke, R.V. and Pease, K. (2002) 'Anticipatory Benefits in Crime Prevention', in N. Tilley (ed.) *Analysis for Crime Prevention. Crime Prevention Studies, Vol. 13*. Monsey, NY: Criminal Justice Press.

Sommers, I. and Baskin, D.R. (1993) 'The Situational Context of Violent Female Offending', *Journal of Research in Crime and Delinquency*, 30(2): 136–62.

Tremblay, P., Talon, B. and Hurley, D. (2001) 'Body Switching and Related Adaptations in the Resale of Stolen Vehicles: Script Elaborations and Aggregate Crime Learning Curves', *British Journal of Criminology*, 41: 561–79.

Tunnell, K.D. (1992) *Choosing Crime: The Criminal Calculus of Property Offenders*. Chicago, IL: Nelson-Hall.

Walsh, D.P. (1980) *Break-Ins: Burglary from Private Houses*. London: Constable.

Weisburd, D., Wyckoff, L.A., Ready, J., Eck, J.E., Hinkle, J.C. and Gajewski, F. (2006) 'Does Crime Just Move Around the Corner? A Controlled Study of Spatial Displacement and Diffusion of Crime Control Benefits', *Criminology*, 44(3): 549–92.

Wortley, R. (2001) 'A Classification of Techniques for Controlling Situational Precipitators of Crime', *Security Journal* 14: 63–82.

Wortley, R. and S. Smallbone (eds) (2006) *Situational Prevention of Child Sexual Abuse. Crime Prevention Studies, Vol. 19*. Cullompton, UK: Willan Publishing.

Wright, R., Brookman, F. and Bennett, T. (2006) 'The Foreground Dynamics of Street Robbery in Britain', *British Journal of Criminology*, 46: 1–15.

3. Situational precipitators of crime

Richard Wortley

Introduction

As we saw in the previous chapter, rational choice is the usual way in environmental criminology to think about the role that immediate environments play in behaviour. According to rational choice perspective, the immediate environment is the source of information that an individual uses to decide whether or not to commit a contemplated crime. Potential offenders weigh up the likely outcomes of illegal behaviour and commit crime if the benefits are judged to outweigh the costs. In this chapter it is argued that rational choice provides only half the explanation for the role of immediate environments. Immediate environments can also actively encourage or induce individuals to commit crimes that they may not have otherwise contemplated at that time. Consider the following scenario:

> Jim arranges to meet his friends at a local nightclub for an evening out. He arrives at the club in good spirits anticipating an enjoyable night. When he arrives at the front door, the door staff are surly and belligerent towards him before eventually allowing him to go inside. When he enters the nightclub he discovers it is packed to capacity. After fighting his way through the crowd he finally locates his friends. There are no tables or chairs left and they are forced stand in the corner with people jostling around them. The music is at full volume and continues without a break, making it impossible to carry on a conversation. The air conditioning cannot cope with the crowd and the room is hot, dark and oppressive. Jim and his friends drink steadily. However, getting to the bar is an ordeal and it can take half an hour to get served. As Jim struggles back from the bar with the latest round of drinks, another patron bumps him and knocks the drinks all over him. Jim's friends urge him to retaliate and hit the man.

Whether Jim decides to commit assault or not can certainly be analysed in terms of rational choice. Perhaps Jim sees a security guard out of the corner of his eye and decides it is too risky to fight. Or perhaps the other man is much bigger than Jim, or is surrounded by his friends, and Jim judges that he will come off worse in a physical encounter. Alternatively, Jim might decide that the benefits of restoring his pride outweigh all the risks, and he elects to throw a punch. However, rational choice does not account for all the situational events leading up to this decision. Since he arrived at the nightclub, Jim has experienced a series of stresses and frustrations that have primed him for aggression. This has been compounded by his alcohol intake, which has lowered his inhibitions, and by the pressure not to back down in front of his friends. The spilled drinks were the final straw. If all of these events had not occurred then the confrontation with the other patron would not have arisen, and there would have been no need to make a rational choice about committing assault. Even if the patron had spilled Jim's drinks, but the night up until then had left Jim in a good mood, he would have been much more inclined to accept the spilling as an accident. As it is, the probability of a violent response has been significantly increased by a variety of situational precipitators.

Table 3.1 compares the rational choice and situational precipitator approaches to analysing crime. First, precipitators are events and influences that occur prior to the contemplated behaviour; rational choices concern the events that are likely to follow the contemplated behaviour. The stresses and pressures Jim experienced are antecedents of action; consideration of whether the security staff will swoop if he throws a punch is to do with the consequences of that action. Second, the function of situational precipitators is to initiate behaviour; in rational choice the immediate environment need only enable the performance of the behaviour. Stress and frustration activate feelings of aggression; whether Jim carries through with an aggressive course of action is regulated by opportunity. Third, precipitating events can supply or intensify the motivation for individuals to commit crime; rational choice assumes that individuals already possess criminal motivations. Jim became aggressive as a direct consequence of his experiences in the nightclub; rational choice is only

Table 3.1 Comparing the rational choice and the situational precipitator approaches to analysing crime

Dimension	Situational precipitators	Rational choice
Focus of analysis	Antecedents of behaviour	Consequences of behaviour
Function of immediate environment	Initiates behaviour	Enables behaviour
Motivation of offender	Situationally dependent	Already motivated
Psychological processes	Sub-cognitive	Conscious
Control by offender	Involuntary	Deliberative

activated once the motivation to commit assault is present. Fourth, precipitators often (although not always) operate below consciousness; rational choices are conscious processes. Jim's rising aggression levels involve physiological reactions to environmental stressors of which Jim may not be fully aware; Jim is quite aware of the possible consequences of getting into a fight. And finally, individuals may have limited control over the effects of precipitators; rational choices are seen as deliberate acts. Jim may feel his stress levels rising but not have the capacity to override the physiological effects; the decision whether or not to proceed with an assault is seen as an active choice.

Situational precipitators and rational choice are not contradictory explanations for crime but can be seen as complementary stages of the offending process (Wortley 2001, 2002). The first stage of offending involves situational forces that ready the potential offender for crime (precipitators); the second stage involves an assessment of the criminal opportunities (rational choice) (see Figure 3.1). Crime may be avoided at either stage if the necessary precipitators or opportunities are absent. The inclusions of precipitators in the situational model provides for a more dynamic picture of criminal behaviour, one that more completely captures the complexity and subtlety of the person–situation interaction as it is understood in psychology (see Wortley and Mazerolle, Chapter 1, this volume). While rational choice explains why criminally-motivated individuals might commit crime on some occasions but not on others, precipitators can help explain changes in criminal propensity within an individual – why, for example, normally law-abiding individuals

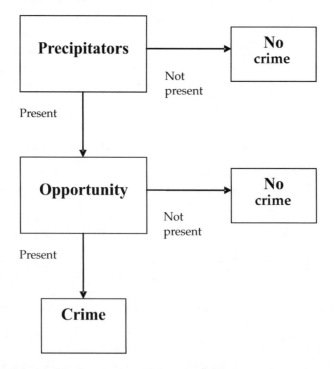

Figure 3.1 Relationship between precipitators and opportunity

might sometimes commit crime. The following section examines the different ways that situational precipitators have been conceptualised in psychology, and the contribution that the concept of situational precipitators makes to understanding the dynamics of criminal behaviour.

Types of precipitators

Psychological theory suggests four main ways that immediate environments might precipitate criminal responses. Learning theory explains how situational cues can *prompt* individuals to perform criminal behaviour. Social psychology examines the social forces that exert *pressure* on individuals to offend. Social-cognitive theory describes how situational factors can help weaken moral prohibitions and so *permit* individuals to engage in normally proscribed behaviour. Finally, environmental psychology outlines how situationally-induced emotional arousal can *provoke* a criminal response. The full classification of precipitators is shown in Table 3.2.

Prompts

Prompts are aspects of the immediate environment that bring to the surface thoughts, feelings and desires that may be lying dormant. Theoretically, the role of prompts in precipitating behaviour is explained by learning theory. Learning theory is concerned with changes in behaviour that result from

Table 3.2 Classification of situational precipitators of crime

Prompts	Pressures	Permissions	Provocations
Triggers e.g. weapons effect	*Conformity* e.g. gang crime	*Minimising the rule* e.g. culture of corruption	*Frustration* e.g. road rage
Signals e.g. 'gay-bashing'	*Obedience* e.g. following corrupt superiors	*Minimising responsibility* e.g. alcohol-related crime	*Crowding* e.g. nightclub violence
Imitation e.g. copy-cat crime	*Compliance/ defiance* e.g. defying security staff	*Minimising consequences* e.g. 'petty' theft	*Territoriality* e.g. turf wars
Expectancies e.g. pubs with violent reputations	*Anonymity* e.g. lynch mobs	*Minimising the victim* e.g. revenge against employer	*Environmental irritants* e.g. riots in heat waves

environmental experiences (Skinner 1953). In criminology, most attention has been given to the way patterns of criminal behaviour are acquired over time, through childhood experiences and the like. However, learning theory also holds that for learned behaviour to be produced on any given occasion it needs to be evoked by an appropriate environmental stimulus. For example, most people will remember the experiment involving Pavlov's dogs. Through the repeated pairing of food and a bell, the dogs learned to salivate when a bell was rung, even when there was no food. One way to stop the dogs salivating is to retrain them by ringing the bell without food until the association is eventually broken and the response is extinguished. But the salivation can be stopped immediately by simply not ringing the bell. That is, the salivation is situationally dependent and only occurs when prompted. Four kinds of environmental prompts are discussed here in relation to criminal behaviour – triggers, signals, models and expectancies.

Triggers

Some environmental prompts elicit involuntary, or reflex, physiological responses. The salivation by Pavlov's dogs is an example of a reflex response. So too in humans the sight of food can make people hungry, viewing erotic images can produce sexual arousal, the sight of blood may make people feel nauseous, the smell of cigarette smoke can make a smoker crave nicotine, listening to a familiar piece of music can arouse feelings of nostalgia, and so on. These physiological reactions can sometimes lead to criminal behaviour. For example, Berkowitz (1983) found that the sight of weapons could trigger feelings of aggression and facilitate violence. Triggers may be particularly important in repetitive behaviours such as sex offending and drug and alcohol abuse. For example, Marshall (1988) reported that one-third of rapists and child-molesters surveyed claimed to have been incited to offend by viewing pornography.

Signals

Environmental cues can provide information about what is appropriate behaviour in a given context. For example, we learn that it is appropriate to drive through an intersection when the traffic light is green but not when it is red. Offenders rely on such signals all of the time to alert them to when crime is 'appropriate'. Uncollected newspapers on the front step are signals to a burglar, outward displays of homosexuality are signals to a 'gay-basher', an open curtain is a signal for a peeping Tom, and so on. Based on the same principle, signals are often introduced into the environment to remind people that certain behaviours are inappropriate. For example, Geller *et al.* (1983) found that honesty prompts attached to self-service newspaper racks significantly reduced thefts.

Models

The observation of someone performing a behaviour can prompt imitation. Children who watch other children play aggressively also play aggressively (Bandura 1965); if one pedestrian crosses the street against a red light others follow (Lefkowitz *et al.* 1955); students emulate teachers who engage in illegal computer activity (Skinner and Fream 1997); workers are more likely to engage in theft from the company if they observe their supervisors doing it (Hollinger 1989; Snyder *et al.* 1991). Models for imitation do not have to appear in person but can be represented symbolically in the mass media. Suicides increase immediately following the portrayal of suicide in popular television programmes (Phillips 1989; Phillips and Carstensen 1990); children become more aggressive immediately after viewing violence on television (Leyens *et al.* 1975; Rosenthal 1990); delinquent homicides surge following the televising of major boxing matches (Phillips 1983).

Expectancies

Expectancy refers to the tendency for individuals to respond to their preconceived ideas about a situation. Individuals can derive expectancies from situational cues. For example, Graham and Homel (1996) argued that nightclubs developed reputations as violent or non-violent establishments based on their physical characteristics, such as level of cleanliness, standard of furnishings and so forth. Patrons visited certain nightclubs anticipating that they would be involved in fights and this expectation acted as a self-fulfilling prophecy. Similarly, in the wider community signs of environmental decay and neglect – litter, vandalism, dilapidated housing and so forth – convey a message of lawlessness that invites criminal activity (Wagers *et al.*, Chapter 13, this volume; Wilson and Kelling 1982). Urban renewal and other environmental beautification programs may reduce crime in these areas by altering the expectations of potential offenders.

Pressures

Situations may exert social pressure on individuals to perform inappropriate behaviour. Social psychology is concerned with the effects of others on an individual's internal psychological processes and overt behaviour. Human beings are social animals who are profoundly influenced by the expectations and demands that are placed upon them in the course of their interactions and affiliations with other members of the species. Social influences have a crucial role in the development of an individual's core attitudes, beliefs and values. More importantly for current purposes, a great deal of behaviour is governed by immediate social settings. We act differently when we are with others from when we are alone. In particular, individuals are subject to pressures to conform to group norms, to obey the instructions of authority figures, to comply with or defy requests, and to submerge their identity within the group.

Conformity

Conformity is the tendency for individuals in groups to adopt group norms and standards of behaviour, even when these contradict personally held beliefs and values. We have all experienced the pressure to go along with the crowd, and offenders may commit crimes in order to avoid social disapproval and to gain group acceptance. In particular, most delinquent behaviour is performed in groups, and peer pressure to conform to subcultural norms is commonly agreed to be an important factor (Akers *et al.* 1979; Warr and Stafford 1991). Similarly, corruption within organisations demonstrates the power of conformity to induce illegal behaviour in otherwise law-abiding adults. A new employee entering an organisation in which corrupt practices are common faces social pressures from co-workers to also engage in those practices (Clark and Hollinger 1983).

Obedience

Obedience is the following of a direct command issued by someone perceived to possess legitimate authority. Of particular interest in psychology is the tendency for individuals to comply with unreasonable commands and to perpetrate all manner of cruelty in the process of following orders. Obedience to authority has been widely used to explain atrocities perpetrated by military regimes, such as the extermination of Jews by the Nazis (Milgram 1974) and the My Lai massacre during the Vietnam War (Kelman and Hamilton 1989). Likewise, corruption within bureaucracies often involves subordinates who act illegally on the orders of superiors, motivated by a misguided loyalty to the organisation. Examples of crimes of authority include cases of governmental abuses of power, and corporate crime (Kelman and Hamilton 1989), police corruption (Fitzgerald 1989) and prison officer brutality (Nagle 1978).

Compliance/defiance

Compliance refers to the acquiescence to the direct request of others. Encouraging compliance is an important factor in face-to-face interactions between potential offenders and official guardians such as police, security guards, nightclub crowd controllers, and correctional officers. Requests and commands are more likely to be followed if they are perceived as fair, consistent and legitimate (Bottoms *et al.* 1995; Lombardo 1989; Sparks *et al.* 1996). However, when attempts to control behaviour are seen as heavy-handed, manipulative or unreasonable, people may fail to comply or may even behave defiantly in the opposite direction (Brehm 1966; Goodstein *et al.* 1984; Sherman 1993). For example, Bensley and Wu (1991) found that high-threat anti-alcohol messages resulted in increased alcohol consumption. Vandalism of public notices (e.g. 'No Skateboarding') is a classic expression of defiance.

Anonymity

Being a member of a group or crowd can create a sense of anonymity and induce disinhibition. Most people have experienced the sensation of becoming immersed in a group and doing things that they would never have done alone. An extreme example of this phenomenon is the herd mentality and frenzied behaviour displayed by members of a lynch mob (Colman 1991). Being a member of a group has two psychological effects. First, people feel that they cannot be personally identified, and they become less concerned with the opinions and censure of others. Second, people experience a decreased ability to monitor their own behaviour, and they lose touch with their usual values. Countering anonymity effects is an important consideration in the policing of crowds. Provocative methods of control can galvanise crowd members and incite collective disorder (Reicher 1991; Shellow and Roemer 1987).

Permissions

Situational factors can help distort moral reasoning processes and so permit individuals to engage in normally forbidden behaviour. According to social-cognitive theory (Bandura 1977; Bandura *et al.* 1996), one of the most powerful constraints on behaviour is self-condemnation. However, on occasions, individuals may make excuses for their bad behaviour and succeed in convincing themselves that their actions are justified. This process is similar to neutralisation theory in criminology (Sykes and Matza 1957). According to neutralisation theory, many offenders do not hold anti-social values, but 'drift' in and out of crime by periodically redefining their behaviour in ways that minimises to themselves their own criminality. Social-cognitive theory extends neutralisation theory by proposing that situational conditions may facilitate this drift. The human conscience is sensitive to feedback from the environment and immediate social groups, and distorted feedback may assist offenders to may make excuses. Bandura (1977) suggested that neutralisations can be grouped into four broad categories: minimisation of the legitimacy of the moral rule, minimisation of the degree of personal responsibility for the behaviour, minimisation of the negative consequences of the behaviour, and minimisation of the worth of the victim (see also Wortley 1996).

Minimising the rule

Offenders may avoid self-blame for their actions by denying the essential wrongness of their actions. Individuals rely on the feedback from peers for guidelines for correct behaviour and may find support for neutralising beliefs from those around them. For example, an individual immersed within a corrupt organisational culture may come to accept corrupt practices as normal, endorsing sentiments such as 'everybody does it' and 'it goes with the job' (Clark and Hollinger 1983; Greenberg 1997). Human beings are also adept at exploiting ambiguity in their own favour when rules are not clear ('I didn't know it was wrong'). The presence of formal codes of conduct can reduce company thefts (Parilla *et al.* 1988), bullying in schools (Elliot 1991) and workplace aggression (Randall 1997).

Minimising responsibility

Offenders may deny their role in the behaviour or blame others. Some people may use alcohol precisely in order to provide an excuse for intended anti-social actions ('I couldn't help it') (Lang *et al.* 1975). Clarke and Homel (1997) suggested thefts from libraries may be related to inefficient book check-out systems that allow thieves to blame the library for causing them to steal ('I wouldn't have to steal if they were quicker'). Bandura (1977) argued that the division of labour within organisations facilitates corruption by allowing individuals to hide behind a collective responsibility. One of the common defences of Nazi prisoners at the Nuremberg trials was that, while they might have played a minor role in the deportation of Jews to the concentration camps, they were not personally responsible for any deaths.

Minimising the consequences

Offenders may deny causing any harm. Greenberg (1997) noted that often people are unable to appreciate the cumulative effect of small offences. For example, when they steal from employers they may comfort themselves with excuses that 'the company can afford it' or 'they will never miss it'. Carter *et al.* (1988) found that posting a graph of theft levels in the employee lunchroom increased awareness of the impact on the company and resulted in a reduction of theft. Sometimes, people are simply ignorant of the full effect of their behaviour. Oliver *et al.* (1985) found providing campers with information on the ecological impact of certain camping practices resulted in a 50 per cent reduction in vandalism. Similarly, Vander Stoep and Gramann (1988) achieved significant reductions in vandalism at historic sites by providing information on the consequences to the environment of destructive behaviour.

Minimising the victims

People find it easier to victimise those who can be stereotyped as subhuman or unworthy. Silbert and Pines (1984) found that rape victims who had attempted to placate their attackers by pretending to be prostitutes found instead that the rapist became even more aggressive and brutal. Indermaur (1996) found that the offering of resistance by victims during a robbery often had the effect of arousing 'righteous indignation' in the offender and escalating the violence. Olweus (1978) found that schoolyard victims of bullying tended to have distinctive signs of weakness or oddness, such as deviations in stature, personal hygiene and dress. When employees feel that they have been badly treated by their company, they may steal, become aggressive, or engage in destructive behaviour as an act of revenge (Greenberg 1990).

Provocations

Situations can create stress and provoke an anti-social response, particularly some form of aggression. The link between situational stress and crime is addressed in environmental psychology. Environmental psychology is concerned with the effects on behaviour of the natural and built environment. Some environmental elements, such as climatic extremes and the correlates of urbanisation, can be sources of stress. According to the environmental stress model (Baum *et al.* 1981), when an organism is under stress it responds in ways to manage or adapt to the aversive conditions and events – the so-called fight or flight response. Responses to environmental stressors may be physiological (e.g. arousal, increased adrenaline activity, physical illness), emotional (e.g. irritability, anxiety, depression) and behavioural (e.g. aggression, withdrawal, suicide). Stress-related crimes can be generated by environmental frustrations, crowding, invasions of territorial boundaries, and environmental irritants such as adverse weather conditions.

Frustration

Frustration is the emotional state produced when an individual is thwarted in their pursuit of a goal. Harding *et al.* (1998) found that incidents of road rage correlated with high traffic volume and were initiated by factors such as encounters with slow drivers, other drivers cutting in and competition for parking spaces. Frustration and stress at work have also been found to be related to increased workplace vandalism and sabotage (Spector 1997). Homel and Clark (1994) found nightclub violence was related to levels of patron boredom, lack of seating, unavailability of food and provocative behaviour of security staff. Boulton (1994) found that schoolyard bullying increased during wet playtimes and recommended improvements the quality of play facilities to reduce frustration levels of students.

Crowding

Crowding is the psychological experience of high density conditions. The distinction can be made between outside density and inside density. Outside density refers to broad population trends at the city or neighbourhood level. Research has shown that urban population density is associated with a range of physical, psychological and behavioural problems, including increased crime rates (Gove *et al.* 1977). Inside density refers to the occupancy of primary living areas. Again, a range of anti-social behaviours have been reported in field studies of specific crowded settings such as prisons (Paulus 1988), college dormitories (Baum and Valins 1977), nightclubs (Macintyre and Homel 1997) and naval ships (Dean *et al.* 1978). The effects of inside density are generally more acute than those of outside density.

Territoriality

Territoriality is the tendency to lay claim to an area and to defend it against intruders. There are two opposing ways that territorial possession might relate to anti-social behaviour. On the one hand, invasion of territory can incite an aggressive response. For example, gang warfare is often caused by aggressive reactions to territorial invasion (Ley and Cybriwsky 1974). On the other hand, possessing territory can inhibit aggression and promote pro-social behaviours. 'Home turf' is a place where people can relax and feel in control over their lives. O'Neill and Paluck (1973) reported a drop in the level of aggression among institutionalised intellectually disabled boys when they were given identifiable territories to call their own. Greater care is taken of housing estates when tenants are given involvement in their management (Foster and Hope 1993).

Environmental irritants

Many factors in the environment influence behaviour because of their aversive nature and the threat they pose to human well-being. Correlations have been reported between temperature and violent crime (Harries and Stadler 1988). Goranson and King (1970) showed that riots were more likely to occur during heatwaves. LeBeau (1994) reported a relationship between domestic disputes and the temperature–humidity index. Atlas (1982, 1984) reported that assault rates in prison are lower for air-conditioned areas and areas with easy access to showers than for areas where no relief from high temperatures is provided. Rotton and Frey (1985) reported an association between air pollution levels and violent crime. Banzinger and Owens (1978) found a correlation between wind speed and delinquency. Laboratory studies have also shown that aversive noise intensifies aggression (Donnerstein and Wilson 1976).

Types of offenders

Both precipitators and rational choice may play a part in every crime, but the relative importance of each may vary from individual to individual. Recently, Cornish and Clarke (2003) proposed an offender typology based on the strength of the offender's criminal disposition and the role that precipitators and rational choice play in his/her offending. Three offender types were suggested – anti-social predators, mundane offenders and provoked offenders:

- *Anti-social predators* are the stereotypical, calculating criminal. These offenders possess ingrained criminal dispositions and their offences involve premeditation and at least some rudimentary planning. They will typically enter the crime scene with pre-existing motivation to commit the crime, and their crimes are carried out intentionally and with a purpose. Their motivations for offending derive from the intrinsically rewarding nature of the crimes they commit. They utilise situational data to make rational choices about the relative costs and benefits of criminal involvement and will actively seek out or create criminal opportunities. Predators may specialise in a particular type of crime or may be criminally versatile, but in any event all will have developed 'knowledge, skills and experience enough to minimize risk and effort, and maximize payoffs' (Cornish and Clarke 2003: 57).

- *Mundane offenders* are ambiguous in their criminal commitment and opportunistic in their offending. They engage in occasional, low-level criminality and may possess generalised impulse control problems. Typically they will commit crime more or less on the spur of the moment with minimal forethought. Like predatory offenders, they seek to derive benefits from their crimes, but they have a greater stake in conformity and are therefore subject to stronger personal and social constraints on their behaviour. These constraints, however, weaken from time to time, and mundane offenders are susceptible to precipitating events that engage their criminal motivations. In particular, to facilitate their performance of morally proscribed behaviour, they may invoke neutralisations for their crimes, especially where situational factors serve to obscure personal responsibility. Mundane offenders vary in their vulnerability to temptation, and hence in the extent of their criminal involvement, but overall both the seriousness and frequency of their offending is less than for predatory offenders.

- *Provoked offenders* are reacting to a particular set of environmental circumstances – situational frustrations, irritations, social pressures and the like – that induce them to commit crimes they would not have otherwise committed. Their crimes include 'crimes of violence that erupt in the heat of the moment; or impulsive ones committed by offenders overcome by temptation, or a temporary failure of self control' (Cornish and Clarke 2003: 70). Provoked offenders may have conventional value systems and lead otherwise law-abiding lives. Their involvement in crime may represent an aberration and would not have occurred if it were not for the precipitating events.

The identification of offender types is a new development in environmental criminology. While the situational approach is conceptually underpinned by psychological theories of behaviour, individual differences have generally played little role in the analysis of crime. The offender has been treated as a constant. Bringing characteristics of the offender into the equation more accurately reflects the view of behaviour as an interaction between person and situation, and offers the potential for better targeted crime prevention strategies. According to the offender typology, the stronger the individual's anti-social commitment, the more likely he/she is to be an active manipulator of – rather than a passive responder to – criminogenic situations (see Figure 3.2). For predatory offenders, situational data primarily inform target selection. They are opportunity-seekers and, if necessary, opportunity-makers. Obstacles to offending are challenges to be overcome and prevention may require 'hard' opportunity reduction. For mundane offenders, situations offer temptations to be seized. They are opportunity-takers. Because of the moral ambivalence of the mundane offender, in the absence of easy opportunity they may not be sufficiently motivated to seek out crime targets. For the provoked offender, situations provide the impetus to offend. They are reactors to the immediate environment. Their engagement in crime requires a kick-start, and relieving the precipitating conditions may be sufficient to prevent offending.

Cornish and Clarke (2003, and Chapter 2, this volume) have argued that the anti-social predator is the default offender type, or at any rate, that thinking about crime as rationally chosen offers the most effective model for situational prevention. However, as Figure 3.2 suggests, an offender type may subsume the offending patterns of the types below it. Thus, predatory offenders are likely also to exploit opportunities and react to precipitators when the situations arise, and in fact may be more likely to do so than are mundane and provoked offenders. Individuals with anti-social dispositions tend to offend across the spectrum. For example, one of Australia's most notorious criminals, Neddy Smith, was ultimately convicted of killing a stranger in a road-rage incident (*Sydney Morning Herald*, 2005). All three types of offenders may at some time commit offences due to situational precipitators.

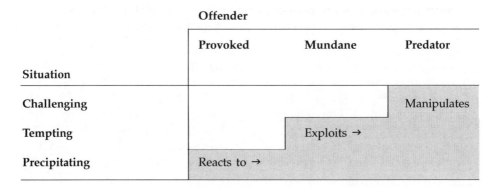

Figure 3.2 Behaviour of the offender as a function of the interaction between offender type and situational characteristics

Types of offences

Just as the role of precipitators may vary among offenders, they may also play a greater or lesser role depending upon the nature of the crime in question. This section highlights two areas in which precipitators make a particular contribution to our understanding the situational dynamics of crime – 'irrational' crime, and crime that occurs within 'capsule' environments.

'Irrational' crime

One of the criticisms often levelled against rational choice is that it only applies to prudent crimes, that is, offences for which the offender is able to calculate a clear benefit (Trasler 1986; Tunnell 2002). It is less applicable, the critics contend, to emotionally-based or pathological behaviour such as violence and sex offending. These behaviours are widely seen to be the product of psychological deficits rather than situational factors. While this criticism of rational choice has been challenged (Clarke 1997; Cornish and Clarke, Chapter 2, this volume), it is true that to date there has been a disproportionate focus in the situational literature on property crime over interpersonal crime. The inclusion of precipitators broadens the scope of the situational approach and provides the basis for a more comprehensive analysis of so-called 'irrational' crimes. Two examples are discussed here – interpersonal violence and child sexual abuse.

Interpersonal violence
Researchers have classically distinguished between instrumental violence – a planned attack with a clearly formulated purpose (e.g. financial gain) – and expressive violence – an impulsive reaction to events carried out in the heat of the moment (e.g. Bowker 1985). Rational choice can clearly help explain instrumental violence but arguably has less to offer in the case of expressive violence. While it has been shown that the distinction between instrumental and

expressive violence is not clear-cut – Tedeschi and Felson (1994), for example, have argued that even expressive violence involves rationality – a great deal of violence undoubtedly has its genesis in interpersonal conflicts and other environmental precipitators, and involves little premeditation. For example, in an analysis of Australian homicide statistics, just 19 per cent of cases were classified as instrumental (Davies and Mousas 2007). Overall, 60 per cent of victims and perpetrators knew one another; around half of all perpetrators were affected by alcohol at the time of the offence; and 35 per cent of cases involving male perpetrators and 58 per cent involving female perpetrators occurred in the course of domestic disputes or other arguments. Even if one retains a role for rational choice in these cases (and it is not suggested that rational choice is irrelevant in expressive violence), the situational events leading up to the homicide have demonstrably impaired the perpetrators' capacity to make a clear-headed decision. There is further examination of the role of precipitators in expressive violence in the discussion of capsule environments below.

Child sexual abuse
The stereotypical image of a child sex offender is of a cunning predator, driven to offend by irresistible psychological urges. In fact, research indicates that many child sex offenders do not possess an entrenched sexual attraction to children. The recidivism rate for child sex offenders is surprisingly low, just 13 per cent after five years at risk (Hanson and Bussiere 1998). Smallbone and Wortley (2001) found that the vast majority (94 per cent) of child sex offenders in their sample abused a child that they already knew, less than a quarter had previous convictions for sexual offences, and almost half had abused just one victim. At the same time, the potential for non-paedophilic adult males, on occasion, to become sexually aroused by children is more widespread than is usually assumed (Barbaree and Marshall 1989; Laws and Marshall 1990). In the absence of strong deviant motivations, immediate environments play an important role in precipitating child sexual abuse (Smallbone *et al.* 2008; Wortley and Smallbone 2006). The sexual impulse is often triggered during intimate care-giving activities – bathing, dressing, comforting, tucking into bed, roughhousing, and so on – which the offender experiences as stimulating. The role of such situational precipitators has been recognised for some time in the sex offender treatment field. In relapse prevention, offenders are taught to avoid or manage situations that they might find sexually stimulating and which might set in train an offending cycle (Pithers *et al.* 1983).

Capsule environments

Capsule environments are bounded locations where people are brought or come together for a specific purpose. They include residential institutions such as prisons, orphanages and boarding schools, and entertainment venues such as nightclubs and sporting arenas. The press of people combined with the enclosed nature of these environments can create pressure-cooker conditions.

With limited options for escaping the capsule, the potential for situational precipitators to generate aberrant behaviour is intensified. Two locations where the role of precipitators has been examined in some detail are nightclubs and prisons.

Nightclubs

The scenario involving nightclub violence that opened this chapter is far from fanciful. Research into nightclub and pub violence clearly points to the crucial role that situational precipitators play. Homel and colleagues (Homel and Clark 1994; Homel et al. 1997; Macintyre and Homel 1997) investigated chronic levels of violence in the nightclub district of a popular Australian tourist resort. Violence was related to the physical conditions of the premises and the alcohol serving policies of management. Homel and Clark (1994) found that violence correlated with a range of aggravating environmental features such as amount of cigarette smoke, lack of ventilation, poor lighting and the demeanour of security staff. Macintyre and Homel (1997) analysed the floor plans of various premises. They found that designs in which the pathway to the toilets intersected the pathway to the bar, thereby increasing the level of jostling, were associated with significantly higher levels of violence. Homel et al. (1997) found that irresponsible alcohol serving practices – excessive discounting, drinking competitions, serving intoxicated patrons, failing to provide alternatives to alcohol – significantly contributed to patron violence. The implementation of a Code of Practice by the licensed premises to encourage responsible serving, and strengthening external regulation to enforce liquor licensing laws, resulted in a significant decrease in alcohol-related violence around the nightclubs.

Prisons

The capacity for 'total' institutions such as prisons to engender pathological behaviour among their residents is well documented (Goffman 1961). The prison environment contains frustrating and aversive experiences for prisoners at every turn (Wortley 2002). Prisons are often crowded and prisoners are forced to live with people they would never socialise with in other circumstances. The architecture is typically drab and spartan, the routine is dull, repetitive and the regime is controlling and sometimes oppressive. In most prisons, prisoners do not have control over the simplest aspects of the environment, such as turning their cells lights on and off and regulating their heating. It is little wonder that prisoners commit twice as many assaults (Cooley 1993) and are more than four times more likely to commit suicide (Ramsay et al. 1987) in prison than on the outside. The traditional way to control prisoner behaviour is through overt security measures, a strategy consistent with rational choice. However, it is clear that consideration of the consequences is not the sole determinant of prison disorder. For example, Allard, Wortley and Stewart (in press) found that CCTV in prison reduced instrumental assaults but not expressive assaults. An alternative strategy is to reduce the situational pressures that precipitate prison disorder.

Implications for crime prevention

The concept of situational precipitators of crime has obvious crime prevention implications, and some of these have been hinted at in the course of the chapter. Take the nightclub example from the beginning of the chapter. This scenario suggests that nightclub violence might be reduced by precipitation control strategies such as training security staff in non-confrontational management techniques (encouraging compliance), restricting patron density (reducing crowding), reorganising the floor plan to facilitate traffic flow (reducing frustration), enhancing patron comfort (controlling environmental irritants), and enforcing responsible alcohol serving policies (clarifying responsibility). However, crime prevention was not the focus of this chapter and a more detailed discussion of controlling situational precipitators can be found elsewhere (Wortley 2001, 2002; Wortley and Smallbone 2006). Recently, too, the concept of situational precipitators has been incorporated into Clarke's situational crime prevention model under the label of reducing provocations (Cornish and Clarke 2003; Clarke and Eck 2003; see also Clarke, Chapter 10, this volume). The purpose of this section is to outline the contributions that the concept of precipitators makes to situational crime prevention. There are five:

1 Consideration of situational precipitators expands the range of techniques available for situational prevention and encourages crime prevention practitioners to think in a more focused way about the antecedents of behaviour. The situational crime prevention task has been traditionally framed in terms of reducing the opportunities for crime. The techniques suggested by the analyses of situational precipitators extend the concept of opportunity reduction.

2 The inclusion of precipitators in the situational model facilitates analyses of behaviours that are not 'rational' or that have otherwise been neglected by situational prevention researchers to date. Critics have contended that behaviours such as interpersonal violence and sex offending are beyond the scope of situational prevention. While this criticism may have always been debatable, it is certainly less true if precipitators are included as part of the situational analysis.

3 Many of the interventions suggested by situational precipitators offer 'soft' prevention options. For example, many suggested precipitation control strategies involve reducing stressful and dehumanising aspects of the environment. A criticism of rational choice is that it leads to an undue focus on target-hardening as a prevention strategy. Critics have equated situational prevention with a 'hard' fortress society. While this criticism can be shown to be unfair (Clarke 1997), precipitators help provide a more balanced image of situational prevention.

4 Precipitators help counter scepticism concerning crime displacement. One of the frequent criticisms of situational prevention is that criminally motivated individuals will simply move to another location or target if one crime opportunity is blocked. Empirically, the amount of crime prevented has been invariably shown to exceed the amount of crime displaced (see Clarke 1997). Precipitators provide an explanation for this. If situations contribute to the potential offender's criminal motivation, then controlling precipitators will reduce the likelihood that he/she will be motivated to seek out alternative crime opportunities.

5 Precipitators help explain and guard against counterproductive situational interventions. Sometimes, opportunity-reduction strategies have the effect of increasing rather than decreasing crime (see Wortley 1998, 2002). For example, too many restrictions on behaviour (such as an overly rigid prison regime) can generate frustration and defiance, and increase levels of expressive violence (for example, a prison riot). That is, under extreme conditions, some opportunity-reduction strategies can transform into precipitators.

Conclusion

The purpose of this chapter has been to show that human behaviour – and criminal behaviour in particular – is inextricably dependent upon its situational context. The role of situations in crime as presented in this chapter, however, differs from the usual way that situations are conceptualised in environmental criminology. In contrast to the rational choice perspective, the psychological theories presented in this chapter emphasise the precipitating role of immediate environments. That is to say, environmental factors may actively induce offenders to commit crimes that they may not have otherwise contemplated at that time. The motivations for crime may be supplied or at least intensified by the situation. Moreover, unlike the deliberative process described in rational choice, according to this perspective immediate environments may influence people at a sub-cognitive level. The offender may be quite unaware of the influence the environment is having upon him/her. It is contended that consideration of the role of precipitators provides for a more faithful rendering of the person–situation interaction, which is a foundational assumption in psychology, and provides for a broader approach to situational crime prevention.

References

Akers, R. L., Krohn, M. D., Lanza-Kaduce, L. and Radosevich, M. (1979) 'Social Learning and Deviant Behavior: A Specific Test of a General Theory', *American Sociological Review*, 44: 636–55.

Allard, T., Wortley, R. and Stewart, A. (in press) 'The Effect of CCTV on Prisoner Misbehaviour', *Prison Journal*.

Atlas, R. (1982) 'Violence in Prison: Architectural Determinism', unpublished doctoral thesis, School of Criminology, Florida State University.

Atlas, R. (1984) 'Violence in Prison: Environmental Influences', *Environment and Behavior*, 16: 275–306.

Bandura, A. (1965) 'Influence of Models' Reinforcement Contingencies on the Acquisition of Imitative Responses', *Journal of Personality and Social Psychology*, 1: 589–95.

Bandura, A. (1977) *Social Learning Theory*. Englewood Cliffs, NJ: Prentice-Hall.

Bandura, A., Barbaranelli, C., Capara, G.V. and Pastorelli, C. (1996), 'Mechanisms of Moral Disengagement in the Exercise of Moral Agency', *Journal of Personality and Social Psychology*, 71: 364–74.

Banzinger, G. and Owens, K. (1978) 'Geophysical Variables and Behavior: Weather Factors as Predictors of Local Social Indicators of Maladaptation in Two Non-urban Areas', *Psychological Reports*, 43: 427–34.

Barbaree, H.E. and Marshall, W.L. (1989), 'Erectile Responses Amongst Heterosexual Child Molestors, Father-Daughter Incest Offenders, and Matched Nonoffenders: Five Distinct Age Preference Profiles', *Canadian Journal of Behavioral Science*, 21: 70–82.

Baum, A. and Valins, S. (1977) *Architecture and Social Behavior: Psychological Studies of Social Density*, Hillsdale, NJ: Erlbaum.

Baum, A., Singer, J.E., and Baum, C.S. (1981) 'Stress and the Environment', *Journal of Social Issues*, 37: 4–35.

Bensley, L.S., and Wu, R. (1991) 'The Role of Psychological Reactance in Drinking Following Alcohol Prevention Messages', *Journal of Applied Social Psychology*, 21: 1111–24.

Berkowitz, L. (1983), 'The Experience of Anger as a Parallel Process in the Display of Impulsive, "Angry" Aggression', in R.G. Green and E.I. Donnerstein (eds), *Aggression: Theoretical and Empirical Reviews*, Vol. 1. New York Academic Press, pp. 103–33.

Bottoms, A.E., Hay, W. and Sparks, J.R. (1995) 'Situational and Social Approaches to the Prevention of Disorder in Long-term Prisons', in T.J. Flanagan (ed.) *Long-term Imprisonment*. Thousand Oaks, CA: Sage, pp. 186–96.

Boulton, M.J. (1994) 'Understanding and Preventing Bullying in the Junior School Playground', in P.K. Smith and S. Sharp (eds) *School Bullying*. London: Routledge, pp. 133–58.

Bowker, L.H. (1985). 'An Essay on Prison Violence', in M. Braswell, S. Dilligham and R. Montgomery (eds) *Prison Violence in America*. Cincinnati, OH: Anderson.

Brehm, J.W. (1966) *A Theory of Psychological Reactance*. New York: Academic Press.

Carter, N., Holström, A., Simpanen, M. and Melin, K. (1988) 'Theft Reduction in a Grocery Store Through Product Identification and Graphing of Losses for Employees', *Journal of Applied Behavioral Analysis*, 21: 385–9.

Clark, J.B. and Hollinger, R.C. (1983). *Theft by Employees in Work Organizations*. Washington, DC: US. Department of Justice.

Clarke, R.V. (1997) 'Introduction', in R.V. Clarke (ed.) *Situational Crime Prevention: Successful Case Studies*, 2nd edn, Albany, NY: Harrow and Heston, pp. 2–43.

Clarke, R.V. and Eck, J. (2003) *Become a Problem-Solving Crime Analyst*. Cullompton, UK: Willan Publishing.

Clarke, R.V. and Homel, R. (1997) 'A Revised Classification of Situational Crime Prevention Techniques', in S. P. Lab (ed.) *Crime Prevention at the Crossroads*. Cincinnati, OH: Anderson, pp. 21–35.

Colman, A. (1991) 'Psychological Evidence in South African Murder Trials', *The Psychologist*, November 482–6.

Cooley, D. (1993) 'Criminal Victimization in Male Federal Prisons', *Canadian Journal of Criminology*, 35: 479–95.

Cornish, D.B. and Clarke, R.V. (2003) 'Opportunities, Precipitators and Criminal Dispositions: A Reply to Wortley's Critique of Situational Crime Prevention', in M.J. Smith and D.B. Cornish (eds) *Theory for Practice in Situational Crime Prevention. Crime Prevention Studies, Vol. 16*. Monsey, NJ: Criminal Justice Press.

Davies, M. and Mousas, J. (2007) *Homicide in Australia: 2005–2006 National Homicide Monitoring Program Annual Report*, Research and Public Policies Series No. 77. Canberra: Australian Institute of Criminology.

Dean, L.M., Pugh, W.M. and Gunderson, E.K. (1978) 'The Behavioral Effects of Crowding: Definitions and Methods', *Environment and Behavior*, 10: 413–31.

Donnerstein, E. and Wilson, D.W. (1976) 'Effects of Noise and Perceived Control on Ongoing and Subsequent Aggressive Behavior', *Journal of Personality and Social Psychology*, 34: 774–81.

Elliot, M. (ed.) (1991) *Bullying: A Practical Guide to Coping for Schools*. Harlow: Longman.

Fitzgerald, G. (1989) *Commission of Inquiry into Possible Illegal Activities and Associated Police Misconduct*. Brisbane: Queensland Government.

Foster, J. and Hope, T. (1993) *Housing, Community and Crime: The Impact of the Priority Estates Project*, Home Office Research Study 131. London: HMSO.

Geller, E.S., Koltuniak, T.A. and Shilling, J.S. (1983) 'Response Avoiding Prompting: A Cost-effective Strategy for Theft Deterrence', *Behavioral Counseling and Community Interventions*, 3: 28–42.

Goffman, E. (1961) *Asylums*. Garden City NY: Anchor Books.

Goodstein, L., MacKenzie, D.L. and Shotland, R.L. (1984), 'Personal Control and Inmate Adjustment to Prison', *Criminology: An Interdisciplinary Journal*, 22: 343–69.

Goranson, R.E. and King, D. (1970) *Rioting and Daily Temperature: Analysis of the U.S. Riots in 1967*. Toronto: York University.

Gove, W.R., Hughs, M. and Galle, O.R. (1977), 'Overcrowding in the Home: An Empirical Investigation of its Possible Pathological Consequences', *American Sociological Review*, 44: 59–80.

Graham, K. and Homel, R. (1996) 'Creating Safer Bars', in M. Plant, E. Single and T. Stockwell (eds) *Alcohol: Minimising the Harm*. London: Free Association Press, pp. 171–92.

Greenberg, J. (1990) 'Employee Theft as a Reaction to Underpayment Inequity: The Hidden Cost of Pay Cuts', *Journal of Applied Psychology*, 75: 561–8.

Greenberg, J. (1997) 'The STEAL Motive: Managing the Social Determinants of Employee Theft', in R.A. Giacalone and J. Greenberg (eds) *Antisocial Behavior in Organisations*. Thousand Oaks, CA: Sage, pp. 85–108.

Hanson, R.K. and Bussiere, M.T. (1998) 'Predicting Relapse: A Meta-analysis of Sexual Offender Recidivism Studies', *Journal of Consulting and Clinical Psychology*, 66: 348–62.

Harding, R.W., Morgan, F.H., Indermaur, D., Ferrante, A.M. and Blagg, H. (1998) 'Road Rage and the Epidemiology of Violence: Something Old, Something New', *Studies on Crime and Crime Prevention*, 7: 221–38.

Harries, K.D. and Stadler, S.J. (1988) 'Heat and Violence: New Findings From the Dallas Field Data 1980–1981', *Journal of Applied Social Psychology*, 18: 129–38.

Hollinger, R.C. (1989) *Dishonesty in the Workplace: A Manager's Guide to Preventing Employee Theft*. Park Ridge, IL: London House.

Homel, R. and Clark, J. (1994) 'The Prediction and Prevention of Violence in Pubs and Clubs', in R.V. Clarke (ed.) *Crime Prevention Studies, Vol. 3*. Monsey, NY: Criminal Justice Press, pp. 1–46.

Homel, R., Hauritz, M., Wortley, R., McIlwain, G. and Carvolth, R. (1997) 'Preventing Alcohol-related Crime Through Community Action: The Surfers Paradise Safety Action Project', in R. Homel (ed.) *Policing for Prevention. Crime Prevention Studies, Vol. 7*. Monsey, NY: Criminal Justice Press, pp. 35–90.

Indermaur, D. (1996) 'Reducing Opportunities for Violence in Robbery and Property Crime: The Perspectives of Offenders and Victims', in R. Homel (ed.) *The Politics and Practice of Situational Crime Prevention. Crime Prevention Studies, Vol. 5*. Monsey, NY: Criminal Justice Press, pp. 133–57.

Kelman, H.C. and Hamilton, V.L. (1989) *Crimes of Obedience*. Binghamton, NY: Yale University Press.

Lang, A.R., Goeckner, D.J., Adesso, V.G. and Marlatt, G.A. (1975) 'Effects of Alcohol on Aggression in Male Social Drinkers', *Journal of Abnormal Psychology*, 84: 508–18.

Laws, D.R. and Marshall, W.L. (1990) 'A Conditioning Theory of the Etiology and Maintenance of Deviant Sexual Preferences and Behavior', in W.L. Marshall, D.R. Laws and H.E. Barbaree (eds) *Handbook of Sexual Assault: Issues, Theories, and Treatment of the Offender*. New York: Plenum.

LeBeau, J.L. (1994) 'The Oscillation of Police Calls to Domestic Disputes with Time and the Temperature Humidity Index', *Journal of Crime and Justice*, 17: 149–61.

Lefkowitz, M., Blake, R.R. and Mouton, J.S. (1955) 'Status Factors in Pedestrian Violation of Traffic Signals', *Journal of Abnormal and Social Psychology*, 51: 704–5.

Ley, D. and Cybriwsky, R. (1974) 'Urban Graffiti as Territorial Markers', *Annals of the Association of American Geographers*, 64: 491–505.

Leyens, J.P., Camino, L., Parke, R.D. and Bekowitz, L. (1975) 'Effects of Movie Violence on Aggression in a Field Setting as a Function of Group Dominance and Cohesion', *Journal of Personality and Social Psychology*, 32: 346–60.

Lombardo, L.X. (1989) *Guards Imprisoned: Correctional Officers at Work*, 2nd edn. Cincinnati, OH: Anderson.

Macintyre, S. and Homel, R. (1997) 'Danger on the Dance Floor: A Study on Interior Design, Crowding and Aggression in Nightclubs', in R. Homel (ed.) *Policing for Prevention: Reducing Crime, Public Intoxication and Injury. Crime Prevention Studies, Vol. 7*. Monsey, NY: Criminal Justice Press, pp. 91–113.

Marshall, W.L. (1988) 'The Use of Explicit Sexual Stimuli by Rapists, Child Molestors and Nonoffender Males', *Journal of Sex Research*, 25: 267–88.

Milgram, S. (1974) *Obedience to Authority: An Experimental View*. New York: Harper and Row.

Nagle, J.F. (1978) *Report of the Royal Commission into New South Wales Prisons*. Sydney: NSW Government Printer.

Oliver, S.S., Roggenbuck, J.W. and Watson, A.E. (1985) 'Education to Reduce Impacts in Forest Campgrounds', *Journal of Forestry*, 83: 234–6.

Olweus, D. (1978) *Aggression in Schools*. Washington, DC: Hemisphere.

O'Neill, S.M. and Paluck, B.J. (1973) 'Altering Territoriality Through Reinforcement', *Proceedings of the 81st Annual Convention of the American Psychological Association*. Montreal, Canada, pp. 901–2.

Parilla, P.F., Hollinger, R.C., and Clark, J.P. (1988), 'Organizational Control of Deviant Behavior: The Case of Employee Theft', *Social Science Quarterly*, 69: 261–80.

Paulus, P. (1988) *Prison Crowding: A Psychological Perspective*. New York: Springer-Verlag.

Phillips, D.P. (1983) 'The Impact of Mass Media Violence on U.S. Homicides', *American Sociological Review*, 48: 560–8.

Phillips, D.P. (1989) 'Recent Advances in Suicidology: The Study of Imitative Suicide', in R.F.W. Diekstra, R. Maris, S. Platt, A. Schmidtke and G. Sonneck (eds) *Suicide and its Prevention*. New York: E.J. Brill, pp. 299–312.

Phillips, D.P. and Carstensen, L.L. (1990) 'The Effects of Suicide Stories on Various Demographic Groups 1968–1985', in R. Surette (ed.) *The Media and Criminal Justice Policy*. Springfield, IL: Charles C. Thomas, pp. 63–72.

Pithers, W.D., Marques, J.K., Gibat, C.C. and Marlatt, G.A. (1983) 'Relapse Prevention with Sexual Aggressives: 'A Self-control Model of Treatment and Maintenance of Change', in J.G. Greer and I.R. Stuart (eds) *The Sexual Aggressor: Current Perspectives on Treatment*. New York: Von Nostrand Reinhold, pp. 214–39.

Ramsay, R.F., Tanney, B.L. and Searle, C.A. (1987) 'Suicide Prevention in High-risk Prison Populations', *Criminology*, 21: 213–32.

Randall, P. (1997) *Adult Bullying*. London: Routledge.

Reicher, S. (1991) 'Politics of Crowd Psychology', *The Psychologist*, November: 487–91.

Rosenthal, R. (1990) 'Media Violence, Antisocial Behavior, and the Social Consequences of Small Effects', in R. Surette (ed.) *The Media and Criminal Justice Policy*. Springfield, IL: Charles C. Thomas, pp. 53–61.

Rotton, J. and Frey, J. (1985) 'Air Pollution, Weather, and Violent Crimes: Concomitant Time-series Analysis of Archival Data', *Journal of Personality and Social Psychology*, 49: 1207–20.

Shellow, R. and Roemer, D.V. (1987) 'No Heaven for "Hell's Angels" ', in R.H. Turner and L.M. Killian (eds) *Collective Behavior*, 3rd edn. Englewood Cliffs, NJ: Prentice-Hall, pp. 115–23.

Sherman, L. (1993) 'Defiance, Deterrence and Irrelevance: A Theory of the Criminal Sanction', *Journal of Research in Crime and Delinquency*, 30: 445–73.

Silbert, M.H. and Pines, A.M. (1984) 'Pornography and Sexual Abuse of Women', *Sex Roles*, 10: 857–68.

Skinner, B.F. (1953) *Science and Human Behavior.* New York: Free Press.

Skinner, W.F., and Fream, A.M. (1997) 'A Social Learning Theory Analysis of Computer Crime Among College Students', *Journal of Research in Crime and Delinquency*, 34: 495–518.

Smallbone, S.W. and Wortley, R.K. (2001) *Child Sexual Abuse: Offender Characteristics and Modus Operandi*, No. 193. Canberra: Australian Institute of Criminology Trends and Issues in Crime and Criminal Justice.

Smallbone, S., Marshall, W. and Wortley, R. (2008) *Preventing Child Sexual Abuse: Evidence, Policy and Practice*. Cullompton, UK: Willan Publishing.

Snyder, N.H., Broome, O.W., Kehoe, W.J., McIntyre, J.T. and Blair, K.E. (1991) *Reducing Employee Theft: A guide to Financial and Organisational Controls*. New York: Quorum.

Sparks, R., Bottoms, A. and Hay, W. (1996) *Prison and the Problem of Order*. Oxford: Clarendon Press.

Spector, P.E. (1997) 'The Role of Frustration in Antisocial Behavior at Work', in R.A. Giacalone and J. Greenberg (eds) *Antisocial Behavior in Organisations*. Thousand Oaks, CA: Sage, pp. 1–17.

Sydney Morning Herald (2005) 'Sydney's Deadliest Pubcrawl' 4 October (www.smh.com.au/news/national/sydneys-deadliest-pub-crawl/2005/10/03/1128191658860.html).

Sykes, G. and Matza, D. (1957) 'Techniques of Neutralization: A Theory of Delinquency', *American Journal of Sociology*, 22: 664–70.

Tedeschi, J. and Felson, R.B. (1994). *Violence, Aggression and Coercive Action.* Washington, DC: American Psychological Association Books.

Trasler, G. (1986) 'Situational Crime Prevention and Rational Choice: A Critique', in K. Heal and G. Laycock (eds) *Situational Crime Prevention: From Theory into Practice.* London: HMSO, pp. 17–42.

Tunnell, K.D. (2002) 'The Impulsiveness and Routinization of Decision-making', in A.R. Piquero and S.G. Tibbetts (eds) *Rational Choice and Criminal Behavior: Recent Research and Future Challenges*. New York: Routledge.

Vander Stoep, G. and Gramann, J. (1987) 'The Effect of Verbal Appeals and Incentives on Depreciative Behavior Among Youthful Park Visitors', *Journal of Leisure Research* 19: 69–83.

Warr, M. and Stafford, M. (1991) 'The Influence of Delinquent Peers: What They Think or What They Do?', *Criminology*, 29: 851–65.

Wilson, J.Q. and Kelling, G. (1982) 'The Police and Neighborhood Safety: Broken Windows', *Atlantic*, 127: 29–38.

Wortley, R. (1996) 'Guilt, Shame and Situational Crime Prevention' in R. Homel (ed.) *The Politics and Practice of Situational Crime Prevention. Crime Prevention Studies, Vol. 5*. Monsey, NY: Criminal Justice Press, pp. 115–32.

Wortley, R. (1997) 'Reconsidering the Role of Opportunity in Situational Crime Prevention', in G. Newman, R.V. Clarke and S.G. Shohan (eds) *Rational Choice and Situational Crime Prevention*. Aldershot, UK: Ashgate, pp. 65–81.

Wortley, R. (1998) 'A Two-stage Model of Situational Crime Prevention', *Studies on Crime and Crime Prevention*, 7: 173–88.

Wortley, R. (2001) 'A Classification of Techniques for Controlling Situational Precipitators of Crime', *Security Journal*, 14(4): 63–82.

Wortley, R. (2002) *Situational Prison Control: Crime Prevention in Correctional Institutions*. Cambridge: Cambridge University Press.

Wortley, R. and Smallbone, S. (2006) 'Applying Situational Principles to Sexual Offending Against Children', in R. Wortley and S. Smallbone (eds) *Situational Prevention of Child Sexual Abuse. Crime Prevention Studies, Vol. 19*. Monsey, NY: Criminal Justice Press.

4. Routine activity approach

Marcus Felson

Introduction

The routine activity approach to crime-rate analysis emerged more than a quarter of a century ago. Since that time the approach has developed and fused with other approaches to crime analysis, as reflected in this volume. This is an account of how the approach was born and how it evolved.

From its inception in the late 1970s, the routine activity approach has been both a micro and macro theory of how crime rates emerge. On a micro level, the theory states that ordinary crime emerges when a likely offender converges with a suitable crime target in the absence of a capable guardian against crime. On a macro level, the theory states that certain features of larger society and larger community can make such convergences much more likely.

The theory was written in the simplest and starkest form as a deliberate attempt to provide an alternative to vague theories about crime (see Cohen and Felson 1979; Felson and Cohen 1980). It was also written to avoid its own ruination. Many crime theories devise a good idea, but over time that idea is ruined through progressive retelling. In the childhood game of telephone, a bunch of kids form a circle, the first one whispering a message to the next, who passes it on, and so on until in the end the message proves to be entirely garbled. So it is with much crime theory. The routine activity approach largely avoided this process because it was too simple to ruin.

Yet the routine activity approach is sometimes misunderstood or trivialised by those who read the one-paragraph textbook version rather than the whole original paper, or who fail to read follow-up papers and books. The original routine activity paper in 1979 was clearly both a general intellectual statement and a middle-level theory of crime. In the general intellectual statement, crime was linked to a broad range of legal activities. Crime was interpreted as part of the broad ecology of everyday life. The theory of human ecology, as stated by Amos Hawley in 1950, was the basis for the routine activity theory.

Clarification and history of the theory

Many people who cite the theory seem totally unaware of this general theoretical basis, or that the original paper presents diverse ideas about how society's technology and organisation affect crime. Thousands cite the routine activity approach but only a smattering of these seem to know more than offender, target, guardian. Indeed, many do not even know that the routine activity approach attributed America's massive crime wave to the dispersion of activities away from family and household as well as technological shifts in goods and services. Fewer realised the linkages to general ecological theory that could apply to other decades and centuries.

Even in micro terms, not all who quote the theory get it right. A guardian is not usually a police officer or security guard. Usually the guardian against crime is anybody whose presence or proximity discourages crime. Usually people protect their own property, however inadvertently. Sometimes people protect relatives or friends, or even strangers. But in the routine activity approach the word 'guardian' is not meant to be 'guard'. The term 'supervision' is less ambiguous, and I have since used it more often. But I was looking for nouns. 'Supervisor' in English implies a boss at the workplace, and so the choice of words is always problematical.

Selection of words

The choice of the word 'target' rather than 'victim' was another interesting decision. Victimology was very popular at the time, and victim research had proliferated. But the word 'victim' did not distinguish victims of direct physical assault from those whose homes were invaded in their absence. The routine activity approach focuses on the offender's viewpoint, not the victim's and not society's. From the property offender's viewpoint, your property is interesting, even without knowing you. To be sure, some property crime is intended as a personal attack, but the direct physical encounter is between the offender and the crime target – sometimes a person and sometimes a thing.

The very selection of the term 'routine activity approach' was necessary because some ordinary words had taken on specialised meanings in criminology. 'Opportunity' was pre-empted, referring to 'economic opportunity'. 'Control' was also taken for other purposes. 'Ecology' was already used to mean local areas rather than interdependencies. And so routine activity became the term. It was a fortunate selection, since it gave the approach uniqueness, while allowing a touch of irony. A crime is a relatively rare event by many calculations. That a rare event can be the outcome of routine events adds a twist and challenge, and that's just what I wanted.

Others now call it routine activity theory, but I preferred 'approach' for one substantive reason and one tactical. My substantive reason was that this was not a full-blown theory. My tactical reason was that I felt the ideas were repugnant enough to conventional criminologists; calling it a theory was like waving a red cape in front of a bull. Calling it an approach made it seem more modest, but of course that fooled nobody. The theory was an overt challenge to conventional criminology, and I had to somehow get it into print. That required sustained effort and substantial resistance.

Difficulty getting published

I wrote up the first drafts of the routine activity paper, and it was over three years before it was published. In the process, a new criminology colleague, Lawrence Cohen, joined our faculty and helped redraft the work to make it more palatable. That failed, at least initially. Even though the routine activity approach is now one of the most cited theories in criminology, the original article was rejected by six leading journals, including the top three sociology journals, the *American Sociological Review*, *American Journal of Sociology* and *Social Forces*. Reviewers' comments included these:

'impressive empirical dribble'

'falls apart in the section devoted to evidence'

'far fetched and premature'

'the human ecology approach ... goes nowhere'

'highly questionable'

'an old theory in new clothes ... a rehash of ... Cloward and Ohlin'

'raises more questions than it answers'

'a bizarre paper'

'too cryptic ... suspiciously glib'

'a bundle of paradoxes'

'long and somewhat boring'

'Can the analysis be saved? I doubt it.'

'[I] recommend that this obviously talented sociologist turn to a problem ... more meaningful.'

At some point in the process, the *American Sociological Review* moved to our campus, the University of Illinois at Urbana-Champaign. Its editor did not like us or our theory, and made no secret of it. Although that journal had turned it down, the associate editor very much liked the paper and allowed an uninvited re-submission. He assigned it to tough but prestigious reviewers, and the editor had no choice but to publish it.

Prior to publication, a version of the paper was presented to the 1978 Annual Meeting of the Academy of Criminal Justice Sciences in New Orleans. The ACJS at that time presented a prize to the single paper of that meeting that was thought to be most likely to have a long-term impact. The Awards Committee strongly recommended the routine activity paper for this award, but was overruled by a committee of higher authority, which then changed the rule to honour the best paper from the *preceding* year.

Resisting 'social disorganisation' theory

After the theory was finally in print in 1979, several people advised me and my co-author to subsume the routine activity approach under conventional criminology. The best way to do that was to 'integrate' it with Shaw and McKay's social disorganisation approach. My co-author and I split and he went back towards conventional sociology, while I moved farther and farther away from my own origins towards a new approach and a new set of intellectual friends, represented in this volume.

Evolution of the theory

Over the years, the routine activity approach has evolved in several ways. First, it has been linked to practical policies against crime (see Felson and Clarke 1998). Second, it has covered many more bases than the original approach.

Linkages to Clarke and the Brantinghams

The original approach stated quite clearly that crime is a function of major changes in the basic structure of society, and that a high crime rate in the contemporary world is virtually inevitable. In the early 1980s I first met Ronald V. Clarke in London, where he challenged this viewpoint. If increased opportunity to commit crimes causes the crime rate to rise, the other side of the coin is that decreased opportunity for crime must push crime rates down. In one sentence he persuaded me that situational crime prevention and the routine activity approach were intertwined. About a year beforehand I had been hosted by Paul and Patricia Brantingham in Vancouver, and I came to realise that all of us, starting from different directions, using different terms, were converging on the same theory (note the other chapters in this volume, including those by Clarke and the Brantinghams).

To make a theory general, one has to cover a multitude of bases. The original routine activity approach applied to 'direct-contact predatory offenses', namely, offences in which one person directly harmed the person or property of another by coming into direct physical contact. Although that is a very broad application, telecommunications crime avoids direct physical contact. More importantly, the original routine activity approach considered micro and macro, but nothing in between. It did not go into the journey to crime, the journey to victimisation, even though it implied all of that. In addition, the routine activity approach implied a decisional offender, but did not make the decision process explicit. Thus it became essential to fuse the routine activity approach with the geography of crime, environmental criminology, situational prevention, and models of offender choices.

Broadening the theory

It became clear in time that routine activity thinking helps understand non-routine crimes, including serial murders and sexual abuses (see Rossmo 1995).

Again, links to the work of others in this volume counters claims that the routine activity approach covers too few bases.

In addition, available crime data and analysis techniques greatly enhanced our ability to study and understand crime. The routine activity approach gained much from these advances. I do not know whether or to what extent the routine activity approach influenced these outcomes, but more and more crime data were incident-based and geo-coded. In time, the theoretical and empirical reliance on community areas, neighbourhoods and census tracts became obsolete, even though many criminologists might not yet realise this. The data of the twenty-first century show great crime variations within so-called high-crime neighbourhoods, with a few addresses contributing most of the local problem. Moreover, offenders and targets move across census tracts every day, rendering the old theories and measures obsolete.

The routine activity theory today has much more to say about offenders than its original rendition. Offenders often cook up crime together, and so co-offending becomes a topic for routine activity theory. Offender convergence settings ('hangouts') are places where offenders find one another, not only committing crimes there but in proximate times and places (see Felson 2003). Many scholars have talked about co-offending in the past, but usually in terms of general influences rather than specific places.

The initial routine activity approach did not come to terms with control theory, and left it largely aside. But in time routine activity theory recognised control on its own terms (Felson 1997). Rather than viewing control as something internalised, it emphasised the presences or absences of others who might supervise a person. Thus parents can influence their children to be good, but not so effectively when the parents are away. The concept of 'handler' was added as a fourth element in routine activity theory. The offender had to first escape the handler (such as his mother), then find a target with a guardian absent. Again, tangible settings became central for understanding crime processes.

Eck's crime triangle

These four elements were elaborated cleverly by John Eck, who devised the 'crime triangle' (also called the 'problem triangle', and depicted in Chapter 12 this volume). This is really two triangles, one engulfing the other. A reduced-size version of the triangle is offered here for reference.

The *inside triangle* has three elements that must converge for a normal crime to occur: the potential offender, the crime target and the place setting for the crime. For a crime problem to occur, the offender needs to find a target in a suitable setting.

The *outside triangle* depicts three sorts of supervisors: the handler, the guardian and the place manager. The handler supervises the offender, the guardian supervises the target and the manager supervises the crime setting. Their absences make a crime feasible. A crime occurs when the offender escapes handlers, finds targets free from guardians in settings not watched by managers. Once more, the routine activity approach has grown well beyond its origins.

Figure 4.1 The crime triangle

Crime and Everyday Life

In *Crime and Everyday Life* (Felson 2002), I broaden the routine activity theory in a number of ways. The most important is to include a critique of how many people think about crime. These are the five main fallacies:

- *The dramatic fallacy*: Emphasising crimes that are most publicised, while forgetting ordinary crimes.
- *The cops-and-courts fallacy*: Overstating the criminal justice system's power over crime.
- *The not-me fallacy*: Thinking you are too good to commit a crime; believing that offenders are from a different population from yours.
- *The ingenuity fallacy*: Overstating the skill required to commit a crime.
- *The agenda fallacy*: Linking crime reduction to your favourite ideology, religion, or political agenda.

These fallacies present a general critique of many conventional approaches to criminology, and explain why modern crime analysis must take a different tack.

Crime in everyday life was interpreted as a kind of social chemistry, depending on who converged when and where, under what circumstances. The crime triangle generalises several possibilities. In another general form, interpersonal violence occurs when disputants converge in the presence of *agents provocateurs*, and the absence of peacemakers. Such convergences lead sometimes to a sort of chemical reaction, with disputes emerging and sometimes escalating into criminal action. This thinking was borrowed from my brother, Richard Felson (see Tedeschi and Felson 1994), then simplified and modified in terms of social chemistry.

Crime and nature

The natural sciences have two broad branches: physical sciences and life sciences. For some time I saw crime in terms of the physical sciences, with offenders and other crime participants converging in space to produce the chemistry for an illicit act.

In time I came to realise that the physical sciences, including chemistry, are too mechanical for understanding criminal behaviour. That does not mean we should dispense with the physical elements. But it does mean that we should allow for more elaborate life processes.

In the physical sciences, every electron is the same as every other and, under the same circumstances, does the same thing. In the life sciences, not every amoeba is the same in every way. The life sciences allow much more variation and hence are more suited to studying crime. Any given stimulus might produce alternative responses. That does not mean that physical processes are no longer central, or that living organisms can do anything they want. But it does allow choices and alternatives, basic to our concept of life itself. In *Crime and Nature* (Felson 2006), I linked crime to a variety of life processes. I used the concepts of the life sciences to organise what we know and need to know about crime, in its full variety. I established that scores of concepts from the life sciences apply very closely in studying crime.

In so doing, I emphasised that the life sciences are much broader than genetics and richer than the biology courses in high school – the farthest most social scientists have gone on these topics. I view conventional biology as a subset of the larger life sciences, with the latter including the study of crime and its prevention.

Conclusion

Despite this growth, the routine activity approach can be taught at an elementary, intermediate and advanced level. The student can accumulate understanding, starting with the original three elements and building up to the full six elements of the crime triangle. The student can start with the micro level, then look at macro changes in society. Then the student studies the intermediate circumstances by which the elements of crime converge or diverge. Taking into account the many features of situational prevention, environmental criminology, crime geography and offender choice, and the relationships among these, the study of crime in tangible terms is quite challenging. Crime's many varieties and processes fit within larger life, and can be studied accordingly.

References

Cohen, L.E. and Felson, M. (1979) 'Social Change and Crime Rate Trends: A Routine Activity Approach', *American Sociological Review*, 44: 588–608.

Felson, M. and Clarke, R.V. (1998) *Opportunity Makes the Thief*, monograph. London: Home Office, Police Research Group.

Felson, M. (2000) 'The Routine Activity Approach: A Very Versatile Theory of Crime', in R. Paternoster and R. Bachman (eds) *Explaining Criminals and Crime: Essays in Contemporary Criminological Theory*. Los Angeles: Roxbury.

Felson, M. (2002) *Crime and Everyday Life*, 3rd edn. Thousand Oaks, CA: Sage and Pine Forge Press.

Felson, M. (2003) 'The Process of Co-offending', in M.J. Smith and D.B. Cornish, (eds) *Theory for Practice in Situational Crime Prevention. Crime Prevention Studies, Vol. 16.* Monsey, NY: Criminal Justice Press.

Felson, M. (2006) *Crime and Nature*. Thousand Oaks, CA: Sage.

Felson, M. (1997) 'Reconciling Hirschi's 1969 Control Theory with the General Theory of Crime', in S.P. Lab (ed.) *Crime Prevention at a Crossroads*. Cincinnati: Anderson.

Felson, M. and Cohen, L.E. (1980) 'Human Ecology and Crime: A Routine Activity Approach', *Human Ecology*, 8: 398–405.

Rossmo, D.K. (1995) 'Place, Space, and Police Investigations: Hunting Serial Violent Criminals', in J.E. Eck and D.L. Weisburd (eds) *Crime and Place: Crime Prevention Studies, Vol. 4.* Monsey, NY: Criminal Justice Press.

Tedeschi, J. and Felson, R.B. (1994) *Violence, Aggression and Coercive Action*. Washington, DC: APA Books.

5. Crime pattern theory

Paul Brantingham and Patricia Brantingham

Introduction

Criminology tries to explain crime and criminal behaviour. This poses long-standing questions: Why do only some people commit crimes? Why are some people re-victimised frequently while others rarely are victims? Why do some places experience a lot of crime while other places experience almost none? These questions seem, to us, to call for an understanding of crime patterns formed by the rich complexities of criminal events formed by law, offender motivation and target characteristic arrayed on an environmental backcloth. Each element in the criminal event has a historical trajectory shaped by past experience and future intention, by the routine activities and rhythms of life, and by the constraints of the environment. Patterns within these complexities, considered over many criminal events, should point us towards understandings of *crime* as a whole.

Understanding complex patterns requires a formalism in which simple rules are proposed and ways of combining the rules are described. Complex theoretical crime patterns are built by composing iterations and combinations of the rules. As complex theoretical patterns are built, they should be continuously compared with observed actual crime patterns derived through a variety of information sources. Observations of actual crime patterns contain noise and blurring that come from the processes available for data gathering and the continual small transformations in the way things are done that are part of the dynamics of everyday living. The basic theoretical rules and the defined processes for combining those rules into formally structured patterns referenced to observations of actual crimes provides a cognitive structure for a much clearer understanding of those patterns and their implications for crime reduction.

This chapter is a summary of crime pattern theory. Guiding rules are presented for: (1) individual offenders; (2) networks of offenders; and (3) aggregations of individual offenders. These rules are placed within a spatio-temporal context. The result of placing the rules within a spatio-temporal context helps explain: (1) crime templates that reflect target/victim assessment; (2) crime locations in spatio-temporal activity spaces based on routine daily movement geographies; (3) crime concentrations that are found along paths to major nodes and are largely restricted to neighbourhood edges; and (4) crime attractors and crime generators. The basics of crime pattern theory are then used to look at offender adaptation and offence displacement and abatement.

Pattern theory sees crime as a complex phenomenon, but, even assuming high degrees of complexity, finds discernible patterns both in criminal events and for criminals that are scale independent. That is, the rules behind the patterns can be found at both detailed and general levels of analysis. *Pattern* is a term used to describe recognisable inter-connectiveness of objects, rules and processes. This inter-connectiveness or linking may be physical or conceptual, but recognising the inter-connectiveness involves the cognitive process of 'seeing' similarity, of discerning prototypes or exemplars of interconnections within cases distorted by local conditions (Churchland 1989). A pattern is sometimes obvious, but sometimes is discernible only through an initial insight, particularly an insight that is embedded within the environment as a whole. Crimes are patterned; decisions to commit crimes are patterned; and the process of committing a crime is patterned.

Pattern theory

Crimes do not occur randomly or uniformly in time or space or society. Crimes do not occur randomly or uniformly across neighbourhoods, or social groups, or during an individual's daily activities or during an individual's lifetime. In fact, arguing for uniformity was once popular but now seems indefensible. There are hot spots and cold spots; there are high repeat offenders and high repeat victims. In fact the two groups are frequently linked. While the numbers will continue to be debated depending on the definition and the population being tested, a very small proportion of people commit most of the known crimes (Carrington *et al.* 2005; Farrington *et al.* 1998; Wolfgang *et al.* 1972) and also account for a large proportion of victimisations (Fattah 1991). The argument for the complete randomness of targets and victims is no longer plausible. Bar fights occur with greater frequency on Friday or Saturday nights than on weekday afternoons; shoplifting occurs during a restricted set of hours in the day and more in some stores than others; and income tax evasions cluster around due dates. Understanding crime requires concepts and models that can be used to account for the patterned non-uniformity and non-randomness that characterises real criminal events.

Individual crime patterns

We will begin working towards understanding complex crime patterns by looking at individual activities. In the first case it will be individual activities of people in general and then the special case of individuals who commit crimes. It should be remembered that people who commit crimes spend most of their day in non-criminal activities. What shapes non-criminal activities helps shape criminal activities.

Rule 1: As individuals move through a series of activities they make decisions. When activities are repeated frequently, the decision process becomes regularised. This regularisation creates an abstract guiding template. For decisions to commit a crime this is called a crime template.

Figure 5.1 provides a summary of Rule 1. Individuals develop routines and, once established, the routines have some stability. The routines may be viewed at many scales and the nature of the formation of routines is scale independent. We all develop routines when we wake up in the morning, make a morning tea or coffee, order our steps towards work or other daily activities. We develop routine travel routes between home, work/school, entertainment, shopping and special events. The process of the formation of the routine is a first, second, third, and continued repetition of a series of small decisions. Routines are disrupted when people move or change jobs or school or when there are other major changes in a life-cycle, but routines are re-established in new circumstances and new routines are influenced by old routines.

The development of routine decision streams, both criminal and non-criminal, involves identification of a series of decisions that work. What works would not necessarily meet objective optimal standards, but satisfy what is wanted (Brantingham and Brantingham 1978; Clarke and Cornish 1985; Cornish and Clarke 1986; Cromwell *et al.* 1991).

In Figure 5.1, the term 'individual' can be changed to 'potential offender' and the word 'decisions' can be expanded to 'crime decisions'. The word 'decision template' can be changed to 'crime template'.

The decision process can be expanded. Crime is an event or series of actions that occur when an individual with some criminal readiness level encounters a suitable target in a situation sufficient to activate that readiness potential, that is, finds that the expected benefits meet the expected costs or risks. When using such words it is important to step back from traditional economics. There is a range of reasons for committing or attempting a crime. Cusson (1983) describes this range in a way that makes it clear that crime can be triggered by anger, revenge, or desire for thrill as well as for economic or emotional benefit. In particular it is important to distinguish between instrumental and affect crimes. In some situations, such as what are called acquisitive crimes for drug addicts and represent an immediate, short-term need for cash to support a drug habit, the instrumental and the affect sides may merge.

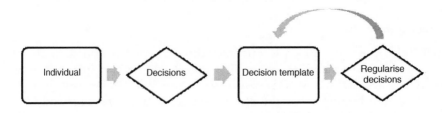

Figure 5.1   Creation of an abstract guiding template

Networks of individuals

Rule 2: Most people do not function as individuals, but have a network of family, friends and acquaintances. These linkages have varying attributes and influence the decisions of others in the network.

Figure 5.2 shows a modification to the process shown in Figure 5.1 when the influence of other people is considered. Figure 5.2 represents a hypothetical relationship between three individuals and how that relationship can influence the decision process and the crime template.

This essentially simple rule, shown in Figure 5.2 for three individuals, becomes remarkably complex in real applications because all its elements are variables. The number of persons in the network varies. The intensity of the relationship between members varies. Readiness to make the decision to commit a crime is not constant: it varies from person to person; and it varies for each individual person across time and space as the backcloth or context varies.

The linked network of affiliations between members has been and continues to be of interest to criminology. At one extreme the networks can be criminal gangs. At another, the network can be composed mostly of law-abiding members forming strong links as guardians, minders and managers of common space-time. Social disorganisation theory (Shaw and McKay 1942); differential association theory (Sutherland 1937) and the collective efficacy movement (Bursik and Grasmick 1993; Sampson and Groves 1989; Sampson *et al.* 1997) are all grounded on strengthening the social network links that inhibit offending and all try to explain crime in terms of network links to other offenders in space and over time.

Rules will be added later in the chapter that place the simple individual and network models within the context of routine movement patterns and explain how the varying context of different cities influence the routine movement patterns. It is with these rules and the associated compositional process that patterns begin to emerge that are similar to actual patterns of crime.

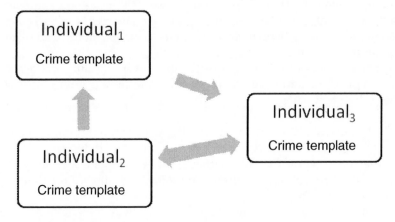

Figure 5.2 Hypothetical relationship between three individuals

Aggregation of individuals

In many instances a researcher is looking at the patterns of crime for specific conceptual groups, such as young males, or conceptual groups of places, like drinking establishments or mass transit stops. In this type of analysis researchers usually take the actions of one individual or an individual at a given location as being independent. In this type of research, the decision process of individuals is aggregated without considering how one individual might influence another. At another level the research might involve the comparison of networks by looking at their aggregate patterns.

> **Rule 3**: When individuals are making their decisions independently, individual decision processes and crime templates can be treated in a summative fashion, that is, average or typical patterns can be determined by combining the patterns of individuals.

Such situations may be common for shoplifting or other property crimes usually committed by individuals. In most cases, it is likely that the crime templates of an individual influence others. The separate and independent creation of crime templates is less likely. Current research tends to look at combinatorial or summative crime templates.

Decision rules

Decision rules are the focus of much excellent theory building and research in environmental criminology. This chapter will not go into depth about decision rules. Basically, there are varying levels of motivation on the part of individuals and in their willingness to engage in different types of offences. Few offenders commit only one type of crime; frequent offenders engage in a variety of offences. What is important to understand is how an individual (or a group) decides that there is some value to be gained by committing a crime. What is particularly important to note is the centrality of opportunity combined with an absence of any formal or informal restrictions on action. *Opportunity Makes the Thief* (Felson and Clarke 1998) is a good summary of the relative availability of potential targets and victims. As Marcus Felson notes, there are situations where there are suitable targets, non-capable guardians and potential offenders.

For the purposes of crime pattern theory it is important to add a rule that reflects the cyclical nature of the process of committing crimes and how that focuses crime templates.

> **Rule 4**: Individuals or networks of individuals commit crimes when there is a triggering event and a process by which an individual can locate a target or a victim that fits within a crime template. Criminal actions change the bank of accumulated experience and alter future actions.

Every person has a knowledge base that is always changing. Successfully committing crimes reinforces existing crime templates and patterns of offending. Lack of success is likely to have little effect the first time. But if lack of success persists, then something is likely to change. Individuals can adapt in a variety of ways: they can change the way they commit a crime to overcome factors that have made successful commission of the crime difficult; they can modify their crime template about the where or the when of a crime; or they can adapt by engaging in non-criminal activities instead. Figure 5.3 represents this pattern of reinforcement or change after a crime is attempted.

Spatial and temporal decision rules

The process varies as the awareness of opportunities to commit a crime varies. Targets are not constant. The types of objects and the categories of people that constitute good targets vary in time and space as the backcloth changes. The distributions of targets vary in time and space. The situation required to activate criminal behaviour also varies with the backcloth and the distribution of targets and the level of a given individual's readiness to commit a crime. Motivation influences the commission of crimes; the characteristics of targets and decisions about the quality of a given opportunity to commit a crime influence motivation.

To understand spatio-temporal patterns that are formed through repetitive activities and occasional and repeat offending it is necessary to take a step back to look at how people make specific decisions about how and when to move about in an urban or rural environment. The focus in this chapter is on urban mobility, but conceptually similar rules work in rural areas.

> **Rule 5:** Individuals have a range of routine daily activities. Usually these occur in different nodes of activity such as home, work, school, shopping, entertainment or time with friends, and along the normal pathways between these nodes.

The daily movement pattern comprises nested movement patterns. That is, within these broader routines and sets of activity nodes, people have more constrained micro-activity and movement patterns. Within their homes, for

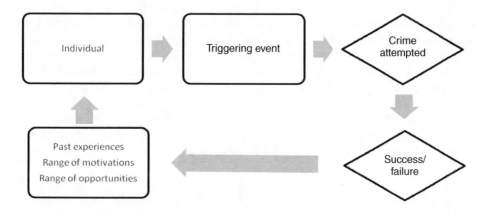

Figure 5.3 Pattern of reinforcement or change after a crime is attempted

instance, people spend time in various locations with more time spent in some rooms than in others. Regular paths are used between these rooms. Within any one of the rooms there is a sub-pattern of movement. In preparing a meal in the kitchen, for example, there is probably a micro-movement pattern between the refrigerator, the stove and the sink. At other times of the day trips to the kitchen may involve making tea or coffee: movement paths to some extent overlap but are different from those used in cooking a meal. Similar micro patterns exist at work and at school, when shopping in a grocery store; and within many other destination nodes.

At a broader scale of resolution, people develop normal daily routines. For one person it might involve going to the gym, then to work, then to visit a nearby set of shops at lunch, then to head straight home after work and then to spend the evening with friends at a pub near home. For another person it could involve going to the university, spending time in classes and the library, meeting friends in the afternoon, eating at a restaurant near the university, and heading home to study for the rest of the evening. For each individual there will be variations but for everyone there is a starting point where that person spent the night, a trip to routine daytime activities, occasional trips for shopping or to see friends in the evening, or to seek outside entertainment and finally a trip back to home for the night.

Going up one more level of resolution, people spend their work days in one pattern of activity and their leisure days in others. Weekend and holiday patterns are different, but for many they are repetitive. In fact, many have routine vacation spots or nodes and even vacation homes.[1]

This pattern of repetitive travel includes learning a route between activity nodes and settling into using it on a continuing basis. Use of that route becomes a routine decision requiring little consideration. Of course, people will try alternatives when there is difficulty following the routine path. Road construction, a traffic accident or unusually heavy traffic, for instance, will cause people to adjust their route choice or modify their allocation of travel time if possible. The range of alternatives available depends on a person's general knowledge of an area and flexibility in the daily schedule.

Figure 5.4 illustrates a set of typical primary node and route choice patterns. For the purposes of this example, the nodes are home, work and shopping and entertainment. Other individuals might well have different sets of primary nodes including, but not limited to, such activity places as a school, a gymnasium or a probation office. The set of normal nodes and the normal paths between them is generally called an *activity space*. The area normally within visual range of the activity space is called the *awareness space*.

> **Rule 6**: People who commit crimes have normal spatio-temporal movement patterns like everyone else. The likely location for a crime is near this normal activity and awareness space.

Criminals are likely to commit their initial crimes near these learned paths or activity nodes or near the paths and activity nodes of their friendship

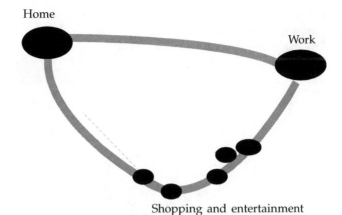

Figure 5.4 A set of typical primary node and route choice patterns

network.[2] Crimes are likely to cluster near these activity spaces, with a higher concentration near the activity nodes. Figure 5.5 shows a hypothetical pattern of offences for an individual.

As with Rule 1 and Rule 2 where individual decision templates are modified by a social network, the target choice location is modified by the activity space and awareness space of a network of friends. It is basically a two-step process. An individual's daily and weekly activity pattern and primary activity nodes are shaped or modified by a network of friends. This network changes over time, as do primary activity nodes like school or work, and with change comes modifications in activity and awareness spaces. Crime occurrence locations will cluster in the overlap of many activity spaces.

Using Rule 3, the aggregation of independent crime templates works as a summative aggregation of individual activity and awareness spaces. This produces some overlapping areas. For example, when youths going to the same school are not friends they still have an overlapping activity space that includes the school and probably other locations near the school or elsewhere in the community. Similarly, a regional shopping centre attracts people from many different locations and the overlaps of their activity and awareness spaces define a major activity node.

Figure 5.6 represents the knowledge and activity space exchanges that occur with the interaction of a network of friends. It should be noted that information exchange that modifies activity spaces and search locations for targets may come from other sources beyond friendship networks. Advertising in the media, verbal exchanges between people who know each other and second-hand information are a few examples.

Target and victim locations

The spatio-temporal movement of victims and targets is similar to the spatio-temporal movement patterns of offenders. Victims are mobile but are frequently victimised at or near one of their own activity nodes. Mobile targets such as

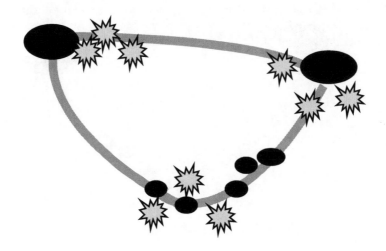

Figure 5.5 A hypothetical pattern of offences for an individual

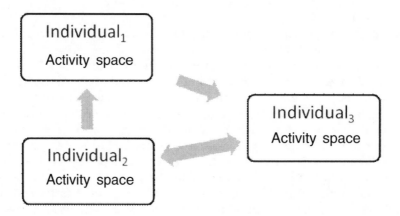

Figure 5.6 Knowledge and activity space exchanges that occur with the interaction of a network of friends

cars or bicycles follow the mobility patterns of their owners. Crimes often occur at nodes where the victim's activity space and the offender's activity space intersect. Targets such as businesses or residences are stationary but have normal catchment areas from which they attract people. They can fall within the activity space of offenders because they are located at a general activity node or are located along a path between general activity nodes and fit a crime template.

Rule 7: Potential targets and victims have passive or active locations or activity spaces that intersect the activity spaces of potential offenders. The potential targets and victims become actual targets or victims when the potential offender's willingness to commit a crime has been triggered and when the potential target or victim fits the offender's crime template.

Victims and offenders need to cross in space and time for a crime to occur. There are situations in which an offender might search for a specific victim or target,[3] but it is overlapping lifestyles or spatio-temporal movement patterns or use of a common node activity area that is more likely to be the reason that a person becomes a victim. The overlap in activity is clear when a victim of a personal crime is a family member or an acquaintance of an offender (or someone who is family or a friend of someone in an offender's network of friends). There is an overlap when the victim and offender are at the same nodal activity point at the same time period or when their routine paths cross.

Targets and offenders need to meet in space and time. This is much easier to understand because targets are often fixed in one location, such as a residence or a business. In these situations, the offender's awareness space includes the target's location. For a crime to occur the offender has to see the target and, with some additional decision steps, find the target suitable and within a crime template.

Just as offenders may commit several types of crimes, individuals and targets may be victims of multiple crimes and several types of crimes. This is a reflection of the overlap in the summative pathways and node activity locations for a range of offenders and the interactive activity spaces of networks of friends.

Urban backcloth

Crimes occur within a context created by the urban form. Roads, land use, the economic forces driving a city, the socio-economic status of residents and workers and the place of the city within a hierarchy of cities in the region are all elements of the backcloth. The urban backcloth is not static. A daytime city is different from a night-time city. Entertainment areas sleep during the day and come alive in the evening and in particular on weekends (Bromley *et al.* 2003; Felson and Poulsen 2003). Shopping areas have high periods and low periods. Similarly, most residential areas have a quiet time during the day.

In all types of urban development forms there are some common components. There is an underlying street network that is often supplemented with walking paths and transit routes. A variety of land uses are arrayed along these road networks and clustered together by city planning rules and zoning by-laws. Businesses are typically clustered within the commercially zoned areas. Factories and warehouses are clustered into industrial zones. Residential areas are often separated into single-family home zones and multi-family housing areas. These basic elements, land uses and travel path networks form the structure of the city and influence where activity nodes are created and which locations are likely to experience concentrations of crime.[4]

Rule 8: The prior rules operate within the built urban form. Crime generators are created by high flows of people through and to nodal activity points. Crime attractors are created when targets are located at nodal activity points of individuals who have a greater willingness to commit crimes.

The clustering of crime relates to the underlying road structure of a city. An area of mathematics called *network theory* provides a mechanism for analysing the impact of the underlying road structures. Networks and network theory drive the internet. People (or messages) flow along certain paths to reach an end point or node. People in cars and trucks and buses follow major roads. Traffic flows, composed of many independent agents, can be modelled using the flow of creeks into streams that flow into rivers. Road networks, like river systems, have quiet areas with smooth flows and congestion points with halting flows.

Figure 5.7 provides examples of alternative road networks. All the networks have centres that are likely to be in high activity areas. These are natural areas for commercial establishments. They also tend to be the areas where non-commercial businesses and government functions concentrate because of their easier access. City planning practice tends to concentrate higher density residential areas near these high activity nodes.

The actual patterning of crime depends on the location of potential offenders. Clustering of prior offenders would produce a nearby clustering of offences, assuming that there are suitable targets near the home locations (Block *et al.* 2007). In situations where the crime is related to a commercial business the crimes would be located in that area. For example, consider that the central locations shown in the four hypothetical street networks in Figure 5.7 are the commercial centres, then commercial crime would be located at the high activity areas.

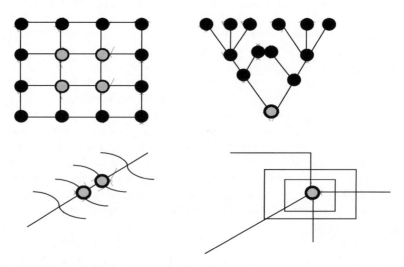

Figure 5.7   Examples of alternative road networks

Stated another way, following similar rules of target choice, offender and population mobility and assuming a similar number of motivated offenders, two cities could have crime patterns that appear to be very different if just viewed as points in space. The patterns are similar when the ways in which people move about in a city, where crime attractors and generators are located and how potential offenders make decisions are considered.

Crime generators and crime attractors are places that become crime hot spots as a result of the processes set out in Rules 1 through to 8. Crime generators are a result of the summative combination of awareness and activity spaces of large numbers of people acting in the course of daily routines. Crime attractors are a result of the cumulative impact of criminal experience and network communication.

Crime generators are particular nodal areas to which large numbers of people are attracted for reasons unrelated to any particular level of criminal motivation they might have or the particular crime they might end up committing. Typical examples might include shopping precincts, entertainment districts, office concentrations, or sports stadiums. Crime generators produce crime by creating particular times and places that provide appropriate concentrations of people and other targets in settings that are conducive to particular types of criminal acts. Mixed into the people gathered at generator locations are some potential offenders with sufficient general levels of criminal readiness that although they did not come to the area with the explicit intent of doing a crime, they notice and exploit criminal opportunities as presented (either immediately or on a subsequent occasion). Both local area insiders and area outsiders may be tempted into committing crimes at crime generator locations.

Crime attractors are particular places, areas, neighbourhoods or districts which create well-known criminal opportunities to which intending criminal offenders are attracted because of the known opportunities for particular types of crime. They become activity nodes for repeat offenders. Examples might include bar districts, prostitution strolls, drug markets, large shopping malls, particularly those near major public transit exchanges, and large, insecure parking lots in business or commercial areas. Crime in such locations is often committed by area outsiders as well as people who live nearby. An accidental encounter or a transfer of knowledge about a target-rich place can put a pull on an area, creating longer trips. Intending offenders will travel relatively long distances in search of a target at a known location. (When insiders commit crimes in such areas, they may have moved to those areas from elsewhere because of their crime-attracting qualities; or, as in many cities, because poor areas are located near commercial areas, thus creating many accessible targets near home.)

It is worth noting that there are also crime-neutral areas in most cities. Crime-neutral areas neither attract intending offenders because they expect to do a particular crime in the area, nor do they produce crimes by creating criminal opportunities that are too tempting to resist. Instead, they experience occasional crimes by local insiders. Simple distance decay and pathway models can describe the geography of crime in such locations. The offence mix is different from the offence mix at either crime attractor or crime generator locations (Brantingham and Brantingham 1994).

It is important to note that areas are unlikely to be pure attractors or pure generators or purely neutral. Most areas will be mixed, in the sense that they may be crime attractors for some types of crimes or some individuals, crime generators for other types of crime or other individuals, and neutral with respect to still other types of crime.

Hot spots and crime displacement

The interplay of the eight rules of crime pattern theory also make it possible to make some broad statements about the general formation of hot spots (Brantingham and Brantingham 1999) and to project displacement potentials when crime control interventions occur at them (Brantingham and Brantingham 2003a).[5]

Hot spots can be predicted at specific locations by taking into account the convergence of eight key elements discussed in crime pattern theory: the residential and activity locations for predisposed offender populations; the residential and activity locations of vulnerable populations; the spatial and temporal distribution of other types of crime targets; the spatial and temporal distribution of different forms of security and guardianship; the broader residential and activity structures of the city; the mix of activity types and land uses; and the modes of transport and the structure of the transport network; as well as the actual transportation flows of people through the city's landscape and timescape.

Displacement depends on the type of hot spot at which the intervention takes place. Intervention at crime generator hot spots is unlikely to result in crime displacement because the crimes that occur there are opportunistic. Displacements from crime attractor hot spots are much more likely and can be encapsulated in three limited statements. First, criminal activity at crime attractors is likely to be displaced into the neighbourhood surrounding the attractor if there are nearby attractive targets or victims. Second, criminal activity that cannot displace to the neighbourhood surrounding the original attractor is likely to be displaced to other important attractor nodes. Third, criminal activity that cannot displace to the neighbourhood surrounding the original attractor, and does not displace to some other important crime attractor, is likely to be displaced back into the offender's home neighbourhood rather than to neighbourhoods nearby and similar to the crime attractor neighbourhood. This is a function of the interplay of awareness spaces with urban form. The result is most likely some abatement and some displacement to a variety of locations. Considering the reverse of the summative awareness spaces that produce major activity nodes, research on displacement from high activity nodes needs to look at nearby areas with embedded targets, nearby similar activity areas, or expect that displacement could be spread over a large catchment area for the original attractor node.

Conclusion

Crime is not randomly distributed in time and space. It is clustered, but the shape of the clustering is greatly influenced by where people live within a city, how and why they travel or move about a city, and how networks of people who know each other spend their time. There will be concentrations of overlapping activity nodes and within those nodes some situations that become crime generators and some that are crime attractors.

When looking at the representation of crime locations, consider individual offenders and their routine activity spaces; consider networks of friends who engage in some crimes and their joint activity spaces; consider the location of stationary targets and the activity spaces of mobile victims and mobile targets and the catchment areas of fixed targets. The patterns are dynamic. Keeping that in mind will make it possible to understand crime patterns so that crime reduction interventions that produce levels of displacement can be designed.

Notes

1 The criminological potential of this is clearly illustrated in Wiles and Costello's (2000) study of Sheffield burglars and car thieves, showing the impact of both a new suburban shopping mall and the impact of a favoured seaside resort on the locations of their routine activities and offences. See also Bromley and Nelson (2002).

2 A remarkable older study illustrating this point is Shaw and Moore's (1931) *Natural History of a Delinquent Career* which illustrates, in passing, the changing location of the subject's crimes as his activity and awareness spaces expand as he grows up and expands his network of friends and associates.

3 On general target search patterns, see Brantingham and Brantingham (1978). For a study demonstrating how time constraints can impose spatial constraints on a criminal's target search, see Ratcliffe (2006).

4 There is a new pattern of mixing land uses in what is called the 'New Urbanism'. This planning practice will increase the activity in some nodes and is likely to produce a tight clustering of crime.

5 For much more detailed treatments of displacement see Brantingham and Brantingham (2003a, 2003b).

References

Block, R., Galary, A. and Brice, D. (2007) 'The Journey to Crime: Victims and Offenders Converge in Violent Index Offences in Chicago', *Security Journal*, 20: 123–37.

Brantingham, P.J. and Brantingham, P.L. (1978) 'A Theoretical Model of Crime Site Selection', in M. Krohn and R. Akers (eds) *Crime, Law and Sanctions*. Beverly Hills, CA: Sage pp. 105–18.

Brantingham, P.J. and Brantingham, P.L. (1984) *Patterns in Crime*. New York: Macmillan.

Brantingham, P.J. and Brantingham, P.L. (1991) *Environmental Criminology*. Prospect Heights, IL: Waveland Press.

Brantingham, P.L. and Brantingham, P.J. (1994) 'La Concentration Spatiale Relative de la Criminalité et son Analyse: Vers un Renouvellement de la Criminologie Environmentale', *Criminologie*, 27: 81–97.

Brantingham, P.L. and Brantingham, P.J. (1999) 'A Theoretical Model of Crime Hot Spot Generation', *Studies on Crime and Crime Prevention*, 8: 7–26.

Brantingham, P.J. and Brantingham, P.L. (2003a) 'Anticipating the Displacement of Crime Using the Principles of Environmental Criminology,' *Crime Prevention Studies*, 16: 119–48.

Brantingham, P.L. and Brantingham, P.J. (2003b) 'Crime Prevention and the Problem of Crime Displacement: Estimating Quantum of Displacement Using a Cohort Component Approach', in H. Kury and J. Obergfell-Fuchs (eds) *Crime Prevention: New Approaches*. Mainz, Germany: Weisser Ring, Gemeinnützige Verlags-GmbH, pp. 356–69.

Bromley, R.D.F. and Nelson, A.L. (2002) 'Alcohol-related Crime and Disorder Across Urban Space and Time: Evidence from a British City', *Geoforum*, 33: 239–54.

Bromley, R.D.F., Tallon, A.R. and Thomas, C.J. (2003) 'Disaggregating the Space–Time Layers of City-centre Activities and their Users', *Environment and Planning A*, 35: 1831–51.

Bursik, R.J. and Grasmick, H.G. (1993) *Neighborhoods and Crime: The Dimensions of Effective Community Control*. New York: Lexington Books.

Carrington, P.J., Matarazzo, A. and de Souza, P. (2005) *Court Careers of a Canadian Birth Cohort*. Ottawa: Statistics Canada, Catalogue no. 85-561-MIE200506.

Churchland, P.M. (1989) *A Neurocomputational Perspective on the Nature of Mind and the Structure of Science*. Cambridge, MA: MIT Press.

Clarke, R.V. and Cornish, D.B. (1985) 'Modeling Offenders' Decisions: A Framework for Research and Policy', *Crime and Justice: An Annual Review of Research*, 6: 147–85.

Cornish, D. and Clarke, R.V. (1986) *The Reasoning Criminal*. New York: Springer-Verlag.

Cromwell, P.F., Olson, J.N. and Avary, D.W. (1991) *Breaking and Entering: An Ethnographic Analysis of Burglary*. Newbury Park, CA: Sage.

Cusson, M. (1983) *Why Delinquency?* Toronto: University of Toronto Press.

Farrington, D.P., Lambert, S. and West, D.J. (1998) 'Criminal Careers of Two Generations of Family Members in the Cambridge Study in Delinquent Development', *Studies on Crime and Crime Prevention*, 7: 85–106.

Fattah, E.A. (1991) *Understanding Criminal Victimization: An Introduction to Theoretical Victimology*. Scarborough, Ontario: Prentice-Hall.

Felson, M. and Clarke, R.V. (1998) *Opportunity Makes the Thief: Practical Theory for Crime Prevention*, Police Research Series Paper 98. London: Home Office.

Felson, M. and Poulsen, E. (2003) 'Simple Indicators of Crime by Time of Day', *International Journal of Forecasting*, 19: 595.

Ratcliffe, J.H. (2006) 'A Temporal Constraint Theory to Explain Opportunity-based Spatial Offending Patterns', *Journal of Research in Crime and Delinquency*, 43: 261–91.

Sampson, R.J. and Groves, W.B. (1989) 'Community Structure and Crime: Testing Social Disorganization Theory. *American Journal of Sociology*, 94: 774–802.

Sampson, R.J., Raudenbush, S. and Earls, F. (1997) 'Neighborhoods and Violent Crime: A Multilevel Study of Collective Efficacy', *Science*, 277: 918–24.

Shaw, C.R. and McKay, H.D. (1942) *Delinquency and Urban Areas*. Chicago: University of Chicago Press.

Shaw, C.R. and Moore, M.E. (1931) *The Natural History of a Delinquent Career*. Chicago: University of Chicago Press.

Sutherland, E. (1937) *Principles of Criminology*, 3rd edn. Philadelphia: Lippincott.
Wiles, P. and Costello, A. (2000) *The 'Road to Nowhere': The Evidence for Travelling Criminals*, Home Office Research Study 207. London: Home Office.
Wolfgang, M.E., Figlio, R.M. and Sellin, T. (1972) *Delinquency in a Birth Cohort*. Chicago: University of Chicago Press.

Part Two

Analysing Crime Patterns

6. Crime mapping and hot spot analysis

Luc Anselin, Elizabeth Griffiths and George Tita

Buffalo, New York, Case 9404: Four male offenders approached a 25-year-old male victim on the street in an apparent robbery. The offenders erroneously believed that the victim, an alleged drug-dealer, was carrying a large sum of money with him. Two of the offenders brandished handguns and shot the victim at point-blank range.

Buffalo, New York, Case 9441: A female victim and her male friend were interrupted in her home by the offender, the victim's ex-boyfriend. Seeking to alert the police, the male friend left the victim's house. The offender sexually assaulted the victim and then shot her with an automatic rifle, before committing suicide.

In 1994, the city of Buffalo recorded its highest homicide count of the twentieth century with a total of 91 incidents. Unfortunately Buffalo was not unique, as most American cities set historical highs for numbers of homicides in the early 1990s. Fuelled by the unprecedented growth in gun homicides involving youth during this period, criminologists and practitioners alike began to employ mapping and spatial analysis in an attempt to better understand the dynamics shaping the violence.

The two Buffalo homicides recounted above occurred about six months apart in time, and about half a mile apart in space. As this example suggests, crime is not randomly distributed across neighbourhoods in cities. Instead, some city neighbourhoods develop the reputation for being 'dangerous' – and they are. In Pittsburgh, PA, for example, in the mid to late 1980s, only one-fifth of all census tracts in the city recorded at least one homicide in any given year. When the homicide rate peaked in 1993 and 1994, the proportion of tracts experiencing any homicide increased only slightly, but the average number of homicides within those tracts increased dramatically. Thus, while youth homicide dispersed (or diffused) to a slightly larger number of tracts, the real impact of the homicide epidemic was that the events became more concentrated within relatively few neighbourhoods of the city (Cohen and Tita 1999).

In this chapter we briefly explore the various theoretical frameworks that aim to explain why crime tends to be concentrated in certain places. We focus on two types of theories: those that view the crime-generating/crime-attracting activities of places as the central mechanism that brings both suitable targets and motivated offenders together in both time and space (e.g. environmental criminology and routine activity theory) and those that place primary importance on the social and economic conditions that foster the commission of crime (e.g. social disorganisation theory). Next we talk about the impact that the development of affordable desktop mapping software has played in the exploration of criminal 'hot spots', especially in terms of how it has been a useful tool within the policing community. Using a dataset comprising homicide events from Buffalo, we outline the basic steps required to map events and identify hot spots. Whether the identification of hot spots is used to better allocate police patrols, or whether it is used by academics to explore the community context of crime, the methodology required to identify concentrated areas of crime is the same.

Finding that violence, or any kind of crime, is concentrated in particular places is not new. The earliest 'spatial studies' of crime were carried out by Quetelet and Guerry in the 1830s (Anselin *et al.* 2000). Early researchers explored the relationship between area social factors, such as poverty and educational attainment, and arrest rates across regions of France. Their results showed that property crime rates were higher in areas with less poverty. This prompted the authors to conclude that offenders in France were targeting wealthier areas where valuables worthy of theft were more prevalent. By the 1930s, researchers at the University of Chicago (the Chicago School) had begun mapping juvenile delinquency patterns across the city by hand, using pins to represent the residence of each juvenile delinquent in Cook County, Illinois. Using this strategy, Shaw and McKay (1942) established that certain zones of the city had consistently high rates of delinquency over decades, despite turnover in the racial and ethnic composition of the population. The finding that crime concentrates in particular areas of cities, and these concentrations tend to remain stable over time, has been one of the more consistent findings to emerge from the field of criminology.

Criminologists have incorporated knowledge about these patterns in developing theories that explain how place influences crime. For example, the central tenets of routine activities theory imply that victimisation risk is heightened around entertainment venues, particularly where drugs or alcohol are present, and in neighbourhoods where residents do not look out for one another (Felson, Chapter 4, this volume). In this case, victims and potential offenders meet in time and space, creating opportunities for crime. Environmental criminologists argue that it is the daily routines of offenders in particular that are worthy of consideration (Brantingham and Brantingham, Chapter 5, this volume). Accordingly, the places where offenders live, work and play, will help to explain geographic offending patterns. In either case, rational offenders, who weigh the costs and benefits of various courses of action, make decisions that are 'bounded' by their immediate environment (Cornish and Clarke, Chapter 2, this volume). Indeed, some research has shown that drug-dealing may be considered rational for some disadvantaged inner-city residents when legitimate opportunities are blocked in offenders' communities (Jacobs 1999).

But place influences crime in other ways as well. We need not focus solely on how place influences whether victims congregate in, or offenders live in or travel through dangerous neighbourhoods. Instead, some criminologists study the characteristics of 'dangerous neighbourhoods' in terms of their local social and economic conditions. High-crime neighbourhoods are typically distinguished by poverty, residential instability, population heterogeneity and family disruption (Sampson and Groves 1989). They lack what Sampson and colleagues (1997) call 'collective efficacy' such that residents show little trust in one another and are unwilling to become actively involved in socially controlling neighbourhood residents and visitors. These neighbourhoods have little social cohesion and are marred by physical disorder; they are littered with trash, vacant and abandoned buildings, graffiti and other signs of neglect. It is precisely in these types of neighbourhoods that crime 'hot spots' most often emerge.

Criminologists define 'hot spots' as geographically bounded spaces of varying size that are associated with heightened victimisation risk and a proportionately greater number of criminal incidents than other similarly sized areas of the city (Eck 2005). Hot spots are usually smaller in geography than neighbourhoods, and comprise block or street segments that experience inordinately high levels of crime and violence. In one of the first studies to identify hot spots, Sherman, Gartin, and Buerger (1989) found that 3.3 per cent of street addresses and intersections in Minneapolis generated 50.4 per cent of all dispatched police calls for service. Similar patterns were apparent in other cities as well (Pierce *et al.* 1988; Sherman 1992; Weisburd and Green 1995).

While much research illustrates that crime concentrates in particular hot spots of cities, it is perhaps more important to explore the types of social characteristics that influence the development and persistence of hot spots. One of the most consistent land use characteristics describing hot spots is the presence of entertainment venues. For example, Roncek and Maier (1991) found a strong and positive relationship between the number of taverns and lounges located in city blocks in Cleveland and index crimes. The taverns' influence on crime was compounded when the taverns were located in areas where residents tended to be strangers or did not look out for one another. Indeed, five out of Sherman *et al.* (1989) top ten hot spots had bars. Similarly, drug hot spots tended to be in areas with nuisance bars, run-down commercial establishments, or areas with poverty and a high proportion of female-headed households (Cohen *et al.* 1993). These kinds of characteristics have also been shown to distinguish the areas where drug homicides occur (Tita and Griffiths 2005).

In addition to aiding scholars in their pursuit to better understand why crime is concentrated in certain neighbourhoods, the identification of crime hot spots has played an important role in the development of policing strategies. Police have responded to hot spots with new enforcement, prevention and investigative techniques. For example, it seems sensible to expect that patrols targeting hot spots during times of peak crime occurrence would be more effective in reducing crime than patrols spread uniformly across beats and time. A small number of studies provide support for this claim (e.g. Koper 1995; Sherman and Weisburd 1995; Koper 1995). The preventative effects of policing hot spots are also associated with both reductions in social disorder and improvements in residents' perceptions of their neighbourhood (Braga 2001). In addition, crime displacement to non-targeted areas nearby is uncommon. Thus, police targeting of hot spots does not simply displace criminal activity to surrounding areas, but actually suppresses it (Braga 2001).

Whether or not the attributes associated with hot spots contribute to crime in a causal way depends on whether or not the elevated levels of crime observed at hot spots are systematic (regular and predictable), and not just random occurrences. If hot spots are random and can occur anywhere, then crime in these locations does not depend on distinctive features found in the observed hot spots, and crime reduction efforts that target these features are likely to be futile.

The role of technology: how do we map crime and what is GIS?

While researchers have expressed interest in the relationship between crime and place for decades, this literature did not significantly influence law enforcement practices until the 1990s. Technological advances relating to computers were the key to this change, notably the proliferation of computerised police information systems and the advent of affordable desktop computer mapping applications and accompanying geographic information systems (GIS). Even without computers, police officers who daily worked the streets in urban areas were aware of the worst crime hot spots – these were the places that generated calls for service on a regular basis. The very high call levels at these chronic locations were hard to miss even by individual officers. More modest hot spots, however, might go unnoticed by individual officers who each saw only a small portion of the activity at a location. This is especially true if the crimes in hot spots tend to occur only during particular times of the day or days of the week.

The advent of police records management systems and computer aided dispatch (CAD) systems to handle 911 calls for service made it possible to systematically quantify varying levels of criminal activity at places within a city. This capability, however, was not an immediate consequence of computerising police data. In their first generation, the focus of CAD and records management systems was still the processing of individual cases, getting police units to the crime scene as quickly as possible and providing access to case-specific information extracted from individual police reports of offences and arrests. However, the documentation and quantification of crime hot spots in Minneapolis – accomplished through special 'outsider' analysis of CAD data in that city – resulted in an important paradigm shift in policing (Sherman *et al.* 1989). For the first time, it was possible to measure the actual concentration of calls for service at relatively few addresses in a city.

The ability to identify these high crime places was further enhanced by the introduction of user-friendly computerised mapping capabilities that allowed easy visual display of data from many crime incidents. The substantial concentration of crime that was observed effectively focused attention on these chronic places, raising questions about whether it might be possible for police to intervene in ways that would reduce or prevent crime at targeted locations. Such an approach was fully compatible with a problem-oriented perspective on policing (Goldstein 1979). While the emphasis in policing remained a reactive mode of clearing crimes after they occur, there was increased interest in also pursuing proactive strategies to diagnose criminogenic features of places and intervene in ways designed to prevent future crimes.

More recent applications of geographic information systems (GIS) to the study of crime has resulted in the development of desktop computer mapping programs that allow for a comprehensive analysis of crime concentrations at places. Researchers are now able to quickly generate dynamically linked maps providing visual representations of the relationship between two or more characteristics, such as poverty rates and crime rates, for instance. In addition, various computer programs allow researchers to determine whether visual hot spots of crime represent statistically significant crime clustering. Such programs are able to determine, with geographic precision, the street boundaries of the hot spot. The practical applications of GIS for both police and scholars illustrate the importance of place in examining the causes of crime and its control.

What is geocoding?

Simply knowing a street address provides limited information about the location of the associated home or business, unless you are familiar with the neighbourhood or have visited the location before. But researchers and law enforcement personnel require much more sophisticated mapping tools to adequately detect areas of concentrated crime, or hot spots. To generate hot spot maps from data comprising street addresses, the addresses must first be geocoded. Geocoding is the method by which an address is transformed into precise geographic coordinates. The most common coordinate systems use latitude and longitude to assign values to the 'x/y' in two-dimensional space. Armed with these coordinates, a crime analyst or researcher can locate crime events with great precision on a projected two-dimensional map of any geographic space on Earth.

Various geographic information systems (GIS) software packages are commercially available to facilitate the geocoding and display of spatially defined data (including ESRI's ArcGIS and MapInfo, among others). In most of these software packages, street networks are previously mapped, projected in coordinate space using one of several universal geographic projections, and divided into street segments. Each segment is defined by four separate pieces of information: the first address and the last address on the right-hand side of the street, and the first address and the last address on the left-hand side of the street. Using a mathematical matching algorithm, GIS analysis locates an address on the appropriate street segment. The resulting geo-spatial coordinates can then be mapped to produce visual representations of the point in space. Furthermore, the points can be characterised (by shape, size or colour) using any of the attributes associated with event at the particular address (e.g. time/date of crime; type of crime; race/ethnicity of victim; weapon usage, etc.). Thus, geocoding provides an automated and significantly less labour intensive method that is equivalent to Shaw and McKay's (1942) manually driven pushpin system for identifying concentrations of crime in geographic space.

Creating a point-pattern map and aggregating points to rates

Once the data have been geocoded, creating a point-pattern map is relatively straightforward. In this section, we will walk through the construction and interpretation of such a map using a dataset comprising all homicides investigated by the Buffalo New York Police Department between 1 January 1990 and 31 December 1999 (Gartner and McCarthy, n.d.). In total, 574 homicides occurred in Buffalo during the 1990s and the homicide rate ranged from a high of 27.75 per 100,000 residents in 1994 to a low of 10.37 per 100,000 in 1999. In total, six homicides that occurred during the 1990s could not be geocoded as the address data could not be matched or were not available in police files. Because homicide is a relatively rare event even during peak years of lethal offending, the data are pooled to represent all homicide incidents occurring during the 1990s.

Figure 6.1 shows the locations of the homicides represented as points on a map that also contains the boundaries of the census tracts. This map is

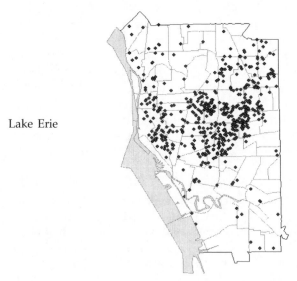

Lake Erie

Figure 6.1 Buffalo homicides point pattern

obtained by combining two spatial layers in a GIS (in our example, ESRI's ArcGIS), one for the points (a so-called point layer) and one for the census tracts (a so-called polygon layer). The map suggests that the homicide incidents in Buffalo were not randomly distributed across the city, but instead appeared to cluster in specific locales. In particular, the spatial patterning of homicide across the city shows a concentration in the centre of the city continuing to the northeastern tip, and along the western shore of Lake Erie north of downtown. While these patterns are apparent to the naked eye, we cannot be sure that this spatial clustering of homicide incidents in Buffalo represents statistically significant clustering, or hot spots, based on these point-pattern maps alone. To determine whether statistically significant clusters of homicide exist, more formal methods must be employed.

In addition, from these point-pattern maps we cannot assess whether the clustering of events (in this case, homicide incidents) is a function of the size of the population at risk. Determining the population at risk is a thorny issue. Most researchers base their rate calculations on the population residing in the area of interest – typically a census tract, street segment, or neighbourhood. While much lethal violence occurs in relatively close proximity to the victim's home, a significant proportion of homicides occur against victims who do not reside in or around the incident location (Tita and Griffiths 2005). As such, rate calculations (e.g. number of homicides divided by the population at risk) are based on a denominator that does not include all potential victims, and that includes some potential victims who reside, but are not present, in the neighbourhood when the homicide occurs. This approach necessarily introduces some measurement error.

Nonetheless, even when calculating homicide rates using the residential population as the population at risk, rate-based maps provide important information that cannot be obtained from the point-pattern maps alone. This is because the number of homicides in two different tracts may be identical, but if the first tract has a population of 1,000 residents and the second tract has a population of 5,000 residents, then the homicide rate (homicides per population) in the first tract will be dramatically higher. A concentration of criminal events in a geographic space may represent a hot spot because the likelihood of criminal victimisation is dramatically higher there than elsewhere, or because a larger number of people reside in the area. In the latter case, the neighbourhood with a larger number of events may actually be 'safer' if the population at risk is also very large, compared to a neighbourhood with fewer events but a much smaller population at risk. In order to determine the distribution of rates across tracts (or any other geographic unit), it is necessary to aggregate the points on the point-pattern map by geographic unit and then divide by the resident population.

Aggregation of points to counts or rates within larger areal units is a simple operation in a GIS. The process involves a 'spatial join' by which the point features (e.g. crime events) are intersected with a polygon feature (e.g. census tracts, neighbourhoods). Each polygon has a unique identifier in the underlying database associated with the feature and through the intersection of point and polygons that unique identifier is appended to the database of the point feature. Next, one can sum the number of times each unique polygon identifier appears in the point feature database to determine how many points fall within each polygon. Once the count is established, the incident rate (crime rate) is computed by dividing by the local population and then standardising (usually by 100,000). The resulting rates can be mapped by areal unit, as in Figure 6.2, which shows the Buffalo homicide rates by census tract. The example given is a choropleth map, a spatial counterpart of a histogram. In the choropleth map, all observations that fall within a given range of values are represented by the same colour. As for a histogram, different ways to classify the observations in intervals or 'bins' will result in different portrayals. In Figure 6.2, the rates are classified into eight categories using the so-called natural breaks (Jenks) algorithm, a commonly used procedure and the default in many mapping software packages. We also show the original points overlaid on the census tracts to illustrate the difference between raw counts and rates (see also below).

Beyond mapping – geovisualisation

Maps, as collections of geographic objects, present information and as such can be abused, taking advantage of design (colours, projections) to trick human perception. Monmonier (1996) provides many interesting examples in

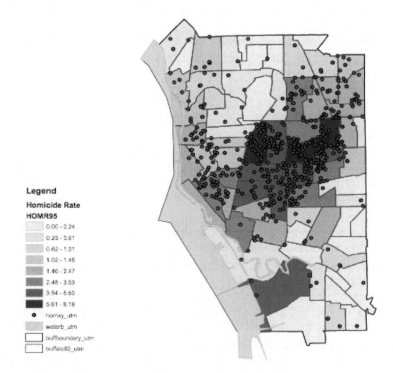

Figure 6.2 Choropleth map of Buffalo homicides by census tract

his book *How to Lie with Maps*. However, if used properly, the tools presented in this chapter allow for the geovisualisation of data that extends mapping as presentational to mapping as an important tool for scientific discovery.

In this section, we illustrate a few techniques that are particularly appropriate to highlight interesting spatial patterns in crime locations and that form the first step towards identifying clusters or hot spots. We limit the discussion to a few of the most commonly used methods and refer the reader to the extensive overview in Anselin *et al.* (2000). We distinguish between crime as observed at individual locations (point maps) and patterns for crime rates, which have been aggregated to a spatial unit such as a census block or tract.

To move from the individual point locations (shown in Figure 6.1) to a smoother representation of the intensity of crime, a kernel density function is a commonly used technique. In essence, the point locations are transformed into a continuous surface that represents an estimate of the expected number of events per unit area. This is accomplished by computing a weighted average (transformation) of the number of points in a moving window. The radius of the window is referred to as the 'bandwidth' and the particular transformation is called a kernel function. Kernel functions differ by the way in which they treat points further away from a reference location (the centre of the moving window). Some kernel functions are continuous (such as the Gaussian kernel), others have a clearly defined cut-off (such as the triangular kernel). The choice of the bandwidth has important repercussions for the results. Broadly speaking, a larger bandwidth yields a smoother function, with a smaller bandwidth resulting in a spikier representation (for technical details see e.g. Waller and Gotway 2004, pp. 130–6 and 164–71).

In Figures 6.3 and 6.4, we show two kernel density functions applied to the Buffalo homicide data, the larger bandwidth Gaussian kernel method and a smaller bandwidth triangular kernel. We computed these using the CrimeStat software package (Levine 2006) and exported the results to a GIS for mapping. Figure 6.3 illustrates the results of choosing a Gaussian kernel. The peak is clearly identified with the core of the urban area and the function shows a smoothly, almost concentric decay from the centre. In Figure 6.4, however, this is less clear, and some peaks appear in other locations, such as close to the lakefront. A careful consideration of a range of bandwidths will bring out some basic patterns in the data. However, the kernel density function as such can be misleading, since it does not account for spatial variations in population at risk.

A better representation of 'homicide risk' is one where both the events (homicides) and the population at risk are taken into account, as in the rate map shown in Figure 6.2. We can move beyond simple mapping and employ so-called statistical maps, which base the classification of observations on characteristics of the statistical distribution of the data. For example, an outlier map is a special kind of quartile map, which extends the idea of a box plot to a choropleth map (Anselin 1999). The objective is to illustrate both the four quartiles as well as those observations in the lowest (first) and highest (fourth) quartiles that are outliers. Outliers are constructed in three steps: (1) compute the interquartile range or IQR (difference between first and third

Figure 6.3 Buffalo homicides, normal kernel

Figure 6.4 Buffalo homicides, triangle kernel

quartile); (2) create fences as either 1.5 times or 3 times the IQR; (3) identify the observations that are less than the lower fence or greater than the upper fence. The box map combines both magnitude and location of the outliers by showing them in a distinct colour on the map.

Figure 6.5 illustrates the need to consider the population at risk with two box maps produced with the GeoDa software for exploratory spatial data analysis (Anselin *et al.* 2006). Figure 6.5a portrays the Buffalo census tracts classified by their homicide counts in the decade of the 1990s. The darkest coloured tracts are outliers, that is, they have counts that are much higher than would be suggested by the overall distribution of values. These census tracts roughly match the highest concentration of the points in Figure 6.1. In Figure 6.5b, the counts have been divided by the population for the census tract and expressed as a rate. As a result, several census tracts are no longer identified as outliers. In other words, the higher count of homicides in those census tracts was primarily the result of a higher population at risk, but not of an elevated level of violence.

Clustering and clusters

Up to now, the analysis of the spatial distribution of homicides has been primarily descriptive. The techniques illustrated suggest interesting patterns and potential clusters or hot spots, but they do not determine in a statistical sense whether or not these patterns are significant. In this section, we move to a more formal treatment and provide some examples of statistical methods that can be applied to detect clusters or hot spots.

The point of departure in the analysis of spatial patterns is the notion of spatial randomness. Simply put, under spatial randomness, any given spatial distribution of events is equally likely as any other one. In other words, location does not matter. Similarly, a spatially random distribution of values across a map (e.g. crime rates for census tracts) is one where the location of

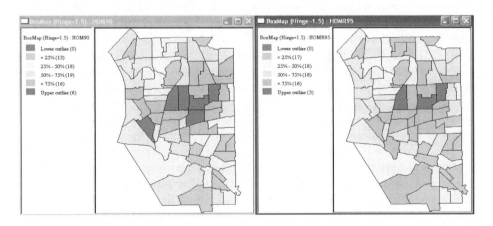

Figure 6.5 Homicide counts by census tract (a) and homicide rates (b)

the value is not important: it does not matter where the high or low values occur. Under spatial randomness, the crime rates observed for particular census tracts can simply be reshuffled to other locations without affecting the results of the analysis. As such, spatial randomness is not a very useful concept. After all, pure randomness cannot be explained. Therefore, the main role of the concept of spatial randomness is as a reference, to make sure that meaningful analysis can be carried out. In sum, our interest is in developing measures and statistics that allow us to reject the null hypothesis of spatial randomness, in favour of a particular type of pattern. We will be interested in rejecting the null in favour of a notion of clustering, that is, a grouping in space of locations of events or of like values that is more than what would be expected under spatial randomness.

In this respect, it is important to make a distinction between clustering, which is a global characteristic of a pattern, and clusters, which are specific locations and thus local characteristics. A global statistic is a single number or graph that indicates whether the null hypothesis of spatial randomness is satisfied for the complete pattern or map. In contrast, a local statistic is designed to detect specific locations of elevated counts (of events) or rates. Such local statistics lend themselves extremely well to mapping, whereas a global statistic is not associated with any given location.

We first consider the study of the distribution of homicide locations as an application of classic point-pattern analysis. Originally, this dealt with points located on a plane which greatly simplified reality (in a so-called isotropic plane, straight line distance is the only aspect that matters). The primary applications were found in the field of ecology, e.g. dealing with locations of tree seedlings, birds' nests, etc. More recently, the location of points on actual street networks has been considered as well (Okabe *et al.* 2006).

We will only illustrate a handful of commonly used techniques that have found their way to standard practice in spatial crime analysis. These methods are incorporated into commonly used software such as CrimeStat (Levine 2006) as well as in specialised open source statistical software such as the Splancs and Spaststat packages of the R framework (http://cran.r-project.org). A classic reference is the book by Diggle (2003). A more introductory treatment of the technical aspects can be found in Waller and Gotway (2004).

Two important departures from the null hypothesis of spatial randomness are point patterns that are more grouped (aggregated or clustered) and patterns that are more regularly distributed over space. Methods to detect such departures are typically based on characteristics of the distribution of inter-point distances. The logic behind this is that departures from randomness will result in many more small distances or many more large distances between points, which will affect the properties of the distribution of inter-point distances. Many such summary statistics have been developed, for example, using the minimum or maximum distance, or focusing on nearest neighbour distances. Perhaps the most commonly used statistic to assess the absence of complete spatial randomness in a point pattern is Ripley's (1976) K function. The K function focuses on so-called second order properties of a point pattern, which are similar to the notion of a covariance. The first order characteristic is simply the intensity of the process, or, the average number of points per unit area. The second order characteristic is then some measure of covariance between intensities at different locations. More precisely, the K function is the ratio of the expected number of additional events within a given distance (h) from an arbitrary event to the intensity of the process. It is often expressed as $\lambda K(h) = E[N_0(h)]$, where λ is the intensity of the process, h is the distance and $N_0(h)$ is the number of points within a distance h from a given event.

The K function is readily calculated by counting the number of points within an increasing radius from each event in the pattern. It is typically computed for a number of distance ranges and plotted against distance. The theoretical shape for the K function under complete spatial randomness can be shown to be πh^2, which can be used to interpret the results. A K function above the curve πh^2 suggests clustering, a K function below the reference curve indicates a more regular pattern. Inference is customarily based on a so-called randomisation envelope, computed for a series of random point patterns with the same intensity. For each of these random patterns, a K function is computed and at each reference distance the highest and smallest value is recorded. These values then form an upper and lower envelope which illustrates the range of K values obtained under randomness (alternatively, sometimes the 2.5 and 97.5 percentiles are used, providing approximately a 95 per cent significance band). When the observed K function is above and outside the envelope, clustering is established. The opposite case, with a K function below and outside the envelope, suggests a regular pattern.

The K function is illustrated for the Buffalo homicide data in Figure 6.6. The solid line is the function calculated from the actual data, and the dashed line

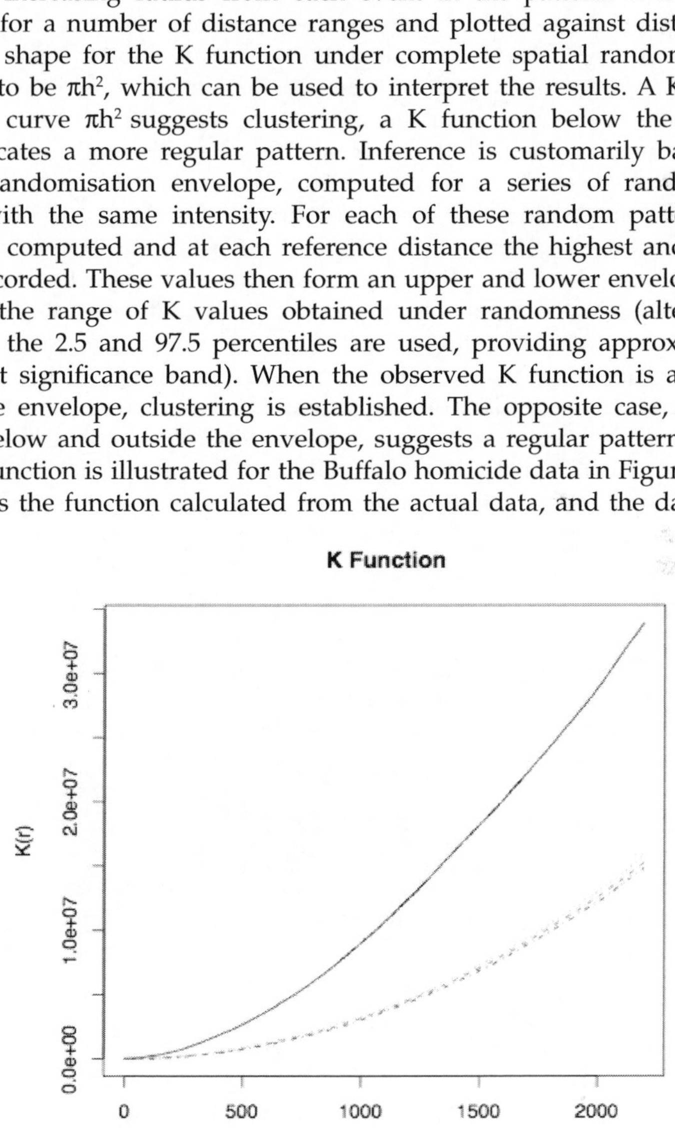

Figure 6.6   K function for Buffalo homicides

corresponds to πh^2, the theoretical value under complete spatial randomness. The dotted and dot/dash lines represent the randomisation envelope. Clearly, the point pattern for the homicides is strongly clustered, and well outside the randomisation envelope for the full range of distances considered.

Recall, however, that the K function or any other global test for clustering does not provide information about the specific location of the clusters. As a global statistic, it only provides insight into the overall pattern of points. Appropriately identifying the specific locations of clusters requires a local approach, which can be implemented by means of a scan statistic.

Scan statistics are designed to detect clusters or hot spots: collections of events that are unusual in a specified sense, such as unlikely to occur under spatial randomness. The general idea behind a scan is to compare the number of events in a geometric shape (typically a circle) to a reference under the null hypothesis (complete spatial randomness). A cluster is identified as such when the count of events in the circle significantly exceeds the reference value. In the Buffalo example, we would interpret a cluster that is identified by a significant scan statistic to represent a homicide hot spot.

Examples of early scan statistics are the Geographical Analysis Machine (GAM) of Openshaw et al. (1987), the space-time analysis of crime (STAC) of Block (1994), and the spatial scan statistics of Kulldorff (1997, 1999). These approaches consist of counting the number of points in a series of overlapping circles and labelling them as significant when the observed count is extreme relative to a reference distribution of simulated points, or based on a more formal likelihood criterion. Uncritical application of scan statistics may suffer from the problem of multiple comparisons (overlapping circles) and they are sensitive to parameter settings (radius of circle, etc.).

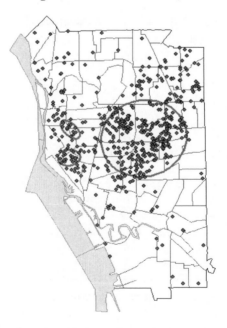

Figure 6.7 STAC ellipses for the Buffalo homicide data

Here, we illustrate a local approach for the Buffalo homicide data using the STAC method as implemented in the CrimeStat software. Clusters are identified and represented by an ellipse centred on the mean location of the cluster points. The elongation and orientation of the ellipse provide a general sense of the shape of the underlying cluster, although it is highly simplified and ignores irregular spatial features that may be present. Nevertheless, as an exploratory tool, the STAC approach provides considerable insight into the location of clusters of elevated homicide activity, or homicide hot spots. In Figure 6.7, STAC identifies the main cluster in the geographic centre of the city, as well as two smaller clusters near the water.

The ellipses shown in Figure 6.7 treat homicide events as points on a map. For spatially aggregate measures such as the rate maps in Figures 6.2 and 6.5(b), we again distinguish between global (clustering) and local tests (clusters).

A spatial autocorrelation statistic is a formal test of the match between attribute similarity and locational similarity. The statistic summarises both aspects and is deemed to be significant if the probability (p-value) that the statistic would take this value in a spatially random pattern is extremely low. Measures of attribute similarity summarise the similarity (or dissimilarity) between the values observed at two locations, for example, as a cross-product $z_i.z_j$ with $i \neq j$. Locational similarity is formalised through a spatial weights matrix, which expresses the notion of neighbour. Spatial weights are not necessarily geographical, but can incorporate social network structures as well.

A spatial weights matrix (W) is an n by n positive matrix where 'n' is equal to the number of spatial units of observations and whose elements are non-zero for neighbours and zero for units that are unconnected. In practice, a common criterion is contiguity, where two observations are considered to be neighbours when they share a common boundary.

By far the best known test statistic for spatial autocorrelation is Moran's I. It is a cross-product statistic, similar to a Pearson correlation coefficient. Formally, the test statistic is $I = [\sum_i \sum_j w_{ij} z_i.z_j / S_0] / [\sum_i z_i^2 / n]$ where the variable z_i is expressed in deviations from the mean and $S_0 = \sum_i \sum_j w_{ij}$ is the sum of the weights. While Moran's I may seem similar to the familiar correlation coefficient, it is different in that its magnitude depends on the spatial weights matrix W (for a technical discussion see e.g. Cliff and Ord 1981). Also, the scaling factors used in numerator and denominator are different, with the sum of the weights used for the former. Inference can be based on analytical approximations, but more easily using a computational technique called permutation. As for the randomisation envelope of the K function, the distribution of the statistic under spatial randomness is approximated by generating many random permutations of the data (i.e. the observed values are reshuffled to different locations) and computing a Moran's I statistic for each case. The actual statistic is then compared to this reference distribution to assess a pseudo significance value. In other words, if the observed Moran's I is extreme (very large or very small) relative to this reference distribution, then the null hypothesis of spatial randomness should be rejected.

When applied to rates, there may be a problem when computing Moran's I in that rates have different variances when the denominator (the population at risk) is not constant, a common occurrence in practice. This may lead to spurious indications of spatial autocorrelation. A correction suggested by Assuncao and Reis (1999) uses an Empirical Bayes approach to standardise each rate and then uses the standardised rates in the computation of Moran's I. This is implemented in popular software such as GeoDa and the R spdep package.

The Moran's I statistic can be easily visualised in a graph called a Moran scatter plot (Anselin 1996). In a Moran scatter plot, the horizontal axis corresponds to the variable of interest and the vertical axis is the average of the values at neighbouring locations, or the spatial lag. The slope of the linear fit through this scatter plot is Moran's I.

In addition, the four quadrants of the scatter plot correspond to four types of spatial autocorrelation. Positive spatial autocorrelation is found in the upper right and lower left quadrant, respectively corresponding to high (above mean) values surrounded by other high values (high-high clusters), or low values surrounded by other low values (low-low clusters). Negative spatial autocorrelation is found in the upper left and lower right quadrants, respectively corresponding to low values surrounded by high values (low-high spatial outliers) and high values surrounded by low values (high-low spatial outliers). This is only suggestive, since no indication of significance is given.

Figure 6.8 illustrates this concept for the Buffalo census tract homicide rates, showing the Moran scatter plot obtained in the GeoDa software. The Moran's I coefficient is 0.51, which is significant with a pseudo p-value of

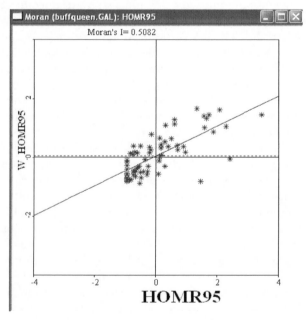

Figure 6.8   Moran scatter plot for Buffalo homicide rates (p < 0.001)

0.001 (permutation results not shown). Note that the positive coefficient suggests clustering, although it does not indicate whether this pertains to high or low values. In effect, this significant and positive Moran's I statistic may be driven either by the clustering of homicide hot spots (high-high clusters) or cold spots (low-low clusters) in the city of Buffalo. After properly correcting for the fact that these are rates with varying populations at risk, the evidence for clustering is much weaker, as shown in Figure 6.9. The coefficient value drops to 0.18 and the pseudo significance is a weak 0.08.

The evidence for overall clustering does not provide information about the nature of the clusters (high or low values) nor their location. This is accomplished by a local indicator of spatial association, or LISA (Getis and Ord 1992; Anselin 1995). A commonly applied local statistic is the local version of Moran's I, or the local Moran statistic, $I_i = (z_i / m_2) \Sigma_j w_{ij} z_j$, where m_2 is the second moment (constant across i). Inference is based on a conditional permutation approach (e.g. holding the value at fixed, and permuting the others). Significance should be interpreted with caution due to the problem of multiple comparisons.

A LISA cluster map shows the four types of local spatial autocorrelation (high-high, low-low, high-low, low-high) for those locations with a significant local Moran statistic. It is a most effective tool to identify spatial clusters and spatial outliers. The LISA cluster map suggests interesting locations but does not provide a way to explain why the patterns occur where they do. Often, such clusters may suggest multivariate relationships. In some cases, they are only indicative of a scale mismatch.

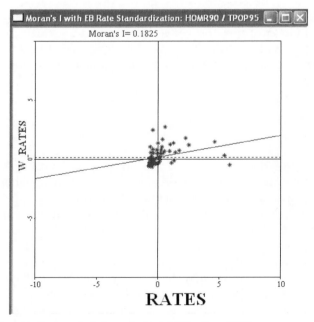

Figure 6.9   Moran's I corrected for rate instability (p < 0.08)

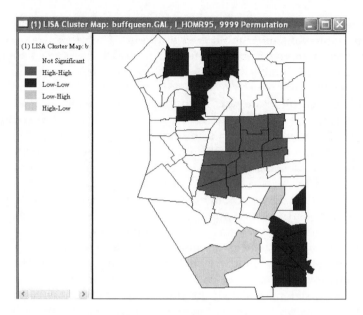

Figure 6.10   LISA cluster map for Buffalo homicides

A LISA cluster map for the Buffalo homicide data is illustrated in Figure 6.10, using a pseudo-significance value of 0.05. The medium-shaded census tracts correspond to clusters of high homicide rates, whereas the dark-shaded tracts are clusters of low homicide rates. There are also two examples of spatial outliers (light shading) where census tract with high homicide rates are surrounded by neighbours with significantly lower rates. From this map, we can statistically determine not only the census tracts that are hot spots for homicide in Buffalo during the 1990s (i.e. the medium tracts), but also those neighbourhoods with considerably less homicide (i.e. the dark tracts) than would be expected under a hypothesis that homicide is randomly distributed across the city.

Conclusion

This chapter provides a basic introduction to the most commonly used methods for determining whether or not a specific phenomenon is clustered in space. We have demonstrated methods that utilise point-pattern analysis as well as methods for determining spatial autocorrelation of homicide rates among areal units. Though these methods are extremely useful for exploring spatial data, it is important to note that a mere convergence in space of high or low crime levels need not reflect a causally meaningful relationship. That is, an apparent relationship may happen by chance. Or it might reflect a spurious relationship in which crime and other observable conditions all result from some other unidentified cause. Affecting crime through interventions

– by police or other agents – requires understanding the contributing factors and the nature of their relationship to crime. This involves going beyond a mere spatial display of crime in maps to more fundamental spatial statistical analyses such as spatial regression analysis. Nonetheless, the techniques for identifying and mapping hot spots illustrated in this chapter are theoretically useful to researchers who can then examine the social characteristics of hot spot clusters, and they are practically useful to police who can target high crime areas for preventative efforts.

References

Anselin, L. (1995), 'Local Indicators of Spatial Association – LISA', *Geographical Analysis*, 27: 93–115.

Anselin, L. (1996) 'The Moran Scatterplot as an ESDA Tool to Assess Local Instability in Spatial Association', in M. Fischer, H. Scholten and D. Unwin (eds) *Spatial Analytical Perspectives on GIS in Environmental and Socio-Economic Sciences*. London: Taylor and Francis, pp. 111–25.

Anselin, L. (1999) 'Interactive Techniques and Exploratory Spatial Data Analysis', in P. Longley, M. Goodchild, D. Maguire and D. Rhind (eds) *Geographical Information Systems: Principles, Techniques, Management and Applications*. New York: Wiley, pp. 251–64.

Anselin, L., Cohen, J., Cook, D., Gorr, W. and Tita, G. (2000) 'Spatial Analyses of Crime', in D. Duffee (ed.) *Measurement and Analysis of Crime and Justice, Criminal Justice 2000, Vol. 4*. Washington, DC: National Institute of Justice, pp. 213–62.

Anselin, L., Syabri, I. and Kho, Y. (2006) 'GeoDa: An Introduction to Spatial Data Analysis', *Geographical Analysis*, 38: 5–22.

Assuncao, R. and Reis, E. (1999) 'A New Proposal to Adjust Moran's I for Population Density', *Statistics in Medicine*, 18: 2147–61.

Block, C.R. (1994) *STAC Hot Spot Analysis: A Statistical Tool for Law Enforcement Decisions*. Illinois Criminal Justice and Information Authority.

Braga, A.A. (2001) 'The Effects of Hot Spots Policing on Crime', *Annals of the American Academy of Political and Social Science*, 578: 104–25.

Cliff, A. and Ord, J.K. (1981) *Spatial Processes, Models and Applications*. London: Pion.

Cohen, J. and Tita, G.E. (1999) 'Spatial Diffusion in Homicide: Exploring a General Method of Detecting Spatial Diffusion Processes', *Journal of Quantitative Criminology*, 15: 451–93.

Cohen, J., Gorr, W. and Olligschlaeger, A. (1993) 'Modeling Street-level Illicit Drug Markets', working paper 93–64. Pittsburgh: H. John Heinz III School of Public Policy and Management, Carnegie Mellon University.

Diggle, P. (2003) *Statistical Analysis of Spatial Point Patterns*. London: Arnold.

Eck, J.E. (2005) 'Crime Hot Spots: What They Are, Why We Have Them, and How to Map Them', in J.E. Eck, S. Chainey, J.G. Cameron, M. Leitner and R.E. Wilson (eds) *Mapping Crime: Understanding Hot Spots*. Washington, DC: US Department of Justice, National Institute of Justice.

Gartner, R. and McCarthy, B. (n.d.) *Homicide in Four Cities Data Set*. Social Sciences and Humanities Research Council of Canada, Grant # 410-94-0756.

Getis, A. and Ord, K. (1992) 'The Analysis of Spatial Association by Use of Distance Statistics', *Geographical Analysis*, 24: 189–206.

Goldstein, H. (1979), 'Improving Policing: A Problem-oriented Approach', *Crime and Delinquency*, 25: 236–58.

Jacobs, B.A. (1999) *Dealing Crack: The Social World of Streetcorner Selling*. Boston, MA: Northeastern University Press.

Koper, C.S. (1995) 'Just Enough Police Presence: Reducing Crime and Disorderly Behavior by Optimizing Patrol Time in Crime Hot Spots', *Justice Quarterly*, 12: 649–72.

Kulldorff, M. (1997) 'A Spatial Scan Statistic', *Communications in Statistics: Theory and Methods*, 26: 1487–96.

Kulldorff, M. (1999), 'Spatial Scan Statistics: Models, Calculations, and Applications', in J. Glaz and N. Balakrishnan (eds) *Scan Statistics and Applications*. Boston, MA: Birkhauser, pp. 303–22.

Levine, N. (2006) 'Crime Mapping and the CrimeStat Program', *Geographical Analysis*, 38: 41–56.

Monmonier, M. (1996) *How to Lie with Maps*, 2nd edn. Chicago: University of Chicago Press.

Okabe, A., Okunuki, K. and Shiode, S. (2006) 'SANET: A Toolbox for Spatial Analysis on a Network', *Geographical Analysis*, 38: 57–66.

Openshaw, S., Charlton, M., Wymer, C. and Craft, A. (1987) 'A Mark I Geographical Analysis Machine for the Automated Analysis of Point Data Sets', *International Journal of Geographical Information Systems*, 1: 359–77.

Pierce, G., Spaar, S. and Briggs, L. (1988) *The Character of Police Work: Strategic and Tactical Implications*, Boston, MA: Center for Applied Social Research, Northeastern University.

Ripley, B. (1976) 'The Second-order Analysis of Stationary Point Processes', *Journal of Applied Probability*, 13: 255–66.

Roncek, D.W. and Maier, P.A. (1991) 'Bars, Blocks and Crimes Revisited: Linking the Theory of Routine Activities to the Empiricisms of "Hot Spots"', *Criminology*, 29: 725–53.

Sampson, R.J. and Groves, B. (1989) 'Community Structure and Crime: Testing Social-Disorganization Theory', *American Journal of Sociology*, 94: 774–802.

Sampson, R.J., Raudenbush, S.W. and Earls, F. (1997) 'Neighborhoods and Violent Crime: A Multilevel Study of Collective Efficacy', *Science*, 227: 918–24.

Shaw, C.R. and McKay, H. (1942) *Juvenile Delinquency and Urban Areas*. Chicago: University of Chicago Press.

Sherman, L.W. (1992) *Policing Domestic Violence: Experiments and Dilemmas*. New York: Free Press.

Sherman, L.W. and Weisburd, D.A. (1995) 'General Deterrent Effects of Police Patrol in Crime Hot Spots: A Randomized, Controlled Trial', *Justice Quarterly*, 12: 625–48.

Sherman, L.W. Gartin, P.R. and Buerger, M.E. (1989) 'Hot Spots of Predatory Crime: Routine Activities and the Criminology of Place', *Criminology*, 27: 27–56.

Tita, G.E. and Griffiths, E. (2005) 'Traveling to Violence: The Case for a Mobility-based Spatial Typology of Homicide', *Journal of Research on Crime and Delinquency*, 42: 275–308.

Waller, L. and Gotway, C. (2004) *Applied Spatial Statistics for Public Health*. Hoboken, NJ: Wiley.

Weisburd, D. and Green, L. (1995) 'Policing Drug Hot-Spots: The Jersey City Drug Market Analysis Experiment', *Justice Quarterly*, 12: 711–35.

7. Repeat victimisation

Graham Farrell and Ken Pease

Mark Dyche murdered Tanya Moore.

> The pair had met at a Young Farmers' ball and were soon engaged.
> But in February 2003 Miss Moore, fed up over Dyche's jealous and
> threatening behaviour, ended the relationship. For a year he waged a
> hate campaign against her, which included repeated threats to kill her.
> In June 2003 he even paid three men armed with baseball bats ... to
> rob and beat her at her family's farmhouse home in Alkmonton, near
> Ashbourne, Derbyshire. Nottingham Crown Court heard that Dyche,
> who has a history of terrorising women, 'wanted her hurting, wanted
> her legs breaking, wanted her eyes gouging out, wanted to be in control'.
> He offered criminal associates £50,000 to kill her but, when no one came
> forward, did it himself, lying in wait on a country road in March 2004
> and blasting her in the face with a shotgun. A few days before she was
> murdered, Miss Moore presented officers with a bundle of threatening
> text messages from Dyche. (*Daily Telegraph* 2006)

On 12 January 2006, a house in Wythenshawe, Manchester, had petrol poured
through its letterbox and ignited. The two adults in the home, Mr and Mrs
Cochrane, died, and their daughter Lucy suffered burns. It emerged that a
hostile family, the Connors, was responsible.

> The 18-month feud began after schoolgirl Natalie Connor developed
> an obsessive hatred of her classmate because of an apparent slight. The
> dispute between the two families, in which Natalie falsely claimed she
> had been bullied by Lucy, came to a head when Michael bought two
> litres of petrol and poured it through the Cochranes' letterbox. A heavy
> drinker, he was goaded by his wife, who plied him with alcohol before
> the attack early on 12 January this year. Five days earlier, Mrs Cochrane
> discovered what appeared to be a flammable liquid on her front door
> and found that someone had tried to uproot a tree from the garden. She
> called the police but no sample of the liquid was taken. Connor and his
> wife were convicted last week on two counts of murder. Their daughter

was found guilty of manslaughter and attempting to cause grievous bodily harm to Lucy. Alistair Webster QC, prosecuting, had told the jury during the six-week trial that Natalie had developed an obsessive enmity towards her classmate that eventually led to her and her mother inciting Connor to start the fire. (*Guardian* 2006)

While the tragic climaxes to these instances of repeat victimisation are thankfully rare, they illustrate a perennial problem, namely that sequences of events, none of which individually gets over the threshold of seriousness which demands police action, may be cumulative in their impact on victims. Mandy Shaw (2001) draws a parallel with the process of bereavement, where victims go through stages in coming to terms with a crime, but can never complete the recovery sequence because the offence (or a variant of it) is repeated. Shaw and Chenery (2007) note the particular distress of men whose families are repeatedly targeted. The general downplaying of cumulative impact is reflected in police performance measurement, in the conventional statistics of recorded crime and even in the conventions of counting series of victimisations within the British Crime Survey, which understates levels of victimisation by capping the number of crimes in a series from whatever is reported by the victim to a maximum of five events (Farrell and Pease 2008). The criminal justice system's need to demonstrate that someone did some specific thing at a specified time and place beyond a reasonable doubt drives the whole official picture of crime away from dreary and sometimes tragic sequences of suffering to dramatic single events. This preamble is by way of pointing out that giving repeat victimisation its proper prominence is to work against the grain of policing and criminal justice practice. Nonetheless, the attempt is worthwhile.

The next section of the chapter provides a brief account of the opportunities afforded by a repeat victimisation perspective, and of some specific obstacles to its realisation. Two contrasting routes by which repeat victimisation may be advanced are then described. Those searching for an account of the research literature in relation to repeat victimisation and its application to crime reduction are directed to Farrell (1995), Pease (1998), Farrell (2006), Eck, Clarke and Guerette (2007) and to the problem-oriented policing website.[1] The writers have nowhere seen in print an account of the directions in which the repeat victimisation enterprise might with profit advance. This chapter constitutes a tentative and partial attempt to do this.

Repeat victimisation: opportunities and obstacles

The more predictable the place and time of crime events, the easier they are to control, by prevention or detection. Therein lies the attraction of sting (see for example Langworthy 1989) or honeypot (see Baumann and Plattner 2002) operations, whereby the police set up a tempting crime opportunity and simply wait for offenders to take advantage of it. One common example of this approach involves setting up a shop and putting out the word that it will not enquire about how the preferred goods had been obtained. Covert CCTV and other evidence then make arrest for handling stolen goods relatively easy. Honeypot websites provide one means of assessing the frequency and tactics of cybercrime attacks.

There are two major problems with most sting operations. First, they take time and resources to set up, rather than forming a routine part of policing. Second, in some manifestations they are vulnerable to the charge of entrapment, for example if the prices offered for stolen goods are so attractive as to constitute an inducement to steal. Of more use to mainstream policing is information about times and places where the risk of crime is predictably high in the short or long term, so that resources can be deployed accordingly. In passing, it should perhaps be noted that (at least in England and Wales) the allocation of policing resources spectacularly fails to achieve proportionality with the presenting crime problem. A doubling of crime is now accompanied by relatively modest increases in police strength at force, police division and beat level (Ross and Pease 2008). This point is mentioned only to emphasise that, despite sophisticated funding formulae, the thinking that underpins honeypot operations is very far from being applied to policing generally.

The phenomenon which can be used to stimulate movement towards well-directed policing is that of repeat victimisation. The near ubiquitous observation that victimisation predicts victimisation does not operate exclusively at the level of the victimised individual or household. The unit of count which can yield a measure of repeat victimisation is flexible. It may be the individual, the household, the street, the town, the police division, the police force or local authority area, or whatever. As for commercial victims, the unit may be (for example) individual bank branches, banking companies, or all banks (or jewellers or betting shops). There is no best unit of count, merely one which is most useful for a particular policing purpose. That said, the smaller the unit of count, the more precisely can risk be assessed.

The matter becomes more subtle when one realises that one is dealing with offender perceptions. There are two consequences of this observation. First, it means that any amount of security hardware is irrelevant insofar as an offender perceives that help will not be summoned or, if summoned, will not arrive. Too little attention has been given to the notion of affordance (see Norman 1999) as used by designers, namely what an object 'invites' the actor to do (as the broken window is deemed to invite further damage). In relation to repeat victimisation, we need to develop our understanding of the circumstances of an offending act which lead to the changes in perception which make repetition more likely (although success is clearly involved, see Everson and Pease 2001).

The second inadequately understood feature of perceptions concern how offenders group things. While criminal careers tend to be diverse, some transitions are more likely than others, with an embezzlement conviction being more likely to be followed by fraud than by robbery, for example. How potential targets are grouped is important, with some targets being functional equivalents of others (for example a racist attack on any Asian being as good as on any other). There was the depressing spectacle in England of a paediatrician being attacked as a paedophile providing a particularly misguided instance. Pease (1998) coined the term 'virtual repeat victimisation' or virtual repeats, to refer to instances where targets are selected because offenders have already moved against targets they perceive as similar or identical. For example, the same make and model of car offers similar prospects to offenders. Cars perceived to afford common opportunities can be targeted as a group (as in the group of those with the tell-tale suction cup impression on the windscreen, bespeaking a probable satellite navigation device in the glove compartment). If the car is parked in a similar location or situation and space is one of the dimensions along which similarity is assessed, the virtual repeat is closer. Nearby households with the same layout are prone to virtual repeats because, for the offender, there is a good chance that the same type of effort and skills are needed, and the risks and rewards are similar. Virtual repeats provide a useful way of thinking about crime prevention: whether virtual repeat victimisation occurs due to a target's design (easy to break-into), its location (in an unlit area) or its high resale value and low traceability (for example a laptop, a portable MP3 player), should influence the choice of preventive tactics. Townsley and Farrell (2007) comment:

> The defining characteristics of the virtual repeat is the replication of the *modus operandi* of an earlier crime. The repetition is of a particular tactic or skill. For instance, if an offender only knows how to pick locks of a certain type or brand then this *modus operandi* is the defining characteristic of what might also be termed a *tactical repeat*.

Given the variety of units of count and the nuances introduced by perception of similarity, repeat victimisation is a mindset rather than a single simple phenomenon. It is properly regarded as integral with other strategies that can be used to focus prevention efforts including targeting hot spots, repeat offenders and hot products. It can also be deployed as an approach to cybercrime. With the mushroom growth of e-commerce, security is increasingly important. Yet attacks and incidents against networks are increasingly common. Potential crimes include fraud, theft (of funds, knowledge and information, or other), account break-ins, malicious damage to users, institutions or networks. Over a quarter (27 per cent) of the 6,684 computer sites studied by Moitra and Konda (2004) experienced at least three attacks, with such sites suffering a mean of twelve attacks each. The ten most victimised sites experienced an average of 369 attacks! Repeat attacks were far more likely to occur within a week of a prior attack. Some types of attack were likely to occur more quickly than others, and repeats were more likely to be the same type of incident (perhaps suggesting the same offenders). Some network domain types experienced more rapid repeats (those ending '.edu' were fastest and those ending '.com' were slowest). Though prevention was not the primary focus of the Moitra and Konda research, the potential is evident. Focusing network security on sites already hacked could prevent a lot of hacking (and the displacement literature suggests that, for various reasons, much of it will not simply move to other networks). Security should be put in place quickly and certain types of domain (.edu sites) should be particularly proactive. There could exist the potential to track and detect returning hackers who, in turn, may well be the most prolific and serious hackers.

A typology of repeats is set out in Table 7.1. Unpacking the various types of repeat victimisation should facilitate the development of appropriate crime prevention practice, and Table 7.1 seeks to promote this effort. It draws upon existing frameworks. The columns of the table – target, location and offender – represent the key elements of Cohen and Felson's routine activity theory (Cohen and Felson 1979; Felson 2002). The rows represent the dimensions of crime identified in Reppetto's analysis of displacement (Reppetto 1974). The typology is a simplification of reality, and in practice many of the types overlap and more than one is present for any given crime. For example, a repeat residential burglary soon after the first is a target, spatial and temporal repeat. If the same repeat offenders gain entry by the same *modus operandi* then it is a tactical repeat.

There is clearly an overlap between target and location in many instances. Domestic violence will often, but not always, occur in the same spatial location, namely the victim's dwelling (whether cohabiting or not). Individual persons may move around and be victimised in different places, but repeats may be more likely to be at the same location.

Table 7.1 incorporates aspects of the lexicon of terms that informs our understanding of how crime repeats. *Virtual repeats* are discussed above and are based on some form of familiarity. *Near repeats* (see Townsley *et al.* 2000, 2003) combine elements of spatial and tactical repeat victimisation. Targets that are similar in design and geographically close are more likely to be victimised (neighbours have a heightened risk of burglary which declines over time) and are detailed further later in this chapter. *Hot dots* (see Pease and Laycock 1996) and *hot spots* are location-based spatial repeats but may be different crime-types. A hot dot is where a static target is repeatedly victimised so that, when represented graphically, a single point (or dot) represents several crimes. In the generic use of the term hot spot, typically neither the absolute nor relative amount of crime or the size of the area is defined. *Risky facilities* (see Eck *et al.* 2007) are spatially prescribed establishments where crimes frequently occur. Whereas most spatial crime analysis is retrospective, Johnson *et al.* (2004) use *prospective hot spotting* to more accurately predict crime based on spatial and temporal proximity. Their techniques have greater accuracy than either retrospective hot spot mapping or simple target repeats. A *series* is typically defined as crimes that are similar. A victim can experience a series of repeat crimes, usually of the same type and by the same offender(s). An offender can commit a series of crimes, usually of the same type against the same target (which if clustered closely in time could be considered a spree). A *crime spree* is a specific form of a crime *series* that is committed by the same offender and typically clustered into a short time period. The number in the series and the length of time over which a spree can occur are not precisely defined. Of necessity, a spree will often contain crimes that are spatially or

Table 7.1 Two-dimensional typology of repeat victimisation

	Target	Location	Offender
Spatial repeat	Same household, person, vehicle, business, target however defined; *hot dots*	Spatially near repeats; *hot spots*; *risky facilities*	Same offender repeating offence at same place
Temporal repeat	Quick repeat against same target, e.g. domestic violence	Quick repeat not necessarily by same offenders, e.g. looting of a prone store by different people	Quick repeat by same offender(s) – as is often the case in domestic violence, for example; can be a *spree*
Crime-type repeat	Same crime-type against same targets, e.g. robbery	Continued drug-dealing in a narrowly defined area	Repeat gasoline drive-off
Tactical repeat	*Virtual repeat* using same tactic (*modus operandi*) leads to 'hot products'	Same tactic facilitated by same place, e.g. theft and pickpocket at a street market	Repeat offending using same tactic (*modus operandi*)

directionally similar – the same neighbourhood, town, city or virtual space, or moving in a particular direction. *Repeat offending* by the same offender may sometimes be against the same target. The sequence of crimes, which has an onset, frequency and duration, and may involve desistence, is the *criminal career* (see e.g. Blumstein *et al.* 1986).[2] *Hot products* (Felson and Clarke 1998) are frequently stolen consumer goods. They are often small lightweight and valuable, such as mobile cell phones, laptops and satnav systems. It is likely that they are often stolen by the same offenders repeating the same tactic (certain types of theft, robbery). While the various concepts share the common starting point of crime's tendency to repeat, there is further work to be done on the integration of concepts, methods and practice for a more comprehensive repeat victimisation perspective to emerge and for it to produce synergies that will further promote crime prevention practice.

Having sought to outline the scope for application of a repeat victimisation perspective on crime generally, let us return to a more prosaic consideration of what has already been established. The following assertions are now largely accepted:

- Crime surveys typically reveal that some 40 per cent of crimes against individual people and against households are repeats, that is, committed against targets already victimised during the same year, with variation by crime type and place.[3]
- Revictimisation of the same target, when it occurs, most often occurs quickly.
- The bulk of repeat victimisation seems to be the work of the same offenders.
- The highest rates of repeat victimisation are found for personal crimes such as domestic violence, sexual victimisation, abuse of elders and children, racial attacks and bullying. These are contexts in which the same targets remain available across time, often in private space.
- High rates of repeat property victimisation are typically found to characterise crimes against businesses. Commercial burglary, robbery and shop theft are prominent examples.
- Although the evidence is not yet as extensive as one would wish, it is consistent in suggesting that repeat attacks against the same target marks out the more prolific offender.
- Rates of repeat victimisation are greater in high crime areas. A case could be made that it is chronic victimisation of the same people and households which is the primary defining characteristic of the high crime area.
- Most repeat prevention programmes have focused on domestic burglary. There is an urgent need to broaden the research base.

The core implication of the repeat victimisation literature is that attention to the prevention of recurrence (and the detection of repeat offenders against the same target) can yield rich dividends in crime reduction. Projects aiming to prevent repeat victimisation have been evaluated and are discussed elsewhere (see Farrell 2006). Some have proven more effective than others, and lessons have been learned relating to establishing levels of repeats and implementation of countermeasures (see Farrell 2006). Some general considerations are set out below which will certainly be encountered by all those seeking to reduce crime by attending to its concentration, reflected in repeats. Let us engage in wishful thinking for a moment by supposing that effective crime reduction measures already exist in the repertoire of those charged with the task. It is an article of belief founded on experience that the supposition is not entirely fanciful, and that the central problem in crime reduction is deploying rather than devising remedies. The particular problems in relation to the prevention of repeat victimisation are as follows.

Camouflaged repeats

Repeat victimisation is not always straightforward to identify, essentially because of shortcomings in police data systems and recording conventions. In a recent training course for police analysts to which one of the writers contributed, the confident assertion by analysts in one heavily burgled area was that repeats were not a problem. Only one had been identified by them in the preceding year. Fortunately, the data were made available which showed 304 repeat burglaries over the year. While this scale of underestimation is unusual, some is endemic in the relevant datasets. Some of the distortions are subtle – for example individual variation among police officers in recording events as 'criminal damage' or 'attempted burglary', or the recording of repeat dog thefts as incidents rather than crimes, depending on the circumstances of loss.

Poorly reported crimes pose a particular problem. A good initiative will show an increase in the number of people reporting crimes like domestic violence but a reduction in repeats. These two will offset each other so that, if one simply measures calls for service, it will look as though the initiative had no effect (see Farrell 2006; Farrell and Buckley 1999).

Premature evacuation

The police function is separated into immediate response and routine support functions. Communication between these is very imperfect. Thus the perception of response to an incident as the first step in a process whose central aim is the prevention of recurrence of a crime requires a reorientation of both attitude and infrastructure. The (imperfect) simile is illness, where the first point of contact with the health service is with a local physician who will refer the case onwards to specialist services where recurrence of a disorder is deemed likely. By contrast, a first officer attending an incident tends to see his or her involvement as the last stage in the process (unless detection of a perpetrator is actively sought) rather than the first step in a protective process. We have taken to referring to this mindset as premature evacuation, in the hope that at least male police officers will come to see it as equally embarrassing with the similarly named sexual dysfunction.

The elusive victim

Where known prevention measures exist, victims or others involved can be difficult to contact or engage with. Indeed, sometimes there is police reluctance to engage with victims. Given the substantial overlap between victimisation and offending, it is not uncommon for those deemed to be prolific offenders to be entitled to help as repeat victims, and the police to be enraged by giving 'goodies to baddies'. Indeed, it is important to acknowledge that among the victims of violence are the serially provocative, and among the victims of most crime types are to be found insurance and compensation fraudsters. Finally, when contacted, some victims (or others involved) do not want, or have the means, to adopt preventive measures. For those (including many commercial organisations) who are simply disinclined to take action to prevent their further victimisation, the problem of offering or withholding subsidy is acute.

Evidence, trials and tribulations

Some of the impetus to the repeat victimisation perspective was given by the success of the Kirkholt burglary reduction initiative (Forrester *et al.* 1988, 1990). The spectacular reductions in domestic burglary achieved led to understandable scepticism that preventing repeats was the 'active ingredient'. The Home Office commissioned David Farrington of the Cambridge Institute of Criminology to reanalyse the data, his conclusion being that the initiative had worked along the lines claimed (Farrington 1992). No other crime reduction programme based on the prevention of repeats has been as successful as Kirkholt, although some have achieved notable reductions (see for example Anderson *et al.* 1995; Chenery *et al.* 1997). While there are many reasons for this shortfall (see Tilley 1993) personal experience suggests implementation failure as important. One of the writers was involved in a project, the findings of which are yet to be published, wherein the first officer attending a domestic burglary completed a basic security survey, which was passed on to the local crime reduction officer for appropriate further action (usually none). Some officers completed the survey conscientiously. Others were contemptuous of the whole process and never completed it. There were roughly one-third fewer repeat burglaries in homes where the process had been set in train than in other homes, and there was no other difference (shift, location, length of officer service) which could account for this reduction.

If, as the security survey study may suggest, repeat victimisation can be reduced by relatively marginal preventive activity, then the possibilities for prevention may be broader than previously envisaged. One line of enquiry is to examine what deters repeat victimisation when it does not occur. Mike Sutton very generously gave us access to unpublished material from 20 interviews he conducted with offenders in the Midlands of England in late summer 2006. Many of the relevant findings echoed those of Ashton *et al.* (1998), wherein offenders detailed how they committed repeats due to the ease, the low risk, and the known rewards. Yet the following, which are selective excerpts from Sutton's field notes, give a glimpse of the possibility of prevention and deterrence. One offender would continue to circumvent security but only up to a certain level:

> [He] said he would go back to the same property on more than one occasion because it was so easy the time before: 'I've done some shops four or five times and all they've done is repaired the fag counter and replaced the window ...' [Then, after describing a series of escalating security measures] He said he was always thwarted in the end. The best way to keep him out was fully shuttered premises with no alarm box on the outside. He said that the alarm systems that had to be turned off by staff once they were inside the fully shuttered shop, where the shutters had to be opened from the inside – were the most effective.

The possibility that adaptation and escalation by offenders is limited was supported in an interview of an offender who committed repeat commercial burglaries but not repeat residential burglaries:

He would do commercial burglaries until the security became too tight. But he never did repeat domestics. 'With a house they tend to have neighbours and they tend to say to the neighbours "I've been burgled – keep your eyes out" or they make sure that someone is in the house all the time.'

A third offender described the occasion when he committed a repeat burglary as being the exception to his rule:

Other than this he says he stuck to a motto of 'never go back'. He says his fear is that he may have been identified by a neighbour on the first occasion that could lead to his rapid arrest if in the area again. He says that lots of burglars think the same way.

One interviewee offered insight into possible push–pull factors underpinning virtual repeats, as: 'He would not do the same house twice due to fear of increased security. But he would do the same *type* of house.' There may be more work to be done to explore whether there are 'push' virtual repeats induced by a fear of the same target or 'pull' virtual repeats induced by the perceived lower risk of a similar target which has become more familiar.

Another of Sutton's interviewees was caught committing a repeat because: 'He went back to same place twice for gold and money. He got caught when a neighbour identified him, and was picked up by police CID.' A sixth confirmed why there is sometimes a lag between repeats when the offender waits for goods to be replaced (a pattern originally found by Polvi *et al.* 1991), while he also explained how he was deterred by improved security. On one occasion:

He went into a house and got a good haul. Two months later, walking by, he saw new stuff so did it again ... took the same stuff (the replacements). 'If I do a place and its got good stuff in it – I think to myself "I'll come back 2 months later". Guaranteed – y'know what I mean, If it's good I'll come back. I did this geezer once three times before he got a [security] system up there ... alarm bell. After I saw the alarm I thought ... ah I'll leave it now.'

While selective and limited in number, such interviews are encouraging for crime preventers. They confirm that deterrence can be induced by security or increasing perceived risks. They also confirm that there may be more work to be done utilising offender interviews to explore the dynamics of repeat victimisation and its prevention.

Ways ahead?

Prospective mapping

The term 'near repeat' derives from the insight that multiple victimisation of the same target was a special case of a general tendency of risk to be communicated across time and space. Early empirical work on the topic was conducted by Shane Johnson and Kate Bowers at Liverpool University and by Mike Townsley and colleagues at Griffith University, Brisbane (Bowers and Johnson 2005; Johnson and Bowers 2004a; Johnson and Bowers 2004b; Townsley *et al*. 2000, 2003). Households close to a burglary have an increased likelihood of suffering the same offence. The increased risk declines with distance from the initial target and with time, typically over 400 metres and one month. Townsley and colleagues used statistical techniques from epidemiology to demonstrate how burglaries are 'infectious'. They found this to be particularly the case in areas with uniform housing type and layout, with higher repeat rates in areas of more diverse housing type. While Townsley and colleagues borrowed techniques from epidemiology, Johnson and Bowers (2004a; 2004b) looked at ecological theory to characterise the burglar as an 'optimal forager'. Consider a grazing animal. It would like to consume the most nutritious grass in the field. However, if the richest patches of grass are spread out across the field, the effort expended in getting to the juiciest stuff must also be taken into account. Starting at the best clump of grass in the field, our ruminant must decide whether the next most promising clump, some way across the field, is a sufficient improvement over the nearby grass to make the amble worthwhile. In optimal foraging, the adequate nearby will be preferred to the optimal but distant. This provides a plausible analogue of burglar behaviour, at least as it can be inferred from patterns of repeats and near repeats. It squares with the following facts:

- Detached houses are disproportionately burgled in areas where terraced housing predominates (the juiciest grass is chosen first).

- Detached houses are repeatedly burgled most in areas where terraced housing predominates (the forager goes back to the juiciest grass when the next juiciest grass isn't very juicy).

- Near repeats are greatest in areas of uniform housing (when the grass is pretty much the same all over the field, you don't bother going very far).

The simile should not be pushed too far. One difference is that burglary is episodic, grazing pretty much continuous. Also the starting point for the burglar is home, not the juiciest burglary target. Nonetheless, there is sheer delight in the importation of ideas from disciplines like epidemiology and ecology into the stifling solipsism of conventional criminology. The heuristic value is immense.

The work of Johnson, Bowers and Townsley has been translated into predictive mapping software which takes the phenomena of repeats and near repeats and puts them to work in prediction (e.g. Bowers *et al.* 2004). The software is called ProMap (for Prospective Mapping) and is revolutionary. So far it has been applied to domestic burglary in several police force areas in the UK with essentially the same results. The patterns which inform ProMap have been identified for burglary in cities all around the world (Johnson *et al.* 2008), motor vehicle crime (Summers *et al.* 2007), bike theft (Johnson, personal communication) and even explosive devices detonated in Baghdad (Townsley *et al.* 2008). Since the burglary research is furthest advanced, it will be used in illustration here.

Traditionally in crime mapping, the past is seen as a direct guide to the future, whether this is by direct extrapolation or by a leading indicators approach. The work on near repeats makes it clear that the relationship of past and future is more subtle. For example, every burglary event confers an elevated level of risk on nearby homes. The closer the home to the one burgled, the greater the risk conferred. This risk is transient, returning to its prior level after a month or so. In ProMap, every burglary event leads to the revision of risk for every nearby home, and every elapsed day leads to a diminution of that risk. Any new burglary event confers transient extra risk on homes nearby. It has already been established that ProMap substantially outperforms the most sophisticated alternatives in predictive accuracy (e.g. Bowers *et al.* 2004; Johnson *et al.* 2007a) and importantly the predictions of police officers serving the area (e.g. McLaughlin *et al.* 2007). It has been trialled operationally with encouraging results (Johnson *et al.* 2007b). However, there are obstacles to the potential of ProMap being realised, the major one being a failure of vision among potential funders. As things stand, ProMap permits police patrolling and short-run preventive measures to be deployed in respect of domestic burglary *or* vehicle crime. What is the optimal pattern for burglary and vehicle crime? This depends on the relative seriousness assigned to the two offence types. A policy decision as to that would permit a presumptive patrolling route to maximise the seriousness of crimes which will take place on and around the patrolling route. So it is a relatively simple matter to produce an optimised patrolling pattern for the two offences taken together. However this still requires a schizoid mindset on the part of patrolling officers, since some crime (violent crime in particular) is excluded from consideration. Officers would have to be in 'burglary-vehicle crime' mode, in which case the presumptive patrolling route would be the best available, or 'other crime' mode, in which case it would not. Toggling between the two is not a skill we should expect them to possess!

The evolution of the eyeball has been taken by intelligent design advocates as a phenomenon which it is difficult for evolution to explain, in that intermediate steps between external photosensitive patch and enclosed eyeball do not confer natural selection advantage. While that argument is ill-founded,[4] there is a problem with incremental changes of ProMap. Until all crimes are incorporated in an optimal presumptive patrolling pattern, it is difficult to forsee its routine and enthusiastic adoption. However, the prospect of real-time information to police patrols and community safety practitioners about the distribution of crime risk, optimally weighted by seriousness, is so palpably useful that it merits support. At the time of writing, only piecemeal funding seems likely.

Rough, ready and roughly ready

ProMap involves detailed and extensive research, sophisticated modelling of the distribution of crime events across space and time, and the design of clever software with a user-friendly front end. Its achievements are already noteworthy. However, there is an alternative strategy by which the fruits of an understanding of repeats and near repeats can be deployed immediately, and which is transparent to those who use it. To call it crude is a compliment in that it takes as its starting point current police data with all their problems and police officers with their tendency to scepticism (like the officer who dismissed ProMap as not telling him anything he didn't already know – an assertion belied by the relative predictive accuracy of police officers and ProMap). It is best exemplified by the work of Alan Edmunds, a former Metropolitan Police inspector who became infected by the repeat victimisation bug, and put it to work. His approach is most evident in Operation Cobra, whose report gained the Herman Goldstein Prize for Problem-Oriented Policing in 2004.[5] The unit of count was the street rather than the individual person or home. The initial analysis showed that 1 per cent of streets hosted 10 per cent of vehicle crime, and 13 per cent of streets accounted for half of all crime. The tactic was simply to talk to the people in the streets, analyse the crime data and take remedial action. Streets with most vehicle crime applied customised warnings to victims, property marking, lighting and structure changes to the streets, and full forensic examination of crime scenes wherever possible. Streets with somewhat less vehicle crime omitted the forensic work, and those with still less crime excluded the structural changes. The crucial point, as seen by Alan Edmunds, was making contact with local citizens who understood the problems and in one case remarked 'What kept you?' to police officers responding to the concentrated problem. The obvious objection, that some streets are longer than others and hence will host more crime on a chance basis, is dismissed by Alan Edmunds. He notes that where a long street is included in Operation Cobra, the offences are clustered at one or two places along it. In the first nine months of Operation Cobra, the number of vehicles stolen declined by 25 per cent, and there was a 33 per cent reduction in thefts from vehicles. This reduction was not experienced elsewhere in the force area. To demonstrate the agency of Cobra in the decline, greater declines were experienced in those streets which had previously hosted most crime, with reductions ranging from 37 per cent to 58 per cent in the previously most victimised streets. Alan Edmunds has since applied the same analytic approach to crimes of violence and criminal damage, showing similar inequality across streets: 4 per cent of streets experienced 25 per cent of damage, and 2 per cent of streets saw 25 per cent of violent offences.

Alan Edmunds is a doer. In common with many high achievers, he finds little time to write up his work. His various PowerPoint presentations are available from him personally.[6] The ease and accessibility of his approach has meant that it promises to penetrate policing practice sooner and more fully than the more sophisticated ProMap approach. He kindly took time to prepare a list of what he sees as advantages of his approach for the practitioner, which is reproduced verbatim.

- Preventing RV can act as the single most important catalyst for partnership development.

- Preventing repeats saves shed loads of money.

- Preventing repeats puts you where the best bangs are to be got for your bucks.

- Preventing RV is a way of proving effective work has been undertaken – a reduction in the prevalence levels and the overall concentration can be a bonus even if crime overall goes up – a number of people will not be blighted by crime in their street so it delivers – assurance in areas where most needed.

- Preventing RV allows new police and partnership neighbourhood teams to sort the wood for the trees – a recent case showed 22 of 166 streets experienced 58 per cent of all crime (cars, burglary, damage, etc.) and when further developed using my system the team could see the streets that had passed the stages set for preventing repeat activity and got on the case.

- Preventing RV that fails and continues allows us to routinely identify street-based 'problems' rather than the rather hit and miss – is it or isn't it so often found on teams.

- Preventing RV allows us to turn the stats into the intelligent programme developed to tackle the issue.

Repeat victimisation and the nature of suffering

As noted at the start of this chapter, the criminal justice system is particularly bad (and arguably getting worse) at dealing with chronic minor criminality. The police are judged in terms of performance indicators which lead chronic minor crime to be overlooked. The Crown Prosecution Service will discontinue cases it deems trivial 'in the interests of justice'. This is an Orwellian horror phrase. Whose interests are served by such discontinuances? Certainly not those of crime victims, nor those of police who want to persuade a community that the bane of their lives is not above the law. Put crudely it seems that legal process changes have the effect of turning a lifestyle into a single event whose occurrence has to be legally established – and sentenced as a one-off event, thus missing the point from a victim's perspective. The means by which this is done include:

- Pressing sample charges rather than charging for each offence committed.
- Allowing offences to be taken into consideration rather than proceeded with.
- The principal offence rule, whereby charging only the offence in a bundle that has the highest maximum sentence.
- The discontinuance of cases by the Crown Prosecution Service 'in the interests of justice' even where the events are elements in a long sequence of predation.

The list below (modified from Laycock and Farrell 2003) provides a host of reasons for preventing repeats, and constitutes the most appropriate coda to the chapter.

Seventeen reasons for policing to prevent repeat victimisation

1 Preventing repeat victimisation is a crime prevention activity and hence pursuant to the most fundamental of police mandates as defined since Robert Peel's original list of policing principles outlined in 1829.
2 Targeting repeat victimisation is an efficient means of allocating, in time and space, scarce police resources to crime problems.
3 Preventing repeat victimisation is an approach that is relevant to all crimes with a target. It has been shown to be a feature of crimes including hate crimes, domestic and commercial burglary, school crime (burglary and vandalism), bullying, sexual assault, car crime, neighbour disputes, credit card fraud and other retail sector crime, domestic violence and child abuse. Even murder can be the repeat of attempted murder or the culmination of harassment.
4 Police managers can use repeat victimisation as a performance indicator (Tilley 1995; Farrell and Buckley 1999). These can range from the national to the local level.
5 Preventing repeat victimisation naturally allocates resources to high-crime areas, crime hot spots, and the most victimised targets (Bennett 1995; Townsley et al. 2000, 2003).
6 Preventing repeat victimisation may inform the allocation of crime prevention to nearby targets (near repeats) and targets with similar characteristics (virtual repeats; Pease 1998).
7 Preventing repeat victimisation is a form of 'drip feeding' of prevention resources (Pease 1991). Since all crime does not occur at once, police resources need only be allocated as victimisations occur from day to day.
8 Preventing repeat victimisation is even less likely to result in displacement than unfocused crime prevention efforts (Bouloukos and Farrell 1997; Chenery et al. 1997).
9 Offenders will be made uncertain and more generally deterred by changed circumstances at the most attractive and vulnerable targets. Hence preventing repeat victimisation may be even more likely to result in a diffusion of crime control benefits than more general crime prevention.

10 Preventing repeat victimisation can generate common goals and positive work between police and other agencies (such as housing, social services, and victim organisations) which may in turn facilitate broader co-operation.

11 Focusing on repeat victimisation empowers police officers to do something tangible and constructive to help crime victims and for policing to become more generally oriented towards victims who are arguably its core consumers (Farrell 2001).

12 Efforts to prevent RV can lead to positive feedback from victims. This is still a relatively rare reward for police in the community. It may promote good community relations.

13 Preventing repeat victimisation is triggered by a crime being reported. Since victims can be asked about prior victimisations, a response does not necessarily require data analysis.

14 Preventing repeat victimisation can sometimes – but not always – use off-the-shelf prevention tactics rather than requiring inventive and sometimes difficult problem-solving.

15 Preventing repeat victimisation can be used to enhance the detection of serious and prolific offenders. Police officers like detecting offenders.

16 Preventing repeat victimisation presents possibilities for preventing and detecting organised crime and terrorism that focuses on vulnerable and rewarding victims and targets – including protection rackets, forced prostitution, loan-sharking, repeat trafficking via certain low-risk locations, art and other high-value thefts and robberies, and terrorist bombings.

17 Targeting repeat victimisation can inform thinking on repeat crimes typically perceived as 'victimless' where the repeatedly victimised target is the state or nation.

Notes

1 www.popcenter.org/Tools/tool-repeat Victimization.htm (accessed 2 May 2007).
2 The hypothetical limiting case of a criminal career would be a single crime which would have no element of repetition. In practice, repeat offending is traditionally the primary concern of criminal career research.
3 This is a conservative estimate based on crime types found in 17 countries from the International Crime Victims Survey (Farrell and Bouloukos 2001). This average includes repeats across as well as within crime-types.
4 For a detailed explanation see Chapter 4 of Dawkins (1986).
5 www.popcenter.org/Library/Goldstein/2004/04-38(W).pdf (accessed 2 May 2007).
6 alanedmunds@btinternet.com

References

Anderson, D., Chenery, S. and Pease, K. (1995) *Biting Back: Tackling Repeat Burglary and Car Crime*, Crime Detection and Prevention Series Paper 58. London: Home Office.

Ashton, J., Brown, I., Senior, B. and Pease, K. (1998) 'Repeat Victimisation: Offender Accounts', *International Journal of Risk, Security and Crime Prevention*, 3: 269–79.

Baumann, R. and Plattner, C. (2002) *Honeypots*. Zurich: Swiss Federal Institute of Technology.

Bennett, T. (1995) 'Identifying, Explaining, and Targeting Burglary '"Hot spots"', *European Journal on Criminal Policy and Research*, 3: 113–23.

Blumstein, A., Cohen, J., Roth, J.A. and Visher, C.A. (1986) *Criminal Careers and Career Criminals*, two vols. Washington, DC: National Academy Press.

Bouloukos, A.C. and Farrell, G. (1997) 'On the Displacement of Repeat Victimization', in G. Newman, R.V. Clarke and S. Shoham (eds) *Situational Crime Prevention and Rational Choice*. Aldershot: Dartmouth.

Bowers, K.J. and Johnson, S.D. (2005) 'Domestic Burglary Repeats and Space-time Clusters: The Dimensions of Risk', *European Journal of Criminology*, 2: 67–92.

Bowers, K.J. and Johnson, S.D. (2004) 'A Test of the Boost Explanation of Near Repeats', *Western Criminology Review*, 5: 12–24.

Bowers, K.J., Johnson, S.D. and Pease, K. (2004) 'Prospective Hot-Spotting: The Future of Crime Mapping?', *British Journal of Criminology*, 44: 641–58.

Chenery, S., Holt, J. and Pease, K. (1997) *Biting Back II: Reducing Repeat Victimization in Huddersfield*, Crime Detection and Prevention Series Paper. London: Home Office.

Cohen, L.E. and Felson, M. (1979) 'Social Change and Crime Rates and Trends: A Routine Activity Approach', *American Sociological Review*, 44: 588–608.

Daily Telegraph (2006) 2 November, p. 12.

Dawkins, R. (1986) *The Blind Watchmaker: Why the Evidence of Evolution Reveals a Universe without Design*. Harlow: Longman.

Eck, J.E., Clarke, R.V. and Guerette, R.T. (2007) 'Risky Facilities: Crime Concentration in Homogeneous Sets of Establishments and Facilities', in G. Farrell, K.J. Bowers, S.D. Johnson and M. Townsley (eds) *Imagination in Crime Prevention*. Cullompton, UK: Willan Publishing.

Everson, P. and Pease, K. (2001) 'Crime Against the Same Person and Place: Detection Opportunity and Offender Targeting', in G. Farrell and K. Pease (eds) *Repeat Victimisation. Crime Prevention Studies, Vol 12*, Monsey, NY: Criminal Justice Press.

Farrell, G. (1995) 'Preventing Repeat Victimization', in M. Tonry and D.P. Farrington (eds) *Building a Safer Society: Strategic Approaches to Crime Prevention, Crime and Justice*. Chicago: Chicago University Press, pp. 469–534.

Farrell, G. (2001) 'How Victim-Oriented is Policing?', in A. Gaudreault and I. Waller (eds) *The Tenth International Symposium on Victimology: Selected Symposium Proceedings*. Montreal: International Symposium on Victimology.

Farrell, G. (2006) 'Progress and Prospects in the Prevention of Repeat Victimisation', in N. Tilley (ed.) *Handbook of Crime Prevention and Community Safety*. Cullompton, UK: Willan Publishing.

Farrell, G. and Bouloukos, A.C. (2001) 'A Cross-national Comparative Analysis of Rates of Repeat Victimization', in G. Farrell and K. Pease (eds) *Repeat Victimization. Crime Prevention Studies, Vol. 12*, Monsey, NY: Criminal Justice Press.

Farrell, G. and Buckley, A. (1999) 'Evaluation of a UK Police Domestic Violence Unit Using Repeat Victimization as a Performance Indicator', *Howard Journal*, 38: 42–53.

Farrell G. and Pease, K. (2008) 'The Sting in the British Crime Survey Tail: Multiple Victimisations', in M.G. Maxfield and M. Hough (eds) *Surveying Crime in the 21st Century*. Cullompton, UK: Willan Publishing.

Farrington, D.P. (1992) 'Evaluation of the Kirkholt Burglary Project', unpublished report to the Home Office. Cambridge: Institute of Criminology, University of Cambridge.

Felson, M. (2002) *Crime and Everyday Life*, 3rd edn. Thousand Oaks, CA: Sage and Pine Forge Press.

Felson, M. and Clarke, R.V. (1998) *Opportunity Makes the Thief*, Police Research Paper 98. London: Home Office.

Forrester, D., Chatterton, M. and Pease, K. (1988) *The Kirkholt Burglary Prevention Project, Rochdale*, Crime Prevention Unit Paper 13. London: Home Office.

Forrester, D., Frenz, S., O'Connell, M. and Pease, K. (1990) *The Kirkholt Burglary Prevention Project: Phase II*, Crime Prevention Unit Paper 23. London: Home Office.

Guardian (2006) 21 December, p. 15.

Johnson, S.D. and Bowers, K.J. (2004a) 'The Burglary as a Clue to the Future: The Beginnings of Prospective Hot-spotting', *European Journal of Criminology*, 1: 237–55.

Johnson, S.D. and Bowers, K.J. (2004b) 'The Stability of Space-time Clusters of Burglary', *British Journal of Criminology*, 44: 55–65.

Johnson, S.D., Bowers, K.J. and Pease, K. (2004) 'Predicting the Future or Summarising the Past? Crime Mapping as Anticipation', in M. Smith and N. Tilley (eds) *Launching Crime Science*. Cullompton, UK: Willan Publishing.

Johnson, S.D., Bernasco, W., Bowers, K.J., Elffers, H., Ratcliffe, J., Rengert, G. and Townsley, M.T. (2007a) 'Near Repeats: A Cross National Assessment of Residential Burglary', *Journal of Quantitative Criminology*, 23: 201–19.

Johnson, S.D., Birks, D., McLaughlin, L., Bowers, K. and Pease, K. (2007b) *Prospective Mapping in Operational Context*, Home Office Online Report 19/07. London: Home Office.

Johnson, S.D., Bowers, K.J., Birks, D. and Pease, K. (2008) 'Prospective Mapping: The Importance of the Environmental Backcloth', in W. Bernasco, D. Weisburd and G. Bruinsma (eds) *Crime and Place*. New York: Springer Verlag.

Langworthy R.H. (1989) 'Do Stings Control Crime? An Evaluation of a Police Fencing Operation', *Justice Quarterly*, 6: 27–45.

Laycock, G. and Farrell, G. (2003) 'Repeat Victimization: Lessons for Implementing Problem-oriented Policing', in J. Knutsson (ed.) *Problem-oriented Policing: From Innovation to Mainstream, Crime Prevention Studies, Vol. 15*: Monsey, NY: Criminal Justice Press, 213–37.

McLaughlin, L., Johnson, S.D., Birks, D., Bowers, K.J. and Pease, K. (2007) 'Police Perceptions of the Long and Short Term Spatial Distribution of Residential Burglary' *International Journal of Police Science and Management*, 9: 99–111.

Moitra, S.D. and Konda, S.L. (2004) 'An Empirical Investigation of Network Attacks on Computer Systems', *Computers and Security*, 23: 43–51.

Norman, D.A. (1999) 'Affordance, Conventions and Design', *Interactions*, 6: 36–43.

Pease, K. (1991) 'The Kirkholt Project: Preventing Burglary on a British Public Housing Estate', *Security Journal*, 2: 73–7.

Pease, K. (1998) *Repeat Victimisation: Taking Stock*, Crime Detection and Prevention Series Paper 90. London: Home Office.

Pease, K. and Laycock, G. (1996) 'Revictimization: Reducing the Heat on Hot Victims', *Research in Action*. Washington, DC: National Institute of Justice.

Polvi, N., Looman, T., Humphries, C. and Pease, K. (1991) 'The Time Course of Repeat Burglarly Victimisation', *British Journal of Criminology*, 34: 411–14.

Reppetto, T.A. (1974) *Residential Crime*. Cambridge, MA: Ballinger.

Ross, N. and Pease, K. (2008) 'Community Policing and Prediction', in T. Williamson (ed.) *Handbook of Knowledge-based Policing*. Chichester, UK: Wiley.

Shaw, M. (2001) 'Time Heals All Wounds?', in G. Farrell and K. Pease (eds) *Repeat Victimization. Crime Prevention Studies, Vol. 12*. Monsey, NY: Criminal Justice Press.

Shaw M. and Chenery, S. (2007) 'Kings and Castles, Cavemen and Caves: The Impact of Crime on Male Victims', in G. Farrell, K.J. Bowers, S.D. Johnson and M. Townsley (eds) *Imagination in Crime Prevention. Crime Prevention Studies, Vol. 21*. Cullompton, UK: Willan Publishing.

Summers, L., Johnson, S.D. and Pease, K. (2007) 'El Robo de (Objetos en) Vehículos y su Contagio a través del Espacio y el Tiempo: Aplicaciones de técnicas epidemiológicas', *Revista Electronica de Investigacion Criminologica* (www.criminologia.net/pdf/reic/REICA1N52007.pdf).

Tilley, N. (1993) *After Kirkholt: Theory, Method and Results of Replication Evaluations*, Crime Reduction Unit Paper 47. London: Home Office.

Tilley, N. (1995) *Thinking About Crime Prevention Performance Indicators*, Crime Detection and Prevention Series Paper 57. London: Home Office.

Townsley M. and Farrell, G. (2007) 'Repeat Victimisation of Prison Inmates', in G. Farrell, K.J. Bowers, S.D. Johnson and M. Townsley (eds) *Imagination in Crime Prevention. Crime Prevention Studies, Vol. 21*. Cullompton, UK: Willan Publishing.

Townsley, M., Homel, R. and Chaseling, J. (2000) 'Repeat Burglary Victimisation: Spatial and Temporal Patterns', *Australian and New Zealand Journal of Criminology*, 33: 37–63.

Townsley, M., Homel, R. and Chaseling, J. (2003) 'Infectious Burglaries: A Test of the Near Repeat Hypothesis', *British Journal of Criminology*, 43: 615–33

Townsley, M.T., Johnson, S.D. and Ratcliffe, J.R. (2008). 'Space-Time Dynamics of Insurgent Activity in Iraq', *Security Journal*.

8. Geographic profiling

D. Kim Rossmo and Sacha Rombouts

Introduction

Attempting to locate an unknown offender is arguably the most important function of the criminal investigative process. Environmental criminology teaches that an interaction in time and place between victim and offender is a necessary prerequisite for crime to occur. The spatial behaviour of both offender and victim may therefore offer important clues which can aid in the identification and apprehension of an unknown offender. The aim of geographic profiling is to use information about crime-related locations to identify the probable location of an offender. The underlying premise here is that the nature of crime-related locations tells us something about the victim, the offender, and how each interacted with the environment during the course of the crime. Crime-related locations can provide information about the level of planning that went into the offence, the offender's familiarity (or not) with the location and broader environment, and the extent to which the offender's use of the crime environment reflects aspects of his non-criminal spatial lifestyle. Geographic profiling is in essence an investigative tool that formally articulates the ways in which environmental criminology and associated research can aid in apprehending unknown offenders. It can be thought of as a support service, a crime analysis product, and an investigative procedure unto itself, and was developed in response to the need to solve serial crimes.

While geographic profiling has traditionally been defined as an investigative aid used to analyse a series of crimes in order to identify the most likely residence of an unknown offender, in the broadest sense it may best be thought of as a strategic information management system designed to support investigative efforts. As this definition implies, its aim is not solely to help apprehend an unknown offender but also to perform other information management functions such as assisting the police with the large volume of information that arises during the course of an investigation. It accomplishes this through an intense focus on the geography of crime, providing a quantitative and qualitative assessment of crime-related spatio-temporal behaviour in order to concentrate investigative efforts geographically. Rather than being a theoretical model unto itself, geographic profiling is instead an applied methodology that draws upon some of the theories presented in previous chapters.

This chapter presents a model of the geographic profiling process. In doing so, a number of key themes are illustrated, including: (1) the use of environmental criminology theories to interpret crime-related spatial behaviour; (2) the use of mathematical/statistical methods to analyse spatial behaviour; and (3) the reliability, validity, and utility of the application of geographic profiling to criminal investigations.

Theoretical underpinnings of geographic profiling

The geographic profiling model is based on the assumption that

> victim selection is spatially biased toward an offender's home location. As a result, criminal acts follow a decay function, such that the farther an offender is from home, the less likely he is to commit a crime. The model also articulates, however, that there is a buffer zone, such that offenders will avoid committing crimes too close to their homes, to avoid incriminating themselves. (Hicks and Sales 2006: 221)

There are four main areas of environmental criminology that contribute in some way or another to the geographic profiling process: journey-to-crime; rational choice theory; routine activity theory; and crime pattern theory.

The journey-to-crime literature supports the notion that crimes more frequently occur closer to an offender's home and follow a distance-decay function (DDF) with crimes less likely to occur the further an offender moves away from his/her home base. According to the least effort or nearness principle, offenders will typically travel limited distances to accomplish their goals. Such 'distance to crime' functions underpin the algorithms that drive most geographic profiling software applications. There are some variations in travel patterns of offenders, however. Travel patterns vary by offence type and offender characteristics (Baldwin and Bottoms 1976; Gabor and Gottheil 1984; Rhodes and Conly 1981; Rossmo 2000). It is also important to recognise that geographic profiling differs from the journey-to-crime research in that the former is concerned with the application of spatial techniques to an individual crime or set of crimes while the latter concerns itself with the analysis of travel patterns of groups of offenders. The distance distributions of aggregated offender crime trips are sometimes mistakenly confused for individual-level distance probability functions; the two are not synonymous (van Koppen and de Keijser 1997).

Rational choice theory provides a foundation for the existence of intentional hunting patterns, emphasising the role of offender perceptions of the environment and purporting a continuum of offender decision-making when interacting with this environment. Concepts relating to offender decision-making that have relevance for geographic profiling include the least-effort principle (that offenders will be more likely to act on the first, or closest, opportunity) and the idea of a buffer zone (that offenders will not want to commit crimes too close to home). Taken together, these concepts suggest that there will be a constant tension between the offender's desire to divert attention away from his/her home base and his/her desire to journey no further than necessary to commit crime. Thus the offender will be periodically conducting cost-benefit analyses, the mechanics of which often occur at a subconscious level, when encountering potential victims at a particular time and place.

The primary tenet of routine activity theory is that an offender and victim must intersect in time and space for a crime to occur and that this intersection generally occurs as a result of both parties' non-criminal spatial activity (Brantingham and Brantingham 1981; Felson 2002; Tita and Griffiths 2005). Consequently, routine activity theory establishes a relationship between non-criminal and criminal spatial patterns, thus providing the geographic profiling method with a rationale for inferring non-criminal spatial behaviour (e.g. a home base) on the basis of the analysis of criminal spatial behaviour. This theory also stresses the importance of using the routine activities of the victim to help establish offender search patterns, resulting in possible combinations of offender, victim and environment interactions.

Brantingham and Brantingham's (1981, 1984) crime pattern theory has exerted the strongest influence over the geographic profiling process. The focus on the selection of crime sites and the relationship between these crime sites and the offender's home base or anchor point highlights that crime locations are not chosen randomly. The emphasis on an interaction between the offender's awareness space (or mental map of his/her spatial surroundings) and the distribution of suitable targets (target backcloth) was the fundamental building block for the development of geographic profiling techniques, providing 'a theoretical basis for the consistency and predictability in the offender/victim/environment paradigm' (Warren *et al.* 1998: 39). Geographic profiling represents an inversion of crime pattern theory whereby the possible journey-to-crime scenarios for every point on a map are evaluated with the end result being a spatial distribution of probabilities of an unknown offender's anchor point. The concept of awareness space further provides a link between the external and internal world of the offender, thereby allowing for the inference of offender decision-making on the basis of known crime site locations.

A process model of geographic profiling

Historically, geographic profiling has developed in the context of the police need to prioritise suspects in the effort to solve serious violent crimes, typically of a high-profile and/or sexual nature. This need typically arises when an investigation is focused on a probable series or pattern of crimes,[1] when such crimes involve offenders and victims with no previous relationship (stranger crimes), and when traditional investigative techniques have been unsuccessful. It is not uncommon for serial stranger crime inquiries to suffer from information overload, amassing hundreds or even thousands of suspects (Rossmo 2000). The criminal investigative process involves two stages: (1) finding the offender; and (2) proving guilt (Rossmo 2006). Geographic profiling can assist in the first stage of this process through the function of suspect or area prioritisation, thereby assisting in the task of information management. The methodology is not designed to solve crimes; that can only be done through a witness, confession, or physical evidence.

Figure 8.1 presents a model of the geographic profiling process. To be able to confidently apply geographic profiling techniques one has to be reasonably certain that most of the crimes being analysed were all committed by the same individual(s). Thus, the initial practical step taken when preparing a geographic profile is to assess and/or develop a linkage analysis. This is followed by the determination of offender–victim–environment interaction through information gathering and mathematical/statistical analyses of the crime locations, the end result being the delineation of a geographic search pattern which has varying probabilities of containing the offender's anchor point or 'base of operations' (i.e. the location from which their criminal search originates). The analysis and interpretation of the offender's spatio-temporal behaviour is underpinned by an environmental criminology framework, thereby guiding hypotheses regarding offender's non-criminal spatio-temporal behaviour and the identification of environmental factors which may exert an influence on offender behaviour. The results of these analyses are collated in the form of a geographic profile – a written report containing both quantitative (usually in the form of colour probability maps) and qualitative components.

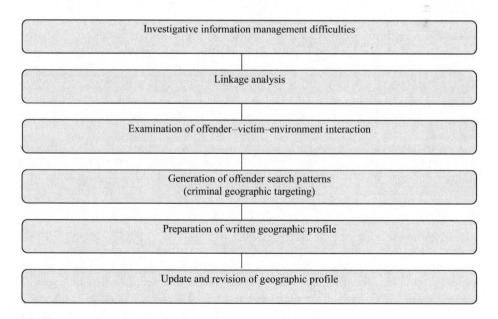

Figure 8.1 A process model of geographic profiling

Linkage analysis

Geographic profiling is reliant on a proper linkage analysis, also known as comparative case analysis. This should be based on physical evidence, victimology, known offender characteristics and the sequence of behavioural events in time and space (e.g. see Hazelwood and Warren 2003). Obviously, the presence of physical evidence at crime scenes offers the most definitive way to link crimes together. However, some crime scenes offer little forensically, necessitating the need to use behavioural analysis to determine connections. The essential aim of linkage analysis is therefore to establish with some certainty which crimes are linked while minimising the background noise created by other similar offences.

A behavioural analysis of the crimes involves examination of *modus operandi* – the method of committing a crime – and unique signature aspects of crime (for a thorough description of signature behaviour see Douglas and Munn 1992; Keppel 1995). This process involves comparing similarities and differences across related and unrelated crimes. Crimes can be reliably linked when they contain more key similarities to each other than differences.

Moreover, crimes that tend to co-occur in time and space tend to be more closely related, which means that linkage analysis will tend to be more successful with crimes that occur in close proximity to one another. For example, recent research found the analysis of geo-spatial data was the most important tool used to link burglary offences, followed by the analysis of temporal data (Bennell and Canter 2002; Bennell and Jones 2005; Goodwill and Alison 2005).

Computerised crime management systems can greatly aid in the identification and linking of serial crimes. Such systems are becoming increasingly prevalent in police departments, and those systems with the capacity to search a large database of crimes on the basis of *modus operandi* have provided the most success (Brahan *et al.* 1998; Ribaux and Margot 1999). While a whole chapter in itself could be devoted to the process of linkage analysis, the key points that have major relevance for the geographic profiling process are that a series of crimes has been established with some confidence (preferably at least five separate offences), that a thorough investigation of *modus operandi* enhances information sharing and identifies common suspects (Rossmo 2000), the recognition that *modus operandi* can change over time, and the utility of integrating automated linkage analysis systems with geographic profiling methodologies.

Examination of offender–victim–environment interaction

The spatial analysis of a series of crimes is what most people associate with the term 'geographic profiling' and indeed comprises the core aspect of the analysis phase. The overall purpose is to determine the offender's likely anchor point by working backwards from the known crime locations to develop an offender search pattern. The type and nature of the spatial data is analysed on the basis of five main parameters specified by environmental criminology theory. According to Lopez (2005), four of these parameters relate to the offender's awareness space: range of operation; distance decay; buffer zone; and travel direction. The final element concerns the offender's opportunity space or target backcloth. Crime sites can contain information about the offender, the victim, and the nature of their interactions, as well as hinting at an unknown offender's non-criminal spatial environment. Crime sites include initial contact, primary crime and post-offence locations.

The preparation of a geographic profile requires the collection and analysis of a diverse range of data, including case file information, a behavioural profile (if available), data on the geography of criminal events (such as crime scene photographs and on-site observations), interviews with police personnel involved with the case, socio-demographic information, transportation hubs and crime statistics relating to the areas in which the offences occurred (see Holmes and Rossmo 1996). These data are not only used to guide the mathematical/statistical modelling component of geographic profiling but also to inform the qualitative analysis, illustrating the ways in which environmental criminology theories may apply to a specific case. For example, knowledge of the above information helps the profiler to determine the relevance of the crime locations to the offender, the role that opportunity space plays in the offences, and the way in which the offender is relating to his or her socio-spatial environment in order to successfully commit his or her offences.

A particular crime site is at some point chosen by the offender for a specific purpose. Crimes are more likely to occur when an offender's awareness space converges with suitable targets. Offenders may then move outward in their search for more targets, with the number of interactions decreasing with distance. The crime location set displayed by a given offender provides information about the way in which he/she operates, the victim/target search process, and methods used to facilitate the commission of the crime. The connections between different crime sites provide further clues as to the offender's mobility and offence skill level. More complex combinations of crime location sets tend to point to a more mobile offender who displays behavioural consistency in the way he/she commits his/her crimes (LeBeau 1985; Rossmo 1997). Different crime sites also differ in their importance and the extent to which they may be known to police. For example, in a murder, while the body dump site is usually known to investigators, the encounter site may have to be inferred.

The choice of crime locations will also be influenced by the opportunity structure afforded to the offender, which in turn is affected by the non-criminal nodes, pathways and edges created by the natural or built environment (Brantingham and Brantingham 1993; LaGrange 1999). Crime locations themselves are embedded in a broader socio-demographic environment whereby different areas will vary in their availability and attractiveness of targets. The spatial opportunity structure generally includes target availability, socio-demographics and temporal factors. The target distribution has a strong influence on the offender's range of operation. Generally, uniform target distributions surrounding crime sites may lead the geographic profiler to an analysis of the offender's activity space to derive clues about his or her anchor point. A non-uniform target distribution, on the other hand, suggests that offending may be more strongly influenced by the opportunity space rather than the offender's activity space (Rengert 1991). In support of this, recent research suggests that in areas where targets cluster more strongly, including a measure of opportunity space may improve the accuracy of geographic profiling techniques (Bernasco 2007). Moreover, research has found that victims of serious crime differ from non-victims on measures of macro-level neighbourhood structures (Dobrin *et al.* 2005). An analysis of victimology therefore guides the accuracy of quantitative and qualitative components of a geographic profile.

Understanding the offender–victim–environment interaction aids the geographic profiler in determining the hunting style of an unknown offender. The ways in which offenders search for victims influence the distributions of crime locations and therefore guide the geographic profiling process. The hunting style of a given offender is based on consideration of four victim search methods (hunter, poacher, troller and trapper) and three victim attack methods (raptor, stalker and ambusher). The reader is referred to Rossmo (2000) for a detailed explanation of hunting styles. It is also important at this point to emphasise that geographic profiling may not be appropriate for every type of crime (e.g. offences committed by 'poachers/commuters'.)[2]

Generation of offender search patterns

The spatial analysis of crime sites constitutes the core analytical component of geographic profiling. This process combines centrographic and journey-to-crime principles, guided by environmental criminology, to derive a subset of geographic space which has the greatest probability of containing an unknown offender's anchor point. The term 'criminal geographic targeting' (CGT) was first used to describe the statistical algorithm guiding the spatial analysis of crime sites (Rossmo 1995, 1997, 2000). CGT essentially divides the hunting area into a grid of 40,000 pixels and calculates the likelihood that each individual pixel contains the offender's anchor point. It is based on the Brantingham and Brantingham (1981) model of crime site selection and on routine activity theory, and uses a distance decay function (DDF) to simulate journey-to-crime behaviour. The algorithm was patented and is incorporated into the Rigel geographic profiling software produced by Environmental Criminology Research Inc. (ECRI).

The Rigel software essentially follows a five-stage process. First, the linked crime locations are used to delineate the offender's hunting area. Second, Manhattan distances (orthogonal distances measured along a street grid) between each grid pixel in the hunting area and each crime location are calculated. Third, these distances are incorporated into a DDF-based algorithm (e.g. CGT) to produce likelihood values. Four, the separate values for the different crime locations are combined to produce an overall score for each pixel in the hunting area. Higher scores indicate a greater probability the pixel contains the offender's anchor point. Finally, these scores are then represented in a both two- and three-dimensional colour probability maps which are used to geographically focus police efforts.

An important step in the profiling process is the development of a valid scenario (i.e. the optimal subset of crime sites to be profiled). Practical rules have been developed to filter out most non-independent crime sites, usually a function of proximity in time and space. Rigel includes the use of these rules in the form of an expert system.

Preparation of a geographic profile

The qualitative component of geographic profiling involves inferring the offender's inner world (e.g. mental map) through analysis of the spatial behaviour present in a series of crimes. The areas that need to be considered in preparing a geographic profile include: (a) the crime locations; (b) offender type; (c) hunting style; (d) target backcloth; (e) arterial roads and highways; (f) bus stops and train stations; (g) physical and psychological boundaries; (h) zoning and land use; (i) neighbourhood demographics; (j) victim routine activities; (k) singularities; and (l) displacement. The method thus attempts to use environmental criminology to provide a more complete account of offender behaviour.

A geographic profile is of little value unless it can be acted upon by police. The written component therefore contains suggestions for modification and design of investigative strategies (see Table 8.1).

Table 8.1 Investigative strategies

Investigative strategy	Description
Suspect prioritisation	Prioritise individuals for follow-up investigation
Patrol saturation and static stakeouts	Basis for directed patrols; effective for hot time periods; stakeouts stationed in crucial areas
Police information systems	Cross-referencing with information in computerised police databases such as ViCLAS
Outside agency databases	Parole/probation offices; mental health professionals; commercial agencies
Zip/postal code prioritisation	Prioritised and used to conduct searches and rankings of address databases; cross-referencing with DMV
Task force computer systems	Cross-referencing with major enquiry databases
Neighbourhood canvasses	Optimising door-to-door and grid searches; information mail-outs
Sex offender register	Cross-referencing with addresses of registered sex offenders
Peak-of-tension polygraphy	Searching areas for victim remains
Bloodings	Geographically focuses DNA testing of potential suspects
Trial expert evidence	The probability of congruence of a series of crimes can be assessed

Evaluation of a geographic profile

It is important for any methodology to meet three criteria: validity, reliability and utility. For a geographic profile to be considered valid, the score associated with the offender's residence should be higher than the scores in the remainder of the grid. Performance is therefore measured by examining the ratio of the total number of pixels with equal or higher scores to the total number of pixels in the hunting area (i.e. 40,000). This hit score percentage (HS%) therefore represents the percentage of the total area that needs to be searched before locating the offender's residence.

The geographic profiling process is limited in a number of ways. First, geographic profiling algorithms are not designed to locate offender residences outside of the hunting area of the crimes, and therefore are not usually appropriate for poaching/commuting offenders.[3] Second, while the rational choice model purports rational offender decision-making, the randomness inherent in human behaviour is emphasised in cases involving only a small number of locations. CGT performance therefore increases (up to a point) with the number of crime sites. The model was tested using Monte Carlo simulations and the subsequent results demonstrated that at least six crime locations were necessary for hit percentages under 10 per cent. The computerisation and mathematical simplicity of the CGT model contribute to confidence in its reliability. Standardised training, testing and certification help minimise the subjectivity present in the choice in crime locations and other qualitative aspects of geographic profiling.

Training

There are two types of geographic profiling training. The International Criminal Investigative Analysis Fellowship (ICIAF) programme provides comprehensive training to members of large police agencies wishing to establish their own geographic profiling capability. It covers training in all crime types including murder, rape and bombing. Suitable candidates start upon a year of study under the tutelage of a mentor who must be a fully qualified geographic profiler. The training programme is divided into four blocks: (1) probability, statistics and computer systems; (2) violent and sexual crime, and offence linkage; (3) violent sexual offenders and criminal profiling; and (4) quantitative spatial techniques and geographic profiling. The first three blocks are done through distance education, under the supervision of the understudy's mentor. The fourth block (16 weeks) is a residency at the mentor's agency, involving both reviews of previous files and casework in active investigations. To successfully conclude the programme, the understudy must pass a qualifying examination at the end of the training period.

The Geographic Profiling Analysis (GPA) training programme was initiated to make the methodology more accessible to local law enforcement agencies by teaching crime analysts and detectives how to geoprofile property crimes (Weiss and Davis 2004). The training involves both classroom courses and field evaluation/mentorship. The GPA curriculum consists of two one-week courses. Week one, 'The Geography of Crime', provides an overview of environmental criminology, the geography of crime, crime linkage, and practical aspects of geographic profiling for property crime. Week two, 'Rigel Analyst', covers the use of the software, developing a geographic profile, casework exercises and report preparation. GPA students are typically crime analysts and property crime investigators (Velarde 2004). Approximately 400 people, representing 200 police agencies from nine countries, have now been trained in geographic profiling analysis. GPA training is currently available internationally through various universities and police agencies.

Case study

For several years the City of Irvine in Orange County, California, suffered from a series of residential break-ins, mainly in middle- and upper-scale neighbourhoods. A single offender was believed responsible, but various approaches used by the Irvine Police Department (IPD) were unsuccessful and the crimes continued. IPD's Special Investigations Unit (SIU) finally decided to employ a proactive approach, combining geographic profiling with crime forecasting and directed surveillance (see Rossmo and Velarde 2007).

The series involved 42 residential burglaries that had occurred over the past 24 months (see Figure 8.2). The offender exhibited a consistent pattern of behaviour. He only chose single-family homes, preferably those that backed on to parks or green belts, allowing him to observe potential targets while

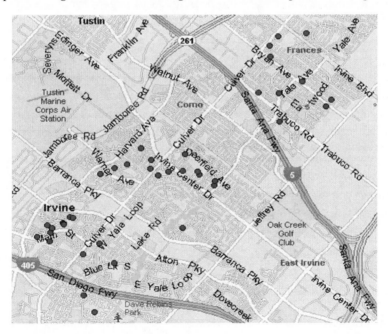

Figure 8.2 Location of 42 residential burglaries over a 24-month period

still on public property. His exit was always at the rear. If the back fence was high, the offender placed a chair next to it. Stolen property was limited to cash, jewellery and easily carried items. It was apparent the offender was a professional burglar.

Rather than attempt to locate the offender in the process of committing his next burglary, an act that typically takes only a very short time, SIU decided to search for him as he hunted for his next target, a process that takes much longer. Crime forecasting predicted the next burglary would be on a Friday, Saturday or Sunday, between 5 and 10. The SIU then had to determine where in the city to deploy its limited surveillance resources; as the crimes covered 44 square kilometres, a geographic focus was necessary.

A geographic profile was prepared which identified a peak area 0.6 square kilometres in size. The anchor point for most criminal searches is the offender's home. But for poachers or commuters, the search base is somewhere else. Irvine is a wealthy community, and its professional criminals come from outside. The neighbourhood demographics in the peak geoprofile area supported the theory of a non-local offender. It was therefore concluded that the geoprofile outlined the area where the burglar began his hunt after his commute to Irvine.

SIU surveillance teams were deployed in the peak area of the geographic profile during the days and times forecasted. The strategy was to identify vehicles by licence plate number. The numbers could then to be used to identify outside individuals for follow-up investigation from California Department of Motor Vehicles (DMV) records.

On the first evening of an operation, an automobile was seen driving in and out of a neighbourhood in the peak area of the geoprofile (see Figure 8.3).

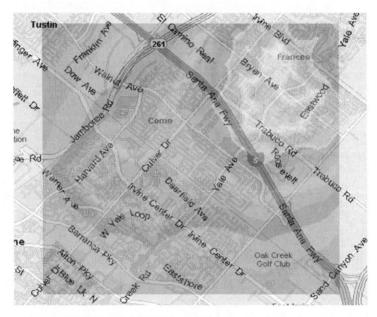

Figure 8.3 Geoprofile based on burglary pattern

The licence plate number was recorded and a subsequent DMV record check revealed the vehicle was a car rental. The driver was Raymond Lopez, an ex-convict living in Los Angeles County. According to the car rental company, Lopez had been renting vehicles weekly for the past 20 years. Lopez was surveilled casing other houses, and after a DNA match to some of the crime scenes, he was arrested.

Detectives seized over half a million dollars' worth of gold, rare coins and jewellery from his home and a nearby pawnshop. The pawnshop owner told police that associates of Lopez had regularly pawned property for the past 20 years. Lopez was responsible for 139 burglaries committed between 2003 and 2005 alone, with a total property loss in excess of $2,500,000. He pleaded guilty to 14 felony counts and was sentenced to 13 years in state prison.

Conclusion

Geographic profiling uses both qualitative and quantitative methods to infer the spatial behaviour of an unknown offender from an analysis of the offender's search and attack patterns. CGT is a statistical process that delineates the most likely area in which the offender's anchor point may be found. Geographic profiling relies on a reliable linkage analysis, and attempts to integrate various sources of geographic information to provide a picture of the spatial interaction between offenders and victims in producing crime. There is sufficient research and operational evidence to justify the use of geographic profiling (Canter *et al.* 2000; Rossmo 1995, 2001, 2005; Rossmo and Velarde 2007; Sarangi and Youngs 2006; Velarde 2005). While it represents an innovative application of environmental criminology theory, it is hoped that geographic profiling will become a standard investigative tool in the hunt for serial criminals.

Notes

1 While geographic profiling may also be useful in examining a single crime containing multiple geographic locations, the focus of this chapter is on serial crime.
2 Studies on the behaviour of serial criminals have found support for a dichotomous classification of offender spatial behaviour into a 'hunting/marauder' style (searching in the area around the home) or a 'poaching/commuter' style (travelling into other neighbourhoods to commit crimes).
3 In the case example that follows, however, geographic profiling was successfully used to arrest a professional burglar poacher who commuted into the target city from his home about 50 kilometres away. The case illustrates the importance of both proper training in the methodology and consideration of the full range of environmental factors in a crime series.

References

Baldwin, J. and Bottoms, A.E. (1976) *The Urban Criminal: A study in Sheffield*. London: Tavistock.

Bennell, C. and Canter, D.V. (2002) 'Linking Commercial Burglaries by *Modus Operandi*: Tests Using Regression and ROC Analysis', *Science and Justice*, 42: 153–64.

Bennell, C. and Jones, N.J. (2005) 'Between a ROC and a Hard Place: A Method for Linking Serial Burglaries by Modus Operandi', *Journal of Investigative Psychology and Offender Profiling*, 2: 23–41.

Bernasco, W. (2007) 'The Usefulness of Measuring Spatial Opportunity Structures for Tracking Down Offenders: A Theoretical Analysis of Geographic Offender Profiling Using Simulation Studies', *Psychology, Crime & Law*, 13: 155–71.

Brahan, J.W., Lam, K.P., Chan, H. and Leung, W. (1998) 'AICAMS: Artificial Intelligence Crime Analysis and Management System', *Knowledge-Based Systems*, 11: 355–61.

Brantingham, P.L. and Brantingham, P.J. (1981) 'Notes on the Geometry on Crime', in P.J. Brantingham and P.L. Brantingham (eds) *Environmental Criminology*. Beverly Hills: Sage, pp. 27–54.

Brantingham, P.J. and Brantingham, P.L. (1984) *Patterns in Crime*. New York: Macmillan.

Brantingham, P.L. and Brantingham, P.J. (1993) 'Notes, Paths and Edges: Considerations on the Complexity of Crime and the Physical Environment', *Journal of Environmental Psychology*, 13: 3–28.

Canter, D.V., Coffey, T., Huntley, M. and Missen, C. (2000) 'Predicting Serial Killers' Home Base Using a Decision Support System', *Journal of Quantitative Criminology*, 16: 457–78.

Dobrin, A., Lee, D. and Price, J. (2005) 'Neighbourhood Structure Differences Between Homicide Victims and Non-victims', *Journal of Criminal Justice*, 33: 137–43.

Douglas, J.E. and Munn, C. (1992) 'Violent Crime Scene Analysis: Modus Operandi, Signature, and Staging', *FBI Law Enforcement Bulletin*, 61(2): 1–10.

Felson, M. (2002). *Crime and Everyday Life*, 3rd edn. Thousand Oaks, CA: Sage.

Gabor, T. and Gottheil, E. (1984) 'Offender Characteristics and Spatial Mobility: An Empirical Study and Some Policy Implications', *Canadian Journal of Criminology*, 26: 267–81.

Goodwill, A.M. and Alison, L.J. (2005) 'Sequential Angulation, Spatial Dispersion and Consistency of Distance Attack Patterns from Home in Serial Murder, Rape and Burglary', *Psychology, Crime & Law*, 11: 161–76.

Hazelwood, R.R. and Warren, J.I. (2003) 'Linkage Analysis: Modus Operandi, ritual, and Signature in Serial Sex Crime', *Aggression and Violent Behaviour*, 8: 587–98.

Hicks, S.J. and Sales, B.D. (2006) *Criminal Profiling: Developing an Effective Science and Practice*. Washington, DC: American Psychological Association.

Holmes, R.M. and Rossmo, D.K. (1996) 'Geography, Profiling, and Predatory Criminals', in R.H. Holmes and S.T. Holmes (eds) *Profiling Violent Crimes: An Investigative Tool*, 2nd edn. Thousand Oaks, CA: Sage, pp. 148–65.

Keppel, R.D. (1995) 'Signature Murders: A Report of Several Related Cases', *Journal of Forensic Sciences*, 40: 670–4.

LeBeau, J.L. (1985) 'Some Problems with Measuring and Describing Rape Presented by the Serial Offender', *Justice Quarterly*, 2: 385–98.

López, M.J.J. (2005) 'The Spatial Behavior of Residential Burglars', in A. van Nes (ed.) *Proceedings of the 5th International Space Syntax Symposium*, TU Delft, Techne Press, Delft (www.spacesyntax.tudelft.nl/media/Long%20papers%20I/manuellopez.pdf).

Rhodes, W.M. and Conly, C. (1981) 'Crime and Mobility: An Empirical Study', in P.J. Brantingham and P.L. Brantingham (eds) *Environmental Criminology*. Beverly Hills: Sage, pp. 16–88.

Ribaux, O. and Margot, P. (1999) 'Inference Structures for Crime Analysis and Intelligence: The Example of Burglary Using Forensic Science Data', *Forensic Science International*, 100: 193–210.

Rossmo, D.K. (1995) 'Geographic Profiling: Target Patterns of Serial Murderers', unpublished doctoral dissertation. Burnaby, BC: Simon Fraser University.

Rossmo, D.K. (1997) 'Geographic Profiling', in J.L. Jackson and D.A. Bekerian (eds) *Offender Profiling: Theory, Research and Practice*. Chichester: John Wiley, pp. 159–75.

Rossmo, D.K. (2000) *Geographic Profiling*. Boca Raton, FL: CRC Press.

Rossmo, D.K. (2001) 'Evaluation of Geographic Profiling Search Strategies', paper presented at the meeting of the American Society of Criminology, Atlanta, GA (November).

Rossmo, D.K. (2005) 'Geographic Heuristics or Shortcuts to Failure?: Response to Snook et al', *Applied Cognitive Psychology*, 19: 651–4.

Rossmo, D.K. (2006) 'Geographic Profiling in Cold Case Investigations', in R. Walton (ed.) *Cold Case Homicides: Practical Investigative Techniques*. Boca Raton, FL: CRC Press, pp. 537–60.

Rossmo, D.K. and Velarde, L. (2007) 'Geographic Profiling Analysis: Principles, Methods, and Applications', in S. Chainey and S. Tompson (eds) *Crime Mapping Case Studies*. Chichester: John Wiley and Sons, pp. 35–43.

Sarangi, S. and Youngs, D.E. (2006) 'Spatial Patterns of Indian Serial Burglars with Relevance to Geographical Profiling', *Journal of Investigative Psychology and Offender Profiling*, 3: 105–15.

Tita, G. and Griffiths, E. (2005) 'Travelling to Violence: The Case for a Mobility-based Spatial Typology of Homicide', *Journal of Research in Crime and Delinquency*, 42: 275–308.

van Koppen, P.J. and de Keijser, J.W. (1997) 'Desisting Distance Decay: On the Aggregation of Individual Crime Trips', *Criminology*, 35: 505–15.

Velarde, L. (2004) 'Applying Geographic Profiling to Property Crimes: The Geographic Profiling Analyst Program', paper presented at the Crime Mapping Research Conference, Boston, MA (April).

Velarde, L. (2005) 'Accuracy and Value of Geographic Profiling in an Operational Context', paper presented at the Crime Mapping Research Conference, Savannah, GA (September).

Warren, J.I., Reboussin, R., Hazelwood, R.R., Cummings, A., Gibbs, N. and Trumbetta, S. (1998) 'Crime Scene and Distance Correlates of Serial Rape', *Journal of Quantitative Criminology*, 14: 35–59.

Weiss, J. and Davis, M. (2004) 'Geographic Profiling Finds Serial Criminals', *Law and Order*, December: 32, 34–38.

Part Three

Preventing and Controlling Crime

9. Crime prevention through environmental design

Paul Cozens

The history of CPTED – major contributors

From early prehistoric cave-dwellers to medieval and modern cities, human settlements have always attempted to provide for the safety, security and well-being of their citizens in terms of design and their location close to water, food and other vital resources. As technology evolved, settlements adapted to reflect new and emerging threats. Initially, topography (e.g. higher ground) and landscaping (e.g. ditches and mounds) were used in early hill forts and a variety of fortification designs for castles (e.g. walls and moats) occurred throughout the Middle Ages and thereafter. In England in 1285 King Edward I enacted the Statute of Winchester to remove areas of concealment provided by ditches and vegetation along highways. Landowners were responsible for removing vegetation and ditches and were also held liable for crimes that may occur due to their negligence in not removing concealment opportunities. The gates of walled cities were also ordered to be closed from sunset to sunrise (Stubbs 1903). Such developments demonstrate that using environmental design to influence human behaviour, and particularly security issues and crime, has a long tradition.

CPTED (pronounced *sep-ted*), also known as 'designing out crime', is an acronym for crime prevention through environmental design, which asserts that 'the proper design and effective use of the built environment can lead to a reduction in the fear and incidence of crime, and an improvement in the quality of life' (Crowe 2000: 46). CPTED is a multi-disciplinary approach, drawing on criminology, planning and environmental psychology, and is specifically located within the field of environmental criminology, deriving theoretical support from opportunity theory such as rational choice theory (see Clarke, Chapter 10, this volume) and routine activities theory (see Felson, Chapter 4, this volume). CPTED is concerned with identifying conditions of the physical and social environment that provide opportunities for criminality, and the modification of those conditions in order to reduce such opportunities (Brantingham and Faust 1976). Its objective is to proactively prevent crime, as compared to the reactive (and often ineffective) strategies of most criminal justice systems (police, courts and correctional facilities) (Wallis 1980).

The term CPTED was originally coined by Jeffery (1971). Jeffery (1976) argued that three key sources can be traced for CPTED. The first is from the academic community, by way of a series of books on environmental design, the geography of crime and the spatial analysis of crime. The second is from Britain, where since the early 1950s the British police have been involved in crime prevention through the manipulation of the physical environment. The third source is from architects, particularly Oscar Newman (1973). Outlined below are the various commentators, theorists and researchers who have contributed significantly towards the development of CPTED in the latter part of the twentieth and early twenty-first centuries.

Wood – Housing Design: A Social Theory

The idea of CPTED began taking shape when Elizabeth Wood (1961) developed security guidelines while working with the Chicago Housing Authority in the 1960s (Colquhoun 2004). An American sociologist, she focused on public housing units and on using physical improvements to enhance visibility. This was applied to the location of seating for adults around child play areas and in entrances to large blocks of flats used as lobbies, reception areas or meeting places. Wood's particular focus was teenagers and their lack of facilities. Somewhat ahead of her time, she recommended the use of vandal-proof materials and designs for facilities, and she encouraged the use of a resident caretaker to liaise with housing management. Her approach suggested that design and 'surveillability' needed to be considered simultaneously.

Jacobs – The Death and Life of Great American Cities

Jacobs' work was an indictment of urban planning that had developed after World War Two. She criticised the separation and zoning of land uses in America, arguing for more diverse and mixed land uses. Following observations in Boston, Jacobs (1961) recommended the clear demarcation between public and private space, and the clarification of the function of space to promote 'territoriality' and a sense of ownership of space by residents. She introduced the concept of 'eyes on the street' (surveillance) whereby residents have enhanced opportunities to 'self-police' the streets in housing configurations, which are oriented to face each other and provide intervisibility of properties and of the streetscape. She observed that busy streets with a diverse mix of land uses provided more 'eyes on the street' and this could potentially reduce opportunities for crime. However, although Jacobs' ideas were innovative for their time and have significantly influenced CPTED and planning policy and practice over the years, her observations were primarily anecdotal and were highly specific to inner-city areas of one large American city. Crucially, she explicitly advised against applying these findings to small cities and suburbs.

Angel – Discouraging Crime Through City Planning

Angel (1968) refined some of Jacobs' assertions and introduced the concept of crime as a function of land-use intensity (see Figure 9.1). He argued that low land-use intensity resulted in low levels of crime since there are limited opportunities for the offender (zone 1). As land-use intensity increases, the number of potential victims increases sufficiently to attract offenders, but there are insufficient 'eyes on the street' acting as guardians to potentially discourage offending. This scenario was identified as the 'critical intensity zone' (zone 2) and according to Angel is when most crime takes place. When land-use intensity increases beyond this threshold, sufficient numbers of guardians are present to deter offenders (zone 3).

Jeffery

The originator of the term 'crime prevention through environmental design' was criminologist C. Ray Jeffery (1969, 1971, 1999). He argued that sociologists had overstated the social causes of crime, neglecting both biological and environmental determinants. He proposed a broad, holistic, systems-based approach to criminology drawing on social, behavioural, political, psychological and biological systems. He argued that the internal environment of the brain was as important as the external physical environment in determining criminality. However, Jeffery (1999) has acknowledged that it has been Oscar Newman's ideas that have been largely adopted in crime prevention and by academics.

Newman – Defensible Space, People and the Violent City

Fundamental to CPTED is the work of Oscar Newman and his concept of 'defensible space' (1973). Newman highlighted the problem of rising levels of crime in urban America and the limited and ineffective responses to the problem that suggested a pessimistic future. This was emphasised particularly

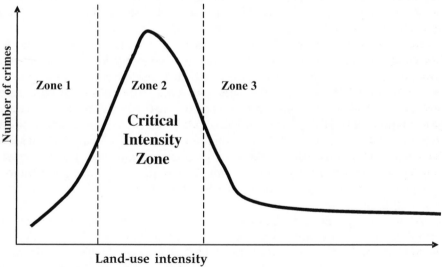

Figure 9.1. Crime as a function of land-use intensity
Source: Adapted from Angel (1968: 16).

by the exodus of a significant proportion of the middle-class community out of the (criminal) inner city to the (law-abiding) suburbs. As a teacher at Washington University in the 1960s, he observed the decline of Pruitt-Igoe, a high-rise (eleven-storey) public housing development of 2,740 units in St Louis, subsequently demolished within ten years of construction. The design followed the planning principles of Le Corbusier and the International Congress of Modern Architects. However, the 'river of trees' and abundance of undesignated communal interior and exterior grounds unintentionally became the focus of litter, graffiti, vandalism and crime. Occupancy levels did not exceed 60 per cent and the residents were predominantly single-parent, welfare families. Newman observed the better-functioning Carr Square development located adjacent to Pruitt-Igoe, which was inhabited by residents of similar social characteristics but was older, smaller and designed as rows of houses. It was fully occupied and relatively trouble-free and Newman implicated the role of design in explaining the difference between these two contrasting residential developments.

In 1960s America, distressing increases in urban crime rates encouraged the President and Congress to pass the Safe Streets Act 1968, which subsequently provided funding for research into new crime prevention techniques. This funding underpinned the research that is documented in Newman's *Defensible Space*. Newman, an architect, claimed: 'this book is about an alternative, about a means for restructuring the residential environments of our cities so they can again become livable and controlled not by police, but by a community of people sharing a common terrain' (1973: 2). *Defensible Space* promotes the use of design to enhance territoriality and promote a 'sense of ownership' by delineating between private and public space using real and symbolic barriers. Building and site design to increase surveillance and 'eyes on the street' and the image of housing were also central to defensible space. The wider environment or 'geographical juxtaposition' was also important to these ideas. The concepts of defensible space are discussed in more detail later in this chapter.

To test his ideas on defensible space, the social housing projects of Brownsville and Van Dyke in New York (considered similar, in social terms) were compared and analysed with regard to recorded crime rates. Van Dyke was a high-rise block (fourteen storeys) while Brownsville buildings were relatively low-level (six storeys). According to the New York City Housing Association (NYCHA) police statistics, Van Dyke project experienced a crime rate of 51.4 per 1,000, while the rate for Brownsville was 28.2 per 1,000. Newman interpreted the higher crime rates in the Van Dyke project as support for his theory. The influence of the environmental design of buildings is suggested as a causal factor to explain the differing crime rates in the two housing projects.

At the time Newman's study was considered by many to be relatively scientific and some have suggested that Newman's work operationalised Jacobs' themes (Jeffrey and Zahm 1993). However, *Defensible Space* was different in that it both highlighted problems and suggested solutions in a pragmatic and scientific approach, uncommon for the period. Nevertheless,

Newman's theory is not without its detractors and critics, particularly for neglecting the role of social factors (Merry 1981; Smith 1986, 1987; Taylor *et al.* 1980) and for making unjustified and unscientific generalisations (Adams 1973; Bottoms 1974; Hillier 1973; Kaplan 1973; Mawby 1977; Mayhew 1979). Later publications by Newman (1980; Newman and Franck 1982) acknowledged that the characteristics of the residents were stronger predictors of crime levels than design features.

Brantingham and Brantingham

Simultaneous to developments in defensible space, Paul and Patricia Brantingham (1975) explored the distribution of offences in Tallahassee, Florida, revealing considerable differences between and within neighbourhoods in terms of levels of recorded burglary. Border blocks, or 'the skin' of a neighbourhood, had higher levels of burglary than inner areas. They also developed theories to explain the search and selection processes that burglars may use and they developed crime pattern theory, which considers how people and objects associated with crime move about in space and time (see Brantingham and Brantingham, Chapter 5, this volume). These ideas stimulated the emergence of environmental criminology (Brantingham and Brantingham 1981, 1991) where CPTED and defensible space are located.

UK Home Office – Designing Out Crime

In the UK, escalating crime levels and the issue of 'problem', 'difficult', or 'run-down' local authority housing estates became a political issue during the 1970s. The Home Office has conducted many studies since the 1970s into how specific crimes can be prevented. Rock (1988) claims Newman's defensible space galvanised many of the responses since there was an affinity between his ideas and those being developed at the Home Office Research Unit (Clarke 1980, 1982; Poyner 1983). While at the Home Office, Clarke and Mayhew (*Designing Out Crime*, 1980) formulated many of the early principles of situational crime prevention, which extends beyond environmental design to focus on specific crimes and issues relating to the management and use of space (see Clarke, Chapter 10, this volume). In *Situational Crime Prevention: Successful Case Studies* (Clarke 1992, 1997), Clarke presents opportunity-reducing techniques aimed at increasing the risk and effort while reducing the rewards, excuses and provocations associated with a specific offence.

Merry and Atlas

Merry (1981) identified 'undefended space', where cultural and social factors reduce the likelihood for resident action and self-policing to such an extent that 'defensible' space is not actively or routinely defended by residents. Social conditions may nurture fear, reduce the inclination to intervene and result in the withdrawal of the individual into the home, which becomes heavily fortified, resulting in undefended space. Crucially, it is not just town planners, designers and police officers who have successfully used the principles of defensible space. Atlas (1991: 65) observed how 'offensible space' may exist where drug dealers and criminals utilise CPTED principles to create safe space within and from which they may carry out their criminal activities protected from detection by CPTED principles. The concept of 'indefensible space', which is incapable of being defended, has also been raised (Cozens *et al.* 2002) and refers to spatial conditions such as extreme urban decay, urban riot and war.

Wilson and Kelling – 'broken windows'

Perhaps one of the most influential theories to be developed within the confines of CPTED is Wilson and Kelling's 'broken windows' thesis (1982). In summary, the theory contends that physical deterioration gives rise to safety concerns in residents and the community may cease to self-police an area. Further delinquency and vandalism occurs, along with increased deterioration and community withdrawal. Finally, potential offenders from elsewhere may then be attracted by the perceived vulnerability of the area. Therefore, what began as one broken window escalates to culminate in physical deterioration and social breakdown (see Wagers *et al.*, Chapter 13, this volume). However, in *Defensible Space*, Newman (1973) explicitly discusses the concept of image and milieu and recognises the importance of the management and maintenance of the urban fabric. The prompt removal of graffiti and rapid repair of vandalism are examples of routine maintenance and this is a significant aspect to the development of defensible space and CPTED ideas.

Coleman – Utopia on Trial

At the Land Use Research Unit (LURU), King's College, London, Alice Coleman's work was influential in the development of designing out crime principles. Her publication *Utopia on Trial: Vision and Reality in Planned Housing* (1985, 1990) was highly controversial, but significantly, received much support from the then Prime Minister Margaret Thatcher. The work of Coleman was perhaps most important in popularising and developing Newman's ideas in Britain. Her ideas were well received, stimulating the multi-million pound Design Improvement Controlled Experiment (DICE), carried out by the LURU to put her theories into practice. Coleman's study of 4,099 blocks of flats and maisonettes in London and Oxford reported sixteen design features (all linked to defensible space), which were problematic for residents and housing managers alike (see Table 9.1). She reported that for locations with concentrations of these defective design features, higher levels of litter, graffiti, vandalism, excrement and urination were found. The willingness of housing authorities to act on Coleman's findings and her ability to attract considerable financial resources for the DICE programme are testament to the influence of Newman's ideas. However, as with defensible space, criticism has focused upon a lack of scientific rigour and many reject her claims that design alone determined behaviour (Smith 1986).

Table 9.1 Coleman's sixteen features of design disadvantage

Overhead walkways	Corridors
Blocks per site	Vertical routes
Spatial organisation (amount and type of private/public space)	Interconnected exits
Access to the site	Stilts and garages
Play areas	Position of the entrance
Number of storeys in the block	Types of entrance
Number of dwellings in the block	Types of door
Dwellings served by each entrance	Storeys per dwelling

(*Source*: Adapted from Coleman 1990: 181–2)

Poyner and Webb – Crime-Free Housing

Poyner and Webb (1991) studied suburbs and new towns in Britain, and put forward twelve design features that were purported to reduce crime – all arguably variations or adaptations of defensible space (see Table 9.2). They argue that design modifications can reduce crime while Coleman (1998) opines that design can actually *cause* anti-social behaviour, and is therefore more deterministic in her opinion.

Crowe – Crime Prevention Through Environmental Design

Criminologist and former director of the American National Crime Prevention Institute (NCPI), Tim Crowe developed and conducted numerous CPTED training programmes providing a practical training tool for police. The publication of *Crime Prevention Through Environmental Design* (1991, 2000) provided a solid foundation for CPTED to progress into the 1990s and beyond.

Key concepts

As has been described, current models of CPTED evolved principally from Newman's model of defensible space. In this section the key concepts of defensible space and CPTED are discussed, with the connections between the two (based on Schneider and Kitchen 2002) summarised in Table 9.3.

Defensible space

Defensible space 'is a surrogate term for the range of mechanisms; real and symbolic barriers, strongly-defined areas of influence, and improved opportunities for surveillance; that combine to bring an environment under the control of its residents' (Newman 1973: 3). There are four elements of defensible space according to Newman, which act individually and in concert to assist in the creation of a safer urban environment (1973: 50):

Table 9.2 Requirements for 'crime-free' housing

Moderate locking security	On-curtilage car parking
Facing windows	A garage at the side of the house
High fences at the sides and the rear	Limit access roads
Front access to a secure yard	Avoid through pedestrian routes
Visible access for deliveries	Surveillance of access roads
Space at the front (garden)	Green spaces outside housing areas

(*Source*: Adapted from Poyner and Webb 1991: 97–101)

Table 9.3 Connections between defensible space and CPTED

Defensible space (Newman 1973)	CPTED (Crowe 2000)
Territoriality and boundary definition	Border definition of controlled space
Territoriality, boundary definition and access control	Clearly marked transitional zones
Surveillance and access control	Attention directed to gathering areas
Image and milieu and geographical juxtaposition	Place safe activities in unsafe areas
Image and milieu and geographical juxtaposition	Place unsafe activities in safe locations
Boundary definition and access control	Reduce use conflicts with natural barriers
Geographical juxtaposition	Better scheduling of space
Surveillance	Increased perception of natural surveillance in spaces by design
Geographical juxtaposition	Overcome distance and isolation by communication

(*Source*: Adapted from Schneider and Kitchen 2002: 102)

- the capacity of the physical environment to create perceived zones of territorial influence;
- the capacity of physical design to provide surveillance opportunities for residents and their agents;
- the capacity of design to influence the perception of a project's uniqueness, isolation, and stigma; and
- the influence of geographical juxtaposition with 'safe zones' on the security of adjacent areas.

The four elements of defensible space can translate the latent territoriality and sense of community of residents into a responsibility to secure and maintain a safe, productive and well-maintained neighbourhood.

For Newman, the impersonal character of large high-rise housing estates (see Figure 9.2) or their 'anonymity' affected crime rates. The number of people using the same entrance rather than population density *per se* and the number of storeys in the block were the important factors. Drawing on Jacobs' concept of delineating between private and public space, Newman (1973) claimed that the extent to which grounds and communal areas around buildings are shared and defended by different households also affects anonymity in that it increases as the number of shareholders increases (see Figure 9.3). Additionally, 'surveillance' (Jacobs' terminology referred to this as 'eyes on the street') involves visibility. The presence of internal corridors (invisible from the street) and the position of the entrance and building in relation to the street are important aspects. Finally, the existence and character of alternative escape routes can prompt criminals to become more audacious. Inter-accessible lifts, staircases and exits are identified and it is claimed that as these multiply, so does crime and the potential for crime. Where a block in Newman's study combined all three of these 'alienating mechanisms', crime would be at its highest. In addition, Newman went on to establish a causal link such that if one or more of the implicated design features was ameliorated, the crime rate would subsequently decline. The high-rise flats in Newman's study (1973) were characterised by a maze of angled corridors and

Figure 9.2　High-rise flats, Pendleton, Salford, UK
(*Source*: www.geograph.org.uk)

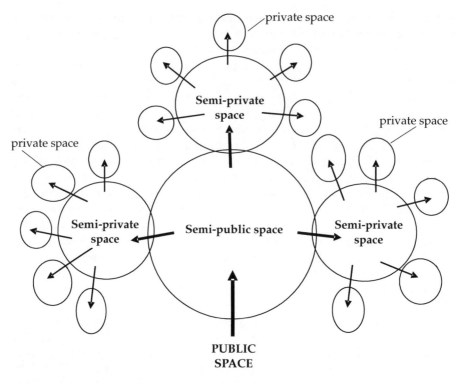

Figure 9.3 Hierarchy of defensible space
Note: Arrows indicate entrance and exit points at different levels of the hierarchy
(*Source*: Adapted from Newman, 1973: levels of the hierarchy).

public areas that provided limited opportunities for surveillance. Significantly, more than half of all crimes were committed in these less visible locations of concealment. The design of high-rise public housing estates also provided offenders with a warren of alternative access and escape routes.

CPTED

As with defensible space, CPTED draws heavily on behavioural psychology, and is concerned with the relationships between people and the environment. The way people react to an environment is commonly influenced by environmental cues, which are variously perceived and decoded. Elements that make normal or legitimate users of a space feel safe (e.g. being visible to others) may discourage abnormal or illegitimate users from pursuing undesirable behaviours (such as robbery or theft from motor vehicles). CPTED requires that natural strategies be incorporated into human activities and space design. Crime prevention has traditionally relied almost exclusively on labour intensive (e.g. security guards and police patrols) and mechanical devices (e.g. security cameras, locks and fences) which increase existing operating costs for personnel, equipment and buildings. Traditionally, the three most common CPTED strategies are territorial reinforcement, natural surveillance and natural access control:

- *Territorial reinforcement* is a design concept directed at promoting notions of proprietary concern and a sense of ownership in legitimate users of space, thereby reducing opportunities for offending by discouraging illegitimate users. Early CPTED ideas, now referred to as first-generation CPTED, considered territorial reinforcement as the primary concept from which all the others are derived. Different forms include symbolic barriers (e.g. signage) and real barriers (e.g. fences or design that clearly defines and delineates between private, semi-private and public spaces). Access control and surveillance will also contribute towards enhancing territoriality by promoting legitimate users' informal social control. CPTED emphasises crime prevention techniques that reduce the opportunities in the environment 'both to naturally and routinely facilitate access control and surveillance, and to reinforce positive behaviour in the use of the environment' (Crowe 2000: 37). These strategies are not independent of one another, but act in concert to use physical attributes to separate public, public-private and private space, to define ownership (e.g. fences, pavement treatments, signs, landscaping and artwork) and define acceptable patterns of usage, in addition to promoting opportunities for surveillance.

- *Natural surveillance* is a traditional concept that has long been used in crime prevention. Opportunities for residents' self-surveillance as facilitated by windows and design can be promoted by physical design and surveillance is part of capable guardianship (Painter and Tilley 1999). If offenders perceive that they can be observed (even if they are not), they may be less likely to offend, given the increased potential for intervention, apprehension and prosecution. Other forms of surveillance include formal or organised (e.g. police and security patrols) and mechanical surveillance strategies (e.g. street lighting and CCTV).

- *Natural access control* is a CPTED concept focused on reducing opportunities for crime using spatial definition to deny access to potential targets and creating a heightened perception of risk in offenders. Formal or organised access control (e.g. security personnel) and mechanical access control (e.g. locks and bolts) strategies were not generally considered as part of the early definitions of CPTED.

Refinement of CPTED has added several other strategies including activity support, image/space management and target hardening:

- *Activity support* involves the use of design and signage to encourage intended patterns of usage of public space. Crowe (2000) notes how, within reason, activity generation and support seek to place inherently unsafe activities (such as those involving money transactions) in safe locations (those with high levels of activity and with surveillance opportunities). Similarly, safe activities serve as magnets for ordinary citizens who may then act to discourage the presence of criminals. This approach clearly contains elements of territoriality, access control and surveillance. Although increased numbers of pedestrians may provide additional 'eyes on the street' and potentially discourage some offences, they may also actually encourage and provide potential targets for crime (e.g. pickpocketing).

- *Image/space management* and routinely maintaining the built environment ensures that the physical environment continues to function effectively and transmits positive signals to all users. The significance of the physical condition and image of the built environment, and the effect this may have on crime and the fear of crime, have long been acknowledged (Lynch 1960; Newman 1973; Perlgut 1983; Wilson and Kelling 1982) and an extensive body of research now exists (Eck 2002; Kraut 1999; Ross and Jang 2000; Ross and Mirowsky 1999). Indeed, vacant premises can become crime magnets (Spelman 1993).

- *Target hardening* increases the efforts that offenders must expend in the commission of a crime and is the most established approach to crime prevention. However, there is much disagreement concerning whether or not target hardening should be considered as a component of CPTED. It is directed at denying or limiting access to a crime target through the use of physical barriers such as fences, gates, locks, electronic alarms and security patrols. Such ideas are often considered as elements of access control at a micro scale (e.g. individual buildings). Crucially, excessive use of target hardening tactics can create a 'fortress mentality' and imagery whereby residents withdraw behind physical barriers and the self-policing capacity of the built environment is damaged, effectively working against CPTED strategies that rely on surveillance, territoriality, image and the legitimate use of space. This fortressification of space is typified by private developments such as gated communities, which appear to be increasingly popular throughout the world.

The key components of CPTED are illustrated in Figure 9.4. It is argued in CPTED that by optimising opportunities for surveillance, clearly defining boundaries (and defining preferred use within such spaces) and creating and maintaining a positive image, urban design and active management can discourage offending. This is explained by the fact that offenders are potentially more visible to law-abiding others, and therefore perceive themselves to be more at risk of observation and subsequent apprehension. Additionally, a well-maintained and appropriately used environment can signify that a sense of ownership and proprietary concern exists within the community and offenders may perceive that residents are more vigilant and more likely to intervene during the commission of a crime.

Popularity and development of defensible space and CPTED

The increasing disillusionment in Britain and America with existing frameworks for tackling crime arguably provided a window of opportunity for Newman and his followers. The necessity to be seen to be intervening and attempting

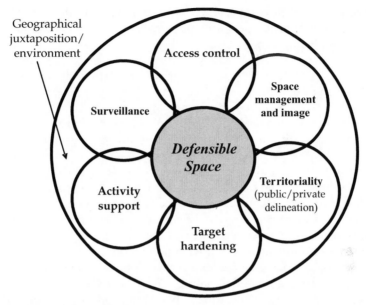

Figure 9.4 CPTED – Key principles
(*Source*: Adapted from Moffatt 1983: 23 and Newman 1973)

to address the problem in political terms cannot be understated. The highly visible nature of implementing design modifications as a potential solution was certainly an attractive characteristic. Newman's theory was explicitly directed at high-rise developments, thereby gaining support from the ever-growing number of critics of such developments. The US Department of Housing and Urban Development and the US Department of Justice both expressed interest in the early writings of Newman (Newman 1973, 1975a, 1975b, 1980; Newman and Franck 1980, 1982).

Despite criticisms (Adams 1973; Bottoms 1974; Hillier 1973; Kaplan 1973; Mawby 1977), Newman's ideas remained popular. Various reasons are suggested for this situation. The ideas inherent within the theory of defensible space can be located firmly within the domains of contemporary thought, and in particular the emphasis in psychology and criminology on the importance of the environment as a cause of behaviour (Labs 1989; Mayhew 1979). On a general level, in comparison with earlier works such as Jacobs (1961), Angel (1968) and Jeffery (1971), Newman's views appeared to be infinitely more attractive in that they did not involve major urban reorganisation. They also seemed to be backed by empirical research (Mayhew 1979). Moreover, Newman's theory (and CPTED) was, and arguably remains, amenable to politicians across the ideological spectrum (Smith 1987). It is attractive to those on the 'right' 'because environmental engineering provides immediate, visible and unambiguous evidence of a commitment to stamp out deviance' (Smith 1987: 147). Furthermore, it does not make any demands to reorganise the social structures of society. For politicians on the 'left', it provides 'a more acceptable scapegoat for today's supposed demise of law and order than the stereotypical vandal, the unemployed working-class youth' (Smith 1987: 147). For any political party, such an approach represents visible, tangible and positive action being pursued.

However, while CPTED had received considerable attention from government, it was to a large extent ignored by criminologists, who showed little interest in design theory (Bottoms and Wiles 1988; Mawby 1977; Reppetto 1976). Clarke (1989) observed that Newman's ideas did not concur with most contemporary criminologists since criminology (particularly in America) is an offshoot of sociology and thus social factors are seen as most important in explaining causation. Newman was not a social scientist and seemed ignorant of the findings of traditional criminology. Reppetto (1976) argued that the field of planning and architecture provided the most committed support for urban design theory. However, given the lack of interaction between urban design theory and criminology, it is not surprising that criminologists were dismissive of the methods and theories employed. For Reppetto, scepticism of CPTED by criminologists is understandable on a theoretical level, but it is another matter to simply ignore its potential policy pay-offs.

Incorrect perceptions of the nature of CPTED have also contributed to its rejection. Reppetto (1976) argued that antipathy may have evolved from a misreading of the theory and an overemphasis on policies such as target hardening and fortification. However, Reppetto claimed that attempts to view urban design theories as forms of government pacification are not supported in the writings of Newman.

Finally, there were concerns with CPTED involving the practical problems of implementing design changes. Construction costs are involved in remodelling or new building projects and delays often occur in the planning, approval and construction cycle. Dislocation of businesses and industry is common, and unknown costs can occur whereby physical changes, which are later proven ineffectual, subsequently prove costly to amend.

Together with some disappointing results from early CPTED experiments, these criticisms justified rejection and neglect (Clarke 1989). Indeed, a Home Office Study conducted by Sturman and Wilson (1976) studied 52 housing estates in London and the findings largely supported Newman's work. However, they discovered that one socio-economic factor was more important than design – the density of children in the environment. British housing authorities and councils began to note this finding and reduce child densities while neglecting design issues (Coleman 1985). The US federal government also lost interest in CPTED for around fifteen years between the beginning of the 1980s and the mid 1990s. Clarke (1989) cites several developments from the early 1980s, which have significantly altered this situation:

- Increasing evidence on the importance of the role of opportunity in crime.

- The development of new criminological theories such as rational choice and routine activity theory, which assign a more significant role to environmental determinants of crime.

- A growing number of case studies demonstrating substantial reductions in crime following environmental modification.

- The displacement of crime following CPTED modifications has not been demonstrated to the extent that critics claimed. Rather than influencing a change in the location, time, tactics, target or type of offending (Hakim and Rengert 1981), a diffusion of the benefits of CPTED to surrounding areas has been observed (Clarke and Weisburd 1994; Saville 1998).

In common with the American experience, results of defensible space initiatives in Britain were mixed. On the one hand, the riot-prone territories in the UK of the 1980s, such as the Broadwater Farm Estate in north London, seemed to vindicate the design-affects-crime approach. This estate was a series of twelve high-rise and deck-access flats interconnected via overhead pedestrian walkways. Residents were socially deprived, the estate was poorly maintained and its design was characterised by dangerously isolated areas, which became hot spots for crime and robbery, providing easy escape routes for criminals. However, in recent years, community initiatives and increased community participation along with some £33 million for redesigning the estate's layout, has transformed the area, and the estate now has significantly lower levels of crime. Improvements included giving each block a unique identity, demolishing the intimidating walkways and installing concierge lobbies, landscaped gardens, a health centre and an enterprise centre.

On the other hand, the Scotswood Estate in the north-east of England did not conform to the design-affects-crime prediction. The estate reflected Coleman's model of defensible space. There were few high-rise blocks (traditionally associated with high crime rates and therefore considered as representing 'bad' design) yet it still experienced relatively high crime rates and eventually a riot. According to Campbell (1993), this example showed that the problems were not about the design of the estate but about the social relationships among residents. She also noted that by the onset of the riots in 1991, almost 400 households had relocated due to feelings of endangerment. It was therefore apparent that effective and ongoing environmental management procedures are required to maintain defensible space – as Newman had suggested (Heck 1987; Newman 1973), if only in relation to the high-rise developments in his original study.

For practitioners, operationalising procedures to create defensible space were attractive features of Newman's thinking. According to Mayhew (1979), these procedures may have influenced the continuing federal governments' financial sponsorship of his work, within the American research programme entitled CPTED. The programme was adopted by the Westinghouse Corporation (1976, 1977a, 1977b) where research extended the defensible space concept to educational and commercial sites, with disappointing results. Jeffery (1977: 45) argues that this may be because territorial behaviour is less natural outside residential settings. Subsequently, government and research interest in CPTED wavered in the 1980s and 1990s. Nevertheless, CPTED has been widely used as a practical training tool for police, associated with the work of Crowe and his associates (Crowe 1991, Crowe and Zahm 1994).

However, defensible space, in the guise of CPTED in America, Canada, Australia and Holland, and Secured By Design (SBD) in Britain, is once again becoming contemporary and fashionable. The resurgence of interest and research has culminated in the establishment of the International Crime Prevention Through Environmental Design Association (ICA), which has now been followed by the UK's Designing Out Crime Association (DOCA), E-DOCA in Europe, the Asia/Pacific CPTED Chapter launched in May 2000 and a Chapter based in Latin America in 2004. Defensible space and CPTED ideas are now commonplace in many planning processes, such as in Florida, British Columbia, Canada and the Netherlands (Saville and Sarkissian 1998), and also in the UK, South Africa, Australia and New Zealand (Cozens 2005).

The application of CPTED

CPTED has been applied in a range of diverse environments, including residential, commercial/retail, schools, universities, hospitals, car parks, offices, convention centres, stadiums and public transport (Crowe 2000). For example, La Vigne (1997) discusses how, using CPTED principles, Metro, Washington's subway station, exhibits significantly lower levels of crime than other stations and the local environment in which it is located. In the UK, the SBD scheme uses CPTED principles in the design of urban environments. Studies by Brown (1999), Pascoe (1999) and Armitage (1999) report significant reductions in crime and the fear of crime (see Cozens *et al.* 2004, 2007 for a review). There is a growing body of evidence that CPTED is an effective crime prevention strategy (Cozens *et al.* 2005; Eck 2002).

The application of CPTED is illustrated by a study of railway stations in the UK (Cozens *et al.* 2003a) that used CPTED principles in the regeneration and redesign of a local rail network. Figures 9.5 and 9.6 illustrate a railway station 'before' and 'after' CPTED design modifications were executed. Clearly, the surveillance of the station platform and waiting areas has been enhanced and the station now provides minimal opportunities for concealment. The installation of signage has clearly designated and defined this space as an operating railway station and the design of the transparent shelter allows the station and passengers to interact with the local community. Additional way-finding information also enhances passengers' sense of personal safety. Significantly, the rail network has witnessed an increase in annual passenger flows and reduced levels of crime and fear of crime. It would not be inappropriate to suggest that a significant proportion of this increase in patronage is attributable to the passenger-led CPTED station improvement programme. Indeed, the new high-visibility shelters not only reduced fear of crime but appear to have also produced higher levels of traveller confidence, and in the short term, higher levels of patronage.

Figure 9.5 Railway station before CPTED modifications
(*Photo*: Author)

Figure 9.6 Railway station after CPTED modifications
(*Photo*: Author)

CPTED – current status and future directions

The traditional focus of CPTED has emphasised physical design. However, along with defensible space, CPTED has expanded to encompass affective, psychological, sociological dimensions to environmental design. These new models are known as second-generation CPTED (Saville and Cleveland 1997) and second-generation defensible space (Taylor and Harrell 1996).

Saville and Cleveland (1997) realised that socio-economic and demographic dynamics can reduce or enhance the efficacy of CPTED strategies. As they put it:

> have we forgotten that what's significant about Jacob's 'eyes on the street' are not the sightlines or even the streets, but the eyes? ... Second-Generation CPTED recognizes the most valuable aspects of safe community lie not in structures of the brick and mortar type, but rather in structures of family, of thought and, most importantly of behavior. (Saville and Cleveland 1997: 1)

According to Saville (1998), second-generation CPTED has resulted in more complete approach to reducing crime. Like first-generation CPTED, Second-Generation CPTED uses risk assessments and environmental strategies to reduce crime opportunities. However, it goes further by encouraging social changes to help maintain crime prevention impacts. Developments in CPTED have involved community building to support physical design modifications (Sarkissian *et al.* 1997; Sarkissian and Perlgut 1994; Sarkissian and Walsh 1994; Saville 1995). The term 'Community CPTED' has been coined (Plaster-Carter 2002) to describe this interaction of selected physical, social and economic conditions.

A key concept in second-generation CPTED is that of an ecological threshold or 'tipping point' (Saville 1996) of a neighbourhood. This is the notion that like any natural ecosystem, it has a limited capacity for certain activities and functions. Environmental decline and increasing rates of vacancy in a given neighbourhood may breach the tipping point and result in the out-migration of residents, social capital and economic resources and set in motion a vicious spiral of decline. This concept of neighbourhood capacity and the tipping point is one of the four principles of second-generation CPTED, the other three being community culture, cohesion and connectivity (Saville and Cleveland 2003a, 2003b). Research investigating this dynamic and temporal dimension to CPTED promises much, as does the study of the after-dark environment, where surveillance opportunities are limited and lighting issues become more significant (for a review of the lighting literature see Cozens *et al.* 2003b).

Researchers have also responded to the common criticism that the application of CPTED relies on the use of generic principles in a one-size-fits-all approach, which ignores local context. Emphasising the point, the UK's Designing Out Crime Association logo is 'context is everything' (see www. doca.org.uk). The type, extent and location of crime risk require systematic consideration before strategies are implemented. Failure to do so is analogous to a medical practitioner prescribing treatment before any illness has been diagnosed. For example, improved lighting can assist in reducing fear of crime and crime in the community. However, in spaces which are illegitimately used by congregating youths and are not overlooked, turning off the lights is often a more appropriate and effective response. As Crowe (2000: 6) observes, 'CPTED is a process for improving planning decisions ... not a belief system.'

Similarly, researchers have increasingly recognised the importance of the perceptual dimension of crime and crime prevention. The growth of crime victimisation surveys in the UK and America influenced the emergence and popularity of the study of fear of crime, as distinct from crime itself. Crucially, Newman's *Defensible Space* (1973: 50) specifically highlights this perceptual dimension in two of his principles – 'the capacity of the physical environment to create *perceived* zones of territorial influence' and 'the capacity of design to influence the *perception* of a project's uniqueness, isolation, and stigma'. Researchers in the field of environmental psychology have contributed much to CPTED in recent years (e.g. Brantingham and Brantingham 1993; Brown and Altman 1983; Brown and Bentley 1993; Brower *et al.* 1983; Fisher and Nasar 1992; Nasar 1994; Nasar and Fisher 1993; Nasar *et al.* 1993; Perkins *et al.* 1990, 1992, 1993; Perkins and Taylor 1996; Vrij and Winkel 1991). Crucially, much of defensible space and CPTED relates to perceptions: of offenders, victims and potential guardians. Indeed, research probing different stakeholder perceptions of crime and the built environment is making a significant contribution to the field (Cozens *et al.* 2001, 2002; Ham-Rowbottom *et al.* 1999; Harris and Brown 1996; MacDonald and Gifford 1989; Tijerino 1998) and promises much for the future direction of CPTED.

There have been a number of other developments. CPTED is increasingly being linked with urban sustainability (Cozens 2002, 2007a; Dewberry 2003; Du Plessis 1999). It has been argued that sustainability will not achieve its full potential unless it explicitly incorporates measures to address the issues of crime and the fear of crime within the community. Indeed, Du Plessis (1999: 33) argues that 'no city can call itself sustainable if the citizens of that city fear for their personal safety and the safety of their livelihood'. As a proactive process, CPTED can assist in achieving development which meets the needs of present and future generations and promotes public health (Cozens 2007b). CPTED has also played an increasing role in premises liability cases. Here, landlords are found negligent in the provision of adequate and reasonable security and CPTED features on their facilities (Kennedy 1993; Gordon and Brill 1996) and in these increasingly litigious times, such a trend is likely to accelerate. Finally, CPTED has been applied to a range of products, to reduce their potential both as targets for crime and as tools for crime (Cozens and Hills 2003; Ekblom 1997; Gamman 2001; Gamman and Pascoe 2004). The Design Against Crime Research Centre at the Central St Martin's College of Art and Design is driving much of this relatively new field of CPTED (see www.designagainstcrime.com and Ekblom, Chapter 11, this volume).

Conclusion

This chapter has provided a classic overview of CPTED, a brief discussion of the major contributors and examples of CPTED applications. CPTED has evolved over the last quarter of a century, merging with other place-based strategies such as situational crime prevention and environmental criminology. The future directions for CPTED are intriguing. The history of CPTED has been one of continuous re-examination and rebuilding, and this dynamic process will no doubt continue.

References

Adams, J. (1973) 'Review of Defensible Space', *Man-Environment Systems*, 10: 267–8.

Angel, S. (1968) *Discouraging Crime Through City Planning*. Working Paper 75. Berkeley, CA: University of California.

Armitage, R. (1999) *An Evaluation of Secured by Design Housing Schemes Throughout the West Yorkshire Area*. Huddersfield, UK: University of Huddersfield.

Atlas, R. (1991) 'The Other Side of Defensible Space', *Security Management*, March: 63–6.

Bottoms, A. (1974) 'Book Review of Defensible Space', *British Journal of Criminology*, 14: 203–6.

Bottoms, A. and Wiles, P. (1988) 'Crime and Housing Policy: A Framework for Crime Prevention', in T. Hope and M. Shaw (eds) *Communities and Crime Reduction*. London: HMSO.

Brantingham, P. and Brantingham, P. (1975) 'Residential Burglary and Urban Form', *Urban Studies*, 12: 273–84.

Brantingham, P. and Brantingham, P. (1981) *Environmental Criminology*. Newbury Park, CA: Sage.

Brantingham, P. and Brantingham, P. (1991) *Environmental Criminology*. Newbury Park, CA: Sage.

Brantingham, P. and Brantingham, P. (1993) 'Nodes, Paths and Edges: Considerations on the Complexity of Crime and the Physical Environment', *Journal of Environmental Psychology*, 13: 3–28.

Brantingham, P. and Faust, F. (1976) 'A Conceptual Model of Crime Prevention', *Crime and Delinquency*, 22: 284–96.

Brower, S., Dockett, K. and Taylor, R. (1983) 'Residents' Perceptions of Territorial Features and Perceived Local Threat', *Environment and Behaviour*, 15: 419–37.

Brown, B. and Altman, B. (1983) 'Territoriality, Defensible Space and Residential Burglary: An Environmental Analysis', *Journal of Environmental Psychology*, 3: 203–20.

Brown, B. and Bentley, D. (1993) 'Residential Burglars Judge Risk: The Role of Territoriality', *Journal of Environmental Psychology*, 13: 51–61.

Brown, J. (1999) 'An Evaluation of the Secured By Design Initiative in Gwent, South Wales', unpublished MSc. Leicester: Scarman Centre for the Study of Public Order, University of Leicester.

Campbell, B. (1993) *Goliath: Britain's Dangerous Places*. London: Methuen.

Clarke, R. (1980) 'Situational Crime Prevention: Theory and Practice', *British Journal of Criminology*, 20: 136–47.

Clarke, R. (1982) 'Chairman's Introduction', in M. Hough and P. Mayhew (eds) *Crime and Public Housing*, Research and Planning Unit Paper 6. London: Home Office.

Clarke, R. (1989) 'Theoretical Background to Crime Prevention Through Environmental Design (CPTED) and Situational Prevention', conference paper, *Designing Out Crime: Crime Prevention Through Environmental Design (CPTED)* Hilton Hotel, Sydney, Australia 16 June. Canberra: Australian Institute of Criminology.

Clarke, R. (ed.) (1992) *Situational Crime Prevention: Successful Case Studies.* Albany, NY: Harrow and Heston.

Clarke, R. (ed.) (1997) *Situational Crime Prevention: Successful Case Studies*, 2nd edn. Albany, NY: Harrow and Heston.

Clarke, R. and Hope, T. (1984) *Coping with Burglary.* Boston, MA: Kluwger-Nijnoff.

Clarke, R. and Mayhew, P. (1980) *Designing Out Crime.* London: HMSO.

Clarke R. and Weisburd D. (1994) 'Diffusion of Crime Control Benefits', in R. Clarke (ed.) *Crime Prevention Studies, Vol. 2.* Monsey, NY: Criminal Justice Press, 165–183.

Coleman, A. (1985) *Utopia on Trial: Vision and Reality in Planned Housing.* London: Hilary Shipman Ltd.

Coleman, A. (1990) *Utopia on Trial: Vision and Reality in Planned Housing*, 2nd edn. London: Hilary Shipman Ltd.

Coleman, A. (1998) 'The Crime Crisis and Preventable Crimino-Genesis', *Journal of Contingencies and Crisis Management*, 6: 102–9.

Colquhoun, I. (2004) *Designing Out Crime: Creating Safe and Sustainable Communities.* Burlington, MA: Architectural Press.

Cozens, P. (2002) 'Sustainable Urban Development and Crime Prevention Through Environmental Design for the British City. Towards an Effective Urban Environmentalism for the 21st Century', *Cities: The International Journal of Urban Policy and Planning*, 19: 129–37.

Cozens, P. (2005) 'Designing Out Crime – From Evidence to Action', conference paper, *Delivering Crime Prevention: Making the Evidence Work*, Australian Institute of Criminology and the Attorney-General's NSW Department, Carlton Crest Hotel, Sydney 21–22 November. Canberra: Australian Institute of Criminology (http://www.aic.gov.au/conferences/2005-cp/cozens.html).

Cozens, P. (2007a) 'Planning, Crime and Urban Sustainability', in A. Kungolas, C. Brebbia and E. Beriatos (eds) *Sustainable Development and Planning III. Volume 1, WIT Transactions on Ecology and the Environment.* Southampton, UK: WIT Press, pp. 187–96.

Cozens, P.M. (2007b) 'Public Health and the Potential Benefits of Crime Prevention Through Environmental Design', *NSW Public Health Bulletin*, 18(11–12): 232–7 (www.publish.csiro.au/nid/226/issue/4094.htm).

Cozens, P. and Hills, J. (2003) 'Form, Function and Dysfunction: Designing for Use and Mis-use', *Journal of Ergonomics in Design*, Winter 11(1): 12–16.

Cozens, P., Hillier, D. and Prescott, G. (2001) 'Defensible Space: Burglars and Police Evaluate Urban Residential Design', *Security Journal*, 14: 43–62.

Cozens, P., Hillier D. and Prescott G. (2002) 'Criminogenic Associations and Characteristic British Housing Designs', *International Planning Studies*, 7: 119–36.

Cozens, P., Neale, R., Whitaker, J. and Hillier, D. (2003a) 'Managing Crime and the Fear of Crime at Railway Stations: A Case Study in South Wales (UK)', *International Journal of Transport Management*, 1: 121–32.

Cozens, P., Neale, R., Whitaker, J., Hillier, D. and Graham, M. (2003b) 'A Critical Review of Street Lighting, Crime and the Fear of Crime in the British City', *Crime Prevention and Community Safety: An International Journal*, 5: 7–24.

Cozens, P., Pascoe, T. and Hillier, D. (2004) 'Critically Reviewing the Theory and Practice of Secured-by-design for Residential New-build Housing in Britain', *Crime Prevention and Community Safety: An International Journal*, 6: 13–29.

Cozens, P., Saville, G. and Hillier, D. (2005) 'Crime Prevention Through Environmental Design (CPTED): A Review and Modern Bibliography', *Journal of Property Management*, 23: 328–56.

Cozens, P., Pascoe, T. and Hillier, D. (2007) 'Critically Reviewing the Theory and Practice of Secured-by-design for Residential New-build Housing in Britain', in R. Mawby (ed.) *Burglary. International Library of Criminology, Criminal Justice and Penology, Second Series*. Aldershot: Ashgate, pp. 345–61.

Crowe, T. (1991) *Crime Prevention Through Environmental Design: Applications of Architectural Design and Space Management Concepts*. Boston, MA: Butterworth-Heinemann.

Crowe, T. (2000) *Crime Prevention Through Environmental Design: Applications of Architectural Design and Space Management Concepts*, 2nd edn. Oxford: Butterworth-Heinemann.

Crowe, T. and Zahm, D. (1994) 'Crime Prevention Through Environmental Design', *Land Development*, Fall: 22–7.

Dewberry, E. (2003) 'Designing Out Crime: Insights from Eco-design', *Security Journal*, 16: 51–62.

Du Plessis, C. (1999) 'The Links Between Crime Prevention and Sustainable Development', *Open House International*, 24: 33–40.

Eck, J. (2002) 'Preventing Crime at Places', in L. Sherman, D. Farrington, B. Welsh and D. Mackenzie (eds) *Evidence-based Crime Prevention*. London: Routledge, pp. 9241–94.

Ekblom, P. (1997) 'Gearing Up Against Crime: A Dynamic Framework to Help Designers Keep Up with the Adaptive Criminal in a Changing World', *International Journal of Risk, Security and Crime Prevention*, 2: 249–65.

Fisher, B. and Nasar, J. (1992) 'Fear of Crime in Relation to Three Exterior Site Features: Prospect, Refuge, and Escape', *Environment and Behavior*, 24: 35–65.

Gamman, L. (2001) *In the Bag: A Design Resource*. London: London Institute.

Gamman, L. and Pascoe, T. (2004) 'Designing Out Crime? Using Practice-based Models of the Design Process', *Crime Prevention and Community Safety: An International Journal*, 6: 37–56.

Gordon, C. and Brill, W. (1996) *The Expanding Role of Crime Prevention Through Environmental Design in Premises Liability*, National Institute of Justice, Research Brief, Washington, DC: US Department of Justice.

Hakim, S. and Rengert, G. (1981) *Crime Spillover*. Beverly Hills, CA: Sage.

Ham-Rowbottom, K., Gifford, R. and Shaw, K. (1999) 'Defensible Space Theory and the Police: Assessing the Vulnerability of Residences to Burglary', *Journal of Environmental Psychology*, 19: 117–29.

Harris, P. and Brown, B. (1996) 'The Home and Identity Display: Interpreting Resident Territoriality from Home Exteriors', *Journal of Environmental Psychology*, 16: 187–203.

Heck, S. (1987) 'Oscar Newman Revisited', *Architects Journal*, 14: 30–2.

Hillier, B. (1973) 'In Defence of Space', *RIBA Journal*, 11: 539–44.

Jacobs, J. (1961) *The Death and Life of Great American Cities*. New York: Vintage Books.

Jeffery, C. (1969) 'Crime Prevention and Control Through Environmental Engineering', *Criminologica*, 7: 35–58.

Jeffery, C. (1971) *Crime Prevention Through Environmental Design*. Beverly Hills: Sage.

Jeffery, C. (1976) 'Criminal Behavior and the Physical Environment', *American Behavioral Scientist*, 20: 149–74.

Jeffery, C. (1977) Crime Prevention Through Environmental Design, 2nd edn. Beverly Hills, CA: Sage.

Jeffery, C. (1999) 'CPTED: Past, Present and Future', paper presented at the 4th Annual International CPTED Association Conference, Mississauga, Ontario, Canada, 20–22 September.

Jeffery, C. and Zahm, D. (1993) 'Crime Prevention Through Environmental Design, Opportunity Theory, and Rational Choice Models', in R. Clarke and M. Felson (eds) Routine Activity and Rational Choice. Advances in Criminological Theory, Vol. 5. New Jersey: Transaction, pp. 323–50.

Kaplan, S. (1973) 'Book Review of Defensible Space', Architectural Forum, 98: 8.

Kennedy, D. (1993) 'Architectural Concerns Regarding Security and Premises Liability', Journal of Architectural and Planning Research, 10: 105–29.

Kraut, D. (1999) 'Hanging Out the No Vacancy Sign: Eliminating the Blight of Vacant Buildings from Urban Areas', New York University Law Review, 74: 1139–77.

La Vigne, N. (1997) Visibility and Vigilance: Metro's Situational Approach to Preventing Subway Crime. Research in Brief. Washington, DC: US Department of Justice.

Labs, K. (1989) 'P/A Technics Deterrence by Design', Progressive Architecture, 11: 100–3.

Lynch, K. (1960) The Image of the City. Cambridge, MA: MIT Press.

MacDonald, J. and Gifford, R. (1989) 'Territorial Cues and Defensible Space Theory: The Burglar's Point of View', Journal of Environmental Psychology, 9: 193–205.

Mawby, R. (1977) 'Defensible Space: A Theoretical and Empirical Appraisal', Urban Studies, 14: 169–79.

Mayhew, P. (1979) 'Defensible Space: The Current Status of Crime Prevention Theory', The Howard Journal, 18: 150–9.

Merry, S. (1981) 'Defensible Space Undefended: Social Factors in Crime Control Through Environmental Design', Urban Affairs Quarterly, 16: 397–422.

Moffat, R. (1983) 'Crime Prevention Through Environmental Design – A Management Perspective', Canadian Journal of Criminology, 25: 19–31.

Nasar, J. (1994) 'Urban Design Aesthetics: The Evaluative Qualities of Building Exteriors', Environment and Behavior, 26: 377–401.

Nasar, J. and Fisher, B. (1993) 'Hot Spots of Fear and Crime: A Multi-method Investigation', Journal of Environmental Psychology, 13: 187–206.

Nasar, J., Fisher, B. and Grannis, M. (1993) 'Proximate Physical Cues to Fear of Crime', Landscape and Urban Planning, 26: 161–78.

Newman, O. (1973) Defensible Space, People and Design in the Violent City. London: Architectural Press.

Newman, O. (1975a) Design Guidelines for Creating Defensible Space. Washington, DC: US Department of Justice, Law Enforcement Assistance Administration.

Newman, O. (1975b) 'Reactions to the Defensible Space Study and Some Further Readings', International Journal of Mental Health, 4: 48–70.

Newman, O. (1980) Community of Interest. New York: Anchor Press/Doubleday.

Newman, O. and Franck, K. (1980) Factors Influencing Crime and Stability in Urban Housing Development. Washington, DC: US Department of Justice.

Newman, O. and Franck, K. (1982) 'The Effects of Building Size on Personal Crime and Fear of Crime', Population and Development, 5: 203–20.

Painter, K. and Tilley, N. (1999) Surveillance of Public Space: CCTV, Street Lighting and Crime Prevention. Monsey, NY: Criminal Justice Press.

Pascoe, T. (1999), Evaluation of Secured by Design in Public Sector Housing. Final Report. Watford: Building Research Establishment.

Perkins, D. and Taylor, R. (1996) 'Ecological Assessments of Community Disorder: Their Relationship to Fear of Crime and Theoretical Implication', *American Journal of Community Psychology*, 18: 83–115.

Perkins, D., Florin, P., Rich, R., Wandersman, A. and Charvis, D. (1990) 'Participation and the Social and Physical Environment of Residential Blocks: Crime and Community Context', *American Journal of Community Psychology*, 18: 83–115.

Perkins, D., Meeks, J. and Taylor, R. (1992) 'The Physical Environment of Street Blocks and Resident Perceptions of Crime and Disorder: Implications for Theory and Measurement', *Journal of Environmental Psychology*, 12: 21–34.

Perkins, D., Wandersman, A., Rich, R. and Taylor, R. (1993) 'The Physical Environment of Street Crime: Defensible Space, Territoriality and Incivilities', *Journal of Environmental Psychology*, 13: 29–49.

Perlgut, D. (1983) 'Vandalism: The Environmental Crime', *Australian Journal of Social Issues*, 18: 209–16.

Plaster-Carter, S. (2002) 'Community CPTED', *Journal of the International Crime Prevention Through Environmental Design Association*, 1: 15–24.

Poyner, B. (1983) *Design Against Crime: Beyond Defensible Space*. London: Butterworths.

Poyner, B. and Webb, B. (1991) *Crime-Free Housing*. Oxford: Butterworth Architecture.

Reppetto, T. (1974) *Residential Crime*. Boston, MA: Ballinger.

Reppetto, T. (1976) 'Crime Prevention Through Environmental Policy – A Critique', *American Behavioural Scientist*, 20: 275–88.

Rock, P. (1988) 'Crime Reduction Initiatives on Problem Estates', in T. Hope and M. Shaw (eds) *Communities and Crime Reduction*. London: HMSO.

Ross, C. and Jang, S. (2000) 'Neighbourhood Disorder, Fear and Mistrust: The Buffering Role of Social Ties with Neighbours', *American Journal of Community Psychology*, 28: 401–20.

Ross, C. and Mirowsky, J. (1999) 'Disorder and Decay: The Concept and Measurement of Perceived Neighbourhood Disorder', *Urban Affairs Review*, 34: 412–32.

Sarkissian, W. and Perlgut, D. (1994) *The Community Participation Handbook*, 2nd edn. Sydney, Australia: Impact Press.

Sarkissian, W. and Walsh, K. (eds) (1994) *The Community Participation in Practice: Casebook*. Perth, Australia: Murdoch University, Institute for Science and Technology Policy.

Sarkissian, W., Cook, A., and Walsh, K. (eds) (1997) *The Community Participation in Practice: A Practical Guide*. Perth, Australia: Institute for Science and Technology Policy.

Saville, G. (1995) *Crime Problems, Community Solutions: Environmental Criminology as a Developing Prevention Strategy*. Vancouver, BC: AAG Publications.

Saville, G. (1996) 'Assessing Risk and Crime Potentials In Neighbourhoods', conference paper, *1st Annual International CPTED Association Conference*, Calgary, Alberta, 30 October–1 November.

Saville G. (1998) 'New Tools to Eradicate Crime Places and Crime Niches', conference paper, *Safer Communities: Strategic Directions in Urban Planning*, Melbourne, Australia, 10–11 September.

Saville, G. and Cleveland, G. (1997) '2nd Generation CPTED: An Antidote to the Social Y2K Virus of Urban Design', paper presented at the 1st Annual International CPTED Association Conference, Orlando, Florida (www.pac2durham.com/resources/schools.pdf).

Saville, G. and Cleveland, G. (2003a) 'An introduction to 2nd Generation CPTED: Part 1', *CPTED Perspectives*, 6(1): 7–9.

Saville, G. and Cleveland, G. (2003b) 'An introduction to 2nd Generation CPTED: Part 2', *CPTED Perspectives*, 6(2): 4–8.

Saville G. and Sarkissian, W. (1998) 'Defensible Space (Book Review)', *Journal of Planning and Education and Research*, 17: 361–3.

Schneider, R. and Kitchen, T. (2002) *Planning For Crime Prevention: A Transatlantic Perspective*. London: Routledge.

Smith, S. (1986) 'Utopia on Trial: Vision and Reality in Planned Housing', *Urban Studies* 23: 244–6.

Smith, S. (1987) 'Designing Against Crime? Beyond the Rhetoric of Residential Crime Prevention', *Property Management*, 5: 146–50.

Spelman, W. (1993) 'Abandoned Buildings: Magnets for Crime?', *Journal of Criminal Justice*, 21: 481–95.

Stubbs, W. (1903) *The Constitutional History of England in Its Origin and Development*, 6th edn. Oxford: Clarendon Press.

Sturman, A. and Wilson, S. (1976) 'Vandalism Research Aimed at Specific Remedies', *Municipal Engineering*, 7 May: 705–13.

Taylor, R. and Harrell, A. (1996) *Physical Environment and Crime*. Washington, DC: US Department of Justice.

Taylor, R., Gottfredson, S. and Brower, S. (1980) 'The Defensibility of Defensible Space: A Critical Review and a Synthetic Framework for Future Research', in T. Hirschi and M. Gottfredson (eds) *Understanding Crime*. Beverly Hills, CA: Sage, pp. 53–71.

Tijerino, R. (1998) 'Civil Spaces: A Critical Perspective of Defensible Space', *Journal of Architectural Planning Research*, 15: 321–37.

Vrij, A. and Winkel, W. (1991) 'Characteristics of the Built Environment and Fear Of Crime: A Research Note on Interventions in Unsafe Locations', *Deviant Behavior*, 12: 203–15.

Wallis, A. (1980) *Crime Prevention Through Environmental Design: An Operational Handbook*, Washington, DC: US Department of Justice.

Westinghouse Electric Corporation (1976) *Crime Prevention Through Environmental Design. CPTED Design Program Manual, Volume 1: Planning and Implementation Manual*. Arlington, VA: Westinghouse Electric Corporation.

Westinghouse Electric Corporation (1977a) *Crime Prevention Through Environmental Design. CPTED Design Program Manual, Volume 1: Strategies and Directives Manual*. Arlington, VA: Westinghouse Electric Corporation.

Westinghouse Electric Corporation (1977b) *Crime Prevention Through Environmental Design. CPTED Design Program Manual, Volume 2: Strategies and Directives Manual*. Arlington, VA: Westinghouse Electric Corporation.

Wilson, J. and Kelling, G. (1982) 'The Police and Neighbourhood Safety: Broken Windows', *Atlantic Monthly*, 3: 29–38.

Wood, E. (1961) *Housing Design: A Social Theory*. New York: Citizens, Housing and Planning Council of New York Inc.

10. Situational crime prevention

Ronald V. Clarke

Situational crime prevention is a highly practical and effective means of reducing specific crime problems. Essentially, it seeks to alter the situational determinants of crime so as to make crime less likely to happen. It is often criticised for being a simplistic, atheoretical approach to crime prevention, but it has a sound basis in the theories of environmental criminology. It is also criticised for not preventing crime, but simply 'displacing' it, that is, moving crime somewhere else or changing its form. However, the criticism is overstated and this chapter shows that many dramatic reductions in crime can be credited to situational prevention. But first the chapter lays out the theory behind situational prevention.

Theoretical background

As said, situational prevention is rooted in the theories of environmental criminology discussed in this book – routine activity theory, the rational choice perspective, crime pattern theory – and more recently it has made use of social and environmental psychological theory. This chapter does not discuss these theories in detail, but rather sets out some of their underlying assumptions that are particularly important for situational prevention.

Crime results from the interaction of motivation and situation

Most criminological theories try only to explain why some people become delinquent or criminal. Whether biological, psychological or sociological in approach, these theories are 'dispositional' because they are seeking to explain a general disposition or propensity to commit crime. But crime is an act, not merely a propensity, and it can only be explained in terms of the interaction between the disposition (sometimes also called 'criminal motivation') and the situation that provides the opportunity for crime to occur.

In early discussions of situational prevention opportunity was used synonymously with situation. However, later discussions recognise that situations provide more than just 'opportunities' for crime; they also provide temptations, inducements and provocations (Wortley 2001) and this recognition has enhanced the scope of situational prevention. Even so, it is convenient to use the term 'opportunity' to refer to the broader roles of situational factors and this chapter adopts this convention.

Crime is always a choice

The interaction between motivation and situation that results in crime is mediated through decisions made by individual offenders. Every time someone commits a crime, they have made a decision to do so (see Cornish and Clarke, Chapter 2, this volume). As Taylor, Walton and Young (1973) pointed out many years ago, nobody is compelled to commit crime. Thus, discrimination and disadvantage do not propel robbers through the doors of the bank; rather, robbers *choose* to rob banks because they want money, and they want large amounts of it.

In fact, people commit crimes because they judge this will bring them some benefit. The benefit is not always financial, but it might be excitement, sex, power, intoxication, revenge, recognition, loyalty, love – indeed, anything that people want. Whether they choose to commit crime depends on a rough calculation of the chances of obtaining the reward and the risks of failure – arrest, punishment, a physical beating, humiliation, etc. Their choices may be made under emotional pressure or when intoxicated. They might also be split-second, foolhardy, ill-informed or ill-advised – but they are choices nonetheless.

If people choose to commit crime, it follows that even those who are more disposed to crime will choose to avoid it when the circumstances are unfavourable. Creating unfavourable circumstances is the objective of situational crime prevention.

Opportunity plays a powerful role in crime

Even when traditional, dispositional theorists have granted some role to opportunity, they have assumed that opportunity is subsidiary to motivation. In their view motivation is the first and most important thing to explain. Environmental criminology, on the other hand, while recognising the importance of motivation gives equal importance to opportunity in explaining crime. Some environmental criminologists, including the author of this chapter, go much further and make important claims, including the following:

- Opportunity plays a part in every form of crime, even carefully planned crimes such as bank robbery and terrorism.
- Opportunity is an important *cause* of crime.
- Criminally disposed individuals will commit a greater numbers of crimes if they encounter more criminal opportunities.
- Regularly encountering such opportunities could lead these individuals to seek even more opportunities.
- Individuals without pre-existing dispositions can be drawn into criminal behaviour by a proliferation of criminal opportunities.

- Generally law-abiding individuals can be drawn into committing specific forms of crime if they regularly encounter easy opportunities for these crimes.
- The more opportunities for crime that exist, the more crime there will be.
- Reducing opportunities for specific forms of crime will reduce the overall amount of crime.

Proof exists for only the first and last of these claims (see Clarke 2005), but they are all generally consistent with environmental criminology, and together they make the case for situational prevention.

Principles of situational prevention

More than making the case for situational prevention, the theory discussed above helps in framing the principles that should guide situational prevention projects. The overriding principle is, of course, that preventive measures should try to change the 'near', situational causes of crime, rather than the 'distant' dispositional causes. Changing near causes is more likely to succeed in reducing crime because the link between cause and effect is more direct. It will also achieve a more immediate effect on crime than will trying to change 'distant' causes such as upbringing or psychological disadvantage. Changing distant causes can only bring crime prevention benefits in the future, whereas reducing opportunities can result in immediate reductions in crime.

Even if they accept these points, dispositional theorists will often claim that situational prevention is not enough; that crime can only be truly prevented if the 'root' causes are also removed. However, not every cause of a crime must be removed for prevention to succeed; it is often enough to remove one small but key ingredient of opportunity. Dispositional theorists find this difficult to accept because they believe disposition is much more important in causation than opportunity. Even if this were true, however, there is no necessary connection between the power of an explanatory variable and its importance for prevention. For example, we might all concede that lack of parental love is an important cause of delinquency, but as James Q. Wilson (1976) pointed out, nobody knows how to make parents more loving. If parental love cannot be manipulated through policy it has no importance for prevention.

Another slightly different argument is sometimes put forward by dispositional theorists to cast doubt on situational prevention and to make the case for changing dispositions. It is that the causes of crime must be fully understood before it can be prevented. This is claimed in countless research proposals for funds to study the causes of delinquency, but it is not true. For example, if traffic engineers want to stop speeding on a stretch of road, they do not need to mount detailed studies of the causes of speeding. All they need do is introduce speed bumps and, as long as they do this carefully with full awareness of other nearby routes that drivers might take instead, speeding will be reduced. This may seem a trivial example, but the same point can be made about some measures that were introduced in the United States in the

1980s to reduce random homicides. These measures consisted of tamper-proof packaging for all medicines and foods in response to an outbreak of deaths resulting from the purchase of painkillers laced with cyanide. The perpetrators of the crimes were not caught and their motivation was never revealed. But a straightforward opportunity-blocking measure eliminated future occurrences (see Clarke and Newman 2005).

With this brief digression on the relationship between causes and preventive measures, we can now turn to principles of situational prevention.

Focus on very specific categories of crime

A situational prevention project will succeed only when it is focused on a specific category of crime, such as juvenile joyriding, rather than some broader category of crime such as 'juvenile delinquency' or 'car thefts'. This is because the situational determinants of any specific category of crime are quite different from those of another one, even one that seems similar. It may also be committed for different motives, by different offenders with quite different resources and skills.

These points can be illustrated by research on residential burglary undertaken by Poyner and Webb (1991) in one British city. They showed that burglaries committed in the suburbs were quite different from those committed in the city centre. City-centre burglaries were committed by offenders on foot who were looking for cash and jewellery. Because most of the housing was built in terraces they could only get in through the front door or a front window. The suburban burglars, on the other hand, used cars and were targeting electronic goods such as videocassette players and TVs. They were more likely to enter through the back windows than through the front. They needed cars to get to the suburbs and to transport the stolen goods. The cars had to be parked near to the house, but not so close as to attract attention. The layout of housing in the newer suburbs allowed these conditions to be met, and Poyner and Webb's preventive suggestions included better surveillance of parking places, improved security at the back of houses and a crackdown on fencing of stolen goods. To prevent inner-city burglaries, on the other hand, they suggested improving security and surveillance at the front of the house. As for disrupting the market for stolen goods, this approach had more relevance to the suburban burglaries, targeted on electronic goods, than to the inner-city burglaries that targeted cash and jewellery.

Understand how the crime is committed

We have just seen that Poyner and Webb could make useful preventive suggestions when they understood *how* the burglaries were committed and what goods were being sought. Notice that they did not spend time researching *why* the burglars wanted to steal goods. It was enough to know that there were some individuals out there with the motivation to steal things from other people's homes.

This brings us to an important distinction between *motivation* and *motive*. Motivation is a longer-term disposition, in this case a criminal motivation.

Motive is a much more immediate driver of behaviour and is a much more tangible concept. The motive for both sets of Poyner and Webb's burglars was financial, but in the case of the city burglars, it was to get small, easy rewards in the form of cash or jewellery. The suburban burglars, on the other hand, were looking for greater rewards by stealing electronic goods even though this involved more work in fencing the goods after they had been stolen. In general, it is helpful for situational prevention to understand the *motives* for particular forms of crime even if it can often ignore the roots of motivation.

In seeking to understand how a specific form of crime is done, it is important to adopt the offender's perspective – seeing the task from the offender's point of view. Sometimes interviews with offenders to ask them about their methods can be helpful, as long as these concentrate on *modus operandi* and do not stray into more general questions such as about the offender's background (Decker 2005). When this cannot be done, an alternative is to 'think thief' (Ekblom 1995). This means putting oneself in the shoes of the offender and trying to think through in detail the decisions that he or she must make to complete the crime. This process reveals another important fact for prevention – committing a crime is not a simple matter of merely snatching a bag or pocketing goods in a store. Rather, it consists of a linked series of steps, each of which involves decisions by the offender (Cornish 1994). To take the shoplifting example, the offender has to decide which store to hit, which goods to steal, how to take them without being seen, how to conceal them, how to escape from the store without being caught, how to sell them (Sutton 2004), what price to ask, who to sell them to and how to make sure that the goods will not be traced back to the offender. For some crimes, of course – take the example of theft of cars for export – the process is much longer and more complicated. The important point is that understanding how a crime is committed helps in finding points of intervention to make the crime more difficult, risky or less rewarding. And the more detailed the understanding of the process, the richer and more diverse will be the possibilities for intervening.

Use an action-research model

Situational prevention belongs to a 'family' of similar preventive approaches deriving from environmental criminology, including design against crime (DAC, see Ekblom, Chapter 11, this volume) and crime prevention through environmental design (CPTED, see Cozens, Chapter 9, this volume). The main difference between situational prevention and these two approaches is that situational prevention seeks to eliminate *existing* problems, whereas DAC and CPTED seek to eliminate *anticipated* problems in new designs on the basis of past experience with similar designs. In fact, the problem-solving methodology of situational prevention is shared by another preventive approach called problem-oriented policing (see Scott *et al.*, Chapter 12, this volume). In both cases, the problem-solving methodology is a form of 'action research' in which the problem is studied, hypotheses about the main determinants are developed, a range of solutions are identified and studied, the chosen measures are put into place, and the results are then evaluated.

Consider a variety of solutions

Later in this chapter the final stage of the action research model is discussed – evaluation of situational prevention. This section concentrates on the preventive solutions. As mentioned, a detailed understanding of the sequential steps involved in committing the crime will yield many possible points of intervention. Generally speaking, a situational prevention project is more effective when it adopts a package of measures, each of which is directed to a particular point of the process of committing the crime. Thus, Poyner and Webb's recommendations to stop suburban burglaries were directed at different points in the process of completing these crimes – better surveillance of places where burglars might park their cars, improved security at the back of houses to stop them breaking in, and a crackdown on local fencing operations to make selling the stolen goods more difficult.

To assist the process of selecting solutions, situational prevention researchers have described and classified the many different ways that exist to reduce crime opportunities. The latest example is shown in Table 10.1. This classification shows 25 opportunity-reducing techniques grouped under five main headings: increase the effort, increase the risks, reduce the rewards, reduce provocations and remove excuses. The first three of these derive from the rational choice perspective (see Cornish and Clarke, Chapter 2, this volume); reducing provocations derives from social and environmental psychological theory (Wortley 2001, and Chapter 3, this volume); and removing excuses derives from Matza's and from Bandura's ideas about the facilitating role in crime of justifications made by offenders for their behaviour (Clarke and Homel 1997).

This discussion of solutions needs to conclude with a harsh fact: situational prevention might be easier to undertake than longer-term efforts to alter dispositions, but it can still be very difficult to implement (Knutsson and Clarke 2006). This is especially the case when situational prevention needs coordinated action among different agencies to be implemented, takes a long time and requires a series of steps, is implemented by staff with little understanding of the problem or the solutions, and lacks either the support of top administrators or a 'champion' to push things forward. Difficulties also occur when the solutions are implemented by an agency that is in turmoil or is poorly resourced and that gains little direct benefit from the work.

Hope and Murphy's (1983) description of a vandalism prevention project undertaken in eleven schools in a British city gives a flavour of these difficulties. The project was not considered a success because the recommendations were only fully implemented in two of the schools; in six schools one or more recommendations failed to materialise; and in the remaining three schools none were put in place. This was partly due to strike action by local government employees during the implementation phase and to the turmoil resulting from a reorganisation of the schools following a decline in pupil numbers. But there were also some more specific reasons, as follows:

Table 10.1 Twenty-five techniques of situational prevention

Increase the effort	Increase the risks	Reduce the rewards	Reduce provocations	Remove excuses
1 *Target harden* • Steering column locks and ignition immobilisers • Anti-robbery screens • Tamper-proof packaging	6 *Extend guardianship* • Go out in group at night • Leave signs of occupancy • Carry cell phone	11 *Conceal targets* • Off-street parking • Gender-neutral phone directories • Unmarked armoured trucks	16 *Reduce frustrations and stress* • Efficient lines • Polite service • Expanded seating • Soothing music/muted lights	21 *Set rules* • Rental agreements • Harassment codes • Hotel registration
2 *Control access to facilities* • Entry phones • Electronic card access • Baggage screening	7 *Assist natural surveillance* • Improved street lighting • Defensible space design • Support whistleblowers	12 *Remove targets* • Removable car radio • Women's shelters • Pre-paid cards for pay phones	17 *Avoid disputes* • Separate seating for rival soccer fans • Reduce crowding in bars • Fixed cab fares	22 *Post instructions* • 'No Parking' • 'Private Property' • 'Extinguish camp fires'
3 *Screen exits* • Ticket needed for exit • Export documents • Electronic merchandise tags	8 *Reduce anonymity* • Taxi driver IDs • 'How's my driving?' decals • School uniforms	13 *Identify property* • Property marking • Vehicle licensing and parts marking • Cattle branding	18 *Reduce temptation and arousal* • Controls on violent pornography • Enforce good behaviour on soccer field • Prohibit racial slurs	23 *Alert conscience* • Roadside speed display boards • Signatures for customs declarations • 'Shoplifting is stealing'

4 Deflect offenders	9 Use place managers	14 Disrupt markets	19 Neutralise peer pressure	24 Assist compliance
• Street closures • Separate bathrooms for women • Disperse pubs	• CCTV for double-deck buses • Two clerks for convenience stores • Reward vigilance	• Monitor pawn shops • Controls on classified ads • License street vendors	• 'Idiots drink and drive' • 'It's OK to say No' • Disperse troublemakers at school	• Easy library checkout • Public lavatories • Litter receptacles
5 Control tools/weapons	**10 Strengthen formal surveillance**	**15 Deny benefits**	**20 Discourage imitation**	**25 Control drugs and alcohol**
'Smart guns' • Restrict spray paint sales to juveniles • Toughened beer glasses	• Red light cameras • Burglar alarms • Security guards	• Ink merchandise tags • Graffiti cleaning • Disabling stolen cell phones	• Rapid repair of vandalism • V-chips in TVs • Censor details of *modus operandi*	• Breathalysers in bars • Server intervention programmes • Alcohol-free events

(*Source*: Clarke and Eck 2003; Cornish and Clarke 2003)

- It was recommended that vulnerable windows in some schools should be replaced with polycarbonate glazing or toughened glass, but not a single pane of either type was installed. It turned out that polycarbonate could prevent escape in the event of a fire and it might give off toxic fumes. Toughened glass had to be cut to size before it was toughened, but the panes came in too many sizes to store a few of each size in readiness. It would also have taken too long to supply a pane to order.

- The municipal agency charged with moving a playground in one school to a less vulnerable area and replacing it with flowerbeds got no further than providing an estimate for the work. The relocation work was then contracted to a private builder, but due to a misunderstanding only half the proposed area was resurfaced. At the end of the project, vandalism was unchanged, there were no flowers, and the school had acquired a useless, narrow strip of concrete.

- Recommendations that were the sole responsibility of the school system's maintenance department were all implemented; however, none of those involving coordination with other departments or agencies ever materialised. For example, two schools developed a plan for encouraging people who lived nearby to report anything suspicious to the police that occurred after hours. This plan required cooperation between the police, the school system administrators, and the staff of the schools. All liked the idea, but no one would take the lead.

- At one badly affected school it was decided to mount a security patrol in the holidays staffed by school maintenance workers. This was immediately successful in reducing vandalism and was extended beyond school holidays to evenings and weekends. Other schools demanded the same protection and more maintenance workers wanted the additional overtime payments. Ultimately the costs became too high and the project was scrapped.

The effectiveness of situational prevention

Many, many case studies using the principles of situational prevention have been published since the concept was first described more than 25 years ago (Clarke 1980). Smith *et al.* (2002) identified 142 situational prevention case studies at 211 sites, most of which involve common property offences of burglary, car theft and vandalism, but which also cover fraud, robbery, street prostitution, drug-dealing, and violent assaults (Homel *et al.* 1997). More recently, situational prevention has applied to child sexual abuse (Wortley and Smallbone 2006), crime and misconduct in prisons (Wortley 2002), internet frauds (Newman and Clarke 2003) and terrorism (Clarke and Newman 2006).

Reductions in the specific crimes addressed have generally been achieved and sometimes the reductions have been dramatic. To take two examples, a plague of bus robberies in New York and eighteen other US cities in the early 1970s was largely eliminated by the introduction of exact fares systems coupled with the installation of drop safes in buses (Chaiken *et al.* 1974; Stanford Research Institute 1970). This form of 'target removal' meant that there was no longer any point in attempting to rob the driver. More recently, US cellphone companies largely wiped out cloning by the introduction of five new anti-cloning technologies (Clarke *et al.* 2001); at its height, this problem had been costing the companies about $800 million per year in fraudulent phone calls (see Figure 10.1).

Probably no other form of crime control can claim this record of evaluated successes, but some critics continue to dispute the evidence. They continue to focus on failures, such as the school vandalism project discussed above, and they argue that situational prevention has been evaluated using only weak research designs; that the reductions claimed are negated by displacement (i.e. the offenders shift their attention to other places, times and targets, use different methods or commit different crimes); that situational prevention results in escalation (i.e. offenders resort to more harmful methods to gain their ends); and that even if displacement does not occur immediately, the criminal population adapts in the long run to reduced opportunities by discovering new ways to commit crime.

Displacement

The most persistent of these criticisms concerns displacement. Because of dispositional assumptions, critics seem to assume that there is a drive to commit crime that cannot be thwarted. But crime is very rarely a compulsion and the displacement thesis is overstated. It may be credible for some crimes, but certainly not for all. Thus, it is highly unlikely that motorists prevented from speeding on a particular stretch of road would seek out another road, somewhere else, on which to speed, or that the shoppers, prevented from

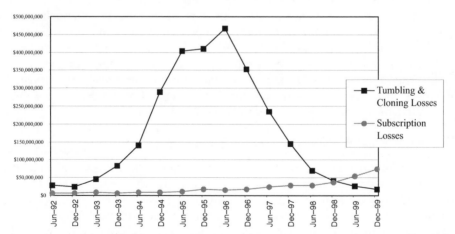

Figure 10.1 Semi-annual fraud dollar losses, United States, June 1992–December 1999

(*Source*: Clarke *et al.* 2001)

stealing at their local supermarket by new security measures, would begin to shop at some more distant store where they could continue to shoplift. Even less likely is that they would turn to mugging senior citizens because shoplifting is easier to rationalise and much less risky than mugging. In fact, almost by definition, any instance of escalation is more costly for offenders. Some of them may be prepared to make more difficult rationalisations or run additional risks, but they will be a minority.

Developments in theory have further undermined claims about the inevitability of displacement and the risks of escalation. If opportunity increases the amount of crime, and crime can result from a variety of situational precipitators, there is every reason to believe that reducing these opportunities and inducements will result in real reductions in crime. In fact, this is the message of the empirical research. Three separate reviews of the evidence on displacement found that it can occur, but it is not inevitable. In the most recent review, Hesseling (1994) found no evidence of displacement in 22 of the 55 studies he examined; in the remaining 33 studies, he found some evidence of displacement, but in no case was there as much crime displaced as prevented.

Much the same would probably be found if his review were repeated today, when many more studies of displacement have been reported. For example, little displacement seems to have occurred to 'subscriber' fraud, the second largest category of cellphone fraud, when cloning was largely eliminated in the United States (see the lower line in Figure 10.1). Subscriber frauds involve the use of a false name and address to obtain cellphone service. They would be difficult to reproduce on a wide scale and would therefore not be attractive to organised groups. Cloned phones, on the other hand, were 'mass produced' by offenders who had learned how to acquire hundreds of legitimate phone numbers and programme them into stolen phones.

We have no way of knowing whether the offenders stopped from cloning turned to other forms of fraud not involving cellphones, but it is possible that many of them were not exclusively dependent on crime for a living. It might have been a sideline for them, or merely a way of making money for a time. When cloning was closed down, they might have had to make do with reduced income – like we all must do from time to time – or they might have turned their energies to legitimate ways of making money. Such positive outcomes from the application of situational prevention become conceivable once freed from dispositional assumptions about crime.

Diffusion of benefits and anticipatory benefits

Another positive outcome of situational prevention is 'diffusion of benefits'. Sometimes described as the reverse of displacement, the term refers to the fact that situational prevention can often bring about reductions in crime beyond the immediate focus of the measures introduced (Clarke and Weisburd 1994). This greatly enhances the practical appeal of situational prevention, especially as the phenomenon is quite general, as shown by the following examples:

- Security added to houses that had been repeatedly burgled in Kirkholt reduced burglaries for the whole of the estate, not just for those houses given additional protection (Pease 1991).

- When 'red light' cameras were installed at some traffic lights in Strathclyde, Scotland, not only did fewer people 'run the lights' at these locations, but also at other traffic lights nearby (Scottish Central Research Unit 1995).

- CCTV cameras installed to monitor car parks at the University of Surrey reduced car crime as much in one not covered by the cameras as in the three that were covered (Poyner 1991).

- When a New Jersey discount electronic retailer introduced a regime of daily counting of valuable merchandise in the warehouse, employee thefts of these items plummeted – but thefts also plummeted of items not repeatedly counted (Masuda 1992).

The explanation for these results seems to be that potential offenders often know that new prevention measures have been introduced, but they may be unsure of their precise scope. They may believe the measures are more widespread than they really are, and that the *effort* needed to commit crime, or the *risks* incurred, have been increased for a wider range of places, times or targets than in fact is the case.

The benefits of diffusion are likely to decay when offenders discover that the risks and effort of committing crime have not increased as much as they had thought. Thus, in a smaller city than Strathclyde, with more local traffic, people might quickly have learned exactly which junctions had red light cameras and the diffusion of benefits might have been short-lived. This means that ways will have to be found of keeping offenders guessing about the precise levels of threat, or quite how much extra effort is needed if they are to continue with crime.

Just as offenders often overestimate the reach of situational prevention, they often believe that prevention measures have been brought into force before they actually have been. This is what is meant by the 'anticipatory benefits' of prevention. Smith *et al.* (2002) found evidence of anticipatory benefits in perhaps as many as 40 per cent of situational prevention projects. Apart from using publicity, little is known about how to deliberately enhance these benefits, but they certainly provide 'added value' to situational prevention.

Adaptation

The concept of criminal adaptation further complicates evaluation of situational prevention. It refers to the process through which offender *populations* discover new crime vulnerabilities after preventive measures have been in place for a while. It is a longer-term process than displacement, which refers to the ways in which *individual* offenders seek to circumvent measures put in place to stop them.

One clear example of adaptation concerns baggage and passenger screening measures introduced in the early 1970s to curb hijackings of airliners between the United States and Cuba. These measures, together with an agreement between the countries to treat hijackers as criminals, quickly eliminated the hijackings (see Table 10.2). Other countries soon adopted the screening measures and hijackings outside the Americas also declined (bear in mind that the table shows actual numbers of hijackings, not rates, and during this period there was a huge increase in the number of airliners and flights). Despite some claims to the contrary, there was no real evidence of any displacement (see Clarke and Newman 2006); in particular, as Table 10.2 shows, there was no increase in sabotage bombings of airlines. However, the screening measures were premised on the assumption that hijackers were not intent on suicide and, anyway, the authorities became increasingly lax over time. This allowed the 9/11 hijackers to find loopholes in the security and seize the airliners. Their attack is a clear example of adaptation to preventive measures. It is not displacement because the 9/11 hijackers were completely different from the offenders (those operating in the 1970s between the United States and Cuba) who made the original introduction of the screening measures necessary.

Social and ethical issues

When first proposed, critics condemned situational prevention for promoting 'big brother' social controls and a 'fortress society'. Since then it has been criticised for 'blaming the victim', for restricting personal freedoms, for 'piecemeal social engineering' (see Tilley 2004 for a discussion), for serving the interests of the powerful, for promoting a selfish exclusionary society and for diverting government attention from the root causes of crime. These criticisms have rarely been spelled out in any detail, though some are discussed in Von

Table 10.2 Numbers of airliner hijackings and sabotage bombings, 1961–2003*

Period	Number of Years	Average hijackings per year US	Average hijackings per year non-US	Average bombings per year worldwide
1961–1967	7	1.6	3.0	1.0
1968	1	20.0	15.0	1.0
1969–1970	2	30.5	58.0	4.5
1971–1972	2	27.0	33.0	4.5
1973–1985	13	9.4	22.7	2.2
1986–1989	4	2.8	9.0	2.0
1990–2000	11	0.3	18.5	0.3
2001–2003	3	1.3	5.7	0.0
1961–2003	43	6.7	17.9	1.6

*Including attempts
(*Source*: Clarke and Newman 2006)

Hirsch *et al.* (2000). Answers can be given to each one of them (for example, see Table 10.3 for summaries), but leaving aside their substance, there are two reasons why the criticisms are misconceived.

First, many of the criticisms are addressed to the *practice* of situational prevention, not its *principles*. Many times opportunity-reducing measures are put into place without the careful analysis and evaluation required by situational prevention. For example, a government might decide for largely political reasons that CCTV should be installed in public places. This can result in it being placed where it offends people's notions of privacy or where it may not be needed, so that there is little effect on crime. Such failures cannot be used to criticise the concept of situational prevention, only the way it has been implemented. Another example is that, in its early days, situational prevention was criticised for being focused only on crimes committed by the 'working class', not by the middle classes ('crime in the streets, not in the suites'). There was some truth to this, partly because situational prevention was developed by government criminologists in the UK's Home Office, who were trying to

Table 10.3 Seven criticisms of situational crime prevention – and rebuttals

Criticism	Rebuttal
1 It is simplistic and atheoretical	It is based on three crime theories: routine activity, crime pattern and rational choice. It also draws on social psychology.
2 It is ineffective; it displaces crime and often makes it worse	Many dozens of case studies show that it can reduce crime, usually with little displacement.
3 It diverts government attention from the root causes of crime	It achieves immediate results and allows time for finding longer-term solutions to crime.
4 It is a conservative, managerial approach to the crime problem	It promises no more than it can deliver. It requires that solutions be economic and socially acceptable.
5 It promotes a selfish, exclusionary society	It provides as much protection to the poor as to the rich. Thus, one of the first applications of situational prevention principles was in public housing (Newman 1972).
6 It promotes Big Brother and restricts personal freedoms	The democratic process protects society from these dangers. People are willing to endure inconvenience and small infringements of liberty when these protect them from crime.
7 It blames the victim	It empowers victims by providing information about crime risks and how to avoid them.

(*Source*: Clarke 2005)

deliver practical crime reduction ideas in a society deeply disturbed by levels of burglary, car theft and vandalism. Twenty-five years later, as more criminologists have become interested in the concept, situational prevention has been applied to a broader range of offences – including frauds, child sexual abuse and drunk driving – committed by people from all walks of life.

Second, the criticisms generally neglect a fundamental point about the action-research *process* of situational prevention – it requires a careful assessment of possible solutions before they are implemented. As explained above, many different solutions can be found for a specific problem of crime and disorder if it is analysed in enough detail. These solutions need to be carefully assessed for their cost and benefits. In all cases, the assessment must go beyond financial considerations and must include a variety of social and ethical costs – intrusiveness, inconvenience, unfairness, discrimination, etc. Even if the assessment is informal, as it usually must be, this stage should never be skipped. Because there are always many different ways to reduce opportunities, there is no necessity to adopt a particular solution if it is found unacceptable in certain respects.

Conclusion

From the start, criminologists have generally shown little interest in situational prevention, for reasons that are not difficult to understand. Apart from the fundamental disagreement about causal theory, situational prevention does little to promote the welfarist, social reform agendas of most criminologists. It also offends many of their attitudes, which include suspicion of governmental authority, distaste for business, fear of corporate power, distrust of wealth and sympathy for the criminal underdog. Moreover, many criminologists are uncomfortable with situational prevention's crime control agenda. They see their role as being simply to understand and explain crime, leaving others to draw out the policy implications. In their view, situational prevention threatens to turn criminology into a technical discourse more in tune with the police and the security industry than with academia.

Some commentators believe that situational prevention is the fastest growing form of crime control worldwide and it might seem that the lack of criminological interest has not harmed situational prevention. On the other hand, if criminologists had laid claim to situational prevention they could take credit for its successes. If more of them had taken an interest in the concept, there would now be an even more solid record of success covering a wider set of crimes. The underlying theories might have been developed more fully and the failures of dispositional explanations might have been exposed sooner (see Weisburd and Piquero, in press). The scientific understanding of crime would also have been enriched by incorporating the wealth of findings about situational determinants. Finally, many more young criminologists would have been launched on rewarding crime control careers, contributing to society and helping to improve the lives of ordinary people, while at the same time bypassing the serious problems of criminal justice sanctioning.

References

Chaiken, J.M., Lawless, M.W., Stevenson and K.A. (1974) *The Impact of Police Activity on Crime: Robberies on the New York City Subway System*, Report No. R-1424-N.Y.C. Santa Monica, CA: Rand Corporation.

Clarke, R.V. (1980) 'Situational Crime Prevention: Theory and Practice', *British Journal of Criminology*, 20: 136–47.

Clarke, R.V. (2005) 'Seven Misconceptions of Situational Crime Prevention', in N. Tilley (ed.) *Handbook of Crime Prevention and Community Safety*. Cullompton, UK: Willan Publishing.

Clarke, R.V. and Eck, J. (2003) *Become a Problem-solving Crime Analyst: In 55 Small Steps*. London: Jill Dando Institute of Crime Science, UCL (accessible at www.popcenter. org).

Clarke, R.V. and Eck, J. (2005) *Crime Analysis for Problem Solvers in 60 Small Steps*. Washington, DC: US Department of Justice Office of Community Oriented Policing Services (accessible at www.popcenter.org).

Clarke, R.V. and Homel, R. (1997) 'A Revised Classification of Situational Crime Prevention Techniques', in S.P. Lab (ed.) *Crime Prevention at a Crossroads*. Cincinnati, OH: Anderson.

Clarke, R.V. and Newman, G. (eds) (2005) *Designing Out Crime from Products and Systems. Crime Prevention Studies, Vol. 18*. Monsey, NY: Criminal Justice Press (accessible at www.popcenter.org).

Clarke, R.V. and Newman, G. (2006) *Outsmarting the Terrorists*. Westport, CT: Praeger Security International.

Clarke, R.V. and Weisburd, D. (1994) 'Diffusion of Crime Control Benefits: Observations on the Reverse of Displacement', in R.V. Clarke (ed.) *Crime Prevention Studies, Vol. 2*. Monsey, NY: Criminal Justice Press.

Clarke, R.V., Kemper, R. and Wyckoff, L. (2001) 'Controlling Cell Phone Fraud in the US: Lessons for the UK "Foresight" Prevention Initiative', *Security Journal*, 14: 7–22.

Cornish, D.B. (1994) 'The Procedural Analysis of Offending, and its Relevance for Situational Prevention', in R.V. Clarke (ed.) *Crime Prevention Studies, Vol. 3*. Monsey, NY: Criminal Justice Press.

Cornish, D.B. and Clarke, R.V. (2003) 'Opportunities, Precipitators and Criminal Decisions', in M.J. Smith and D.B. Cornish (eds) *Crime Prevention Studies, Vol. 16*. Monsey, NY: Criminal Justice Press (accessible at www.popcenter.org).

Decker, S.H. *Using Offender Interviews to Inform Police Problem Solving. Problem-Oriented Guides for Police*, Problem Solving Tools Series, No. 3. Washington, DC: US Department of Justice. Office of Community Oriented Policing Services (accessible at www.popcenter.org).

Eck, J., Clarke, R.V. and Guerette, R. (2007) 'Risky Facilities: Crime Concentrations in Homogeneous Sets of Establishments and Facilities', in G. Farrell, K. Bowers, S. Johnson and M. Townsley (eds.) *Imagination for Crime Prevention. Crime Prevention Studies, Vol 21*. Monsey, NY: Criminal Justice Press (accessible at www.popcenter. org).

Ekblom, P. (1995) 'Less Crime, by Design', *Annals of the American Academy of Political and Social Science*, 539: 114–29.

Hesseling, R.B.P. (1994) 'Displacement: A Review of the Empirical Literature', in R.V. Clarke (ed.) *Crime Prevention Studies, Vol. 3*. Monsey, NY: Criminal Justice Press.

Homel, R., Hauritz, M., McIlwain, G., Wortley, R. and Carvolth, R. (1997) 'Preventing Drunkenness and Violence around Nightclubs in a Tourist Resort', in R.V. Clarke (ed.) *Situational Crime Prevention: Successful Case Studies,* 2nd edn. Albany, NY: Harrow and Heston.

Hope, T. and Murphy, D. (1983) 'Problems of Implementing Crime Prevention: The Experience of a Demonstration Project', *The Howard Journal,* 22: 38-50.

Knutsson, J. and Clarke, R.V. (eds) (2006) *Putting Theory to Work. Crime Prevention Studies, Vol 20.* Monsey, NY: Criminal Justice Press (accessible at www.popcenter. org).

Masuda, B. (1992) 'Displacement vs. Diffusion of Benefits and the Reduction of Inventory Losses in a Retail Environment', *Security Journal,* 3: 131–6.

Newman, G.R. and Clarke, R.V. (2003) *Superhighway Robbery: Preventing E-commerce Crime.* Cullompton, UK: Willan Publishing.

Newman, O. (1972) *Defensible Space: Crime Prevention Through Urban Design.* New York: Macmillan.

Pease, K. (1991) 'The Kirkholt Project: Preventing Burglary on a British Public Housing Estate', *Security Journal,* 2: 73–7.

Poyner, B. (1988) 'Video Cameras and Bus Vandalism', *Journal of Security Administration* 11: 44–51.

Poyner, B. (1991) 'Situational Prevention in Two Car Parks', *Security Journal,* 2: 96–101.

Poyner, B. and Webb, B. (1991) *Crime Free Housing.* Oxford, UK: Butterworth Architect.

Scottish Central Research Unit (1995) *Running the Red: An Evaluation of the Strathclyde Police Red Light Camera Initiative.* Edinburgh: The Scottish Office.

Smith, M.J., Clarke, R.V. and Pease, K. (2002) 'Anticipatory Benefits in Crime Prevention', in N. Tilley (ed.) *Analysis for Crime Prevention. Crime Prevention Studies, Vol. 13.* Monsey, NY: Criminal Justice Press (accessible at www.popcenter.org).

Stanford Research Institute (1970). *Reduction of Robbery and Assault of Bus Drivers. Vol. III, Technological and Operational Methods.* Stanford, CA: Stanford Research Institute.

Sutton, M. (2004) 'Tackling the Roots of Theft: Reducing Tolerance Toward Stolen Goods Markets', in R. Hopkins Burke (ed.) *Hard Cop, Soft Cop.* Cullompton, UK: Willan Publishing.

Taylor, I., Walton, P. and Young, J. (1973) *The New Criminology.* London: Routledge and Kegan Paul.

Tilley, N. (2004) 'Karl Popper: A Philosopher for Ronald Clarke's Situational Crime Prevention', *Israeli Studies in Criminology,* 8: 39–56.

Von Hirsch, A., Garland, D. and Wakefield, A. (eds) (2000) *Ethical and Social Issues in Situational Crime Prevention.* Oxford: Hart Publications.

Weisburd, D. and Piquero, A.R. (in press) 'Taking Stock of How Well Criminologists Explain Crime: A Review of Published Studies', *Crime and Justice.* Chicago: University of Chicago Press.

Wilson, J.Q. (1975). *Thinking about Crime.* New York: Basic Books.

Wortley, R. (2001) 'A Classification of Techniques for Controlling Situational Precipitators of Crime', *Security Journal,* 14: 63–82.

Wortley, R. (2002) *Situational Prison Control: Crime Prevention in Correctional Institutions.* Cambridge: Cambridge University Press.

Wortley, R. and Smallbone, S. (2006) *Situational Prevention of Child Sexual Abuse. Crime Prevention Studies, Vol. 19.* Monsey, NY: Criminal Justice Press (accessible at www. popcenter.org).

11. Designing products against crime

Paul Ekblom

Introduction

Consider these examples of 'bad' crime preventive design:

- Distinctive earphones telling criminals 'here's an expensive music player'.
- The player itself having little or no inbuilt security so it will play promiscuously for anyone who possesses it, legitimate or otherwise.
- Frustrating-to-use ticket machines which may provoke retaliatory vandalism.
- Syringes which can be re-used, facilitating cross-infection between drug addicts.
- A range of banknotes whose denominations are so similar in appearance that people unfamiliar with them can easily be short-changed.

Consider, too, these 'good' designs from Central Saint Martins College of Art and Design:

- The 'Karrysafe' bag range (Gamman and Hughes 2003) including this backpack (Figure 11.1), designed to look stylish while resisting a range of perpetrator techniques including slashing (by anti-rip material), grabbing (by reinforced handle) and 'dipping' (by replacing the normal flap or clasp top with a Velcro roll-top, which requires two hands to open and makes a noise when doing so).

- The 'Stop Thief' café chair (Figure 11.2, with Karrysafe handbag), following a classic style, with notches cut to enable bags to be secured beneath the knees, 'locked' in place by the user's legs, located where thieves find it risky to reach and users will be alert.

- The 'Puma Bike' (Figure 11.3) folding bicycle whose down-tube is replaced by a tensioned steel cable, which can be unlocked and passed round a stand to secure the bike; cutting the cable to release the bike destroys the bike's integrity and hence its use or resale value.

- The 'CaMden' bicycle stand (Figure 11.4) that forces people to lock their bikes to it in a secure way, i.e. with both wheels and the frame attached.

- The 'Grippa' clip (Figure 11.5), for securing bags to bar tables, designed to match bar decor, and easy and safe to use for customers, hard to release for thieves.

Figure 11.1   The 'Karrysafe' bag

Figure 11.2   The 'Stop Thief' café chair

Figure 11.3 The 'Puma Bike'

Figure 11.4 The 'CaMden' bicycle stand

Figure 11.5 The 'Grippa' clip

Bad designs can sometimes lead to good – vehicle security has greatly improved over the last 20 years and vehicle crime has markedly fallen (Sallybanks and Brown 1999; Webb 2005). In both good and bad instances, of course, the design is not the only contributor to raised or lowered crime risk, but adds to, or interacts with, other social and physical influences, such as the kinds of place in which it is exposed to crime hazards, and the lifestyle of the people who carry the products. One-dimensional 'design determinism' is not advocated here.

'Design against crime' (DAC, also known as designing out crime) uses the tools, processes and products of design to work in partnership with agencies, companies, individuals and communities to prevent all kinds of criminal events – including anti-social behaviour, drug abuse/dealing and terrorism – and to promote quality of life and sustainable living through enhanced community safety. It does so through designs that are 'fit for purpose' and contextually appropriate in all other respects.

The term 'products' has a wide sense in which it encompasses 'anything that has been designed' – places, systems, communications and so on. This chapter, however, focuses on the design of 'movable' or free-standing products in two dimensions (like banknotes or street signs) or three (such as cellphones or handbags/purses).

The review begins with some history. The next part discusses the nature of design; the following section covers the role of products in crime, risk factors identifying which products feature in crime, and how product design can prevent crime. Then two kinds of challenge posed by design against crime are reviewed: how to make the *designs* work and keep working in diverse contexts and changing circumstances; and how to make the *designers* (and the design decision-makers who call the tune) work on DAC in terms of their awareness, motivation and capacity. A brief review of issues of impact evidence precedes the conclusion.

In this chapter various practical conceptual frameworks are introduced or referred to. Up-to-date information on these is maintained at www. designagainstcrime.com – click on 'Crime Frameworks'. In many cases, further detail on the issues discussed here can be found in Ekblom (2005a) and other papers listed in the references.

History ancient and modern

Designing products against crime has a long history closely intertwined with technological progress and commodity prices – well illustrated by the evolution of money. Shortly after the Greeks introduced silver coinage in around 600 BC, someone produced a silver-plated bronze forgery (James and Thorpe 1994). The anti-counterfeit design feature of apparently accidental micro-marks on coins is of equal antiquity. The potential harm from undermining the currency, for example by clipping the edge from hammered silver coins, provoked harsh punishment, but technological/design interventions such as milled edges may have had greater impact. Interestingly, monetary design has long incorporated self-evident 'help the user' security features, culminating in today's foil strips as well as arcane 'help the bank' ones.

Changes in material composition have also made coins more secure – silver was removed to repay British wartime debts to the USA; inflation removed much of the remaining symbolic value relative to the risk, cost and effort of counterfeiting. However, as commodity prices fluctuate, even bronze coins' intrinsic value can outstrip their symbolic value, making them targets for melting down in their turn.

Other 'historically hot' products have included jewellery and clothing, motor vehicles and, more recently, consumer electronics. Like legitimate demand, criminal demand follows fashion (there is even a clothing brand called Criminal, doubtless sought by wearers of Police sunglasses). This applies to phones as much as to fancy trainers. Both legitimate and criminal demand for a new product peaks, then diminishes with market saturation when everyone owns one (Felson 1997; Pease 2001) – until, that is, fashion changes revive both, by imparting artificial scarcity value to the latest model. This is good for neither crime prevention nor sustainability.

Preventing vehicle crime through design has come far since early ordinances required drivers to leave cars unlocked should they have to be moved. Specific interventions on steering column locks (Mayhew *et al.* 1976) and speculative ideas on 'crime-free cars' (Ekblom 1979) led in the UK to research on the practicalities of mass-market vehicle security (Southall and Ekblom 1985) and, through publication of a car theft index (Houghton 1992), successful attempts to name and shame lax manufacturers while awakening and guiding consumer choice. To this was added pressure from insurers who started to increase premiums for insecure models.

More strategic interest in designing products against crime lagged behind the emergence of crime prevention through environmental design (CPTED). That changed in the late 1990s in the UK at least, with initiatives under the national Crime Reduction Programme. These included:

- Research into the state of design against crime (Design Council 2000), and subsequent case studies and guidance materials building on that (Design Council 2003).
- Student design competitions through the Royal Society of Arts.
- An interest in products in the UK Foresight Programme's Crime Prevention Panel. (Department of Trade and Industry 2001).

Around the same time, Clarke (1999) published the seminal 'hot products' concept (described below), identifying which were at greatest risk of theft. However, strategic UK work was halted soon after as government funds were drained to control a street-crime panic. Ironically, although the crime wave was heightened by insecure product and system design of cellphones, the solution was an expensive and unsustainable boost of police overtime.

Research on cellphone vulnerability and security nevertheless continued in the UK (Harrington and Mayhew 2001) and USA (Clarke et al. 2001); and in Australia on product design more generally (Lester 2001). And 'practice-led' design studies began to emerge in the UK under an initiative led by Lorraine Gamman (e.g. Gamman and Pascoe 2004) at Central Saint Martins College of Art and Design. The European Commission, which had introduced a directive requiring member states to legislate for compulsory factory-fitted vehicle immobilisers from 1998, showed renewed interest in 'crime proofing' of domestic electronic products (such as music players), funding Project MARC (Armitage and Pease 2007; Ekblom and Sidebottom 2007) to pursue an approach to security rating suggested by Clarke and Newman (2005a). The UK Home Office has now incorporated DAC within its national crime reduction/safety strategy (Home Office 2007a: 33–7) and in 2007 inaugurated a Design and Technology Alliance involving designers, industrialists and academics, to take this forward.

Products and crime – the future

Major trends towards shifting value from outright ownership of products to leasing of serviced products may cause further changes in the role of products in crime, whether an outright reduction or a link to identity and service theft. 'Pervasive computing' (processor chips embedded in virtually any product), plus wireless connections of products to the internet for access to services, upgrades, etc., offer enormous scope for 'piggybacking' security functions at

200

little manufacturing cost, much as immobiliser functions have hitched a ride in vehicle engine management computers. Another trend with crime implications is 'mass-customising', where products are personalised via computer control of the production line. Which thief would risk being caught with personalised products when frisked by police on the street? Who would want to buy a stolen phone with someone else's partner's picture indelibly embedded in it?

Design fundamentals

What is design?

The full scope of design is enormous, potentially embracing all human productive and artistic activity in every medium. Focusing on the applied side, design is a generic *process* of creating some new or improved product which:

- Is materially possible to make (e.g. it doesn't fall apart, obeys the laws of science and respects the behaviour of its constituent materials).
- Is fit, or fitter than predecessors, for some specified primary purpose.
- Does not significantly interfere with other purposes or with wider requirements of social and economic life and the environment, including in cost terms.

Under this broad definition (adapted from Booch 1993) lies enormous variety among processes or approaches to design. At one end of the scale, say, we could envisage someone jamming a nail into a window frame to hastily secure it; at the other, a complex and sophisticated vehicle immobiliser system developed over years by large professional teams whose work has to be integrated by explicit managerial processes.

The *purpose* of the designed product can vary from utilitarian to aesthetic and the conveyance of image, lifestyle and value. Playful and subversive designs are also possible. A creative crime prevention example was one entry to the Royal Society of Arts' Student Design Award, which disguised the real openings in a rucksack with false, deterrent ones revealing apparent dirty underwear. The classic principle of 'form following function' can at times be supplanted by 'form following emotion'. In crime, of course, emotions are not always positive, hence (using Wortley's (2001) two-stage 'precipitation' model of situational prevention) a poster may provoke vandalism, or a knife prompt aggression.

Broadening horizons – drawing on design in the crime preventive process

Previously designers have been urged to 'think thief' about their products (Ekblom 1995, 1997; Design Council 2003). The emphasis here is more on encouraging crime preventers, and students of prevention, to 'draw on design' both practically and conceptually. Mapping out the nature and diversity of design is important, too, because crime preventers often have quite limited assumptions about what design means. Many will be familiar with the built environment interventions advocated by the CPTED (crime prevention through environmental design) movement, and with the design of locks, bolts and other security fittings. Both of these demonstrate the obvious relationship between DAC and situational crime prevention. However, DAC is far more than a set of products or buildings, important though they are. Understanding and applying the design *process*, the designer's way of capturing requirements and formulating and solving problems, can greatly benefit all crime prevention practitioners.

Products and crime

How products feature in crime

Unsurprisingly, products can feature in crime in myriad ways. Practical approaches must be systematic. Two linked frameworks can aid this (see Crime Frameworks at www.designagainstcrime.com). The Conjunction of Criminal Opportunity (Ekblom 2001), a more detailed equivalent of the crime triangle (Clarke and Eck 2003), can be used to define the broad types of role played by products in causing criminal events in general. Products can be:

- Targets.
- Target enclosures (e.g. houses, cars, containers, packaging or handbags).
- Environments (with products, e.g. the designed interior of trains, bus shelters or phone boxes).
- Resources for offending (e.g. tools, weapons – see Ekblom and Tilley 2000; Gill 2005) equivalent to 'facilitators' (Clarke and Eck 2003).

The Misdeeds and Security framework (Ekblom 2005b) describes how products feature as object, subject, tool or setting for particular *kinds* of criminal behaviour. Products can be:

- Misappropriated (stolen for themselves, their parts or materials).
- Mistreated (damaged, destroyed).
- Mishandled (counterfeited, copied, sold when stolen, or smuggled).
- Misused.
- Misbehaved with.

Criminal misuse or misbehaviour could implicate cordless drills as tools for burglary, cellphones for drug-dealing or illicitly photographing young swimmers, laser pointers as weapons, aerosol paint cans spraying graffiti on walls, computer programs controlling re-chipping of stolen phones, jewellery as props in confidence tricks.

Combining the frameworks generates permutations which can be used to organise what we know and (by providing boxes to fill) anticipate new risks. For example, targets of crime can be misappropriated, mistreated or mishandled. Enclosures can be mistreated by being broken into or carried off for their contents. Some products are heavily implicated in crime. Table 11.1 shows combined analysis of the roles played by motor vehicles.

Risk factors – which products feature in crime?

Not all classes of product are at equal risk of involvement in crime. Domestic consumer electronics items are at greater risk than domestic 'white goods' (washing machines, etc.). Likewise within a single class, not all makes and models are at equal risk, as the UK *Car Theft Index* (Home Office 2004) reveals. The 'classic' risk factor approach within situational crime prevention is Clarke's (1999) 'hot products', which covers theft. According to this model, based on a mix of statistical and theoretical analysis, the risk of theft is raised if the product is CRAVED:

- Concealable (by the offender).
- Removable.
- Available (lots of such targets about in accessible places).
- Valuable.
- Enjoyable.
- Disposable (via resale).

The best example is the cellphone. The value of CRAVED is in guiding the targeting of preventive effort: it is only reasonable to ask manufacturers to build additional security into a particular new product if it is likely, on sound research grounds, to be at high risk of theft.

A recent study (Armitage and Pease 2007) sought to incorporate CRAVED into a practical system of crime-proofing. The aim, following proposals by Clarke and Newman (2005a), was to encourage manufacturers of domestic electronic products judged to be at high risk of theft, to bestow upon them commensurately high security. Various difficulties were encountered, however, especially in development of a rating system for security. Ekblom and Sidebottom (2007) have attempted to learn from these experiences by evolving a wider suite of definitions of risk and security, and a range of different languages (e.g. technical, mechanistic, functional). They also drew on Cornish's (1994) concept of *crime scripts* to argue that designers need to consider the different risks to the product at different stages of the theft process (seek, see, take, escape, realise value). While concealability of a cellphone at the escape stage aids the thief, the same property at the seek/see stages helps the legitimate owner, who doesn't want the thief to spot it. Product design must envisage, and address, the whole sequence and any such design conflicts within it.

How does it work? How product design can prevent crime

Product security uses design and technology to reduce the risk of criminal events. Risk divides into *probability* of criminal events, and various kinds of *harm*

Table 11.1 The motor vehicle as criminogenic product

Nature of crime risk[2]	Motor vehicle as causal ingredient of crime[1]			
	Target of crime	Target enclosure	Environment	Resource/facilitator for crime
Misappropriation	Theft of car for resale	Theft from car	Pickpocketing in bus	Theft of car for misuse/misbehaviour
Mistreatment	Vandalised car	Damage to achieve entry; assassination of passengers	Assault/sexual assault on bus	Damage during misuse/misbehaviour
Misuse				Getaway, car, ram-raiding, drug-dealing, car bomb
Mishandling	'Ringing' of car identity smuggling, counterfeit spares	Delivery scams, falsifying weight of load carried by truck	Car burnt out to destroy DNA evidence	Avoidance of paying speeding fines, etc. by cloned number plate
Misbehaviour	Obscene messages in dirt on vehicle paintwork	Illegal use of cellphone when driving	Rowdy behaviour/taking drugs in stretch limo	Joyriding, speeding, drink driving

[1] From Conjunction of Criminal Opportunity Framework.
[2] From Misdeeds and Security Framework.

from those events to the product, the owner or others (see 'Crime Frameworks' at www.designagainst crime.com). The focus here is on probability.

Reducing the probability of crime by product design may work either by making the products objectively harder, riskier or less rewarding for the offender to exploit, or making them *perceived* as such by the offender – this is standard situational prevention. Obviously real resistance is more durable: offenders will eventually see through any pretence. However, the 'semiotics', or capacity to convey meaning, of design makes a significant additional contribution. Giving an objectively resistant product a robust appearance can confer the additional advantage of deterring or discouraging criminal *attempts*, and any damage they may cause (Whitehead *et al.* 2008). Think also of the winking red light indicating, faintly menacingly, an armed vehicle alarm. This strategy is used in nature by wasps which supplement stings with warning colouration (Ekblom 1997, 1999; Felson 2006).

There are four broad ways of objectively securing products against crime: designing them to be inherently secure, adding on security products, securing the immediate situation in which other products or people are at risk, and making remoter interventions.

Designing inherently secure products

Products designed to be inherently secure will incorporate specific 'security adaptations' – components, structural features or materials whose explicit purpose is to confer the security. Using the labels which are the 'security' counterpart of 'misdeeds', they may be:

Secured against misappropriation
- Spatially fragmented, e.g. computers whose terminals are cheap with the main processing done in a secure or remote location; or in-car entertainment systems whose components are distributed throughout the vehicle requiring more time, effort and knowledge to extract as a saleable set.

- Less distinctive or prompting targets to offenders at the 'seeking and seeing' stages of crime scripts, e.g. in-car entertainment systems that are camouflaged by a flap that descends when the vehicle is locked.

- More distinctive to law enforcers at the 'using and selling' stages of crime scripts, countering the anonymity of mass production and increasing risk to offender and secondary purchaser. This perhaps incorporates deliberately traceable features such as 'property marking' (Sutton *et al.* 2001). Advanced equivalents exist including incorporating multilayered paint spots with unique, registered colour sequences into the material of the product.

- Discriminating in allowing access to their value. This can include mechanical lockability, password operation, or intelligent systems that recognise they are not in the location they are meant to be, and shut down.

- Building on the last example, actively enhancing risk to offenders, and aiding recovery of loot, by sending tracking signals or internet messages to some system designed to receive and act on them.

Safeguarded against mistreatment
- Non-provocative, e.g. street signs that avoid couching regulations in confrontational terms.

- Physically resistant or resilient, such as laminated glass, street furniture that pops back into shape after being kicked in, or graffiti-resistant surfaces. Note that targets can be *softened* as well as hardened – a swivel on old-fashioned pocket watch fastenings prevented thieves applying force to snap them off, a technique used today to protect vehicle fuel caps (when locked, they spin free of the screwthread).

Scam-proofed against mishandling
- Indicative of loss or tampering. Examples include paint cans whose lids reveal they have been opened, by rupture of a thin membrane, preventing them being returned, refilled with water, for refund (Design Council 2003: case studies).

- Resistant to interception of information – e.g. fold-over airline baggage labels that conceal holidaymakers' addresses from professional burglars' touts.

- Resistant to fraud. Ticket machines on the London Underground were modified (Clarke 1997) so the last coin in became the first coin out in the eject mechanism. This frustrated offenders' fraudulent trick of putting a low-value 'slug' into the slot and ejecting a high-value coin in exchange. Security designs on official documents such as certificates of ownership or importation are made difficult to copy (Burrows and Ekblom 1986).

Shielded against misuse or misbehaviour
- Resistant: once-only syringes; beer glasses made from plastic that cannot be 'weaponised' (Design Council 2003: case studies); guns that fire only for the registered owner through a fingerprint scanner in the grip; colour photocopiers that recognise, and refuse, attempts to copy banknotes; waste bins that reveal their contents – including hidden bombs – or deflect blast upwards.

- Indicative: food or medicine containers with sealed or pop-up lids, a design response to the infamous Tylenol painkiller case where poison was substituted for medicine (Clarke and Newman 2005b); emergency alarms on trains which activate an appropriate CCTV camera.

- Non-provocative: sound insulation that prevents earphones annoying fellow travellers, thereby avoiding the occasionally serious conflict.

Inherent security, at one extreme, is an intrinsic property of a product: the massive inertia of some home cinema televisions makes them unlikely loot for opportunist burglars (see Cohen and Felson 1979). This could hardly be accredited to deliberate design as the weight is simply a by-product of other considerations such as the requirement to use plasma screens. However, future displays could perhaps be rolled up and carried off under the arm. Reliance on intrinsic security features should then be supplanted by designed-in security adaptations.

In the middle of the range inherent security can be achieved via simple and clever system design, such as the lighting tubes on London Underground trains which use a different voltage from domestic supply. This makes them unattractive to (moderately intelligent) thieves. At the other extreme are specialised security components, like holographic labels for brand protection of vodka (Design Council 2000); or the integration of the immobiliser function into, say, a vehicle engine management computer.

Adding on security products

Products which themselves are insecure can be protected by dedicated add-on security products, often fitted after a crime problem has become apparent.

- Laptops can be secured against theft by low-tech anchor-cables, or high-tech wireless sensors (transmitter incorporated in laptop, sensor in owner's pocket, which protests if the computer is moved).

- Add-on car alarms or steering-wheel locks can protect vehicles.

- Grilles and screens can safeguard street furniture against vandal damage.

- Expensive consumer items liable to counterfeiting can be scam-proofed by hard or expensive to copy packaging, e.g. using codes that only appear when body warmth is applied (Design Council 2000). However, the international nature of product piracy means factories in places like China are well appointed to copy even these – the practice has been both low risk and suited to mass-market sales.

Security add-ons may not provide the best solution to security, as the final part of the chapter discusses.

Securing the immediate situation in which products are at risk

Otherwise-insecure products can be kept in situations which have been made secure. This may involve the use of additional products, or environmental design, with little recourse to human intervention:

- Security products such as safes provide secure enclosures for storage; cages, e.g. for computer projectors in school classrooms, enable secure use.

- Physical or electronic access control methods can prevent unauthorised people from reaching the target products.

- Items readily to hand, which can be misused as an impromptu resource for crime, can be restricted. For example, designing lockable rubbish hoppers so they cannot be used as a temporary stash for stolen goods; securing 'emergency escape hammers', misused to break car windows, behind a screen sufficiently monitored to deter offenders; designing litterbins so empty bottles cannot be extracted for use in fights.

Often, however, designs are intended to work with human crime preventers and against crime promoters. The requirement to mobilise preventers may either be an on-cost of bad design, as with cars so vulnerable to theft they need guarding, realistic admission of a product design's limitations in particular circumstances, or positive exploitation of the human element:

- Some products, whose main function does not concern prevention, can be modified to alert and empower people in various kinds of crime preventer role. Guardians of targets can be aided in protecting their own bags in bars by the 'stop thief' chairs and table clips illustrated above. These can be called 'securing products'.

- Other products can constrain or influence people from unintentionally acting as crime promoters (those who do not commit the central offence being considered but who, perhaps through inaction, make it more likely). The M-shaped bike stand illustrated above forces cyclists to lock their bike securely (both wheels and the frame) rather than relying on a single lock in the middle of the crossbar, which leaves the wheels removable and the frame liable to misuse in the service of its own misappropriation – as a lever to snap the lock. User-friendly electronic locks on car doors remove obstacles of effort to securing the vehicle when parking.

- Inherently insecure products can be designed to compensate by prompting securing behaviour by their guardians. Vehicles nowadays give various (often intensely annoying) audio reminders e.g. to remove the key on leaving the car. As inbuilt intelligence increases in hot products such as music players, one can anticipate the incorporation of the same nag-functions. This is because they may be a cheaper solution to getting manufacturers off the moral/legal hook for theft prevention and deflecting responsibility on to the owner, than is incorporating inherent security.

- But human preventers can be unreliable. Some security functions have been designed to remove people from the loop: the car radio aerial built into the window glass does not require the driver to telescope it shut on leaving the vehicle. Removing human intermediaries more generally is not always beneficial. As Pease (2001) notes, the arrival of digital photography removed the employee-based surveillance from photographic development services which once kept paedophilic activities in check. And if circumstances change, the flexibility of human guardianship may be lacking.

- Preventers' presence, alertness, motivation, empowerment and direction could all fit within the design of some *integrated security system* (Tilley 2005). A familiar example is a retail security environment with an interior designed for surveillance, and where products or their packaging are fitted with tags which, if not neutralised by sales staff, activate detectors at the exit, bring security guards running, and provide legal evidence of ownership for the court.

Securing products by remote interventions

Vulnerable and valuable products can also be protected by actions beyond the immediate crime situation:

- Making it hard to obtain specialist tools used to remove a target product. Unfortunately, this goes against modern trends to hire out virtually anything, no questions asked. However, concerns about terrorist misuse of everyday items (like fertiliser) have begun to prompt a counter-trend of registration and identification.

- Limiting knowledge of where the target products can be found and what their vulnerabilities are. Again, this is counter to contemporary trends except for very high value, dangerous or 'critical infrastructure' products.

- Restricting the activities of deliberate crime promoters such as fences via a range of interventions including property marking and registration, tracking devices, etc. Specific laws have been enacted (e.g. in UK) forbidding recoding of stolen cellphones, or even possession of requisite equipment.

- The last can be part of a wider market-reduction approach to crime prevention (Sutton *et al.* 2001), where various actions on or through buyers, sellers, second-hand shops, etc. are explicitly combined with product identification techniques (which themselves could involve product or packaging design) and registration systems.

Together, the approaches described in this 'how does it work?' section exemplify most of the 25 techniques of situational crime prevention (Clarke and Eck 2003). Underlying these techniques they engage the familiar 'rational choice' mechanisms of increasing effort, cost, time and risk of harm to offender, and reducing reward. In some cases, however, the situational influences are directed towards changing not the offender's behaviour but that of preventers/promoters. But besides treating humans as 'active agents' in all these ways, design may also act through methods that are more 'causal', such as those that *provoke* criminal motivation (Wortley 2001).

The challenges of design against crime

Someone designing coffee machines must address manufacturing and shipping considerations, changing fashion, changing values (e.g. sustainability), evolving technology, the products of competitors and much more. Those designing products additionally to be crime resistant must squeeze in yet another, distinctive, set of requirements. Worse, they must cope with, or preferably anticipate, adaptive adversaries who may develop countermoves against the resistance.

Designs fit-for-purpose: troublesome trade-offs

Despite public concern about crime, when it comes to everyday priorities of consumers, crime prevention is often way down the list. People want a car that is stylish, high performance, economical, safe and cheap – and by the way, one that does not get stolen or broken into. A major challenge, therefore, is how to design products that are secure without jeopardising their main purpose or interfering with many other criteria. Designers must consider how incorporation of security interacts with a product's manufacture, safe and economic delivery through the supply chain, marketing, installation and ultimate disposal. Recognising, and reconciling, the range of potentially competing and conflicting requirements at (and between) all these stages is the heart of the industrial designer's skill. Several such 'troublesome trade-offs' are particularly significant. While presented in a product design context here, they can apply to all kinds of crime prevention intervention or problem-oriented policing solution.

- *Aesthetics*: A familiar negative image of DAC is the 'fortress society'. Originally applied to built environments (blockhouses, heavy shutters), this could equally cover movable products: hideous armoured computer cases, ugly moneybelts, or chains on music players signalling 'uncool' risk-aversion. Crude fortification can happen, of course, through thoughtless commissioning and bad or compartmentalised design. But as seen earlier, for example, perfectly aesthetic handbags can be designed that are secure in diverse ways against dipping and slashing (Gamman and Hughes 2003), and window-embedded car radio aerials can be designed without obvious protective engineering features.

- *Legal and ethical issues*: Designers against crime must also consider whether their proposal violates privacy or unacceptably constrains freedom. One example is a mobile phone that reports on someone's movements without their awareness or free consent. Communicating lack of trust may also be an issue, as in over-intrusive anti-shoplifting devices.

- *Sustainability*: Crime prevention requirements sit alongside environmental/energy considerations. One approach to preventing shoplifting of small, pocketable goods is to put them in a big package; this consumes materials and energy. One item to receive this treatment (Design Council 2000) was a small torch, but cleverly, the packaging material came from surplus plastic from manufacturing the product itself.

- *Nuisance*: This is another trade-off in the quality of the social environment. Whereas designing insecure cars may export costs of crime on to victims and the rest of society (Hardie and Hobbs 2005; Roman and Farrell 2002), poorly designed car alarms export the costs of crime *prevention*.

- *Safety*: With efforts to stop drink-driving or restrict weapon use, safety and crime prevention are on the same side (intelligent cars can recognise and act on drink-diminished skills and intelligent weapons fire only for their registered owner). However, safety (and failsafe) considerations can collide with security. Nobody wants a crime-proof car that occupants cannot be rescued from. But creative leaps can serve both safety and crime prevention. The bottom run of some fire escape stairs are drawn up from street level, thwarting burglars but sliding down under the weight of fleeing occupants.

- *Convenience*: Design against crime must be simultaneously user-friendly while abuser-unfriendly (Ekblom 2005a). Elaborate security procedures, forgettable passwords and awkward locks rapidly destroy a product's allure. They will also conflict with inclusive design (see www.designcouncil. org.uk/en/About-Design/Design-Techniques/Inclusive-design/), which aims to make products and places readily and unobtrusively usable by the elderly or disabled. Indeed, difficult security features may well be bypassed. Who has not seen a seedy advertisement on a street stall for unblocking of cellphones?

- *Cost*: Every additional feature in a product imposes extra cost on the design process and manufacture. In fiercely competitive sectors like automotive design or consumer electronics even additional pence may be unacceptable. But some security features only require thought at the design stage. An example is the road sign for the River Uck, which (as can be imagined) is quite provocative of graffiti. Presumably after wearying experience, the local council devised the sign shown in Figure 11.6 to deny writing space for the offending extra letter.

Figure 11.6   River Uck sign

Ingenuity apart, the earlier crime considerations are raised in the design process, the easier to optimise troublesome trade-offs. Security features will be less obtrusive, hence more aesthetic and less vulnerable to counterattack; operation may be more user-friendly; constraints on design freedom less, and costs reduced.

Sometimes, new technology can relax these trade-offs. In cars, the arrival of cheap, reliable miniature electric motors allowed the discriminant function of locks to be physically detached from the actuator devices that latch the doors, removing size, space and reliability constraints on the design of door security. But technology and engineering must yield to wider design requirements. Superficial, 'bolt-on-drop-off' techno-fixes or clunky, awkward engineering solutions like heavy grilles are unfortunately encountered and spoil the reputation of DAC (Ekblom 2005a).

Anticipating risk

Continual arrival on the market of new, naively insecure products generates what Pease (2001) calls 'crime harvests', followed by hasty retrospective efforts to cope with the crime and clumsily patch the damage by remedial design. The classic example has been with cellphones (Clarke *et al.* 2001). Although older leaks are now plugged, arguably the early vulnerabilities enabled the establishment of a crime market, with criminal expertise, criminal service providers and criminal networks. Advances in technology also produce a steady stream of new resources for crime, like cordless drills, or pocketable 12V batteries (which can be misused to energise car door locks). Previously secure items become vulnerable overnight.

Anticipation could avoid many of these problems. Clarke's (1999) 'hot products' concept was conceived to predict which new products could be prone to theft. And to match the largely empirical identification of risk factors underlying CRAVED, the more theoretical approach of routine activity theory (Cohen and Felson 1979; Felson 1997; Pease 1997) and the Conjunction of Criminal Opportunity framework (Ekblom 2002, 2005b; see 'Crime Frameworks' at www.designagainstcrime.com) can be applied.

Offenders fight back

As every discussion of displacement acknowledges, offenders are adaptable: potentially able to circumvent crime prevention methods by changing location, target or (most relevant to DAC) tactics. The word *potentially* is significant, because reviews of the more conventional kinds of displacement over the shorter term (e.g. Hesseling 1994) show it is rare or only partial. In DAC, however, the wider picture of offender adaptation is not so clear, although quantitative evidence is lacking. Offenders can respond to crime-resistant design at several levels:

- Making tactical countermoves *in situ* – spraying quick-setting foam in car alarms to deaden the sound.

- Turning crime prevention devices to their own advantage – anti-shoplifting mirrors work both ways; communal CCTV in blocks of flats has been misused by residents to spot which neighbours are going out, prior to burgling their flat.

- Turning designer themselves and developing tools as described above; perhaps doing sophisticated reverse engineering of locks to understand and defeat the mechanism.

Crime prevention is a kind of arms race (Ekblom 1997, 1999) between crime preventers and adaptive offenders who innovate, exploit change and enjoy the obsolescence of familiar crime prevention methods. A good illustration (Shover 1996) is the unfolding history of safes and safe-crackers. A more recent example concerns credit-card fraud (Levi and Handley 1998) where the game shifts from one *modus operandi* (such as theft and misuse of card) to another (e.g. 'card not present', as with internet purchases) as each successive loophole is closed.

In the longer term, crime levels depend on which side is innovating, and mainstreaming their innovations, faster than the other. And offender innovation is accelerating. Previously, techniques were often learned in prison, but guides on making bombs or picking locks now regularly appear on the internet. Preventers can, however, catch up by learning from other 'evolutionary struggles' including military, predator versus prey, antibiotic versus bacteria, and pest versus pest control. Ekblom (1997, 1999, 2005a) explores these issues in depth, and see also Felson (2006).

Involving designers in DAC

Few crime prevention interventions in the 'civil' world of work, leisure, travel and shopping are directly implemented by police and other professional crime preventers. Usually, the professionals aim to get other people or institutions to take responsibility for implementing and sometimes designing the intervention. This is the sphere of *involvement*. Involvement in turn has three main aspects – climate-setting, partnership (as between government and insurance companies, well developed in the Netherlands – see www.theccv.eu) and mobilisation. The first two are touched on below, but mobilisation is the key. One generic framework for mobilising crime preventers, CLAIMED (see 'Crime Frameworks' at www.designagainstcrime.com), sets out the following steps for mobilisation:

- Clarify the crime prevention tasks or roles that need doing, e.g. implementing the intervention itself; alleviating constraints; and supplying enablers.

- Locate the individuals or organisations best placed to undertake them, including designers, manufacturers, marketers and consumers. Then:

- Alert them that their product could be causing crime, or that they could help stop unrelated crimes.

- Inform them in detail of the risks.

- Motivate them.

- Empower them. And, where appropriate,

- Direct them.

This process can be done locally or nationally, by government, police or other institutions with an interest in crime prevention. Let's assume by this point that we have clarified the crime prevention tasks and roles, and located the designers and design decision-makers we wish to mobilise. What exactly do we do next?

Alerting designers, clients and customers to the role of design in crime

The cultural and political focus on the offender as problem, and 'cops, courts and corrections' as solution, has allowed designers and the manufacturers that commission them to get away with statements like 'don't blame my design, but the people who use it'; and the media, politicians and the public go along with this complicity with crime. The first stage in getting designers and design decision-makers to 'think thief', is to give them the right mindset. This is best done with a range of 'why didn't I think of that?' illustrations like those that opened this chapter.

Individual examples may have localised effects. Strategically it is important to establish a pervasive public climate of expectation that designers and manufacturers will have responsibility for addressing crime through effective product design, as has happened with vehicle security (Webb 2005).

Informing designers through intelligence on risk and design

For governments and insurers to act directly against insecure designs, or to get manufacturers, retailers and service providers to do likewise in a way that is efficient and proportionate to harm, it is necessary to know which products are insecure, to what degree, and why. Such evidence is also needed to inform the detail of design itself. There are three main approaches to obtaining it.

- *Deriving comparative risk rates* requires combining two kinds of information: the numbers of different makes and models (preferably by year, as production details change quite rapidly) exposed to crime, say, theft; and the numbers actually stolen. This is to index out a simple effect of numbers at risk – the more music players on the streets, the more would likely get stolen irrespective of design. This approach was successfully used to generate the UK *Car Theft Index* (e.g. Home Office 2004), intended to mobilise consumer pressure to encourage manufacturers to increase security levels. Vehicles, however, may be a special case – it was relatively straightforward to get the datasets on exposure (number of cars of each make and model on the road) and crime (from police records of this highly reported offence). It is hard to envisage any equivalent index for, say, laptops being easy to produce and reliable, although there may be scope with cellphones if manufacturers/ service providers are pressed to pool data. However, the situation may improve as products increasingly incorporate web-enabled electronics, and automated registration of ownership grows.

- *Attack testing* of products uses the tools and perpetrator techniques that offenders employ currently or are likely to adopt in the near future. The Association of British Insurers does just this for automobiles. Models rated insecure are assigned to a higher insurance premium band – as can be imagined, this concentrates the minds of the manufacturers because of its influence on consumer purchasing choice. Apart from on vehicles and financial systems, attack testing remains rare.

- *Systematic scrutiny of design and construction* of the products themselves seeks to identify vulnerabilities and assess whether security is commensurate with risk; and thence to assign a security rating. Such certification has been done with houses and other buildings (as with the UK Secured By Design scheme, and the equivalent Dutch Police Safe Housing). But attempts to develop ways for rating the security of movable products have yet to reach a practicable state, as experience with consumer electronics recently showed (Armitage and Pease 2007; Ekblom and Sidebottom 2007).

Both attack testing and systematic scrutiny draw on various kinds of background research. This can include literally picking up the pieces of some stolen product and looking at them forensically to see how the offender overcame any resistance; obtaining descriptions of perpetrator techniques from crime reports (sadly, rarely well documented); interviewing product-servicing people; and interviewing offenders to explicitly obtain this 'preventive intelligence'.

Motivating designers and others to take on crime

Much has been written on the problem of 'incentivising' crime prevention in general (e.g. Home Office 2006). Motivation of designers has been attempted through various awards (e.g. the Royal Society of Arts Student Design Awards, now Design Directions) and simply by stimulating them with the challenges of the task outlined above. But converting student enthusiasm into sustained interest and career commitment requires that for designers, crime pays; and that they see their crime-resistant designs consistently welcomed and put into production. The attention thus turns to design decision-makers.

Motivation of manufacturers to make their products secure can be achieved by hard or soft incentives, including an image of corporate social responsibility, naming and shaming, 'polluter-pays' taxes (Roman and Farrell 2002), awakening consumer expectations and pressures and imposing insurance costs, and legislation (Design Council 2000; Clarke and Newman 2005a). Hardie and Hobbs (2005) and Webb (2005) give good descriptions of how a combination of many of these pressures led to radical improvements in car security.

But none of the supply-side motivators are 'intrinsic' to the core profit motive of manufacturers and will always remain precarious. The closer the desire to incorporate crime resistance can be aligned to this 'natural' motivation, the more consistently, sustainably and creatively the task will be done. The general answer is to look towards demand-side motivation. However, while encouraging consumers to preferentially buy secure products is theoretically plausible (Design Council 2000), it has yet to convincingly demonstrate effective influence on choice, let alone showing that those choices go on to induce manufacturers to reduce crime.

Government intervention remains a vital corrective to 'market failures'. Clarke and Newman (2005b) assess various roles governments could undertake to support modification of criminogenic products, including acting as socially responsible large-scale procurers for their own needs, managing incentives and ensuring a level playing-field, so that socially responsible manufacturers do not lose out.

Empowering designers to make products crime resistant

Compared with the CPTED field, guidance for product designers has been sparse – but that is changing. The earlier Design Council guidance is increasingly being supplemented. With the founding of the DAC Research Centre in 2005, Central Saint Martins College has produced a range of materials in various media (www.designagainstcrime.com), including 'Know the Enemy', an animated guide to perpetrator techniques for stealing bicycles. Work to develop more sophisticated guidance on prevention of bike crime through more secure bikes and parking facilities is currently under way and will be available on www.bikeoff.org. Other British institutions have entered the field, including Loughborough University, which has been developing ways of assessing security features of cellphones (Whitehead *et al.* 2008); and the UK-Italian team of Project MARC (Armitage and Pease 2007) have taken forward the security rating process.

Directing designers – standards

Standards are an important implementation tool for government policy; but rigid requirements may make designs difficult to adapt to individual contexts and slow to adapt to change. And variety of preventive methods is important in running arms races. Enhancing design freedom is therefore vital in tackling crime. The paradox can be resolved if performance standards are used rather than technical or construction standards and if those performance standards are future-proofed. For example, a vehicle security specification would not be for 'hardened steel lock surrounds', but for 'locks which resist offenders, armed with the latest tools, for at least five minutes'. Such criteria are preferred by the UK Loss Prevention Certification Board, and the European CEN standards organisation.

DAC – evidence of impact

Assessment and feedback from studio tests, field trials, user and service engineer experience, and ultimately sales, profitability and market leadership are, of course, an inherent part of the evolutionary process that is product design. In evaluation and cost-effectiveness, terms normally applied to crime prevention, however, there is unfortunately little hard evidence to report that relates to product design as opposed to 'target-hardening' and other situational approaches in general (see, e.g. Clarke 1997; Ekblom 1998; Welsh and Farrington 2000). Such evidence as exists is often characterised by weak research designs; formally evaluated products are summarised in Clarke and Newman (2005b, Table 4). Circumstantial evidence (Sallybanks and Brown 1999; Webb 2005) points to the contribution of vehicle security technology towards the substantial and sustained reduction of theft of cars in the UK in recent years. British Crime Survey figures (Home Office 2007b: Table 2.01) show theft of vehicles reduced by 65 per cent from 1995 to 2006–7 following the design of improved security into the vehicle. Other evidence is anecdotal but, as Clarke and Newman (2005b) note, almost entirely self-evident. For example, remedial plastic housing was recently put on the end beams of train carriages to stop boys riding there, at mortal peril. The most superficial glance reveals that there is now simply nowhere for them to stand.

One research project currently under way (at Central Saint Martins College, evaluated by the Jill Dando Institute and mainly funded by UK Arts and Humanities Research Council) is, however, attempting a rigorous field evaluation of second-generation anti-theft clips to secure customers' bags to bar tables. The more such hard evidence can be obtained, the better DAC will fare in securing sustained funding and attention from government. The evidence may also help convince consumers to prefer products so designed and manufacturers to include security in their requirements capture.

Conclusion

The study and practice of designing products against crime lets us view the familiar with fresh eyes. It also leads to unfamiliar territory. DAC as a whole is simultaneously a relatively narrow domain of intervention within situational prevention, and a broad approach that can contribute to every kind of intervention and indeed to every stage of the preventive process.

DAC interventions can never be the complete answer to crime (although hard evidence either way is sorely needed). Implementation, too, is a major issue – how to mobilise producers and users to make the crime-resistant choice, and to realise it well. However, DAC will continue to help reduce all kinds of crime in ways that complement place management or offender-oriented interventions. The boundaries of its competence will surely undergo some drastic shifts as new technology and, especially, inbuilt or ambient web-based intelligence make their presence felt in everyday products and the systems and places they are embedded in.

References

Armitage, R. and Pease, K. (2007) 'Predicting and Preventing the Theft of Electronic Products', *European Journal on Criminal Policy and Research*, DOI:10.1007/s10610-007-9039-2.

Booch, G. (1993) *Object-oriented Analysis and Design with Applications*, 2nd edn. Boston, MA: Addison-Wesley Professional.

Burrows, J. and Ekblom, P. (1986) *Preventing Car Crime: An Initiative Affecting Vehicle Import Procedures,* Home Office Research Bulletin 21. London: Home Office.

Clarke, R.V. (1997) *Situational Crime Prevention: Successful Case Studies,* 2nd edn. New York: Harrow and Heston.

Clarke, R.V. (1999) *Hot Products: Understanding, Anticipating and Reducing Demand for Stolen Goods,* Police Research Series Paper 112. London: Home Office.

Clarke, R.V. and Eck, J. (2003) *Become a Problem Solving Crime Analyst: In 55 Small Steps.* London: Jill Dando Institute, University College London (www.jdi.ucl.ac.uk/publications/manual/crime manual content.php).

Clarke, R.V. and Newman, G. (2005a) 'Secured by Design. A Plan for Security Coding of Electronic Products', in R.V. Clarke and G. Newman (eds) *Designing Out Crime from Products and Systems. Crime Prevention Studies, Vol. 18.* Monsey, NY: Criminal Justice Press.

Clarke, R.V. and Newman, G. (2005b) 'Modifying Criminogenic Products – What Role for Government?', in R.V. Clarke and G. Newman (eds) *Designing Out Crime from Products and Systems. Crime Prevention Studies, Vol. 18.* Monsey, NY: Criminal Justice Press.

Clarke, R.V., Kemper, R. and Wyckoff, L. (2001) 'Controlling Cell Phone Fraud in the US: Lessons for the UK "Foresight" Prevention Initiative', *Security Journal,* 14: 7–22.

Cohen, L. and Felson, M. (1979) 'Social Change and Crime Rate Changes: A Routine Activities Approach', *American Sociological Review,* 44: 588–608.

Cornish, D. (1994) 'The Procedural Analysis of Offending and its Relevance for Situational Prevention', in R.V. Clarke (ed.) *Crime Prevention Studies, Vol. 3.* Monsey, NY: Criminal Justice Press, pp. 151–96.

Department of Trade and Industry (2000) *Turning the Corner.* Report of Foresight Programme's Crime Prevention Panel. London: Department of Trade and Industry (downloadable from www.foresight.gov.uk/previous rounds/foresight 1999 2002/crime prevention/reports/index.html).

Design Council (2000) *Design Against Crime,* A Report to the Design Council, the Home Office and the Department of Trade and Industry. Cambridge, Salford and Sheffield Hallam Universities (www.shu.ac.uk/schools/cs/cri/adrc/dac/designagainstcrimereport.pdf).

Design Council (2003) *Think Thief. A Designer's Guide to Designing Out Crime.* London: Design Council. See also case studies at www.designcouncil.org.uk/webdav/servlet/XRM?Page/@id=6016&Session/@id=D 5tNN7DzIbDAh8FVsL8C5&Document/@id=1250).

Ekblom, P. (1979) *A Crime-free Car?,* Home Office Research Bulletin 7. London: Home Office.

Ekblom, P. (1995) 'Less Crime, by Design', *Annals of the American Academy of Political and Social Science*, 539: 114–29 (special review edition edited by Professor Wesley Skogan, Northwestern University).

Ekblom, P. (1997) 'Gearing up Against Crime: A Dynamic Framework to Help Designers Keep up with the Adaptive Criminal in a Changing World', *International Journal of Risk, Security and Crime Prevention*, 2: 249–65.

Ekblom, P. (1998) 'Situational Crime Prevention', in P. Goldblatt and C. Lewis (eds) *Reducing Offending: An Assessment of Research Evidence on Ways of Dealing with Offending Behaviour*, Home Office Research Study 187. London: Home Office.

Ekblom, P. (1999) 'Can We Make Crime Prevention Adaptive by Learning from other Evolutionary Struggles?', *Studies on Crime and Crime Prevention*, 8(1): 27–51.

Ekblom, P. (2001) *The Conjunction of Criminal Opportunity: A Framework for Crime Reduction Toolkits*. Online at Crime Reduction website (www.crimereduction.gov.uk/learningzone/cco.htm).

Ekblom, P. (2002) 'Future Imperfect: Preparing for the Crimes to Come', *Criminal Justice Matters*, 46, Winter: 38–40.

Ekblom, P. (2005a) 'Designing Products against Crime', in N. Tilley (ed.) *Handbook of Crime Prevention and Community Safety*. Cullompton, UK: Willan Publishing.

Ekblom, P. (2005b) 'How to Police the Future: Scanning for Scientific and Technological Innovations which Generate Potential Threats and Opportunities in Crime, Policing and Crime Reduction', in M. Smith and N. Tilley (eds) *Crime Science: New Approaches to Preventing and Detecting Crime*. Cullompton, UK Willan Publishing.

Ekblom, P. and Sidebottom, A. (2007) 'What Do You Mean, "Is it Secure?" Redesigning Language to be Fit for the Task of Assessing the Security of Domestic and Personal Electronic Goods', *European Journal on Criminal Policy and Research*, (DOI: http://dx.doi.org/10.1007/s10610-007-9041-8").

Ekblom, P. and Tilley, N. (2000) 'Going Equipped: Criminology, Situational Crime Prevention and the Resourceful Offender', *British Journal of Criminology*, 40: 376–98.

Felson, M. (1997) 'Technology, Business, and Crime', in M. Felson and R.V. Clarke (eds) *Business and Crime Prevention*. Monsey, NY: Criminal Justice Press.

Felson, M. (2006) *Crime and Nature*. Thousand Oaks, CA: Sage.

Gamman, L. and Hughes, B. (2003) "Thinking thief' – Designing out Misuse, Abuse and "Criminal" Aesthetics', *Ingenia* 15 (www.raeng.org.uk/news/publications/ingenia/issue15/Gamman.pdf).

Gamman, L. and Pascoe, T. (eds) (2004) *Seeing is Believing, Crime Prevention and Community Safety Journal*, 6/4 (special issue).

Gill, M. (2005) 'Reducing the Capacity to Offend: Restricting Resources for Offending' in N. Tilley (ed.) *Handbook of Crime Prevention and Community Safety*. Cullompton, UK: Willan Publishing.

Hardie, J. and Hobbs, B. (2005) 'Partners against Crime – The Role of the Corporate Sector in Tackling Crime', in R.V. Clarke and G. Newman (eds) *Designing Out Crime from Products and Systems. Crime Prevention Studies*, Vol. 18. Monsey, NY: Criminal Justice Press.

Harrington, V. and Mayhew, P. (2001) *Mobile Phone Theft*, Home Office Research Study 235. London: Home Office.

Hesseling, R. (1994) 'Displacement: An Empirical Review of the Literature', in R.V. Clarke (ed.) *Crime Prevention Studies*, Vol. 3. Monsey, NY: Criminal Justice Press.

Home Office (2004) *The Car Theft Index 2004*. London: Home Office (www.crimereduction.homeoffice.gov.uk/cti/cit2004.pdf).

Home Office (2006) *Changing Behaviour to Prevent Crime: an Incentives-Based Approach*. Online report 05/06 (www.homeoffice.gov.uk/rds/pdfs06/rdsolr0506.pdf).

Home Office (2007a) *Cutting Crime. A New Partnership 2008–2011*. London: Home Office.

Home Office (2007b) *Crime in England and Wales 2006/7*, Statistical Bulletin 11/07. London: Home Office.

Houghton, G. (1992). *Car Theft in England and Wales. The Home Office Car Theft Index*, Crime Prevention Unit Paper 33. London: Home Office.

James, P. and Thorpe, N. (1994) *Ancient Inventions*. London: Michael O'Mara.

Learmont, S. (2005) 'Design Against Crime', in R.V. Clarke and G. Newman (eds) *Designing out Crime from Products and Systems. Crime Prevention Studies, Vol. 18.* Monsey, NY: Criminal Justice Press.

Lester, A. (2001) *Crime Reduction Through Product Design*, Trends and Issues in Crime and Criminal Justice No. 206. Canberra: Australian Institute of Criminology, (www.aic.gov.au/publications/tandi/tandi206.html).

Levi, M. and Handley, J. (1998) *The Prevention of Plastic and Cheque Fraud Revisited*, Home Office Research Study 182. London: Home Office.

Mayhew, P., Clarke, R., Sturman, A. and Hough, J. (1976) *Crime as Opportunity*, Home Office Research Study 34. London: Home Office.

Pease, K. (1997) 'Predicting the Future: The Roles of Routine Activity and Rational Choice Theory', in G. Newman, R.V. Clarke and S.G. Shoham (eds) *Rational Choice and Situational Crime Prevention: Theoretical Foundations*. Dartmouth, UK: Ashgate.

Pease, K. (2001) *Cracking Crime Through Design*. London: Design Council.

Roman, J. and Farrell, G. (2002) 'Cost-benefit Analysis for Crime Prevention: Opportunity Costs, Routine Savings and Crime Externalities', *Crime Prevention Studies*, 14: 53–92.

Sallybanks, J. and Brown, R. (1999) *Vehicle Crime Reduction: Turning the Corner*, Police Research Series Paper 119. London: Home Office.

Shover, N. (1996) *Great Pretenders: Pursuits and Careers of Persistent Thieves*. London: Westview Press/HarperCollins.

Southall, D. and Ekblom, P. (1985) *Designing for Vehicle Security: Towards a Crime Free Car*, Crime Prevention Unit Paper 4. London: Home Office.

Sutton, M., Schneider, J. and Hetherington, S. (2001) *Tackling Theft with the Market Reduction Approach*, Crime Reduction Research Series Paper 8. London: Home Office.

Tilley, N. (2005) 'Crime Prevention and System Design', in N. Tilley (ed.) *Handbook of Crime Prevention and Community Safety*. Cullompton, UK: Willan Publishing.

Webb, B. (2005) 'Preventing Vehicle Crime' in N. Tilley (ed.) *Handbook of Crime Prevention and Community Safety*. Cullompton, UK: Willan Publishing.

Welsh, B. and Farrington, D. (2000) 'Monetary Costs and Benefits of Crime Prevention Programs', in M. Tonry (ed.) *Crime and Justice: A Review of Research, Vol. 27*. Chicago: University of Chicago Press.

Whitehead, S., Mailley, J., Storer, I., McCardle, J., Torrens, G. and Farrell, G. (2008) 'Mobile Phone Anti-theft Designs: A Review', *European Journal on Criminal Policy and Research*, 14: 39–60.

Wortley, R. (2001) 'A Classification of Techniques for Controlling Situational Precipitators of Crime', *Security Journal*, 14: 63–82.

12. Problem-oriented policing and environmental criminology

Michael Scott, John Eck, Johannes Knutsson and Herman Goldstein

Introduction

Problem-oriented policing is a comprehensive framework for improving policing. It originated at the University of Wisconsin Law School and was first articulated by Goldstein (1979) in a journal article titled 'Improving Policing: A Problem-oriented Approach'. This article was itself a result of several decades of legal research at the University of Wisconsin and elsewhere about the realities of the law in action and how reality was so different from ideal notions about how the legal system was supposed to function.

This original articulation of the problem-oriented approach opened with an observation about police organisations, one not unfamiliar to many other types of organisations. That is, over time they tend to become preoccupied with the *means* of conducting their business and lose sight of the *ends* that the organisation is supposed to achieve. Goldstein illustrated the phenomenon with reference to a story about a bus company whose drivers failed to pick up waiting passengers (the end goal of a bus company) so as to keep on schedule (a means toward the end). This was an example of the *means-over-ends syndrome*, for which there are many examples in the police business, though perhaps not quite as ludicrous as the bus example.

There is an important difference between the bus business and police business. In the bus business the ends are fairly clear, obvious and simple: bus companies (at least privately owned ones) exist to transport people from one place to another and to do so profitably. But while the ends of policing might seem clear and obvious to some people – to fight crime, to enforce the law – in reality its ends are far less clear and obvious, and far more complex, certainly than those of a bus company.

If one believes that the ends of policing are clear, obvious and simple, then one need not spend a great deal of time thinking more about those ends; one needs to spend time thinking about the means by which those ends will best be achieved. For police officers and police administrators who believe that the ends of policing are clear, obvious and simple – such as to enforce the law, to fight crime, to chase and catch bad guys – the only interesting questions are how best to accomplish these ends. For that mission the police profession has developed some basic means, or strategies.

Standard policing strategy

Until the advent of problem-oriented policing, the police profession relied heavily on three major strategies (or means) for achieving the ends of policing: random preventive patrol, rapid response, and follow-up criminal investigation. These three strategies remain central to policing today, but from (at least) the 1940s through to the 1970s they comprised nearly the whole of American police strategy. These three strategies were logical means to the end of controlling crime through enforcement of the law. Each of these three strategies was calculated to maximise the ability of the police to enforce the criminal law, which was believed to be the most effective way to control crime (through the mechanism of deterrence).

Random preventive patrol posited that by having uniformed police officers drive, walk, or otherwise get around a specified area in unpredictable patterns, two positive results would be achieved. First, rapid response would control crime by increasing the likelihood that police officers would interrupt a crime in progress or apprehend a criminal fleeing the scene of a crime. Second, it is hypothesised that criminals would be more hesitant to commit crimes knowing that police were only moments away. For this reason, having police officers in patrol cars was preferable to having them on foot or other slower modes of transportation. Speed was deemed critical to deterrence. An extra benefit would be that law-abiding citizens would feel safer seeing uniformed police officers seemingly everywhere. The random movement of police officers could serve effectively as a force multiplier: law-abiding citizens and criminals alike would come to believe that there were more police officers on patrol than there actually were.

Furthermore, it was considered that follow-up criminal investigation that allowed police officers to dedicate time to search for evidence increased the probability that they would identify and apprehend the offenders. This, along with subsequent criminal prosecutions and convictions, would result in a reduction in crime. More criminals would be taken off the streets, thereby reducing crime by incapacitating criminals, and criminals would be deterred from committing crimes in the first instance, knowing that police would be hot on their trail.

Rethinking the ends and means of policing

By the 1970s, a growing body of research was calling into question some long-held assumptions about the means by which police went about their business and the very ends or goals they were trying to achieve.

Getting back to the ends of policing, the new law in action research stream was revealing that the ends of policing were not clear, obvious or simple. The notion that police existed merely to fight crime or enforce the law were proving grossly inadequate characterisations of a much broader and more complex mission. Below are some specific findings that emerged from this body of research, accompanied by some logical conclusions that follow from these findings:

- *The police are expected by the public to deal with much more than just crime.* Police are called upon to manage the flow of vehicle and pedestrian traffic; to settle a wide range of disputes – between family members, employers and employees or customers, friends, landlords and tenants, neighbours, and so forth; to take temporary care of lost children, the intoxicated, homeless and mentally ill, and vulnerable elderly people; to enforce a wide range of non-criminal government regulations over such matters as dispensing liquor, carrying guns, holding parades and protests, controlling animals and parking vehicles; and to provide a range of ancillary public services such as maintaining and distributing official records, checking criminal records on behalf of other agencies, running youth recreation programmes, and teaching crime prevention. The breadth of duties for which the police have been given some responsibility is truly astounding, and in fact, only a relatively small portion of their total time is spent dealing with actual criminal matters. Thus, while crime fighting might be an important part of the police mission, judging by what police actually do, it cannot be the whole mission.

- *Police officers do not always enforce the law when they have the legal grounds to do so.* Even the most junior police officers, particularly those working on the front lines in patrol and detective operations, exercise a tremendous degree of personal discretion in their enforcement decisions. Moreover, even when arrests are made by police, they are not always made for the express purpose of seeing the offender prosecuted. Arrest sometimes serves other purposes such as protecting persons from further harm or administering the summary punishment of a night in jail. Indeed, police officers' decisions not to arrest, and prosecutors' decisions not to charge, even where there exists a legal basis for doing so, is essential to enabling many local criminal justice systems to continue to operate with any degree of efficiency. But wholly unregulated police discretion provides abundant opportunities for abuse of authority as well.

- *The police are heavily dependent on many systems in addition to the criminal justice system* in order to effectively discharge their duties. They depend on the systems of schools, civil regulation, mental health, emergency medicine, alternative dispute resolution, child protection services, detoxification and drug treatment, juvenile justice and so forth. The police as an institution are really integral to many systems, not solely the criminal justice system with which they are most closely identified.

- *The ends, or objectives, that police seek to attain are varied, and sometimes in conflict with one another.* A modified version of the American Bar Association's articulation of police objectives described the police as an institution seeking to attain all of the following objectives:

  (a) To prevent and control conduct threatening to life and property (including serious crime).
  (b) To aid crime victims and protect people in danger of physical harm.
  (c) To protect constitutional guarantees, such as the right to free speech and assembly.
  (d) To facilitate the movement of people and vehicles.
  (e) To assist those who cannot care for themselves, including the intoxicated, the addicted, the mentally ill, the physically disabled, the elderly and the young.
  (f) To resolve conflict between individuals, among groups, or between citizens and their government.
  (g) To identify problems that have the potential for becoming more serious for individuals, the police or the government.
  (h) To create and maintain a feeling of security in the community.

This characterisation of the police function is far more complex and nuanced than simplistic characterisations of the police function as one of fighting crime or enforcing the law.

- *Interestingly, enforcing the law does not even appear on the list of police objectives above*, not because police don't do it, but because, upon reflection, it makes more sense to think of enforcing the law as but one means among many that police have for achieving these other ends. This insight alone had the potential to turn much of policing, as conventionally understood, right on its head. Police were not merely a 'law enforcement' agency, but rather a special institution with a broad mandate relating to matters of public safety and security, and only one of a number of government agencies with law enforcement authority. Moreover, law enforcement was not, and could not possibly be, the only means available to police to get its job done.

Another body of research called into question some of the most basic assumptions about the effectiveness of the three basic elements of police strategy (random preventive patrol, rapid response and follow-up criminal investigation). The research concluded that random preventive patrol was neither controlling crime nor making citizens feel safer. Rapid response was proving to be valuable to apprehending criminals in only a very small proportion of incidents, partly because of citizen delay in calling the police. And follow-up criminal investigations by specialised detectives were not as effective at solving cases as was commonly believed.

It was in the context of these discoveries that a wholly new approach emerged. This new approach understood both the demands placed on the police and the appropriate strategies to meet these demands.

Defining problem-oriented policing

The groundwork for problem-oriented policing was laid in the book *Policing a Free Society* (Goldstein 1977); then described in detail in the 1979 journal article; then expanded upon in the book, *Problem-oriented Policing* (Goldstein 1990); and then summarised in one paragraph in 2001 in an unpublished conference presentation entitled 'Problem-oriented Policing in a Nutshell' (Goldstein 2001). We will use this one paragraph summary description of problem-oriented policing as the basis of a fuller explanation of the concept.

> Problem-oriented policing (POP) is an approach to policing in which *(1) discrete pieces of police business* (each consisting of a cluster of similar incidents, whether crimes or acts of disorder, that the police are expected to handle) are subject to *(2) microscopic examination* (drawing on the especially honed skills of crime analysts and the accumulated experience of operating field personnel) in hopes that what is freshly learned about each problem will lead to discovering a *(3) new and more effective strategy* for dealing with it. POP places a high value on new responses that are *(4) preventive* in nature, that are *(5) not dependent on the use of the criminal justice system*, and that *(6) engage other public agencies, the community and the private sector* when their involvement has the potential for significantly contributing to the reduction of the problem. POP carries a commitment to *(7) implementing the new strategy, (8) rigorously evaluating its effectiveness, and, subsequently, (9) reporting the results* in ways that will benefit other police agencies and that will ultimately contribute to *(10) building a body of knowledge* that supports the further professionalization of the police. (Goldstein 2001)

> Problem-oriented policing (POP) is an approach to policing ...

Problem-oriented policing is not a particular policing tactic, nor even a crime control strategy. Accordingly, it is not an alternative to law enforcement, preventive patrol, criminal investigation, foot patrol, saturation patrol, undercover sting operations, or any of the many other tactics and strategies police employ. There are no distinctly problem-oriented policing tactics. It is neither a specific prescription for how police should carry out their duties, nor is problem-oriented policing a criminological theory, for it does not seek to explain the causes of crime and disorder.

Problem-oriented policing is a theory of police organisations, rooted in the fields of public administration and organisational behaviour rather than in the social sciences. It posits that the problem-oriented approach is more effective than competing approaches to carrying out the police function. As such, it constitutes a system of thought, a framework, a set of principles, for understanding and doing police work and administering police agencies. Accordingly, problem-oriented policing is open to a wide range of crime theories and police tactics and strategies, so long as they are employed in a fashion consistent with the core principles of problem-oriented policing.

... in which (1) discrete pieces of police business (each consisting of a cluster of similar incidents, whether crimes or acts of disorder, that the police are expected to handle) ...

Police work, like nearly all types of work, comprises units of work. In other fields units of work might be cars manufactured (automobile manufacturing), houses sold (real estate), at-bats taken (baseball), patients seen (medicine), articles published and courses taught (academia), and so forth. Defining what constitutes a unit of work is important in any field for several reasons. First, it is usually the thing that gets counted, and typically, the more units any worker and work organisation produces, the more the worker or work organisation is rewarded. Second, it sets the parameters for measuring the quality of work: each car should be of high quality, each house sale should net a profit for the broker, each at-bat should result in a hit, and so forth. Third, the work unit constitutes the thing around which the organisation should be managed: enough workers must be hired to produce a desired number of units; enough resources must be allocated to allow each work unit to be produced well. In sum, it is around the standard work unit, however defined, that the worker and the work organisation are oriented. Nearly everything else revolves around a common understanding of the standard work unit.

Problem-oriented policing conceptualises the standard police work unit in a new way, as something referred to as a *problem*. The term problem, of course, has a general definition: any situation that presents difficulty. But in the context of problem-oriented policing, it has a more precise definition: a problem is a cluster of harmful incidents (e.g. calls-for-service or cases of a similar nature or revolving about a place or person, or occurring at the same time of day, or in conjunction with a given event) that the public expects the police to handle. Among the important elements of a problem are that it constitutes something more than a single incident, and that it is something that concerns the public because it threatens public safety or security. This distinguishes a problem from a simple call-for-service or a criminal case, as well as from matters that are solely the concern of police (typically, internal organisational matters).

... are subject to (2) microscopic examination (drawing on the especially honed skills of crime analysts and the accumulated experience of operating field personnel)...'

In the context of problem-oriented policing we are not talking about police examining or investigating cases and calls-for-service – important work though that is – but rather, we are talking about police examining, investigating or analysing *problems*. 'Microscopic examination' of problems means that police seek an understanding of the connections among the incidents that comprise the problem, and an understanding of what is causing the problem to occur. This sort of examination, or analysis, draws upon the principles and methods of the social sciences. Police are called upon to analyse problems in far greater detail and depth than they are accustomed to doing. Furthermore, the approach

emphasises the need for making use of properly trained crime ar
well as the need for tapping into the knowledge and insights of the
police officers who handle the calls-for-service and cases. Problem-
policing seeks to link the work of line personnel, analysts and admini
within the police agency, and experts and citizens outside the police ag   -y.

> ... in hopes that what is freshly learned about each problem will lead to
> discovering a (3) new and more effective strategy for dealing with it.

This element of problem-oriented policing explains its very rationale. The
whole point of taking a problem-oriented approach to police business is so
that the response to the particular problem at hand – whether by the police
or others – is more effective in controlling that problem than previous efforts
to address the problem. In this respect, problem-oriented policing is outcome-
focused. Indeed, this principle should strongly guide how problems are
examined or analysed. It is practically oriented, as it seeks the knowledge and
understanding of problems that will lead to more effective practical solutions
to problems. This overriding emphasis on effectiveness largely explains the
links between problem-oriented policing and situational crime prevention.
Both concepts are principally interested in knowledge that will help those
responsible for dealing with crime do so more effectively. For example,
neither problem-oriented policing nor situational crime prevention are much
interested in knowing that people steal because humans are inherently evil
(a philosophical matter about which police can do nothing), nor that people
commit crimes because they lacked nurturing parents (a socio-psychological
matter about which police can do little), but are very likely to be interested
in knowing that people steal because the items they desire are left so
unprotected from theft (a crime prevention matter about which police can
often do something).

A concern about effectiveness merits a few words about two related
concerns: efficiency and equity (or fairness). While problem-oriented policing
emphasises the effectiveness of responses to problems, it is also very much
concerned with equity. From among a range of possibly effective responses
to a problem, a problem-oriented approach would call for the response that
equitably apportions the burdens placed upon various people and groups for
addressing the problem, as well as equitably apportioning the benefits of the
new responses to the problem. It recognises, though, that questions of equity
are not for the police to decide alone, nor are they questions that science
can always answer. Equity, or fairness, is a judgement about which police
have something to say, but which ultimately is for the larger community to
determine.

Regarding efficiency, problem-oriented policing would naturally favour more
efficient responses than inefficient ones. Conserving scarce resources is nearly
always desirable. But the concept pointedly makes efficiency subservient to
effectiveness. For example, one might conclude that private security officers or
video surveillance cameras are more efficient than police patrol for watching
over a particular space, but unless they are more effective (say at reducing

the number of crimes occurring in that space) then the efficiency gains are of limited value.

POP places a high value on new responses that are (4) preventive in nature …

Police work is and always has been partly remedial and partly preventive. Remedial aspects of police work are those that seek to fix, correct or punish after harm has already occurred. Preventive aspects of police work are those that seek to avoid or minimise harm before it occurs. Criminal investigation emphasises the remedial aspects of policing: discovering who committed crimes and holding them to account. Most victim services are also remedial, rather then preventive: helping victims recover physically, emotionally and financially. Police patrolling emphasises prevention by discouraging potential criminals from committing crimes and encouraging law-abiding citizens to be out in public spaces. Few police activities are categorically one or the other – remedial or preventive; most are a combination of both. Arresting offenders, for example, serves remedial purposes in holding people to account for the harm they have caused, but also serves preventive purposes by deterring those offenders as well as others from committing future offences.

In problem-oriented policing, addressing any problem typically entails doing several things. It may well entail improving the procedures by which police respond to certain types of incidents (e.g. improving evidence collection procedures in sexual assault cases). Such responses are remedial in nature. But, problem-oriented policing calls for police to give greater attention than they have in the past to developing responses to problems that reduce the likelihood of future incidents occurring or reducing the severity of harm arising out of future incidents.

If the problem is a rash of armed robberies around automated teller machines (ATMs), police should not be content to arrest some offenders who are committing the robberies, but should also implement measures to reduce the future risk of robbery around ATMs. When the public demands that police react strongly to recent egregious incidents, police are encouraged to leverage heightened public interest in the problem by pressing also for adoption of new preventive measures.

… that are (5) not dependent on the use of the criminal justice system …

Among the most important findings of the seminal American Bar Foundation 1950s study of the criminal justice system was that the resources of the criminal justice system are quite often stretched thinly. In many jurisdictions there are far too many cases for the system to address fairly or effectively. Consequently, each of the actors comprising the criminal justice system – police included – are compelled to seek out means of disposing of cases short of giving them the full treatment implied in an ideal model of the system. Police opt not to arrest all offenders, even where probable cause to do so can be established.

Prosecutors opt not to file formal criminal charges against all persons arrested by police, dropping some cases altogether and diverting others to alternative systems. Courts impose rules and apply pressures such that only a small percentage of cases formally charged result in full-blown trials. Corrections agencies emphasise non-custodial sentences (probation, parole, house arrest, electronic monitoring, work release, community service, etc.) to help manage scarce jail and prison space.

Not only does the criminal justice system often lack resources, it often lacks competence. The criminal justice system is principally designed to handle conventional crime involving malevolent offenders preying upon innocent victims. As a general proposition, these sorts of cases are easier to prove and more obviously warrant punitive sanctions. But an awful lot of the incidents that police handle are not prototypical crimes. The offenders might be mentally ill or addicted to drugs or alcohol, in which cases proving criminal intent might be difficult, and even if proven, incarceration might either be ineffective or perhaps make matters worse. Many other incidents police handle involve disputes or offences that are too petty in nature to justify the expenditure of resources necessary for the full criminal justice treatment.

Accordingly, problem-oriented policing, while not ruling out the use of arrest, prosecution, or incarceration, encourages police to search for alternatives to the full use of the criminal justice system as means for addressing problems.

> ... and that (6) engage other public agencies, the community and the private sector when their involvement has the potential for significantly contributing to the reduction of the problem.

Much of the discussion of problem-oriented policing focuses on what the police should do to improve their effectiveness. Indeed, the very term implies that the police are at the hub of responses to public safety problems. But this focus is premised upon a deeper reality: that the police institution is ultimately limited in what it can do by itself toward promoting public safety. The police, however important, are a relatively small force within the whole of society. For instance, in the United States, police personnel constitute something like a mere three-tenths of 1 per cent of the total population (one million police personnel out of 300 million citizens), and only about a fifth of the police are on duty at any one time. Moreover, however much authority we grant to the police, in Western democracies we are nearly equally obliged to constrain such authority, taking care not to make the police too powerful.

Problem-oriented policing challenges police to leverage their own authority and resources by selectively tapping into the far vaster authority and resources that are diffused throughout the rest of society; by encouraging the increased use of other forms of established social control. The sort of engagement with other public agencies, the community and the private sector imagined will variously mean that police solicit input from others about the nature and importance of public safety problems, solicit information from others necessary to analysing problems, and solicit assistance from others in responding to problems.

229

Police engagement with others is encouraged not for its own sake or for the sake of increasing public support for the police, but for the sake of more effectively addressing problems. With regard to some problems a very high level of external engagement may be warranted. Exactly which public agencies and which segments of the community and the private sector should be engaged by police should depend on the particulars of each problem.

POP carries a commitment to (7) implementing the new strategy ...

Problem-oriented policing employs a form of what is known as action research. Action research is a type in which the researcher has an interest in achieving a particular outcome and is often an integral part of a team working toward that outcome. Accordingly, problem-oriented policing emphasises the next step: putting a new plan into action. While this sounds simple enough, research and experience tells us that even the best-laid plans can go awry, for various reasons.

In a problem-oriented approach, police are encouraged to anticipate obstacles to implementing a new plan of action and both to shape the plan in anticipation of some obstacles and to make special effort to overcome other obstacles. Among the various factors police are encouraged to take into account when formulating a new plan of action are: the financial costs; the availability of personnel to implement responses; support for the plan within and without the police agency; legality, practicality and simplicity of the responses; the likelihood that new responses will be more effective than the *status quo*; and the likelihood that the new plan will prevent future harm in addition to remedying past harm.

... (8) rigorously evaluating its effectiveness ...

Again, the problem-oriented approach has as its overriding concern the effectiveness of the police in controlling crime and disorder problems. It follows that relative effectiveness must be measured. But this presents a significant challenge for police as there is an absence of a well-established history of rigorous evaluation in the police profession. Making progress requires police agencies to develop new internal capacities for evaluation, as well as new partnerships with external evaluators. It may well require additional funding to support evaluations. It will require a new spirit of self-reflection, openness to critique, understanding of the benefits and limitations of evaluation, and willingness to adapt to new knowledge, both within and without police agencies. It will require the further development of and experimentation with evaluation methods that are adapted to the particular conditions of the policing environment.

... and, subsequently, (9) reporting the results in ways that will benefit other police agencies ...

Story-telling is an essential component of problem-oriented policing. Certainly, policing has many interesting stories to tell. The stories that need to be told are not just the 'war stories' that police officers share with one another, nor the 'who done it' mysteries, but the action research stories about police problem-solving. Getting these stories told in a reliable and responsible way will require the development of new habits and new systems within police agencies and within the police profession. Staff with the requisite skills will be needed to write the stories. Venues must be established to disseminate the stories inside and outside the police agency. And police agencies must get in the habit of searching for and reading other agencies' stories, and then applying their lessons to the local situation. Importantly, no single police agency can be expected to study all of its problems, so sharing of knowledge is essential – lessons from one agency can help many other agencies address similar problems.

> ... and that will ultimately contribute to (10) building a body of knowledge that supports the further professionalization of the police.

Every field of endeavour that purports to be a profession, along with many of the skilled trades, depends quite heavily on its practitioners having access to the accumulated knowledge of the field, both when they are students or apprentices studying to become practitioners, and when they are practising and seeking to apply knowledge to the practical problems at hand. This access to an accumulating body of knowledge helps practitioners deliver quality service and solve problems by providing them with the cumulative knowledge gained from past research and practice.

In comparison to many other professions and skilled trades, the body of knowledge in policing remains rather thin and inaccessible to its practitioners. Problem-oriented policing is in part a call to fatten up the police body of knowledge: to systematise it, standardise it, improve its rigour, and make it more accessible and essential to current practitioners.

The application of problem-oriented policing

We have described the theory of problem-oriented policing. For this theory to work it needed to be made operational so that members of police agencies could carry it out in their daily work. This operationalisation has developed over more than twenty years and is still evolving. One of the first major steps was the development of the SARA (Scanning, Analysis, Response, Assessment) process. Another was the development of the problem triangle and adaptation of principles of environmental criminology to police work. A third aspect of operationalisation was the creation of educational material written specifically for police practitioners that incorporated the findings from research and practice. We will look at each of these and other developments in turn. Though there is a rough chronology to these efforts, all overlap to some extent.

A problem-solving process

In 1984 the Newport News (Virginia) Police Department, with support of the National Institute of Justice (the research branch of the US Department of Justice) began to implement problem-oriented policing across the force. Though there were many uncertainties, the Newport News Police Department could draw on the experiences of three other more limited efforts. The Madison (Wisconsin) Police Department, guided by Herman Goldstein and his colleagues and students, examined two problems: drunk-driving and serious sexual assaults (Goldstein and Susmilch 1982). Though much was learned about these problems, and credible innovative approaches to addressing sexual assaults by repeat offenders were implemented, it became clear that if the police were to undertake a problem-oriented approach they would need considerable guidance. The London Metropolitan Police also undertook pilot problem studies with some success. But the internal report to the police commissioner warned that the existing police organisational framework would need to be substantially changed to undertake problem-oriented policing as a general strategy (Hoare *et al.* 1984). Also in the early 1980s, the Baltimore County (Maryland) Police Department established three problem-solving teams to address fear problems in the three police command areas of the county. These special units developed standard protocols for identifying, analysing and responding to problems as well as for conducting citizen surveys to measure fear before and after implementing possible solutions. An evaluation of these units showed they had considerable success at reducing fear and crime (Cordner 1986).

Drawing on these earlier experiences the members of the Newport News Police Department suggested that a clear set of procedures be developed for handling problems. Working with two consultants they developed the SARA process (Eck and Spelman 1987). SARA is an acronym for a four-stage problem-solving process based on similar processes used in business and planning.

- *Scanning*: At this first stage a problem is discovered and defined well enough so that further action can be taken. The definition may be revised as more information is developed at later stages. There is no single source of information to identify problems. Rather, officers are encouraged to use multiple sources including crime data, community members, elected officials and news media accounts. The definition of a problem has evolved over time, though most of its basic features have remained constant. A problem is a recurring set of harmful events that the police are reasonably expected to handle. This allows both crime and non-crime problems to be included. Single one-off events that are not expected to repeat are excluded. The definition explicitly points to the public as an important feature in this definition. There does not need to be a community consensus on the problem, but some members of the community need to feel that the police should deal with the issue.

- *Analysis*: The second stage involves collecting information about the problem and police experiences at addressing it. Much of this information is local:

immediately around the problem. But police problem-solvers must also examine information from other police agencies, social science research, and other institutions and individuals that are relevant to the problem. The objective is to know how the problem arises and to locate pinch points that suggest ways of reducing the problem.

- *Response*: A cardinal rule of problem-solving is that the problem-solver must examine a broad range of possible solutions, and select from these possible solutions those that fit the facts shown by the analysis. In this third stage, the problem-solver uses the analysis findings to judge the options available, select the most appropriate option and then implement it.

- *Assessment*: If the police are to avoid the means-over-ends syndrome, then it is important to judge the success of a problem-solving effort by the impact on the problem, rather than the nature of the response selected. While the response may be innovative and fit the facts, these are no guarantees of success. Consequently, the final stage in the problem-solving process is to evaluate the response and determine if the problem changed for the better, if it is smaller or if the problem has been rendered less harmful.

Though the SARA process may appear to be a simple linear process, in fact it contains numerous feedback loops (see Figure 12.1). The analysis might require a redefinition of the definition established in the scanning stage. A response might reveal new facts about the problem that change the analysis conclusions, or even redefine the problem. The assessment may show that the response was ineffective, thus forcing reconsideration of any one or all of the earlier stages. In fact, a problem-solving effort could start at any stage. In a crisis, for example, an immediate temporary response might initiate the SARA

Figure 12.1 The SARA problem-solving process
(*Source*: Clarke and Eck 2005)

process to control the problem and assure the public. The analysis that follows might redefine the problem, which in turn suggests further analysis and the creation of a revised sustainable response. Assessment may be ongoing to track the level of the problem and determine the effectiveness of each new response.

The SARA process has become so widespread that it has become synonymous with problem-oriented policing. This is unfortunate. It is only one way of providing practical guidance to police problem-solvers. For example, the Royal Canadian Mounted Police use a process called CAPRA: the letters stand for Client (or community), Acquiring and analysing information, Partnerships, Response, Assessment (RCMP 2000). Other police agencies have split the response stage of SARA into two stages – designing a response and implementing the response. But whether the process is SARA or some variation, the important point is that the process is simple enough to use while capturing the critical features of problem-oriented policing.

The problem triangle and environmental criminology

As it was implemented in various agencies it became clear that problem-oriented policing was vague about how to analyse problems and locate responses. Police were left with the impression that if they simply collected data that seemed relevant, somehow they would gain insight into the problem and possible solutions would appear. Unfortunately, this was seldom the case, except for a few police officials who appeared to be natural problem-solvers. Basing a policing strategy on a few people who could intuit problems and solutions would doom the strategy to failure. A second theory was needed – a theory about the substantive nature of problems – that would complement the theory of problem-oriented policing.

While most criminological theories were of little practical value to the police, a small but growing movement called environmental criminology was developing a set of theories that were useful. These theories are described in greater detail in other chapters in this book. Here we will focus on routine activity theory and situational crime prevention.

Routine activity theory was originally described in the same year (Cohen and Felson 1979) that problem-oriented policing was first formally articulated (Goldstein 1979). Since that time routine activity theory has been elaborated upon. In the early 1990s Rana Sampson was training police in problem analysis by showing routine activity theory as a single triangle consisting of offender, target and place: the inner triangle of Figure 12.2 (Eck 2003). This simple illustration pointed out that for a crime or disorder incident to exist, all three of these elements needed to come together. If these elements came together repeatedly then there is a problem. Analysis should proceed by collecting information on all three sides of the triangle and the objective was to design a response that controlled at least one side of the triangle: that is, keeping targets and offenders from meeting at the same place. Evidence about the commonality of repeat offending, repeat victimisation, and repeat places lent credence to this idea. Repeat offending problems could be addressed by going after the offenders. Repeat victimisation problems could be addressed by helping victims, and repeat place problems could be addressed by attending to the physical and social aspects of the location (Eck 2003).

Later Eck (2003) expanded this graphical motif to form a double triangle (see Figure 12.2). Where the inner triangle's elements show the conditions necessary for a problem, the outer triangle's elements showed what could be added to suppress a problem. These outer elements represent people who can control their corresponding inner element.

A handler is someone to whom the offender is emotionally or legally attached and thus is in a position to dissuade or deter the offender. Common examples of handlers who exercise control through emotional attachment (i.e. informal social control) are parents, neighbours and sports coaches. Common examples of handlers who exercise control through legal attachment (i.e. formal social control) are police officers probation and parole officers, and judges). When devoid of handlers, offenders are more likely to offend than when handlers are present.

A guardian protects a target – a human, animal or thing. The absence of guardianship was one of the original insights in the first versions of routine activity theory. When a guardian is present, a crime or act of disorder is much less likely. Common guardians include friends protecting friends, individuals protecting their belongings or household, hired security guards, and of course, the police.

A manager regulates the functioning of a place. As part of their duties, they may be attentive to situations that could lead to crime and disorder, and act to head them off. However, much of place management influences crime and disorder indirectly. Decisions about the seating, entertainment and prices in bars may be made for reasons of profit, but can influence the amount of

Figure 12.2 The problem triangle
(*Source*: Adapted from Clarke and Eck 2005)

drunkenness, thievery and violence in the bar (Madensen 2007). Common managers include store clerks, life guards, airline flight attendants, teachers in classrooms, janitors, and anyone who owns a place or is employed by an owner.

Routine activity theory draws attention to the situation that gives rise to a problem, from the perspective of the problem-solver. Situational crime prevention looks at the same situation from the perspective of the offender, and is described in detail in another chapter in this book (see Cornish and Clarke, Chapter 2, this volume). Situational crime prevention became very important for problem-oriented policing for several reasons. First, both perspectives call for the careful analysis of crime patterns and problems. Second, both situational crime prevention and problem-oriented policing are detail-oriented – small things can create big problems so it is important to know the details. Third, situational crime prevention operates on the same timescale as policing: solutions that will have quick or near-term pay-offs, rather than produce results in years or decades. Fourth, situational crime prevention's focus is on causes close to the problem, like most police work. Fifth, there is a large and growing body of evidence that situational interventions by police and others reduce crime.

Just as situational crime prevention can be used by many non-police organisations, police problem-solvers are not limited to situational crime prevention. In principle, any approach to crime prevention that works could be employed by the police. The major limitation to using other crime prevention strategies is finding one that has evidence of effectiveness. Nevertheless, police problem-solvers have partnered with a variety of other human services organisations to reduce harms to victims and divert offenders into treatment or other services. Just as problem-oriented policing improved with the development of situational crime prevention, the development of other effective crime prevention strategies would also aid problem-oriented policing.

Center for Problem-Oriented Policing

Around the beginning of the new millennium the Office of Community-Oriented Policing Services (COPS) of the US Department of Justice funded a group of researchers who then founded the Center for Problem-Oriented Policing (POP Center) to develop and disseminate information on problem-solving. The POP Center has produced, as of the time of writing, over 50 problem-specific guides. Each guide examines a concrete type of problem: for example, street drug markets, speeding in residential neighbourhoods, college student drinking riots, robberies of convenience stores, and false alarms. The guide authors follow a protocol that requires careful examination of the scientific evidence as well as the experiences of police and other institutions in addressing the problem. Each guide summarises what is known about the problem, including its causes and contributing factors; sets out questions local problem-solvers should ask in examining that problem type at the local level; and describes what responses are known to be relatively effective or ineffective in addressing that problem type.

In addition to the problem specific-guides, the POP Center produces guides on classes of responses (for example, police crackdowns and crime prevention publicity campaigns) that also draw on science and experience to describe for which problems and under which circumstances the response can work and when it is likely to fail.

Finally, there is a set of problem-solving tools guides that explain analytical techniques and procedures that can be used during analysis, response or assessment. These include guides on how to evaluate a response, how to apply repeat victimisation analysis and methods for addressing risky facilities.

In 2002 the Jill Dando Institute for Crime Science, with funding from the UK Home Office, commissioned the development of a manual for British crime analysts that would improve their ability to address problems. The manual, co-authored by Ronald Clarke and John Eck (2003), is entitled *Become a Problem-solving Crime Analyst: In 55 Small Steps*. In 2005 the authors revised the manual for a US audience (Clarke and Eck 2005) and published it under the auspices of the POP Center. Both manuals have been distributed widely. As of this writing, these two manuals have been or are being translated into eleven other languages.

The POP Center's website (www.popcenter.org) now contains all the above guides and manuals plus interactive problem-solving learning exercises, a library of problem-solving case studies from the United States and the United Kingdom, an online system to aid problem-solvers diagnose their specific problems, a model academic curriculum in problem-oriented policing and situational crime prevention, and a library of articles and reports on problem-oriented policing and situational crime prevention.

Problem-oriented policing and scientific development

The linking of problem-oriented policing to environmental criminology, combined with the work of the Center for Problem-Oriented Policing, has created something new to policing: a policing strategy linked to a community of scientists dedicated to creating and testing practical crime reduction theories and practices. Uniquely among police reform movements, problem-oriented policing retains a coherent core set of principles but has increased the knowledge base with which to apply these principles.

Perhaps the best example of how problem-oriented policing and social science combined to develop useful knowledge is the history of place in crime prevention. In the late 1980s, when problem-oriented policing was first being field-tested, few police officials were aware of the importance of identifying the owners of troublesome locations. Problem-solving efforts in Oakland (Green 1995) and San Diego (Capowich and Roehl 1994), California suggested that civil law could be applied to compel property-owners to assist police and local governments in reducing problems occurring at and near those properties. Sherman and colleagues (1989), as well as Pierce and colleagues (1988), had already demonstrated that crime is highly concentrated at a relatively few places, even in high-crime neighbourhoods. These insights led to the modification of routine activity theory to include place managers, as described earlier (see Figure 12.2). Studies of violent bars also pointed to the importance of managers (Eck 2002). Increasingly, police were looking at the behaviours of place-owners when they tackled place hot spots. Now, in the first decade of the twenty-first century, the importance of places and their management is well established within policing. Many police officers who are not engaged in problem-solving but who are coping with a hot place can name the owner of the location and understand how the owner's management practices contribute to the problem. Though these officers may not be aware of it, their actions are being guided by the experiences of problem-solving officers and research by social scientists. As information from the experiences of police moved into environmental criminological research the science of places advanced. Moreover, as findings from this research moved into police problem-solving, policing advanced.

The intertwining of problem-oriented policing and environmental criminology is probably responsible for the effectiveness of the approach. In 2004 the National Academy of Sciences panel on Police Policy and Research released its report, *Fairness and Effectiveness in Policing: The Evidence* (National Research Council: 2004). Summarising three decades of research in the ability of the police to reduce crime, disorder and fear of crime, the panel showed that where there was research evidence to support the proposition that problem-oriented policing was probably more effective than standard policing, community policing without problem-solving, and even hot-spots policing. Since then, other reviews of the scientific evidence have demonstrated that problem-oriented policing is effective at reducing crime (Mazerolle *et al.* 2007; Weisburd *et al.* 2007). Importantly, most of the research reviewed in these studies was conducted prior to the explosion of guidance now available from the Center for Problem-Oriented Policing. It seems highly likely that continued improvements in our understanding of problems, and increased police application of this new knowledge, will further enhance and substantiate the effectiveness of problem-oriented policing.

Awards

There are two major professional awards for police problem-solving. The Herman Goldstein Award for Excellence in Problem-Oriented Policing was established in 1993 by the Police Executive Research Forum (and assumed by the Center for Problem-Oriented Policing in 2004). Police departments from around the world can submit projects for consideration. Each is judged by a panel of police practitioners and researchers. The awards are made at the Annual Problem-Oriented Policing Conference.

The Tilley Award (named in honour of British crime scholar Professor Nick Tilley) was established in 1999 and is sponsored by the British Home Office. Though most submissions are from police agencies, these awards are open to any partnership addressing crime problems. The judging process is similar to the Goldstein Award and the winners are announced at an annual conference on problem-oriented partnerships. In recent years, the Lancashire Constabulary has won a number of the Tilley Awards, as well as several Goldstein Awards. The Lancashire Constabulary also has its own awards process and an annual conference, underscoring its long-term commitment to a problem-oriented approach.

All submissions, including award winners, for both the Goldstein and Tilley awards are accessible at the Center for Problem-Oriented Policing website. These documents provide a wealth of information on what does and does not work in addressing a variety of problems. Consequently, they are used extensively in the development of problem-specific guides. So these awards not only provide recognition for quality problem-solving, they also provide knowledge for use in other problem-oriented projects.

Implementing problem-oriented policing

Many police agencies around the world have tried to apply problem-oriented policing, including police agencies in North America, the UK, Scandinavia, Continental Europe, South America, Africa, Australia and New Zealand. Scott (2000) has reviewed the US experience to the end of the twentieth century and Bullock *et al.* (2006) have examined the UK experience. Though much progress has been noted, these authors have shown that problem-solving often does not meet expectations. We can see the variety of experiences and results by examining three experiences in the Nordic countries, by way of example.

The Nordic experiences with problem-oriented policing

One of the boldest introductions was carried out by the Swedish police in the mid 1990s. In an extensive reform about half the strength of the police force was assigned to community policing, with one of the primary tasks to prevent crime. The officers were instructed to use problem-oriented policing as the tool. But the reform was met with less success than had been hoped. There were two explanations: first, the officers had not been adequately trained in problem-oriented policing, and second, the central authority (Rikspolisstyrelsen) did not have a basic understanding of problem-oriented policing and what was required to support the organisation for such an undertaking. Beginning in 2005, the National Police Academy began to give crime analysts a thorough training in crime analysis and crime prevention, where problem-oriented policing is an important element. Elements of problem-oriented policing are also included in the Police Intelligence Model for police operational leaders. Thus, in Sweden problem-oriented policing was given a second chance.

Denmark introduced problem-oriented policing somewhat later. The introduction was made stepwise, where first a few police districts in 1998 started to work according to a somewhat modified model. The trial was extended in 2002 and several more police districts were included. Finally,

239

in 2007 all districts, as part of a greater reform of the Danish police, were expected to work under a problem-oriented approach to policing. Though the central authority (Rigspolitiet) considered the implementation to be successful, an examination showed that the quality of the projects was limited: some projects could not be classified as problem-oriented. Among those projects that could be called problem-oriented, many displayed weaknesses in analysis and assessment (Hammerich 2007). These results were similar to those found by Scott (2000) in the United States.

In 2002 the Norwegian Police Directorate (Politidirektoratet) instituted problem-oriented policing as the main approach for the Norwegian police to prevent crime. Although Norway began implementing problem-oriented policing after Sweden and Denmark, and could have learned from shortcomings of other forces, there were still barriers to successful implementation. Thomassen (2005) mentions five such obstacles: (1) lack of understanding of problem-oriented policing; (2) lack of analytical skills; (3) lack of real incorporation of problem-oriented policing into the organisation; (4) lack of incentives to carry out problem-oriented policing; and (5) barriers in the police culture, where crime fighting has high status and crime prevention not. Nevertheless, the education in problem-oriented policing provided by the Norwegian Police University College at basic level is probably the most extensive that exists. Further, even if many problem-oriented policing projects have weaknesses, there are also well-documented successful projects. Some have been fed back into police training. For example, Vestfold's (2004) examination of a gypsy cab problem is now used in a textbook written to teach students in Norway and Sweden about the principles of POP (Knutsson and Søvik 2005).

Ways of implementing problem-oriented policing

Problem-oriented policing has been implemented in four distinct ways. The most common approach is to have all front-line police officers engaged in problem-solving. The Newport News (Virginia) Police Department in the 1980s, the San Diego Police Department in the 1990s, and the Hampshire and Lancashire Constabularies in the UK in the 2000s are all examples of agencies using this approach. While such an approach holds the promise of making problem-oriented policing the central strategy of a police department, problem-solving projects tend to be rather superficial (Clarke 2002; Leigh et al. 1998). Nevertheless, Braga and Weisburd (2006) have noted that superficial problem-solving can be effective. So even if beat-level problem-solving by line police officials does not reach the standards envisioned by proponents of problem-oriented policing, it is still very much worthwhile. There is another reason for superficiality not being a serious objection, and that is, the assessments of problem-solving describe the average, modal or typical problem-solving effort. There are notable exceptions to the norm. Both the Hampshire and Lancashire Constabularies have produced some exceptional problem-solving efforts, as evidenced by their receiving both Tilley and Goldstein Awards for problem-solving excellence. The distribution of quality may be typical of any profession: (a) operational quality lags behind theoretical expectations;

(b) operational quality improves slower than the science supporting it; and (c) the highest quality outputs are rare relative to the large number of middle and lower quality outputs.

A second approach to implementing problem-oriented policing is to designate some officers within the patrol ranks as neighbourhood (or community) patrol officers. These officers have the advantage of being given a clear geographic area for which they are responsible, and are relatively undistracted by routine incidents and most emergencies. This approach has been used in conjunction with community policing. In the late 1980s and early 1990s the New York City Police Department used this approach, first in several experimental beats and then throughout the department. The Swedish example above also fits this model. The disadvantage of this approach is that such officers can often be distracted by the processes of community meetings and other public relations, and end up addressing few problems.

A third approach is to create a special unit whose function is to address problems. The Baltimore County Police Department had a very well-regarded problem-solving unit in the 1980s. It had three squads – one for each command area – whose functions were to identify, analyse and resolve problems related to crime and fear of crime. An independent evaluation suggested that these squads were quite effective (Cordner 1986). Among the limitations of such an approach is that problem-oriented policing becomes isolated in an elite unit, and elite units tend to alienate regular patrol officers. These were some of the reasons the Baltimore County Police Department disbanded its units, despite evidence of their effectiveness. Another possible limitation is that the specialised squad becomes a tactical unit with a superficial problem orientation. The unit emphasises enforcement to suppress the problem, but then does little to make sure that the problem does not recur. Thus the unit must cycle back on hot spots that were once addressed, but whose problems have reincarnated.

The fourth approach to implementing problem-oriented policing is to create or augment the crime analysis unit so that it can identify and take on serious problems. This approach locates the technical nature of problem-oriented policing within a unit that has the technical capabilities to conduct analysis. By locating the unit within the administration of the agency, larger problems can be taken on. Though the analysis unit must coordinate with other parts of the police department and others outside the department this is also true of any other police unit applying problem-solving. The Crime Analysis Unit of the Chula Vista (California) Police Department, for example, has taken on disorder in parks, vehicle theft and hotel/motel crime. The drawback of this approach is that smaller, beat-level problems may not get addressed. Interestingly, while this approach is relatively new in its implementation, it was central to the original conceptualisation of and experimentation with the problem-oriented approach (Goldstein 1979; Goldstein and Susmilch 1982). The crime analysis guides by Clarke and Eck (2003, 2005) were developed to foster this form of problem-solving.

Since its inception police have struggled with implementing a problem-oriented approach. There are many good reasons for this. First, problem-

241

oriented policing redefined police work, so it was difficult to embed in organisations that were founded on alternative definitions of police work. Second, problem-oriented policing is simultaneously simple and complex. The basic ideas behind problem-oriented policing seem self-evident. The process of careful analysis, response and assessment, however, can be quite complex. Third, police agencies are not structured to analyse problems and make tailored solutions. These human and technical capacities need to be developed. And while progress has been made, there is a long way to go. Case studies of addressing thefts from construction sites and thefts from vehicles illustrate many of these difficulties (Clarke and Goldstein 2002, 2003). Fourth, to address problems police must work closely with other public and private institutions. In the UK national legislation in 1998 mandated local crime reduction partnerships among police and other institutions, and this has greatly facilitated the implementation of problem-oriented policing (though here too progress is slow, see Leigh *et al.* 1998). Fifth, while there have been advances in the problem-solving knowledge base, these have been recent developments, since the founding of the Center for Problem-Oriented Policing. Consequently, much of the early effort was seat-of-the-pants trial and error progress. Sixth, local government leadership is marked by long periods of inattention to policing and short bursts of calls for the police to adopt the latest fad. It is a testament to the validity of problem-oriented policing that it has endured and developed over more than two decades, while many other ideas for policing have sprouted, bloomed, withered and dried up. Nevertheless, these fad reform efforts impede real progress by frustrating the police themselves. Seventh, the fad mentality to police reform infects the way many police administrators take on problem-oriented policing. Typically, the implementation involves a limited amount of training for line officers and immediate supervisors, little guidance to higher ranks as to how they should manage problem-solving and hold officers accountable, virtually no attention to infrastructure that could facilitate problem-solving, and no attempt to assure that the reforms will outlive the tenure of the chief executive who implemented them.

Conclusion

Problem-oriented policing is a policing strategy that redefines the police role from one of merely handling incidents to addressing problems. In doing so it focuses attention on the prevention of crime through the field application of scientific principles. It draws heavily on environmental criminology for structuring analysis, identifying responses and evaluating results. Over the last quarter of a century, a dedicated cadre of researchers and practitioners has maintained the core principles of the concept, while developing new knowledge about problems and methods for resolving them. Consequently, problem-oriented policing has not suffered from the drift that seems to have undermined community policing and appears to be infecting CompStat and intelligence-led policing. Indeed, since 1984 all new proposals for comprehensive policing strategies have embraced many of the core principles of problem-oriented policing, and there have been no efforts to advocate a policing strategy in opposition to problem-oriented policing. Community policing is defined by the US Department of Justice's COPS Office as including problem-solving (Office of Community Oriented Problem Solving 1998). Similarly, the Chicago Police Department built problem-solving into its community policing strategy (Skogan *et al.* 1999). Kelling and Sousa (2001) claim that problem-solving is an integral part of 'broken windows' policing (see Wagers *et al.*, Chapter 13, this volume). Advocates for CompStat suggest that police should be highly flexible in looking for ways of handling crime concentrations (Silverman 1999). Indeed, the Anaheim (California) Police Department is explicitly combining problem-oriented policing and CompStat (Welter 2007). Ratcliffe describes how intelligence-led policing overlaps with problem-oriented policing (Ratcliffe, Chapter 14, this volume). Indeed, Weisburd *et al.* (2003) claim that strategic problem-solving is a widespread core element of late twentieth and early twenty-first century new policing strategies.

Each of these reform efforts emphasises some element of problem-oriented policing. Community policing emphasises community institutions and public participation, as well as the need for the police not to take their legitimacy for granted. Broken windows policing emphasises the need to address disorder as a means for addressing crime. CompStat emphasises accountability for reducing crime and the use of data to focus resources and measure results. Intelligence-led policing emphasises the role of offenders in general, and offender networks in particular. All of these reform movements simplify the police reform task, creating a 'light' version of problem-oriented policing that is easier to adopt without major organisational change (Weisburd *et al.* 2003). And in all cases, the reforms are predicated on vaguely defined ideas that have at most limited supporting evidence: community policing and broken windows policing seem to be founded on the notion that community dysfunction can be quickly remedied by an injection of policing (though they disagree on the form of that policing). CompStat seems to be based on the notion that rapid allocation of resources to fast-breaking crime patterns is sufficient to prevent crime. While research on hot spots seems to support this idea, CompStat has no theory of how to solidify short-term gains. To rescue intelligence-led policing from its weak theoretical foundations, Ratcliffe (Chapter 14, this volume) places it on a foundation compatible with problem-oriented policing.

What this suggests is that despite the slow progress in improving the quality of problem-solving, the core ideas are slowly taking hold within police agencies throughout Western democracies. There is no longer a dispute about the importance of crime concentrations for allocating police resources. Similarly, there is no dispute over the need for data and evidence to drive police operations. There is also a widespread recognition that the police can get more done through collaboration with other institutions, and that they need to look for innovative approaches to reducing crime and disorder. Although in a weakened form, most policing strategies now emphasise the concept of problems. However, the overly simple versions of problem-oriented policing ignore the complexities inherent in the police function, the many different problems that the police must handle and the serious limitations of using the criminal law as the principal means for crime reduction.

In retrospect, this should not be surprising. If the police are to be in the crime prevention business (as opposed to simply responding to crime emergencies), then they need a business model that facilitates the production of prevention. And that business model needs to take into account the limited capacity of the criminal justice system to process offenders. To produce sustainable reductions in crime, the police will have to rely more on other institutions – government, business and community – to help analyse and solve problems. This allows more judicious use of the unique enforcement powers of the police. To date there is no alternative policing strategy to problem-oriented policing that addresses the wide array of concerns the public brings to the police. In addition, there is no other theory of crime that is as useful to the police as those encompassed within the framework of environmental criminology.

References

Braga, A. and Weisburd, D. (2006) 'Problem-oriented Policing: The Disconnect between Principles and Practice', in D. Weisburd and A. Braga (eds) *Police Innovation: Contrasting Perspectives*. New York: Cambridge University Press, pp. 133–54.

Bullock, K., Erol, R. and Tilley, N. (2006) *Problem-oriented Policing and Partnerships: Implementing an Evidence Based Approach to Crime Reduction*. Cullompton, UK: Willan Publishing.

Capowich, G.E. and Roehl, J.A. (1994) 'Problem-oriented Policing: Actions and Effectiveness in San Diego', in D. Rosenbaum (ed.) *The Challenges of Community Policing: Testing the Promises*. Thousand Oaks, CA: Sage, pp. 127–46.

Clarke, R.V. (2002) *Problem-oriented Policing, Case Studies. Report to the US Department of Justice*, Document 193801 (www.popcenter.org/Library/RecommendedReadings/POP-SCP-Clarke.pdf).

Clarke, R.V. and Eck, J.E. (2003) *Become a Problem-solving Crime Analyst: In 55 Small Steps*. London: Jill Dando Institute of Crime Science.

Clarke, R.V. and Eck, J.E. (2005) *Crime Analysis for Problem Solvers in 60 Small Steps*. Washington, DC: Office of Community Oriented Policing Services, US Department of Justice.

Clarke, R.V. and Goldstein, H. (2002) 'Reducing Theft at Construction Sites: Lessons from a Problem-oriented Project', in N. Tilley (ed.) *Analysis for Crime Prevention. Crime Prevention Studies Vol. 13*, Monsey, NY: Criminal Justice Press, pp. 89–130.

Clarke, R.V. and Goldstein, H. (2003) 'Thefts from Cars in Center-City Parking Facilities: A Case Study in Implementing Problem-oriented Policing', in J. Knutsson (ed.) *Problem-oriented Policing: From Innovation to Mainstream Crime Prevention Studies, Vol. 15*. Monsey, NY: Criminal Justice Press, pp. 257–98.

Cohen, L.E. and Felson, M. (1979) 'Social Change and Crime Rate Trends: A Routine Activity Approach', *American Sociological Review*, 44: 588–605.

Cordner, G. (1986) 'Fear of Crime and the Police: An Evaluation of a Fear-Reduction Strategy', *Journal of Police Science and Administration* 14: 223–33.

Eck, J.E. (2002) 'Preventing Crime at Places', in L.W. Sherman, D. Farrington, B. Welsh and D.L. MacKenzie (eds) *Evidence-based Crime Prevention*. New York: Routledge, pp. 241–94.

Eck, J.E. (2003) 'Police Problems: The Complexity of Problem Theory, Research and Evaluation', in J. Knutsson (ed.) *Problem-Oriented Policing: From Innovation to Mainstream. Crime Prevention Studies, Vol. 15*. Monsey, NY: Criminal Justice Press, pp. 67–102.

Eck, J.E. and Spelman, W. (1987) *Problem-solving: Problem-oriented Policing in Newport News*. Washington DC: Police Executive Research Forum.

Goldstein, H. (1977) *Policing a Free Society*. Cambridge, MA: Ballinger.

Goldstein, H. (1979) 'Improving Policing: A Problem-oriented Approach', *Crime and Delinquency*, 25: 236–58.

Goldstein, H. (1990) *Problem-oriented Policing*. New York: McGraw-Hill.

Goldstein, H. (2001) 'Problem-oriented Policing in a Nutshell', presentation at the International Problem-oriented Policing Conference, San Diego, CA.

Goldstein, H. and Susmilch, C.E. (1982) *Experimenting with the Problem-oriented Approach to Improve Police Service: A Report and Some Reflections on Two Case Studies*. Madison, WI: University of Wisconsin, Law School.

Green, L. (1995) 'Policing Places with Drug Problems: The Multi-agency Response Team Approach', in J.E. Eck and D. Weisburd (eds) *Crime and Place. Crime Prevention Studies, Vol. 4*. Monsey, NY: Criminal Justice Press, pp. 199–216.

Hammerich, M. (2007) *Problemorientert Politiarbeide – Når Tjenesten Tilladet det*. Afgangsprojekt, Diplomuddannelsen i kriminologi, Köbenhavns universitet.

Hoare, M.A., Stewart, G., and Purcell, C.M. (1984) *The Problem Oriented Approach: Four Pilot Studies*. London: Metropolitan Police, Management Services Department.

Kelling, G.L. and Sousa, W.H. Jr (2001) *Do Police Matter? An Analysis of the Impact of New York City's Police Reforms*, Civic Report. New York: Manhattan Institute for Policy Research (www.manhattan-institute.org/html/cr–22.htm).

Knutsson, J. and Søvik, K.E. (2005) *Problemorientert Politiarbeid i Teori og Praksis*. Politihøgskolen 2005: 1, Oslo: Politihøgskolen.

Leigh, A., Read, T. and Tilley, N. (1998) *Brit Pop II: Problem-oriented Policing in Practice*, Police Research Series Paper 93. London: Home Office.

Madensen, T. (2007) 'Bar Management and Crime: Toward a Dynamic Theory of Place Management and Crime Hotspots', PhD dissertation. Cincinnati, OH: Division of Criminal Justice, University of Cincinnati.

Mazerolle, L., Soole, D.W. and Rombouts, S. (2007) *Disrupting Street-level Drug Markets*, Crime Prevention Research Reviews No. 1. Washington DC: US Department of Justice, Office of Community Oriented Policing Services.

National Research Council (2004) *Fairness and Effectiveness in Policing: The Evidence*, W. Skogan and K. Frydl (eds) Committee to Review Research on Police Policy and Practices, Committee on Law and Justice, Division of Behavioral and Social Sciences and Education. Washington, DC: National Academies Press.

Office of Community Oriented Policing Services (1998) *Problem-solving Tips: A Guide to Reducing Crime and Disorder Through Problem-solving Partnerships*. Washington, DC: US Department of Justice, Office of Community Oriented Policing Services.

Pierce, G., Spaar, S. and Briggs, L. (1988) *The Character of Police Work: Implications for the Delivery of Police Service: Final Report to the National Institute of Justice*. Boston, MA: Northeastern University, College of Criminal Justice.

RCMP (Royal Canadian Mounted Police) (2000) *RCMP Employee's Handbook – Developing Your Learning Strategy*. RCMP, Learning and Development Branch (www.rcmp-learning.org/download/e_book.pdf).

Scott, M. (2000) *Problem-oriented Policing: Reflections on the First 20 Years*. Washington, DC: US Department of Justice, Office of Community Oriented Policing Services.

Sherman, L.S., Gartin, P.R. and Buerger, M.E. (1989) 'Hot Spots of Predatory Crime: Routine Activities and the Criminology of Place', *Criminology* 27: 27–55.

Silverman, E.B. (1999) *NYPD Battles Crime: Innovative Strategies in Policing*. Boston, MA: Northeastern University Press.

Skogan, W.G., Hartnett, S.M., DuBois, J., Comey, J.T., Kaiser, M., and Lovig, J.H. (1999) *On the Beat: Police and Community Problem Solving*. Boulder, CO: Westview Press.

Thomassen, G. (2005) *Implementering av Problemorientert Politiarbeid*, Noen Sentrale Utfordringar. (www.nsfk.org/downloads/seminarreports/researchsem_no47.pdf).

Vestfold Police District (2004) *Gypsy Cabs in Tønsberg – A Case for Problem Oriented Policing*. Vestfold Police District, Norway (www.popcenter.org/Library/Goldstein/2004/04-35(F).pdf).

Weisburd, D., Eck, J.E., Hinkle, J.C. and Telep, C.W. (2007), 'Does Problem-oriented Policing Reduce Crime and Disorder? A Systematic Review', Campbell Collaborative Annual Meeting. Maryland: University of Maryland.

Weisburd, D., Mastrofski, S.D., McNally, A.M., Greenspan, R. and Willis, J.J. (2003) 'Reforming to Preserve: COMPSTAT and Strategic Problem Solving in American Policing', *Criminology and Public Policy* 2: 421–56.

Welter, J.T. (2007) E-mail correspondence with Eck.

13. Broken windows

Michael Wagers, William Sousa and George Kelling

Introduction

Environmental criminology emphasises the understanding of criminal events at the local level. As such, environmental criminologists are less concerned with aggregate crime trends, and more concerned with particular problems occurring at specific places. By developing knowledge of crime at the local level, interventions can be more effectively tailored to prevent future occurrences at those locations (Clarke 1997). This micro-level approach has important implications for communities – depending on the unique characteristics of neighbourhoods and their problems, efforts can be made to reduce criminal opportunities.

Understanding local problems is especially critical for public police. While police must be concerned with the prevention of serious offences and crimes of violence, they must also respond to citizen demands to maintain order and improve neighbourhood quality of life. Thus, not only is it important for officers to understand the unique characteristics of crime at specific locations, they must also appreciate the nature of disorder in different communities.

In this chapter we describe a strategy for managing crime and disorder in local neighbourhoods. Our discussion revolves around the broken windows hypothesis, an argument that describes the relationship among disorder, citizen fear and crime. Here, we re-examine the central tenets of the original article.

Overview of broken windows

The broken windows argument grew out of research on police foot patrol in Newark, New Jersey by George Kelling and built upon earlier writings on the complexities of police work by James Q. Wilson (Pate *et al.* 1981; Wilson 1968). The original concept was published in the literary and cultural magazine *Atlantic Monthly*, under the title of 'Broken Windows: The Police and Neighborhood Safety'. Wilson and Kelling (1982) speculated that just as a broken window in a building left untended is a sign that nobody cares and invites more broken windows, disorder left untended is a sign that nobody cares and leads to fear of crime, withdrawal from public spaces, a breakdown of community controls, and more serious crime. Wilson, commenting about the developmental sequence described in the *Atlantic* article, notes that the argument and process behind the public order premise is intended to capture 'how neighborhoods might decay into disorder and even crime if no one attends faithfully to their maintenance' (1996: xv).

The broken windows metaphor is an intellectual extension of research conducted in the 1960s by psychologist Phillip Zimbardo. Among his findings was that when a car was abandoned in an ostensibly stable neighbourhood, it took only a few hours for the car to be almost completely destroyed once the first window was broken by the researcher; while it went untouched for weeks prior to that. Conversely, a car left in a crime-ridden neighbourhood was attacked within ten minutes (Wilson and Kelling 1982). Zimbardo's research provided a glimpse into the psychology of urban life. The supposition was that individuals engage in deviance when there is evidence that an area is without controls *vis-à-vis* visual cues indicating that criminal behaviour is acceptable. The surprise was not that the car in the crime-prone neighbourhood was vandalised within minutes of being abandoned – there were already signals that indicated crime occurs in that neighbourhood. More instructive was the effect that the abandoned car had in the stable neighbourhood. Once a window was broken it was a sign that communal barriers were beginning to break down.

The publication of broken windows came on the heels of a relatively new but burgeoning body of social science research on the profession of policing. A number of evaluations, for instance, questioned the efficacy of the standard and accepted police strategies of random patrol and rapid response to citizen calls for service. The prevailing wisdom was that unpredictable patrols created a perceived feeling of police omnipresence and, thus, deterred crime. Kelling *et al.* (1974), however, found no link when they tested this idea in an experiment in Kansas City. Adding or removing the number of police cars randomly patrolling an area did not affect the level of crime or citizen fear. As Sparrow, Moore, and Kennedy (1990: 15) write about the experiment: 'The results dumbfounded the police world. The variations in patrol seemed to have no appreciable impact at all.' Around the same time, another hallmark of policing was challenged: that quicker response times to a scene of a crime increase the chances of catching a fleeing offender. To the contrary, analyses indicated that the crime-control benefits of increasing response times were negligible, and that citizen reporting time most influenced the probability of an on-scene arrest, not police response time (Kansas City Police Department 1977; Spelman and Brown 1981). Sparrow *et al.* (1990: 16) sum up the impact of the findings from this early police research:

> By relying on patrol to prevent crime and rapid response to catch criminals, police had backed themselves into an isolated, reactive corner. The beat officers of old had naturally seen crime on their beats in terms

of patterns: they were responsible for all incidents on their turf, and a rash of burglaries or overdoses signaled a burglar or a dealer who needed to be dealt with. Modern officers, tied to their radios, saw crime as an endless string of isolated incidents. Fourteen burglaries in the same neighborhood might draw fourteen different cars.

These and other police studies followed the publication of *The Challenge of Crime in a Free Society* by the 1967 President's Commission on Law Enforcement and the Administration of Justice. Prior to the report, there was scant scientific research on police. The subsequent years produced an 'extraordinarily productive period of intellectual effort' on understanding police work (Committee to Review Research 2004: 20). A short review of the empirical findings illuminates the extent of this intellectual effort.

A variety of studies throughout the 1980s and 1990s sought to examine the broken windows thesis. Skogan's (1990), study of 40 cities is most often cited as providing empirical support for broken windows. He found a statistically significant relationship between fear, disorder and crime. It was changes in police practices in New York City during the 1990's, however, that provided the first real-world test of the approach called for by the broken windows metaphor. If disorder causes crime, as the research suggests, could the policing of disorder prevent crime? Beginning in the subways in the early 1990s, and then citywide in the mid 1990s, broken windows policing became an integral part of the overall strategy of the transit and city police to reduce crime and restore order in public space (Bratton 1998; Kelling and Coles 1996).

In the New York City subway system, the Metropolitan Transit Authority, among other things, began trying to combat the vandalism problem. They aggressively removed graffiti from subway cars under the Clean Car Program: cars would be taken out of service and cleaned of graffiti almost immediately. Graffiti artists were not allowed to see nor were others allowed to view their 'art'. However, the unruly behaviour continued. Bratton, who was brought in as chief of the transit police department, summed up the situation as follows:

> At the time, three and a half million people rode the New York subway system every day. However, those numbers had been declining dramatically because of a combination of fear of the system – at the time there was very little maintenance of the system, and every day there were fires on the tracks and train derailments – and every day they would encounter the subway version of the squeegee pest, or the petty criminal who vandalized the turnstiles, so that in order to get into the subway you had to go through the adjacent gate, and a beggar or petty criminal would be standing there with his hand out, intimidating you to give him money in much the same way that his counterpart at street level with a squeegee was intimidating you when you were stopped at a red light. (Civic Bulletin 2004: 4)

It was not until transit police began addressing problems with turnstile jumpers, aggressive panhandlers, and other forms of uncivil behaviour that conditions changed. They began to police disorderly behaviour. As Bratton continues:

> Once our program was underway, officers discovered that one out of every seven people we were arresting for fare evasion was wanted on a warrant. Often times, these warrants would be for very serious crimes: murders, rapes, and so on. One out of every twenty-one fare-evaders, at least initially, was carrying some type of weapon – ranging from a straightedge razor on up to Uzi submachine guns. Eventually this process excited police because they had a good chance of catching significant offenders without exorbitant effort. (Civic Bulletin 2004: 5)

Because of this type of policing – with its focus on disorderly behaviours and conditions – crime dropped and ridership increased (Kelling and Coles 1996). Crime in the subway system is down by almost 90 per cent from what it was in 1990; the number of daily riders has increased exponentially (Civic Bulletin 2004).

The problems on the streets of New York City mirrored the chaos of the subways. There were over 2,200 murders in the city in 1990; at the same time, the city led the country in number of robberies per 100,000 residents (Karmen 2000). Lardner and Reppetto (2000: 297) summarise what surveys about crime showed public perceptions to be during this time: 'It's out of control and nothing is being done.' A famous *New York Post* headline pleaded with then-mayor David Dinkins to address the situation. It read: 'DAVE, DO SOMETHING!'

Rudolph Giuliani beat Dinkins in the 1993 election, largely running on a law and order platform. He appointed Bratton commissioner of the New York Police Department in 1994. Under Bratton, the NYPD institutionalised broken windows policing. 'Policing Strategy Number 5: Reclaiming the Public Spaces of New York' became the blueprint. Quoting Wilson and Kelling, the 1994 NYPD document outlines how broken windows policing would become the linchpin of the department's efforts to reduce crime and disorder in the city. The strategy notes that 'by working systematically and assertively to reduce the level of disorder in the city, the NYPD will act to undercut the ground on which more serious crimes seem possible and even permissible' (New York Police Department 1994: 7). New York City experienced a 12 per cent reduction in crime the year the strategy was introduced; in both 1995 and 1996 crime dropped by 16 per cent each year (Silverman 1999: 6–7). Overall crime is down by over 70 per cent since the year before broken windows was introduced (1993–2005) (NYPD 2006).

But what exactly did police in New York City, both underground and on the city streets, do? How does a metaphor translate into an operational strategy? Broken windows policing can be described as the assertive enforcement of misdemeanour offences (Kelling and Coles 1996). It is frequently used synonymously with the term order-maintenance or quality-of-life policing. Sousa and Kelling (2006: 78) refer to broken windows policing as 'a police emphasis on disorderly behavior and minor offenses, often referred to as "quality of life" offenses like prostitution, public urination, and aggressive panhandling'. Based on observational research of what NYPD officers do when engaged in broken windows policing, they also describe it as 'paying attention' to minor offences (Sousa and Kelling 2006; Kelling and Sousa 2001). They note: 'Sometimes paying attention to minor offenses involved formal action – such as arrest or citation – but more often than not it involved no official action at all. While officers did not ignore disorderly behavior, they were much more likely to informally warn, educate, scold, or verbally reprimand citizens who violated minor offenses' (Sousa and Kelling 2006: 89). These are similar to the observations made during the Newark Foot Patrol experiment, which served as much of the basis for the idea of broken windows.

The New York City experience was not, of course, an experiment with random assignment. This has spawned an intense debate about what actually happened. Proponents claim that broken windows was one part of the success story (Giuliani 2002; Bratton 1998; Kelling and Coles 1996). Competing explanations have been offered for why crime dropped, and continues to decline, in New York. Improving economic conditions, demography, the decline of violent crack markets, and even the legalisation of abortion in the 1970s, have all been cited (Levitt and Dubner 2005; Blumstein and Wallman 2000). There have been attempts to parcel out the contribution of broken windows policing to the overall crime drop. For example, Kelling and Sousa (2001) link the reduction in crime, after examining precinct and borough-level data, to increased misdemeanour arrests; a proxy for broken windows policing.

Along with the debate about the impact of broken windows policing on the reduction in crime in New York City, some scholars have criticized Skogan's research, which has provided the strongest empirical support for the ideas contained within the broken windows thesis (see Harcourt 2001). Research by some scholars, such as Raudenbush and Sampson (2005, 1999) report that macro-level factors are more closely correlated with fear and crime than with disorder. Other scholars have argued that there are unintended consequences produced by broken windows policing. Harcourt (2001: 207) contends that broken windows re-criminalises quality- of-life offences, such as loitering and panhandling, from that of being 'mere nuisances and annoyances into seriously harmful conduct ...' The thesis has been described as an approach to define certain people out of the community and as a middle-class yearning for order and decorum (Kunen 1994; McCoy 1986). Bowling (1999) declares that broken windows clears the way for police to 'kick ass'. Wilson and Kelling themselves recognised in the *Atlantic* article the inherent ethical dilemmas posed by enforcing disorderly infractions such as disturbing the peace, loitering and vagrancy: offences that are usually only punished by fines or community service. They were concerned about how such an approach can be undertaken while ensuring that 'police do not become agents of neighborhood bigotry'. Additionally, Wilson and Kelling (1982: 35–6) were concerned about community controls turning into 'neighborhood vigilantes'.

In the following section, we describe why Wilson and Kelling speculated in the original article that disorder matters; and why police should pay attention to minor crimes. By discussing the core ideas described in the *Atlantic* article, we also counter many of the points critics have missed when criticising broken windows.

The original idea of broken windows

Broken windows was originally stated as a hypothesis by Wilson and Kelling in 1982. They speculated that untended disorder led to fear and more serious crime (Wilson and Kelling 2006). Kelling and Coles (1996) expanded upon these ideas in their book, *Fixing Broken Windows: Restoring Order and Reducing Crime in Our Communities*. The essence of the broken windows argument is that disorder that is not addressed leads to an increase in fear of crime. This increased fear causes neighbourhood residents to withdraw from using public spaces and to take various protective measures. For example, citizens may move to the other side of the street when rowdy youths approach or homeowners may place bars on the windows of their homes for added security and stop using their front porch or stoop as a place to congregate. Accordingly, this diminishes informal social control exerted by community members, merchants and other neighbourhood caretakers. It also decreases the possibility that citizens will informally warn or scold people for their behaviour, such as youth acting wildly in a local park, littering and the use of profane language by young children. It is a tacit recognition (bars on windows are an explicit sign) that conditions have become such that fear overrides the sense of community that once may have existed.

This breakdown in community controls in combination with disorder in turn provides fertile ground for more serious crime to take place. Wilson and Kelling (1982) argue that relatively minor problems, like graffiti and aggressive panhandling, are the equivalent of, in a literal sense, broken windows in a building. Furthermore, these types of minor infractions, when they begin to aggregate, send a signal to would-be offenders that an area is not controlled by those that live or work in the area or the police. This invites more crime because it is a demonstrable cue that the risk of detection or apprehension is low. Wilson and Kelling (1982: 34) write:

> Muggers and robbers, whether opportunistic or professional, believe they reduce their chances of being caught or even identified if they operate on streets where potential victims are already intimidated by prevailing conditions. If the neighborhood cannot keep a bothersome panhandler from annoying passersby, the thief may reason, it is even less likely to call the police to identify a potential mugger or to interfere if the mugging actually takes place.

Broken windows puts forth a model wherein disorder indirectly leads to more serious crime. Some researchers have misspecified the model, interpreting the thesis as one that argues that disorder is *directly* linked to crime (for example, Jang and Johnson 2001). But a reading of the original article makes evident that 'broken windows postulates that disorder *indirectly* leads to crime via weakened community and neighborhood controls' (Sousa and Kelling 2006: 84; emphasis in original).

The eight core ideas

To better understand the broken windows argument, it is useful to go back to the writing of Wilson and Kelling (1982). Sousa and Kelling (2006: 79) have outlined the eight core ideas of broken windows; they are taken from the original article in the *Atlantic*. The eight core ideas of broken windows are:

1 Disorder and fear of crime are strongly linked.
2 Police (in the examples given, foot patrol officers) negotiate rules of the street. 'Street people' are involved in the negotiation of those rules.
3 Different neighbourhoods have different rules.
4 Untended disorder leads to the breakdown of community controls.
5 Areas where community controls break down are vulnerable to criminal invasion.
6 The essence of the police role in maintaining order is to reinforce the informal control mechanisms of the community itself.
7 Problems arise not so much from individual disorderly persons as it does from the congregation of large numbers of disorderly persons.
8 Different neighbourhoods have different capacities to manage disorder.

1 Disorder and fear of crime are strongly linked

Disorder triggers the developmental sequence: disorder leads to an increase in fear of crime. Wilson and Kelling (1982) refer to disorderly behaviours and conditions such as graffiti, aggressive panhandling and rowdy youths. Kelling and Coles (1996: 14) say that: 'In the broadest social sense, disorder is incivility, boorish and threatening behavior that disturbs life, especially urban life.' LaGrange, Ferraro and Supancic (1992: 312) define disorder as incivilities that are 'breaches of community standards that signal an erosion of conventionally accepted norms and values'. In more general terms, most researchers characterise disorder along two dimensions: physical and social (Ferraro 1995; Skogan 1990). Physical disorder refers to visible, easily identifiable conditions such as litter, abandoned buildings and cars, graffiti, broken and barricaded windows, and unkempt lots. Social incivilities, according to Ferraro (1995: 15), can be defined as 'disruptive social behaviors such as the presence of rowdy youth, homeless people, beggars, drunks ("riffraff" on the streets) or, perhaps, inconsiderate neighbors'. Disorder can be behavioural – an act a person engages in that violates the values of a community – or environmental, such as graffiti. Skogan has defined disorder the following way:

> Social disorder is a matter of behavior: you can see it happen (public drinking or prostitution), experience it (catcalling or sexual harassment),

or notice direct evidence of it (graffiti or vandalism). Physical disorder involves visual signs of negligence and unchecked decay: abandoned or ill-kept buildings, broken streetlights, trash-filled lots, and alleys strewn with garbage and alive with rats. *By and large, physical disorder refers to ongoing conditions, while social disorder appears as a series of more-or-less episodic events.* (1990: 4, emphasis added)

Does disorder cause fear? Fear of crime is 'defined as an emotional reaction of dread or anxiety to crime or symbols that a person associates with crime' (Ferraro 1995: 4). The 1967 President's Commission noted the disjuncture between direct victimisation and fear and also the influence of ecological factors. The Commission (1967: 160) reports:

We have found that attitudes of citizens regarding crime are less affected by past victimization experiences than by their ideas about what is going on in their community – fears about a weakening of social controls on which they feel their safety and broader fabric of social life is ultimately dependent.

For the most part, empirical research has consistently linked fear with disorder. Lewis and Maxfield (1980) found that citizens' perception of local crime conditions is more affected by disorder than by actual crime. Stinchcombe *et al.* (1980) argued that fear of crime differs from other fears insomuch as citizens make a connection between crime and environmental cues. Kenny (1987) found that riders of the New York City subway system who were fearful also thought disorderly behaviours, such as public drunkenness and loitering, were problems. Hope and Hough (1988) found a strong and statistically significant relationship between disorder and fear in their examination of data from the British Crime Survey. They found that rates of perceived incivilities are more strongly related to levels of fear than the level of victimisation.

Xu, Fielder and Flaming (2005) reported similar findings. They found that disorder is a more important source of fear than is serious crime. They gathered survey data from a large Midwestern city that included measures of neighbourhood disorder, crime, victimisation, fear, perceptions of community environment, and evaluations of police effectiveness and accountability, finding that 'perceived disorder is a significant facilitator of citizens' fear' (2005: 171).

Skogan's (1990) analysis of survey data from six cities (40 urban neighbourhoods) also produced empirical evidence that disorder is significantly related to fear of crime. Where neighbourhood disorder was high, people did not feel safe. The direction and strength of this relationship remained when other factors, such as neighbourhood stability, poverty and racial composition were taken into account. This increased fear is attributed to disorder being an indicator of crime which, when perceived, heightens an individual's perception of risk (Skogan 1990; Skogan and Maxfield 1981). Disorderly behaviours and conditions elevate a person's sense that the neighbourhood or community is a high-crime area where potential offenders are and past criminal behaviour has taken place. Moreover, disorder provides some indication about the level of social control, both informal and formal, in an area, further influencing perceptions of risk and fear.

2 Police negotiate rules of the street

The second core idea is that police negotiate the rules of the street. This is more of a description of what police do when engaged in broken windows policing (at least, as described in the original publication) than part of the developmental sequence. What this core idea describes is the process for how disorder is defined and enforced. It also highlights the distinction between broken windows and a zero-tolerance policing approach. In the former, discretion is part of police officer decision-making. In the latter, it is not (Clarke and Eck 2005).

The police officer described by Wilson and Kelling (1982) enforced – by formal and informal means – the agreed-upon standards of behaviour for the area he patrolled. As they described it, 'These rules were defined and enforced in collaboration with the "regulars" on the street' (Wilson and Kelling 1982: 30). Because the officer was assigned to a specific beat he was able to get to know the people, the problems in the area, and developed a common understanding of community standards. For instance, drinking was permitted, but only off the main intersection and if the liquor/beer was contained in a brown bag. It was acceptable for disreputable individuals to sit on stoops but they could not lie down. Also, panhandling was permissible, but not from people standing still or waiting at a bus stop (Wilson and Kelling 1982). Hence, within this discretionary and negotiable context, certain (generally) undesirable behaviours became permissible under certain circumstances.

These contextual or situational factors have been found to be important factors in observational studies of broken windows policing. Kelling and Sousa (2001), for example, found that NYPD officers routinely assessed the circumstances surrounding minor offences before, during and after making enforcement decisions. In negotiating the rules of the street, officers would typically explain the circumstances for their decisions regarding minor offences. Consider the following observation of officers citing individuals for public alcohol use in an entertainment district of New York City:

> At one point, one male asks, 'What is the big deal? It's harmless, it's just a beer – it's minor and victimless'. The officer replies, 'Yes, it is just a beer, but if you had been here a few years ago, and it was a little later and you were a little drunker, maybe you bump into someone accidentally who also was drinking, and that's how fights start and how violence breaks out. The reason why we're so strict now is because we're trying to prevent that from happening.' (Kelling and Sousa 2001: 17)

This observation demonstrates the ability of NYPD officers to have a somewhat educational function, providing advice about appropriate rules in public places. It also marks a distinction between broken windows policing and traditional (or standard) police practice. The officer's mention of 'a few years ago' is a reference to a period before NYPD's adoption of broken windows policing, when officers would respond to incidents of serious assault – but would do relatively little to prevent them from initially occurring.

3 Different neighbourhoods have different rules

Closely linked to the core idea discussed above (police work with regulars in an area to negotiate rules of the street) is the idea that different public spaces, whether residential neighbourhoods, apartment complexes, business districts, or parks, have differing behavioural expectations. Behaviour that is acceptable in one setting (both in space and time) may not be in another. For example, the types of behaviour that are part of the norm in the Ironbound section of Newark, New Jersey, which has a lively outdoor street scene along its main commercial corridor, Ferry Street – a mix of Portuguese and Brazilian restaurants, shops, and apartments – are not acceptable in other, quieter residential settings in Newark, such as the North Ward.

In Lakewood, New Jersey, as we have observed, police allowed residents in public housing apartments to drink beer and liquor within a limited radius of their building if they were doing so responsibly. As the officers described it, they allowed the residents to do so because they have little or no private outdoor property of their own. However, they were not allowed to drink in the parking lots or on the sidewalks that lined the major streets in the area. This was one of the agreed-upon rules of that area, worked out between police and residents.

This core idea, and the idea that police negotiate rules of the street, points to the importance of police working with the community. Officers need to have a relationship with the regulars of an area – shopkeepers, youth, homeless people, residents – in order to understand the characteristics of a public space and to collaborate with those regulars to define and address problems in an area.

4 Untended disorder leads to the breakdown of community controls

An important element in the broken windows developmental sequence is the relationship between disorder, fear, the breakdown of community controls, and crime. Disorder and fear lead to the inability for a community to regulate itself; when this happens, social atomisation sets in. Kelling and Coles (1996: 20) describe the chain of events as follows:

> [D]isorderly behavior unregulated and unchecked signals to citizens that the area is unsafe. Responding prudently, and fearfully, citizens will stay off of the streets, avoid certain areas, and curtail their normal activities and associations. As citizens withdraw physically, they also withdraw from roles of mutual support with fellow citizens on the streets, thereby relinquishing social controls they formerly helped to maintain within the community as social atomization sets in.

Research into the relationship between community characteristics and crime is nothing new. Its origins date back to the early twentieth century when scholars at the University of Chicago began applying ecological theory to the study of crime. In what became known as the Chicago School, sociological theories of crime developed around the idea that social disorganisation – where neighbourhoods were characterised by relationships that were impersonal, superficial and transitory – caused crime (Williams and McShane 1993). In one of their classic writings, Shaw and McKay (1942: 445) note: 'Communities with high rates have social and economic characteristics which differentiate them from communities with low rates.' The contribution of this perspective in criminology and of significance to broken windows is that it focuses attention on the importance of informal social controls on neighbourhood stability (Taylor 2001).

Bursik and Grasmick (1993), Sampson and Raudenbush (1999) and others have conducted research in the tradition of the Chicago School, seeking to further explain the relationship between neighbourhood deterioration and crime. Bursik and Grasmick (1993) point to not only the importance of control mechanisms within a neighbourhood but also to how that neighbourhood is connected to external processes, such as being able to funnel resources – public services, for example – into that neighbourhood. Sampson and Raudenbush (1999) describe community controls in terms of 'collective efficacy'. Collective efficacy describes the differential ability of neighbourhoods to realise common values and maintain effective social controls, and is hence the source of crime and violence in communities. Sampson and Raudenbush (1999), in fact, conclude that the level of collective efficacy in a neighbourhood is a stronger predictor of crime than disorder.

Where theories that have their foundation in the Chicago School differ from the developmental sequence described by broken windows is that they believe that structural variables matter more than disorder (see Sampson and Raudenbush 1999). Others, such as Taylor (2001), call for a more integrated perspective, one that takes into account these larger forces, including race and class, and an incivilities thesis. Taylor (2001: p. 23) argues that public officials responsible for urban redevelopment 'ought not hope that grime-fighting initiatives by themselves will restore the fundamental fabric of neighbourhoods which has been damaged by decades of inadequate city services, declining employment opportunities for its adults, and declining educational opportunities for it youth'. Broken windows does not argue against the need for improving the lot of social forces that impinge upon the fabric of urban neighbourhoods. What broken windows offers, however, is a framework for addressing crime in the near-term, so that other stabilising forces – such as schools, churches, social service agencies and businesses – can function properly.

5 Areas where community controls break down are vulnerable to criminal invasion

Disorderly public spaces attract would-be offenders. Disorder signals to potential offenders that an area is an opportunistic place to commit crime. There are physical signs, such as graffiti, trash-strewn sidewalks, boarded-up houses and security bars over windows. There are also social signs: groups of rowdy youth hanging out on street corners; aggressive panhandlers accosting citizens; homeless people sleeping in doorways. These circumstances set the stage for an abundance of offenders (and targets) to converge in one place. The place could be, for example, a neighbourhood, a park, a downtown business district, or a subway system.

Wilson and Kelling believe that this invasion of prospective offenders into public places is more likely in places where informal controls have broken down. They note that in an environment where people are not confident they cannot regulate behaviour: 'drugs will change hands, prostitutes will solicit, and cars will be stripped' (Wilson and Kelling 1982: 32).

6 The essence of the police role in maintaining order is to reinforce the informal control mechanisms of the community itself

According to this core idea, the role of the police is to support the community. Wilson and Kelling (1982) note that police cannot replace community controls. They write: 'The police cannot, without committing extraordinary resources, provide a substitute for that informal control' (1982: 34). Jane Jacobs recognised this in her groundbreaking work, *The Death and Life of Great American Cities* (Sousa and Kelling 2006). She writes about the vitality of urban neighbourhoods, observing that order is not kept principally by the police. She explains that: '[Order] is kept primarily by an intricate, almost unconscious, network of voluntary controls and standards among people themselves, and enforced by the people themselves' (Jacobs 1961: 40). What Jacobs describes as the normal, casual enforcement by citizens is also embodied in this core idea. Citizens are responsible for social control. The role of the police is to exert authority, when necessary, to support community controls (and standards) and to provide assistance when communal barriers against crime breakdown.

7 Problems arise not so much from individual disorderly persons as it does from the congregation of large numbers of disorderly persons

One or two drunks in a public space, such as a park, begging for money from passersby might not be a problem. When the number reaches a certain point – and that point depends on a number of contextual factors – that space can reach a tipping point, changing from an orderly place, where users of the space are not fearful and coexist with a certain level of disorder, to one where crime begins to occur more frequently. Wilson (1996: p. vx) describes the congregation phenomenon this way:

> A public space – a bus stop, a market square, a subway entrance – is more than the sum of its human parts; it is a complex pattern of interactions that can become dramatically more threatening as the scale and frequency of those interactions increase. As the number of unconventional individuals

increases arithmetically, the number of worrisome behaviors increases geometrically.

The aggregation of disorder sets the stage for more serious crime to follow. Broken windows does not prescribe taking action against one or two disorderly persons who are not causing immediate harm to someone. (A panhandler aggressively soliciting money near an automatic teller machine at night is a different situation). It is concerned with the effect that a congregation of disorderly persons do. In the original article, Wilson and Kelling (1982: 35) write: 'Arresting a single drunk or a single vagrant who has harmed no identifiable person seems unjust, and in a sense it is.' They go on to say that 'failing to do anything about a score of drunks or a hundred vagrants may destroy an entire community. It makes no sense because it fails to take into account the connection between one broken window left untended and a thousand broken windows'.

8 Different neighbourhoods have different capacities to manage disorder

This issue was basic in the original *Atlantic* article and re-emphasised in *Fixing Broken Windows*. Some neighbourhoods have an enormous capacity to manage disorder. An example of this is Harvard Square in Cambridge, MA. Harvard Square has more than its share of street people, hustlers, and aggressive panhandlers, yet it can absorb their behaviour without major threat to citizens' sense of security, commerce, or community life. One can find many other neighbourhood centres, however, that would grind to an economic and social halt if they had *half* of the disorder that characterises Harvard Square.

True, Harvard Square is a relatively wealthy neighbourhood surrounded by what is perhaps the world's most prestigious university. Still, as Sampson and his colleagues have demonstrated (1997), reiterating a key theme of the Chicago School, even neighbourhoods that are socially and economically disadvantaged but that are characterised by *collective efficacy* – that is, the capacity for informal social control – can manage and reduce disorderly behaviour and serious crime. The mechanisms include disapproval of anti-social behaviour, intervention to mediate fights, discouragement of truancy, the presence of capable guardians, neighbourhood design and uses of public spaces, and others.

Conclusion

It has been more than 25 years since the publication of the original broken windows article. In some respects, it has become conventional wisdom among policy-makers and practitioners, although we are quick to add that broken windows has been criticised by many academics and civil libertarians. Here, we have gone back to the original article and summarised its central tenets – tenets that both critics and advocates have often misrepresented or ignored.

In retrospect, little has happened, whether in research or practice, that would lead us to back away from these eight central points. In our view they both stood in the traditions of community justice and community policing and gave further impetus and substance to those inchoate movements during their critical early stages. To sum, we quote Wilson and Kelling (2006: 172):

> The broken windows idea does two things, one indisputably good and the other probably effective: it encourages the police to take public order seriously, something that the overwhelming majority of people ardently desire, and it raises the possibility that more order will mean less crime. The first goal requires no evidence. The second does, and so far most studies suggest that more public order (along with other factors) is associated with less predatory street crime.

References

Blumstein, A. and Wallman, J. (eds) (2000) *The Crime Drop in America*. Cambridge: Cambridge University Press.

Bowling, B. (1999) 'The Rise and Fall of New York Murder: Zero Tolerance or Crack's Decline', *British Journal of Criminology*, 39: 531–54.

Bratton, W.J. (1998) *Turnaround: How America's Top Cop Reversed the Crime Epidemic*. New York: Random House.

Bursik, R. and Grasmick, H. (1993) *Neighborhoods and Crime: The Dimensions of Effective Community Controls*. New York: Lexington Books.

Civic Bulletin (2004) *This Works: Crime Prevention and the Future of Broken Windows Policing* (No. 36). New York: Manhattan Institute.

Clarke, R.V. (1997) *Situational Crime Prevention*, 2nd edn. Albany, NY: Harrow and Heston.

Clarke, R.V. and Eck, J.E. (2005) *Crime Analysis for Problem Solvers in 60 Small Steps*. Washington, DC: Office of Community Oriented Policing Services.

Committee to Review Research on Police Policy and Practice (2004), *Fairness and Effectiveness in Policing: The Evidence*. Washington, DC: National Academies Press.

Ferraro, K.F. (1995) *Fear of Crime: Interpreting Victimization Risk*. Albany, NY: State University of New York Press.

Giuliani, R.W. (2002) *Leadership*. New York: Hyperion Books.

Harcourt, B.E. (2001) *Illusion of Order: The False Promise of Broken Windows Policing*. Cambridge, MA: Harvard University Press.

Hope, T. and Hough, M. (1988) 'Area Crime, and Incivility: A Profile from the British Crime Survey', in T. Hope and M. Shaw (eds) *Communities and Crime Reduction*. London: HMSO.

Jacobs, J. (1961) *The Death and Life of Great American Cities*. New York: Vintage Books.

Jang, S.J. and Johnson, B.R. (2001) 'Neighbourhood Disorder, Individual Religiosity, and Adolescent Use of Illicit Drugs: A Test of Multilevel Hypotheses', *Criminology*, 39(1): 109–44.

Kansas City Police Department (1977) *Response Time Analysis*. Kansas City, MO: Kansas City Police Department.

Karmen, A. (2000) *New York Murder Mystery: The True Story Behind the Crime Crash of the 1990s*. New York: New York University Press.

Kelling, G.L. (1998) 'Crime Control, the Police, and Culture Wars: Broken Windows and Cultural Pluralism', *Perspectives on Crime and Justice: 1997–1998 Lecture Series*. Washington, DC: National Institute of Justice.

Kelling, G.L. and Coles, C.M. (1996), *Fixing Broken Windows: Restoring Order and Reducing Crime in Our Communities*. New York, NY: Free Press.

Kelling, G.L. and Sousa, W.H. (2001) *Do Police Matter? An Analysis of the Impact of New York City's Police Reform*, Civic Report No. 22. New York: Manhattan Institute.

Kelling, G.L., Pate, A., Dieckman, D. and Brown, C. (1974) *The Kansas City Preventive Patrol Experiment: Summary Version*. Washington, DC: Police Foundation.

Kenny, D.J. (1987) *Crime, Fear, and the New York City Subways*. New York: Praeger.

Kunen, J.S. (1994) 'Quality and Equality: The Mayor Tries Something that Works, at a Cost', *The New Yorker* (28 November): 9–10.

LaGrange, R.L., Ferraro, K.F. and Supancic, M. (1992) 'Perceived Risk and Fear of Crime: Role of Social and Physical Incivilities', *Journal of Research in Crime and Delinquency*, 29: 311–34.

Lardner, J. and Reppetto, T. (2000) *NYPD: A City and Its Police*. New York: Henry Holt Company.

Levitt, S.D. and Dubner, S.J. (2005) *Freakanomics*, New York: William Morrow.

Lewis, D.A. and Maxfield, M.M. (1980), 'Fear in the Neighborhoods: An Investigation of the Impact of Crime', *Journal of Research in Crime and Delinquency*, 17: 160–89.

McCoy, C. (1986) 'Policing the Homeless', *Criminal Law Bulletin*, 22: 266.

New York Police Department (1994) *Policing Strategy Number 5: Reclaiming the Public Spaces of New York*. New York: NYPD.

New York Police Department (2006) www.nyc.gov/html/nypd/pdf/chfdept/cscity.pdf (accessed 14 November 2006).

Pate, T., Ferrara, A. and Kelling, G.L. (1981) 'Foot Patrol: A Discussion of the Issues', in *The Newark Foot Patrol Experiment*. Washington, DC: Police Foundation.

President's Commission on Law Enforcement and Administration of Justice (1967) *The Crime Commission Report: The Challenge of Crime in a Free Society*. Washington, DC: US Government Printing Office.

Sampson, R.J. and Raudenbush, S.W. (1999), 'Systematic Social Observations of Public Spaces: A New Look at Disorder in Urban Neighborhoods', *American Journal of Sociology*, 105: 603.

Shaw, C.R. and McKay, H.D. (1942) *Juvenile Delinquency and Urban Areas*. Chicago: University of Chicago Press.

Silverman, E.B. (1999) *NYPD Battles Crime: Innovative Strategies in Policing*. Boston, MA: Northeastern University Press.

Skogan, W.G. and Maxfield, M.M. (1981) *Coping with Crime*, Beverly Hills, CA: Sage.

Skogan, W.G. (1990) *Disorder and Decline: Crime and the Spiral of Decay in American Neighborhoods*. New York: Free Press.

Sloan-Howitt, M. and Kelling, G.L. (1992) 'Subway Graffiti in New York City: Getting Up vs. Meanin it and Cleaning it', in *Situational Crime Prevention: Successful Case Studies*. Albany, NY: Harrow and Heston.

Sousa, W.H. and Kelling, G.L. (2006) 'Of Broken Windows, Criminology and Criminal Justice', in D. Weisburd and A. Braga (eds) *Police Innovation: Contrasting Perspectives*. Cambridge: Cambridge University Press.

Sparrow, M., Moore, M. and Kennedy, D. (1990) *Beyond 911: A New Era for Policing*. New York: Basic Books.

Spelman, W. and Brown, D. (1981) *Calling the Police: A Replication of the Citizen Reporting Component of the Kansas City Response Time Analysis*. Washington, DC: Police Executive Research Forum.

Stinchcombe, A.L., Adams, R., Heimer, C., Scheppele, K., Smith T. and Taylor, D.G. (1980) *Crime and Punishment in Public Opinion*. San Francisco: Jossey-Bass.

Taylor, R.B. (2001) *Breaking Away from Broken Windows: Baltimore Neighborhoods and the Nationwide Fight Against Crime, Grime, Fear, and Decline*. Boulder, CO: Westview Press.

Williams, F.P. and McShane, M.D. (1993) *Criminological Theory: Selected Classic Readings*. Cincinnati, Ohio: Anderson.

Wilson, J.Q. (1968) *Varieties of Police Behavior*. Cambridge, MA: Harvard University Press.

Wilson, J.Q. (1996) 'Forward', in G. Kelling and C. Coles (eds) *Fixing Broken Windows: Restoring Order and Reducing Crime in Our Communities*. New York: The Free Press.

Wilson, J.Q. and Kelling, G.L. (1982) 'Broken Windows: The Police and Neighborhood Safety', *Atlantic Monthly*, March: 29–38.

Wilson, J.Q. and Kelling, G.L. (2006) 'A Quarter Century of Broken Windows', September–October.

Xu, Y., Fielder, M. and Flaming, K. (2005) 'Discovering the Impact of Community Policing: The Broken Windows Thesis, Collective Efficacy, and Citizens' Judgment', *Journal of Research in Crime and Delinquency*, 42: 147–86.

14. Intelligence-led policing

Jerry H. Ratcliffe

Introduction

The word *intelligence* seems to summon up the wrong image in just about everyone. To the public it can suggest subterfuge, a clandestine and covert activity conducted by officers of a shady disposition and involving a degree of moral ambiguity. To patrol officers, it is a peripheral activity that seems to have little relevance to their daily job and is mainly used by specialised units employing wire taps and surveillance. To senior police officers, it is of tangential value, a tool for investigative case support that has little influence over strategic decision-making. But to crime intelligence analysts, it represents a rare objective voice that understands the criminal environment, a lone whisper that is maligned, misunderstood or simply ignored by an institutional milieu yet to come to terms with policing in the post-9/11, information-rich world. Misuse of the term *intelligence-led policing* can further increase confusion by reinforcing preconceived notions (such as those mentioned above), encumbering this new conceptual framework and business model for policing with all of the characteristics embodied by however the individual originally viewed *intelligence*.

Wardlaw and Boughton argue that 'the concept of intelligence-led policing is now widely espoused by police services as a fundamental part of the way they do business. But for such a widely talked about concept, there is remarkably little clarity about its definition and fundamental concepts' (2006: 134). This chapter therefore aims to wade through the conceptual fog by outlining the origins of intelligence-led policing and from this move towards clarifying its central tenets and how they differ from other models of policing.

Origins

It is claimed by some in law enforcement that they have been doing intelligence-led policing for ages. For much of the history of policing, however, criminal intelligence has been utilised in a haphazard and inconsequential manner

)04; Grieve 2004). As such, intelligence played little role
del of policing that favoured a reactive and investigative
ather than a preventative one (Weisburd and Eck 2004).
iminal intelligence was rarely used in any coordinated,
was used on a case-by-case basis to gather evidence to
In many respects, this was worse than 'policing-led
2004) and was really a 150-year illustration of *investigation-
...ligence*, a demotion that pushed criminal intelligence and the analytical
process into the wilderness of the law enforcement world and subverted it to
the role of case support: a minor adjunct to investigations.

So how did the use of crime analysis and criminal intelligence emerge from
a peripheral activity employed by specialised police units, into the pivotal
position at the heart of the business model that intelligence-led policing has
become today? The exact path from investigation-led intelligence to intelligence-
led policing is a little unclear; however, it does have some signposts and one
or two significant milestones (Gill 1998). Signposts include:

• *The demand gap and the failure of traditional policing.* The standard model of
reactive, investigative policing was unable to contain the huge spike in crime
that hit the US starting in the mid 1960s and which manifested itself as a
failure of the criminal justice system in the 1970s (Weisburd and Eck 2004).
Similarly in the mid 1970s, the UK experienced a demand gap that saw
requests for police attention and assistance far outstrip any corresponding
increases in police resources or personnel (Flood 2004). These challenging
times provided the impetus for problem-oriented policing, community
policing, team policing and a host of other attempts to be more effective
with existing resources.

• *Improvements in information technology.* The period since the mid 1970s has
seen police departments slowly adopting greater technological solutions for
their information management needs. While originally spurred to collect
statistics for governmental purposes and to manage the information needs
of agencies outside policing (Chainey and Ratcliffe 2005; Ericson and
Haggerty 1997), it became apparent to innovators within law enforcement
that the vast volumes of data collected internally could be used to influence
police decision-making. Crime analysts (often separate from intelligence
officers) began cropping up in police departments as a group adept at
using this 'new knowledge' (Ratcliffe 2008b) to provide tactical support for
mid-level commanders and create a strategic picture of crime for senior
management.

• *Pressure for greater managerial professionalisation.* The demand gap coincided
with, and was related to, greater calls on the police for effectiveness and
efficiency. The growth in the UK of the 'new public management' movement
saw government take an active interest in the day-to-day business of policing
for the first time (Crawford 1997). Police executives fell under far more
scrutiny than ever before, such that decisions had to be tempered by a risk

management assessment of likely fall-out to the police service. This need to manage risk required greater access to information and drove significant changes in the business of policing (Ericson and Haggerty 1997). As Flood notes, 'in the face of an established social trend that seems to disallow honest mistakes, apportions blame and makes sure that someone "pays" whenever misfortune strikes, it is nothing more than common sense to ensure that police actions should be based, wherever possible, on rigorously evaluated intelligence of known provenance rather than on intuition, even where the latter may have its roots in long experience' (Flood 2004: 43).

- *The growth of serious and organised crime.* The breakdown of national boundaries at the end of the last century, coupled with the end of the Cold War, led to rapid changes on an international level. Greater internationalism of illicit commodities, the rise of globalisation, the creation of electronic financial transactions and the internet, all facilitated an increase in transnational crime. No longer could police departments remain isolated from their colleagues in other jurisdictions. The resultant move to a more collaborative approach to serious and organised crime has left police departments contemplating organisational restructuring as well as seeking out new models of policing as a conceptual framework on which to orientate themselves (see for example Ratcliffe and Guidetti, 2008). Federal intelligence agencies have desks specifically to examine groups such as South-East Asian organised crime and the Russian mafia, and there is now a range of federal and national agencies that have directives to interdict transnational organised crime organisations and to link domestic and international intelligence on these groups (Wardlaw and Boughton 2006). Internationally, organisations with mandates that stretch beyond traditional national borders are becoming common, including; the myriad agencies under the Department of Homeland Security (US), the UK Serious and Organised Crime Agency (SOCA), Criminal Intelligence Service Canada (CISC), and the Australian Crime Commission (ACC) and Australian Federal Police (AFP).

While these drivers (the demand gap, improvements in information technology, new public managerialism, and the growth of organised crime) were responsible for creating an environment conducive to intelligence-led policing, there are specific milestones that map the route to the current law enforcement landscape. One is the publication in 1993 of *Helping with Enquiries: Tackling Crime Effectively* by a British government financial oversight body (Audit Commission 1993). Their recommendations sought to achieve the greatest value for money from the police in the fight against crime and looked to move the police away from a reactive, crime focus to a proactive, offender focus. *Helping with Enquiries* had three main arguments (Ratcliffe 2003):

- Existing policing roles and the levels of accountability lacked integration and efficiency.
- The police were failing to make the best use of resources.

- Greater emphasis on tackling criminals would be more effective than focusing on crimes.

Helping with Enquiries included a raft of statistical data that appeared to support the case for proactive policing. Some researchers questioned the validity of the case proposed by the Audit Commission (see for example Dunnighan and Norris 1999 and related work by Townsley and Pease 2002), but the government had already gathered vocal and enthusiastic support, especially from within the police. Intelligence-led policing provided an argument for police to re-engage with what they considered to be core business: fighting crime and arresting serious offenders. Further publications (Amey *et al.* 1996; HMIC 1997; Maguire and John 1995) provided a framework for implementation and the experiences of police in Kent, under the leadership of David Phillips with the Kent Policing Model (Anderson 1994; Collier 2006), demonstrated that proactive policing could be applied to high-volume property crime as well as to organised crime. To promote the idea to all forces, Her Majesty's Inspectorate of Constabulary identified the central tenets of a successful intelligence-led model (1997: 1):

- Enthusiastic and energetic leadership that endorses intelligence-led policing and promotes it through a Director of Intelligence.

- A published strategy that sets the intelligence agenda for a force, as well as explains what is meant by 'proactivity'.

- An integrated intelligence structure so that analysts can work at the hub of operational policing activities.

- Criteria to measure performance to determine the effectiveness of the introduction of the crime intelligence function and the tasking of operational units.

- The forging of effective partnerships with local agencies that may be able to help police combat local crime and disorder problems.

Beyond the UK, the events of September 11th 2001 (9/11) served to fuel a growing international interest in intelligence-led policing. Realising that a reactive, investigation-focused approach was of increasingly less comfort to a public seeking prevention and disruption of future incidents (rather than swift investigation), police in a number of countries began exploring intelligence-led policing as a framework for the reduction, disruption and prevention of crime. In particular, based on recommendations from the Criminal Intelligence Sharing Summit held in Spring 2002, senior US law enforcement officers called for a National Intelligence Plan to promote information sharing and intelligence-led policing (IACP 2002). Intelligence-led policing was now firmly established into the worldwide policing lexicon (Ratcliffe 2003).

Definition

Possibly the easiest way to begin to explain what intelligence-led policing is, it to start by addressing what it is not. Intelligence-led policing is a business process and not an intelligence-gathering technique. Both inside and outside policing, there is a belief that surveillance and confidential informant use constitutes intelligence. This is not the case, as both surveillance (physical and electronic) and information from confidential human sources are more accurately described as covert information-gathering techniques. There is an important distinction between gathering information and using intelligence to influence the decision-making of crime reduction practitioners. Intelligence-led policing does involve an extension of what constitutes traditional information resources to include more sources than an investigation-oriented, case-support analyst might consider. For example, 'the interpretation of crime and incident data through analysis, and community information on a range of issues, as well as the more commonly used information gleaned from various sources on the activities of known or suspected active criminals' (Oakensen *et al.*, 2002: 7) are all considered valid information sources under an intelligence-led policing regime.

In the US, some members of the public (and some in law enforcement) view the word *intelligence* within the context of policing with some suspicion. This caution has its origins in the abuses of police intelligence activity in the 1950s and 1960s. Investigations of political and non-violent war protest organisations were brought to public notice when it was revealed that public figures such as John Lennon and Dr Martin Luther King Jr had been kept under police surveillance. Some organisations (such as the US National Institute of Justice) therefore prefer the use of the term *information-led policing* in lieu of intelligence-led policing. This is, however, inaccurate and confusing because it does not do justice to the continuum from data to intelligence. To build on and extend the ideas of Davenport (1997), intelligence is the end result of a process that starts with data, becomes information, that itself can become knowledge, and – if employed to have an impact on decisions affecting the criminal environment – becomes intelligence. For example, a computer database can store locations of drug-related incidents and arrests. These computer records are *data*. When a crime analyst accesses the data and recognises a new pattern of drug market incidents at a particular street corner, then this becomes *information*. Information is data given meaning and structure. If the analyst talks to a narcotics officer and shares this information, and the narcotics officer remembers that this was a favourite corner for a particularly violent drug set and that the gang leaders have just been released from prison, this collective understanding of the context of the drug corner now becomes *knowledge*. Finally, when the analyst and the officer take their knowledge to a senior commander who agrees to mount both a surveillance operation to arrest ringleaders and a problem-oriented policing project to identify and resolve why the particular corner is attractive to drug-dealers, then this actionable knowledge becomes *intelligence*. Intelligence is therefore knowledge that is geared towards action.

So what is intelligence-led policing if it is neither information-led policing nor investigation-led intelligence (where covert information-gathering techniques support investigations)? When originally proposed in the early 1990s, intelligence-led policing was seen as a conceptual model that used crime analysis and criminal intelligence in a strategic manner to determine offenders for targeting. Crime reduction tactics would concentrate on enforcement and the prevention of offender activity with a particular interest in using crime intelligence against the activities of prolific and serious offenders. The techniques to be deployed included an expanded use of confidential informants, analysis of recorded crime and calls for service, surveillance of suspects and offender interviews. Where intelligence-led policing was revolutionary was in the use of intelligence derived from covert information as a strategic planning resource rather than as a means to develop case-specific evidence, as had traditionally been the case. Furthermore, intelligence-led policing became synonymous with the greater integration of criminal intelligence and crime analysis.

In the last few years, the implementation of intelligence-led policing appears to suggest a widening definition that is moving towards integration with the tenets of problem-oriented policing. While still remaining true to the core ideas that police should avoid expending substantial resources in reactive, individual investigations, intelligence-led policing has now evolved into a business model that can include greater emphasis on information-sharing with local partnerships and on strategic problem-solving. The police are still central to the process and the core activity of disrupting recidivists and serious offenders remains pivotal, but there is also an increased desire to work with partners in order to develop collaborative, strategic solutions to crime problems. In summary:

> Intelligence-led policing is a business model and managerial philosophy where data analysis and crime intelligence are pivotal to an objective, decision-making framework that facilitates crime and problem reduction, disruption and prevention through both strategic management and effective enforcement strategies that target prolific and serious offenders. (Ratcliffe 2008a: 89)

Distinctive features

Readers familiar with other chapters in this book, as well as the broader policing literature, will recognise some familiarity in the internal and external drivers introduced at the beginning of this chapter. These drivers helped promote intelligence-led policing but also acted as forces that influenced the development of other conceptual frameworks of policing, such as community policing, broken windows theory, problem-oriented policing and Compstat. Problem-oriented policing and broken windows are addressed in preceding chapters. However, some definitional clarity is required in order to establish that there is clear daylight between these differing views on how to control crime.

Table 14.1 describes particular dimensions of five common policing models. Of course, any attempt to highlight the distinctive tenets of any policing model requires both a considerable degree of generalisation and some latitude in this attempt to distil into a simple table the varying policing models; inevitably the table suggests differences that appear more severe than they often are in reality.

The first is the standard model of policing, an approach that:

> relies generally on a 'one-size-fits all' application of reactive strategies to suppress crime and … is based on the assumption that generic strategies for crime reduction can be applied throughout a jurisdiction regardless of the level of crime, the nature of crime, or other variations. Such strategies as increasing the size of police agencies, random patrol across all parts of the community, rapid response to calls for service, generally applied follow-up investigations, and generally applied intensive enforcement and arrest policies are all examples of this standard model of policing. (Weisburd and Eck 2004: 44)

While still the most common way to conduct policing in America, many of the tenets of the standard model have been found to be unsuccessful in promoting long-term crime control. For example, research from the 1970s and 1980s went a considerable way to debunking the myth that random patrol had any significant crime prevention benefits (see for example Kelling 1981; Kelling *et al.* 1974).

Community policing (the second model) evolved not just as a response to the limitations of the standard model but mainly as a way to re-establish police legitimacy in communities that had lost confidence and trust in the police. This approach, one that believes the police should consult with the public in determining operational policing priorities as well as collaborate with them in the search for solutions (Bennett 1994), was supported by significant funds from federal and state governments in the US. In the ensuing scramble for dollars (nearly nine billion were on offer from the US federal government alone) a wide array of policing tactics and approaches were labelled as community policing such that it has become impossible to determine what is, and what is not, community policing. The neighbourhood level empowerment of community officers working with local people on priorities determined by the community is certainly attractive to politicians and the media, but the lack of clear criteria for success has hampered efforts to label community policing a success. Community policing has been unable to overcome a lack of enthusiasm from a police culture that does not regard community policing as real police work, as well as resistance from mid-level commanders in some police departments. In addition, some departments have been unable to appropriately staff community policing units, a number of evaluations have not found significant crime reduction benefits from community policing efforts, and it has been difficult to sustain the interest of the public in community policing (Skogan and Hartnett 1997).

Table 14.1 Key dimensions of five policing models

	Standard model of policing	Community policing	Problem-oriented policing	Compstat	Intelligence-led policing
Easily defined?	Yes	No	Fairly easy	Yes	Fairly easy, but still evolving
Easily adopted?	Yes	Superficially	Difficult	At the technical level, but managerially challenging	Managerially challenging
Orientation?	Police administrative units	Neighbourhoods	Problems	Police administrative units	Criminal groups, prolific and serious offenders
Hierarchical focus?	Top down	Bottom up	As appropriate for the problem	Top down	Top down
Who determines priorities?	Police management	Community concerns/demands	Sometimes crime analysis, but varies from problem to problem	Police management from crime analysis	Police management from crime intelligence analysis
Target?	Offence detection	Unclear	Crime and disorder problems, and other areas of concern for police	Crime and disorder hotspots	Prolific offenders and crime problems, and other areas of concern for police
Criteria for success?	Increased detections and arrests	Satisfied community	Reduction of problem	Lower crime rates	Detection, reduction or disruption of criminal activity or problem
Expected benefit?	Increased efficiency	Increased police legitimacy	Reduced crime and other problems	Reduced crime (sometimes other problems)	Reduced crime and other problems

(*Source:* Ratcliffe 2008a)

Unlike community policing, intelligence-led policing is a top-down managerially driven approach to crime control. It concentrates on prolific offenders and criminal groups identified as threats through crime intelligence analysis, as opposed to specifically working to alleviate community concerns and address issues of public trust. This is not to say that there is no possibility of overlap, but rather that a community's concerns are not permitted to perpetually trump an objective assessment of the criminal environment. Furthermore, like problem-oriented policing but unlike community policing, community involvement in a crime control solution is not a requirement of intelligence-led policing.

Problem-oriented policing's focus is more objective than community policing, as it employs crime analysis as a major determinant of problems to be addressed. While applicable to a broad range of issues, both the requirement to stick with problems until they are resolved and the common approach of empowering rank-and-file members of the police department as the action arm of the model require a considerable cultural change for many police departments. Chapter 12 in this book describes problem-oriented policing in greater detail.

The last decade has seen the term Compstat cemented into the dictionary of policing. Like the standard model, Compstat is a managerial accountability process, but is oriented towards the crime reduction aspect of police business. With Compstat, mid-level commanders are required to be accountable to the top brass for the control of crime in their basic command units. By encouraging and requiring accountability, the theory runs that precinct captains and managers will have to make use of regular, detailed crime analysis (often in the form of crime maps) in order to determine an appropriate crime reduction strategy.

Because it is focused on police managerial levels, Compstat is organised along police administrative units and is very much a top-down approach to effecting change. Commanders survive in Compstat meetings by demonstrating their knowledge of the crime situation in their area, and ideally showing that they have lowered crime rates in the worst locations, at least in the short term. Few Compstat meetings review crime patterns from more than the preceding meeting, so commanders rarely have to worry too much about crime that occurred before the last assembly. Priorities are determined by commanders reviewing crime and disorder hot spots identified by crime analysis; this use of analysis by senior police commanders to drive the actions of officers under their command makes Compstat, in a broad sense, similar to, but not the same as, intelligence-led policing.

So where does intelligence-led policing fit into the picture, and how is it unique from these other attempts to control crime? As Table 14.1 shows, intelligence-led policing is relatively easy for a police department to adopt, at least from the perspective of police culture: Inhibiting the activities of serious and prolific offenders and disrupting their criminal activity is definitely the type of work for which most police officers joined the job. Existing managerial cultures, however, may take some time to adapt to intelligence-led policing. It is a management philosophy and business model that employs a top-down management approach, employing the existing rank structure, where strategic priorities derived from a combination of crime analysis and criminal intelligence are used to focus tactical outcomes with the aim of achieving crime reduction and prevention and the disruption of offender activity. This is a business model because the combined crime analysis and criminal intelligence (collectively termed crime intelligence) are used to objectively direct police resource decisions. As said earlier, it is this resource allocation and prioritisation that makes intelligence-led policing different from previous uses of criminal intelligence: what used to be a myopic, case-specific, evidence-gathering tool is now used for strategic planning at a higher organisational level.

A conceptual model of intelligence-led policing

While Table 14.1 outlines intelligence-led policing, there is some latitude in the definition from a conceptual sense. This section therefore outlines the *three-i model* (Ratcliffe 2003, 2004b), a simplified conceptual framework of how crime reduction is achieved in an intelligence-led policing environment. The model is shown in Figure 14.1.

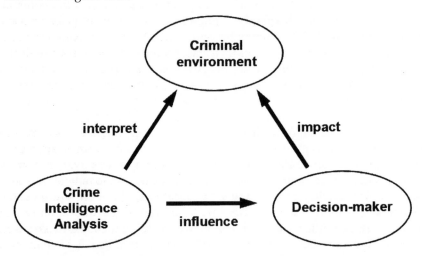

Figure 14.1 The three-i model
(*Source*: Ratcliffe 2003)

In the three-i model (interpret, influence, impact), the analytical arm of the police department actively *interprets* the criminal environment in order to determine who the main players are, and what are the significant and emerging threats. In the model, the arrow runs from the intelligence analysis unit to the criminal environment. While this frustrates some analysts who are more used to viewing their role as part of a cycle, it is a reflection of the reality of crime intelligence analysis. While a *push model*, where analysts send out information requests and wait for that information to come back to them is nice in theory, the push model does not work well in practice. The bureaucratic structure and culture of law enforcement agencies militates against the effective communication of intelligence requirements. The culture also thwarts the push model because large volumes of intelligence remain tacit, 'inside officers' heads', rather than recorded in intelligence records which can be shared at the push of a button. (Higgins 2004: 80)

As a result of this failure, crime intelligence analysts have to resort to a *pull model* for information collation. This approach entails the analyst actively seeking intelligence from contributors and actively seeking out the information they require by interviewing investigating officers and debriefing handlers of confidential informants.

The second arrow runs from the intelligence function to the decision-maker. The three-i model does not make a determination as to who is the best decision-maker; that is for the individual analyst to figure out for themselves. Many decision-makers are not the people who initially commissioned the intelligence product, and many are also outside of the immediate law enforcement environment. For example, mobile phone thefts in the 1990s were predominantly thwarted by the activities of the cellphone industry rather than the enforcement actions of the police (Clarke *et al.* 2001). This illustration is an example of what Wood and Shearing (2007) call 'nodal governance': networks of actors both within law enforcement and from outside agencies such as government and the private sector, all of whom having responsibilities to provide security. The *influence* part of the three-i model requires analysts to influence the thinking of decision-makers – whoever they determine decision-makers to be.

Influencing decision-makers is a tricky area for many analysts. Analysts with a traditional intelligence background often feel that their role is simply one of investigative case support, providing output and descriptive analyses of wire taps, intelligence gleaned from individual investigations, and grading information that detectives receive from confidential informants. The notion of providing commanders with recommendations as to targets and action can seem quite alien and many analysts feel that this is outside of their remit. Making recommendations for action is especially difficult for civilian analysts in a sworn-officer world; however, the analysts often have a sense of the broader perspective and are less reliant on experiential knowledge, one of the major causes of policing-led intelligence (Cope 2004). However, from the perspective of the three-i model, making recommendations is a crucial part of the analyst's job in an intelligence-led policing environment. Cope points out the importance of differentiating 'the capacity to make *recommendations based on analysis and research* and the *capacity to make decisions about adopting recommendations and directing action*' (2004: 191, emphasis in original). Crime intelligence analysts are quite entitled and usually qualified to make the former: the latter is an issue for decision-makers.

Intelligence-led policing does not occur if interpret and influence are the only components of the three-i model that occur. For crime reduction to result, decision-makers must bring about an *impact* on the criminal environment. The process can break down at any stage in the three-i model; however, the last stage is particularly troublesome because of the lack of education and training available for senior officers in law enforcement. As the literature on problem-oriented policing demonstrates (for an overview see Sampson and Scott 1999; Scott 2000; Scott *et al.*, Chapter 12, this volume; and www.popcenter.org), many tactics that effectively reduce crime over the long term do not involve operational policing. Regretfully, operational commanders too often rely on traditional policing tactics (such as investigations and saturation patrolling) as the only response to crime problems. The cause for this lack of tactical imagination is likely to be a general sense that if a commander has made it to the higher echelons of law enforcement, then that commander must know how to do crime prevention. This probably explains why one of the leading providers in police education in the US in 2004 offered only one course dedicated to crime prevention from a total of 68 available courses (Ratcliffe 2004a).

For crime prevention, reduction or offender disruption to occur, all three *i* components of the three-i model must occur: the crime intelligence analysts must *interpret* the criminal environment, the analysts must then use that intelligence to *influence* decision-makers, and decision-makers must direct resources effectively in order to have a positive *impact* on the criminal environment.

Implementing intelligence-led policing

In the UK, it is almost impossible to discuss the concept of intelligence-led policing without making reference to the National Intelligence Model (NIM). While the National Intelligence Model is not entirely synonymous with intelligence-led policing, the NIM has been adopted as a business model through which to implement the conceptual framework of intelligence-led policing. Released by the National Criminal Intelligence Service in 2000 and becoming the policy of the Association of Chief Police Officers in the same year, the NIM became the required business model of police services in England and Wales in April 2004, courtesy of the Police Reform Act 2002. The NIM has also been adopted in the UK by the Serious and Organised Crime Agency (SOCA), the Immigration Service, and it is also used by the Crime and Disorder Reduction Partnerships established by the 1998 Crime and Disorder Act to create partnerships between the police and relevant local authorities such as the probation service, health authorities and the local community.

The NIM is designed to work on three levels. At the local level, neighbourhood policing teams handle their own crime and disorder problems, gather information and use local resources to address problems in the local area and immediate region. This is level one of the NIM. Level two NIM operations occur at the cross-border area where offenders are operating in more than one jurisdictional area or affecting more than one region such that additional resources are required to combat their criminal activity (Sheptycki 2004a). Level three is designed for the types of serious and organised crime activity that operate at national or international levels. Offenders operating at this level may have to be identified by more proactive methods and the targeting and response is directed primarily through the work of dedicated units (NCPE 2005a). Within each level, the NIM is conceptualised to operate in roughly the same way. Figure 14.2 shows NIM business process, derived from the original model that accompanied the roll-out of the NIM from the National Criminal Intelligence Service (an agency now incorporated into SOCA). The diagram shows that the tasking and coordinating process is central to the model, but that importance is also placed on the need to have knowledge, system, source and people assets to support the model. Expected outcomes address community safety, reduced crime, limiting criminality and reducing disorder.

For this process to work, analysts have to create products that feed into the tasking and coordinating process, products that influence the thinking of managers who are able to deploy resources and engage partnerships. Intelligence products feed into the model at two levels of tasking and coordination: strategic and tactical.

The Strategic Tasking and Coordination Group usually comprises senior management of the local police area and, according to the National Centre for Policing Excellence (NCPE 2005a), should also include the commanders responsible for operations, roads policing, business and administration, training, technology, forensics, intelligence management and analysis. It is also possible that members of the local police authorities, prosecution service and local Crime and Disorder Reduction Partnerships can be invited to attend. This group is expected to meet at least every six months (NCPE 2005b). The strategic group sets the Control Strategy, a document that lays out the region's long-term priorities for crime prevention, enforcement and intelligence gathering.

The Tactical Tasking and Coordinating Group takes the Control Strategy and uses it as the guiding document that dictates the day-to-day priorities for resource allocation. The role of the tactical group is also to identify crime hot spots for attention, try and identify linked series of crimes, and identify and target prolific and serious offenders, all within the broad mandate from the strategic assessment.

From the perspective of a police analyst, the NIM provides the first real guidance as to how crime intelligence products directly link to the decision-making process. It is also beneficial because the NIM requires only four specific types of output. As Flood notes, 'the NIM's emphasis is deliberately on formal intelligence products. Intelligence process in law enforcement cannot be merely a voyage of discovery but demands predictability in the delivery and content of intelligence products for managers' decision-making' (2004: 48). The strategic tasking group are influenced by the *strategic assessment* (the main strategic intelligence product), prepared every few months and used to indicate long-term priorities and intelligence gaps. The three other products have more operational functions: the *tactical assessment* supports the business of the tactical tasking and coordinating body and is essentially an update document that charts progress towards the Control Strategy; the *problem*

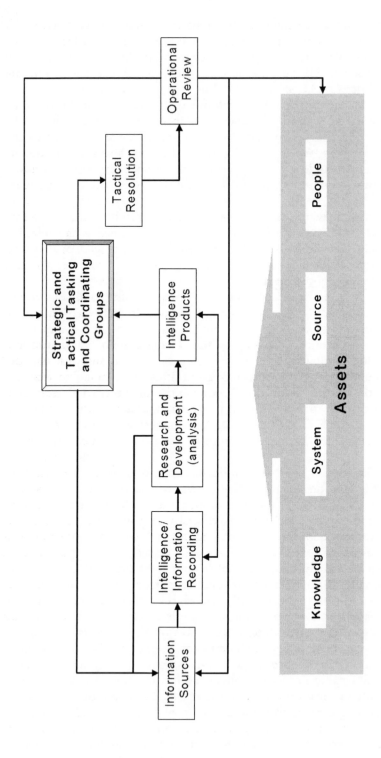

Figure 14.2 The National Intelligence Model Business Process
Source: (Adapted from NCPE 2005a: 14)

profile is an operational document that describes linked series of crimes or the problems surrounding a crime hot spot (an area of higher intensity crime volume); and the *target profile* is a product that directs law enforcement to tackle the offenders responsible for causing the significant disruption that often causes a problem profile.

Outside the UK, attempts to integrate intelligence-led policing into the thinking of police organisations have been less dramatic than the British approach of forcing the move through legislation. However, a number of police departments are actively moving towards intelligence-led policing as a conceptual framework for conducting operations and determining strategy.

One such example is the New Jersey State Police (NJSP). The NJSP performs patrol, traffic, criminal investigative, homeland security, technical services and emergency management responsibilities for the state of New Jersey. The state adjoins New York City and with thriving ports and a major casino complex in Atlantic City the state has received the unfortunate attention of a number of organised crime families. The state is also a major thoroughfare for illicit contraband and a staging post for criminal activity between New York, Philadelphia and up and down the Interstate-95 corridor between Boston and Washington DC. Combating these threats is one task of the NJSP Investigations Branch.

Branch commanders recognised that their organisational structure was one that reflected a model of bureaucratic efficiency but was not one that reflected the criminal environment they were trying to tackle. For example, individual units existed within their own silo of operations: a street gang bureau looked at street gangs, a narcotics bureau addressed drug crime, and an intelligence bureau focused on organised crime families. Within each group there was certainly expertise, but this tight specialisation had two significant negative outcomes. First, the organisational structure did not reflect the criminality performed by the groups targeted. For instance, street gangs were often involved in the distribution of narcotics, and organised crime families were involved in political corruption and sometimes wholesale narcotics distribution. Second, the organisational architecture encouraged intelligence-hoarding and information silos (Sheptycki 2004a) where if particular bureaus found evidence of activities conducted by their targets that fell outside their specialised remit, they did not necessarily pass this information on.

To resolve this problem, the Investigations Branch has reorganised the entire structure of the department so that commanders are in charge of geographic regions of the state, and within those commands fall units that address street gangs, organised crime and narcotics. Each command has their own tactical intelligence group so that the intelligence for the region can be pooled to address any overlaps in criminal activity. Furthermore, the branch has created a strategic intelligence group to address the strategic planning needs of senior executives (for more information see Ratcliffe and Guidetti, 2008).

The formation of a tactical intelligence group at the regional level and a strategic intelligence group situated within the branch level command are strongly reminiscent of the tactical and strategic tasking and coordinating groups of the NIM. The reorganisation of the structural architecture of the branch is a way to overcome some of the problems that specialisation in an intelligence-led policing environment can cause. As Sheptycki (2004a) pointed out, close inspection of the intelligence process often finds that it is not as rationally ordered as would appear on the surface. The NJSP response has been to structure the organisation so that intelligence products have the greatest chance of influencing the commanders who need them.

Evaluating intelligence-led policing

As Table 14.1 indicated, intelligence-led policing is still evolving in a definitional sense. The recent UK move to greater incorporation of partnership work and problem-solving into the NIM is a good indication of this. As a result, an evaluation of intelligence-led policing is currently difficult as the goalposts are still moving. The situation is further confounded by the fact that intelligence-led policing is not in itself a tactic, like the use of CCTV cameras or hot-spot policing. It is a business model, and therefore to date evaluations of the National Intelligence Model have tended to examine its ability to provide for effective information-sharing and a better ordering of crime reduction priorities, in lieu of the model's direct ability to deliver crime reduction. Some studies have identified implementation problems associated with intelligence-led policing. At the strategic intelligence level problems include technical, organisational and cultural factors that are inhibiting a rapid adoption of the central tenets of intelligence-led policing (Sheptycki 2004a, 2004b). Moreover, recent moves within the UK towards reassurance policing and the competition between a localised, neighbourhood approach to policing and crime reduction targets set by government have driven a shift back towards more reactive approaches to policing (Maguire and John 2006). While there appears to be a considerable overlap between problem-oriented policing and intelligence-led policing – at least in terms of overall crime reduction aim and the use of analysis as the fundamental cornerstone of problem identification – it may be that reassurance policing (with its overtones of community policing) is some way from the original conceptualisation of intelligence-led policing. Either way, the success of intelligence-led policing in the UK may be intertwined with the perceived accomplishments of the National Intelligence Model.

Outside the UK, adopting intelligence-led policing can appear to be little more than adoption of rhetoric rather than a true integration of the central tenets into business practice. While a number of police departments are experimenting with vastly different organisational philosophies, priorities and configurations, some claims to be intelligence-led are rather dubious, often simply based on the police department conducting a successful prosecution of a big case rather than any evidence that the case was the result of priorities set at the managerial level based on a strategic assessment of the criminal environment. Unfortunately, many such approaches tend to stress the intelligence aspect of intelligence-led policing rather than emphasising *policing*; in doing so they relegate the value of crime intelligence to a sideshow rather than as central to forming organisational goals.

Studies that have examined intelligence management find that many police departments have to undertake significant organisational change in the process. For example, there were significant organisational implications to improved management of resources in response to crime problems in Edmonton Police Service, Canada (Clarke 2006), while another study found flaws in intelligence management processes of three divisions of the New Zealand Police (Ratcliffe 2005). It is too early to say if the sweeping changes often found necessary are worth the investment; however, the signs are extremely promising. For example, when the Australian Federal Police, based in the capital city of Canberra, conducted a burglary reduction operation that employed many tactics associated with intelligence-led policing (surveillance of recidivist offenders, targeted policing in crime hot spots, and extensive use of confidential informants to identify targets) the operation resulted in statistically significant reductions in burglary (Makkai *et al.* 2004). The burglary reduction was not only associated with the operational period but also for a further 45 weeks after the operation, with evidence of a diffusion of benefits to other crime types and nearby areas (Ratcliffe 2008a; Ratcliffe and Makkai 2004).

Voices of concern occasionally surface from people concerned that the police are adopting a business model that places greater emphasis on the use of confidential informants and physical and electronic surveillance. In Australia, for example, a number of well-publicised corruption inquiries have damaged the reputation of more than one police service (Ratcliffe 2002). While policing has a long tradition of using informants, their strategic use as a planning tool is quite new. The increased use of confidential sources has been questioned, both in terms of the cost benefits of using paid informants and in terms of the moral and legitimacy considerations (see for example Dunnighan and Norris 1999). To some degree these objections stem from a misconception of the distinction between tactics used to gather information, and the management strategy used to determine priorities that is intelligence-led policing.

Most concerns have largely been ignored in the post-9/11 environment. In the current politically charged atmosphere that sees terrorism as a substantial threat, policing has recognised that reactive models may be insufficient to address future significant criminality, and that a more proactive risk management strategy is required. While never designed to specifically address counter-terrorism management, the advantage of intelligence-led policing is that as a business model it may be equally efficient as a terrorism prevention model as it is in addressing the day-to-day crime problems of neighbourhoods and communities. Intelligence-led policing represents a model that looks to provide objective crime intelligence that allows decision-makers to better manage risk, and as such is certainly attractive to police executives looking to return to the preventative paradigm that originally fuelled the development of modern policing in 1829. To achieve this, crime analysis and criminal intelligence will need to be merged to create a more complete picture of the criminal environment, and greater information-sharing is essential. It remains to be seen if a traditional police resistance to sharing information, especially from confidential sources, can be overcome to help fulfil this holistic objective.

References

Amey, P., Hale, C., and Uglow, S. (1996) *Development and Evaluation of a Crime Management Model*. Police Research Series Paper 18. London: Home Office.

Anderson, R. (1994) 'Intelligence-led Policing: A British Perspective', in A. Smith, (ed.) *Intelligence Led Policing: International Perspectives on Policing in the 21st Century*. Lawrenceville, NJ: International Association of Law Enforcement Intelligence Analysts.

Audit Commission (1993) *Helping With Enquiries: Tackling Crime Effectively*. London: HMSO.

Bennett, T. (1994) 'Community Policing on the Ground: Developments in Britain', in D.P. Rosenbaum (ed.) *The Challenge of Community Policing: Testing the Promises*. Thousand Oaks, CA: Sage, pp. 224–46.

Chainey, S. and Ratcliffe, J.H. (2005) *GIS and Crime Mapping*. London: John Wiley.

Christopher, S. (2004) 'A Practitioner's Perspective of UK Strategic Intelligence', in J.H. Ratcliffe (ed.) *Strategic Thinking in Criminal Intelligence*, Sydney: Federation Press.

Clarke, C. (2006) 'Proactive Policing: Standing on the Shoulders of Community-based Policing', *Police Practice and Research*, 7: 3–17.

Clarke, R.V., Kemper, R. and Wyckoff, L. (2001) 'Controlling Cell Phone Fraud in the US: Lessons for the UK "Foresight" Prevention Initiative', *Security Journal*, 14: 7–22.

Collier, P.M. (2006) 'Policing and the Intelligent Application of Knowledge', *Public Money and Management*, 26: 109–116.

Cope, N. (2004) 'Intelligence Led Policing or Policing Led Intelligence?: Integrating Volume Crime Analysis into Policing', *British Journal of Criminology*, 44: 188–203.

Crawford, A. (1997) *The Local Governance of Crime: Appeals to Community and Partnerships*. Oxford: Clarendon Press.

Davenport, T.H. (1997) *Information Ecology: Mastering the Information and Knowledge Environment*. New York: Oxford University Press.

Dunnighan, C. and Norris, C. (1999) 'The Detective, the Snout, and the Audit Commission: The Real Costs in Using Informants', *Howard Journal of Criminal Justice*, 38: 67–86.

Ericson, R.V. and Haggerty, K.D. (1997) *Policing the Risk Society*, Oxford: Clarendon Press.

Flood, B. (2004) 'Strategic Aspects of the UK National Intelligence Model', in J.H. Ratcliffe (ed.) *Strategic Thinking in Criminal Intelligence*. Sydney: Federation Press, pp. 37–52.

Gill, P. (1998) 'Making Sense of Police Intelligence? The Use of a Cybernetic Model in Analysing Information and Power in Police Intelligence Processes', *Policing and Society*, 8: 289–314.

Grieve, J. (2004) 'Developments in UK "Ciminal Intelligence"', in J. H. Ratcliffe (ed.) *Strategic Thinking in Criminal Intelligence*. Sydney: Federation Press, pp. 25–36.

Higgins, O. (2004) 'Rising to the Collection Challenge', in J. H. Ratcliffe (ed.) *Strategic Thinking in Criminal Intelligence*. Sydney: Federation Press, pp. 70–85.

HMIC (1997) *Policing with Intelligence*. London: Her Majesty's Inspectorate of Constabulary.

IACP (2002) 'Criminal Intelligence Sharing: A National Plan for Intelligence-led Policing at the Local, State and Federal Levels', *IACP Intelligence Summit*. Alexandria, VA: COPS and International Association of Chiefs of Police.

Kelling, G.L. (1981) *The Newark Foot Patrol Experiment*. Washington, DC: Police Foundation.

Kelling, G.L., Pate, T., Dieckman, D. and Brown, C.E. (1974) *The Kansas City Preventative Patrol Experiment: A Summary Report*. Washington DC: Police Foundation.

Maguire, M., and John, T. (1995) *Intelligence, Surveillance and Informants: Integrated Approaches*, Crime Detection and Prevention Series, Paper 64. London: Home Office.

Maguire, M. and John, T. (2006) 'Intelligence Led Policing, Managerialism and Community Engagement: Competing Priorities and the Role of the National Intelligence Model in the UK', *Policing and Society*, 16: 67–85.

Makkai, T., Ratcliffe, J.H., Veraar, K., and Collins, L. (2004) *ACT Recidivist Offenders'*, Research and Public Policy Series, 54. Canberra: Australian Institute of Criminology.

NCPE (2005a) *Guidance on the National Intelligence Model*. Wyboston, UK: National Centre for Policing Excellence on behalf of ACPO.

NCPE (2005b) *National Intelligence Model: Minimum Standards*. London: National Centre for Policing Excellence.

Oakensen, D., Mockford, R. and Pascoe, C. (2002) 'Does There Have to be Blood on the Carpet? Integrating Partnership, Problem-solving and the National Intelligence Model in Strategic and Tactical Police Decision-making Processes', *Police Research and Management*, 5: 51–62.

Ratcliffe, J.H. (2002) 'Intelligence-led Policing and the Problems of Turning Rhetoric into Practice', *Policing and Society*, 12: 53–66.

Ratcliffe, J.H. (2003) 'Intelligence-led Policing', *Trends and Issues in Crime and Criminal Justice*, 248: 6.

Ratcliffe, J.H. (2004a) 'Crime Mapping and the Training Needs of Law Enforcement', *European Journal on Criminal Policy and Research*, 10: 65–83.

Ratcliffe, J.H. (2004b) 'The Structure of Strategic Thinking', in J. H. Ratcliffe (ed.) *Strategic Thinking in Criminal Intelligence*. Sydney: Federation Press, pp. 1–10.

Ratcliffe, J.H. (2005) 'The Effectiveness of Police Intelligence Management: A New Zealand Case Study', *Police Practice and Research*, 6: 435–51.

Ratcliffe, J.H. (2008a) *Intelligence-Led Policing*. Cullompton, UK: Willan Publishing.

Ratcliffe, J.H. (2008b) 'Knowledge Management Challenges in the Development of Intelligence-led Policing', in T. Williamson (ed.) *The Handbook of Knowledge Based Policing: Current Conceptions and Future Directions*. London: John Wiley.

Ratcliffe, J.H. and Guidetti, R. (2008) 'State Police Investigative Structure and the Adoption of Intelligence-led Policing', *Policing: An International Journal of Police Strategies & Management* 31: 109–28.

Ratcliffe, J.H. and Makkai, T. (2004) 'Diffusion of Benefits: Evaluating a Policing Operation', *Trends and Issues in Crime and Criminal Justice*, 278: 1–6.

Sampson, R. and Scott, M.S. (1999) *Tackling Crime and Other Public-safety Problems: Case Studies in Problem-solving*. Washington, DC: US Department of Justice Office of Community Oriented Policing Services.

Scott, M.S. (2000) *Problem-oriented Policing: Reflections on the First 20 Years*. Washington DC.

Sheptycki, J. (2004a) 'Organizational Pathologies in Police Intelligence Systems: Some Contributions to the Lexicon of Intelligence-led Policing', *European Journal of Criminology*, 1: 307–32.

Sheptycki, J. (2004b) *Review of the Influence of Strategic Intelligence on Organised Crime Policy and Practice*. London: Home Office Research and Statistics Directorate.

Skogan, W.G. and Hartnett, S.M. (1997) *Community Policing, Chicago Style*. New York: Oxford University Press.

Townsley, M. and Pease, K. (2002) 'How Efficiently Can We Target Prolific Offenders?', *International Journal of Police Science and Management*, 4: 323–31.

Wardlaw, G. and Boughton, J. (2006) 'Intelligence-led Policing: The AFP Approach', in J. Fleming and J. Wood (eds) *Fighting Crime Together: The Challenges of Policing and Security Networks*. Sydney: University of New South Wales Press, pp. 133–49.

Weisburd, D. and Eck, J. (2004) 'What Can Police Do to Reduce Crime, Disorder, and Fear?' *Annals of the American Academy of Political and Social Science*, 593: 43–65.

Wood, J. and Shearing, C. (2007) *Imagining Security*. Cullompton, UK: Willan Publishing.

Index

Added to a page number 'f' denotes a figure and 't' denotes a table.

evaluation of a geographic profile
144
as strategic information management
system 136–7
theoretical underpinnings 137–8
training 144–5
see also crime mapping
Geographic Profiling Analysis (GPA)
training programme 144–5
Geographical Analysis Machine (GAM)
110
'geographical juxtaposition' 156
geovisualisation 104–7
Giuliani, Rudolph 250
global statistics 108
good enough theorising 38
government intervention, product design
216
graffiti 156, 158, 249, 252
Grippa clip 196, 198f
group membership 54
guardians 235
guardianship 12
Guerry, André-Michel 4

habituation 28, 31, 32f, 42
Hampshire Constabulary 240
handlers 74, 235
hangouts 74
Harvard Square 259
*Helping with Enquiries: Tackling Crime
Effectively* 265–6
herd mentality 54
Herman Goldstein Award for Excellence
in Problem-Oriented Policing 238,
239
high-crime neighbourhoods 99
high-rise housing estates 156, 161–2
histograms 104
Home Office (UK) 157
home turf 57
homicides *see* Buffalo homicides
honeypot operations 118–19
hot dots 13, 121
hot products 122, 199, 200
hot spot analysis
displacement 90
policing strategies 99–100
repeat victimisation 12–13
see also crime mapping
hot spots 99, 121

housing
and burglary 127, 181
crime-free 159, 160t
Housing Design: A Social Theory 154
housing estates
child densities 166
high-rise 156, 161–2
How to Lie with Maps 105
human crime preventers 208
human ecology movement 4–5
human settlements, security 153
hunting style (offenders) 142

image/space management 164
immediate environments 48–9, 61
immigrant smuggling 14
*Improving Policing: A Problem-oriented
Approach* 221
'incentivising' crime prevention
215–16
indefensible space 158
see also defensible space
individual crime patterns 79–87
informal control 258
information 267
information gathering 267
information silos 277
information technology 264
ingenuity fallacy 75
inherent product security 205–7
initiation 28, 29–31, 39
inside density 57
instrumental violence 60–1
integrated security systems 208
intelligence 263, 264, 267
informing designers through 214–15
intelligence hoarding 277
intelligence management 279
intelligence-led policing 14, 263–79
conceptual model 272–4
definition 267–8
distinctive features 268–72
emphasis on role of offenders 243
evaluating 278–9
implementing 274–8
misuse of term 263
origins 263–6
intentionality 23
inter-connectiveness 79
International Congress of Modern
Architects 156